John Wyclif:
On the Truth of Holy Scripture

Commentary Series

General Editor

E. Ann Matter, University of Pennsylvania

Advisory Board

The Commentary Series is designed for classroom use. Its goal is to make available to teachers and students useful examples of the vast tradition of medieval commentary on sacred scripture. The series will include English translations of works written in a number of medieval languages and from various centuries and religious traditions. The series focuses on treatises which have relevance to many fields of Medieval Studies, including theories of allegory and literature, history of art, music and spirituality, and political thought. The translations strive for clear, straightforward English prose style. Notes are meant to provide sources and to gloss difficult passages rather than to give an exhaustive scholarly commentary on the treatise. The editions include short introductions which set the context and suggest the importance of each work.

John Wyclif:
On the Truth of Holy Scripture

Translated with an Introduction and Notes by
Ian Christopher Levy

Published for TEAMS
(The Consortium for the Teaching
of the Middle Ages)

by

Medieval Institute Publications

WESTERN MICHIGAN UNIVERSITY

Kalamazoo, Michigan—2001

Library of Congress Cataloging-in-Publication Data

Wycliffe, John, d. 1384.
[De veritate Sacrae Scripturae. English]
On the truth of Holy Scripture / John Wycliff ; translated with an introduction and notes by Ian Christopher Levy.
p. cm. -- (Commentary series)
Includes bibliographical references.
ISBN 1-58044-031-2 (pbk. : alk. paper)
1. Bible--Evidences, authority, etc. I. Levy, Ian Christopher.
II. Title. III. Series.

BS480 .W9313 2001
220.1--dc21

2001045024

ISBN 1-58044-031-2 (paperbound)

Second Printing 2003

Printed in the United States of America

Cover design by Linda K. Judv

for Kenneth Hagen—

doctor verus in fide et amicus meus in Christo

Contents

Preface

Some years ago, a church historian remarked to me that "John Wyclif was a very interesting fellow who wrote as if he wasn't." While there may be some truth to that, Wyclif nonetheless remains an intriguing and resourceful, though enigmatic, writer whose resilient and often provocative character presses out from the pages and across the centuries. And so it is perhaps the most unfortunate aspect of John Wyclif's legacy that while much has been written about him, few people actually read what he has written. One need only glance through the indices of countless books on medieval and Reformation history to find his name, which means, in turn, that many students and scholars must surely be coming into contact with his thoughts regarding scriptural interpretation, sacramental theology, and ecclesiology. Yet how many of these same readers then open one of Wyclif's own books on these topics? The number drops markedly, and for some good reasons. Only the smallest handful of his works has been translated from the original Latin. And while the Wyclif Society produced an impressive set of critical editions of his Latin works, making one's way through a volume can be hard going. Wyclif did not systematically structure his works in the style of Aquinas's *Summa Theologiae*, for example. Thus if one is looking for an exposition broken into short, conveniently labeled passages one will be disappointed. Instead, the reader is confronted with long, sometimes rambling discourses, divided merely into untitled chapters (to their credit, his modern editors do provide side notes and erudite introductions).

It is with those reasons in mind that I first proposed this condensed translation of *De veritate sacrae scripturae* three years ago. Happily the proposal was quickly accepted by the TEAMS editorial board, and I am grateful to them. This volume is much longer than was anticipated, and yet many significant pages of the original could not be included—although, for the sake of organization and reference I have provided titles for all thirty-two chapters in this present edition. Nevertheless, what is here will, I believe, provide the reader with a substantial representation, sufficient to gain a genuine understanding of Wyclif's ideas on biblical exegesis and the role of Scripture in the Church. In that respect, I think the present volume should be useful, though the most desired effect is that it will inspire some readers to still further study of Wyclif in his many facets. These readers are sure to be rewarded as they encounter the sort of powerful and complex ideas that defy the facile reductions frequently offered in textbooks.

There are indeed a number of people to whom I am indebted. First and foremost, I must thank the series editor, Dr. E. Ann Matter, for her diligent efforts. From start to finish, Dr. Matter was exceptionally responsive, offering expert advice regarding the method and style of translation. The production editor, Julie Scrivener, was invaluable. Carefully reading the text and putting it into its current handsome form, she corrected my numerous errors and inconsistencies. Any that remain are entirely my own responsibility. I am grateful as well to Dr. Rita Copeland for reading and commenting upon the completed manuscript. Dr. Julian Hills was kind enough to read a draft of the proposal I sent to TEAMS. Fr. John P. Donnelly, S.J., and Dr. Stephen Beall graciously helped me with a few perplexing passages. Lastly, I would like to thank my dear friend, Wendy Bright, for her continual prayers and encouragement.

IAN CHRISTOPHER LEVY
MILWAUKEE, WISCONSIN
AUGUST 2001

Introduction

John Wyclif's *On the Truth of Holy Scripture* must be numbered among those works which one could not imagine being written by anyone but the author himself, bearing as it does the indelible stamp of his character, borne out in the style and substance of one man's strength of conviction, range of thought, and abiding obsessions. And yet for all his force of personality and copious production it is not always easy to offer a satisfactory definition of Wyclif when pressed to exceed trite definitions and banal classifications. Indeed, anyone who sets out to study Wyclif soon realizes that there is little about him which will lend itself to summary judgment. While appearing in numerous studies of the late Middle Ages, Wyclif is just as likely to appear in studies of medieval heresy, and even those devoted to the Protestant Reformation. But this is hardly surprising considering the sheer volume of Wyclif's own writings, the massive and powerful works devoted to the questions of ecclesiology, sacramental theology, and the role of Scripture. And if this were not enough, there are the logical and metaphysical works which comprise his earlier scholastic efforts, none of which the modern scholar of late medieval philosophy can bypass.

The fourteenth century was a fractious period, one that witnessed dissent and schism in the wider Church, and a persistent strain of skepticism within the confines of the universities. Wyclif lived in both of these worlds, speaking as he did on everything from the virtues of metaphysical realism to the nature of the true Church, from the proper interpretation of Scripture to the right ordering of Christian society. Yet for Wyclif they were all of one piece, all matters that fell under the domain of divine truth, and thus thoroughly contiguous. To pull a thread from any one section is to begin unraveling the entire sacred tapestry. Perhaps it is precisely because he was at once schoolman, biblical exegete, reformer, and finally even heretic, that he remains such an enigmatic figure to this day. Wyclif sought the restoration of an idealized past even if that meant taking revolutionary steps in the present to recover what had been lost. His 1377–78 *On the Truth of Holy Scripture* represents such an effort in reform: the recognition of the inherent perfection and veracity of the Sacred Page which serves as the model for daily conduct, discourse, and worship, thereby forming the foundation upon which Christendom itself is to be ordered.

From the perspective of fourteenth- and fifteenth-century English ecclesiastics contending with Wyclif himself and those who took up his mantle, he was a heretic, in fact a heresiarch, who had forced them into the uncomfortable position of rooting out his influence and even sending some of his Lollard followers to burn at the stake.[1] Yet with the onset of the Protestant Reformation in the sixteenth century, English Protestants like the martyrologist John Foxe found in Wyclif the Reformation's "morning star," a courageous witness to evangelical truth.[2] The most common categorization of Wyclif over the last two centuries has been that of a "pre-reformer," or "forerunner of the Reformation," whose ideas anticipated Christendom's coming upheaval.[3] And it is true that as one who called attention to perceived corruption in the Church, and offered a program of correction, however drastic or unrealistic, Wyclif can be considered a significant medieval reformer. For those nineteenth-century Protestant scholars to whom modern Wyclif studies are so indebted, such as Lechler, Buddensieg, and Loserth, Wyclif is the man who kindled the flames of Luther's brilliant bonfire, while the Czech reformer Jan Hus is largely written off as Wyclif's poor relation, playing the illuminated moon to Wyclif's dazzling sun.[4] Yet even Lechler admits the world would have to wait for Luther to hear the Protestant doctrine of justification by faith alone.[5] This is true; and in all fairness, Wyclif can hardly be expected to answer questions he had never been asked about this matter. It is for this reason that we must exercise considerable caution when assessing any influence Wyclif may have had on the Reformation of the sixteenth century. For not only was the Reformation theologically multifarious, it was conditioned by so many varying social and political realities as to preclude any positive judgments regarding Wyclif's role. That he can be credited as being the progenitor of the Lollard movement, however, is much more certain.[6] What we can say with assurance is that he was the quintessential late medieval man, perfectly suited for an age of rebellious peasants, renegade friars, skeptical schoolmen, grasping kings, and schismatic popes. Striking out into the fray, he sought to remedy the persistent corruption of the apostolic ideal which, in his estimation, had only accelerated in recent centuries. No doubt some of the measures he proposed were of a radical sort, and perhaps quite unrealistic, but in recognizing the need for genuine reform he was hardly alone. Calls for reform echoed at every level of the Church, from heretical sects to nationalist movements, and lastly the Conciliarists who convened the Council of Constance—ironically the very council that burned the Czech reformer Jan Hus, and posthumously condemned forty-five propositions attributed to Wyclif.[7]

Life of Wyclif

Born ca. 1327 in Yorkshire, Wyclif was ordained a priest by 1351. A secular cleric, it must be admitted that Wyclif spent little time in residence at the benefices he held, receiving the customary dispensations which allowed him to pursue his academic career at Oxford. He began by taking his Bachelor of Arts at Merton College in 1356, becoming Master of Balliol by 1360. Having devoted himself to philosophical studies for some time, he took his Bachelor's degree in Theology in 1369, and his Doctorate in 1372. From 1361 to 1368 he was rector of Fillingham, Lincolnshire. There was a brief and tumultuous period spent as warden of Canterbury College, a strife-ridden composition of secular clergy and monks, which he held from December 1365 until the Benedictines secured his deposition from the post in 1367; he was finally ejected by 1371. By 1368, however, he had secured the rectory of Ludgershall, Buckinghamshire, which he held until his death. In 1374 he also received the rectory of Lutterworth in Leicester, to which he retired in 1381 and where he died in 1384.[8]

Wyclif's era was marked by boldness on the part of the schoolmen in the face of ecclesiastical authorities, Oxford enjoying considerable freedom from the bishop of Lincoln. By the 1370s the university was under the watchful eye of Canterbury, while arousing deepening mistrust regarding its orthodoxy. In 1382 Archbishop Courtenay would diligently set himself to rooting out Lollardy in the university after Wyclif's departure the prior year. Even so, Courtenay's successor Arundel would still be embroiled in such efforts during the first quarter of the fifteenth century.[9] When Wyclif arrived at Oxford in the middle of the fourteenth century, the university was still vital, though past the high-point of intellectual achievement it had known in the first third of the century. Throughout the 1370s Wyclif was the university's preeminent scholar, a time when realist metaphysics held sway, and Scripture, rather than the venerable authorities, was increasingly given pride of place in theological discourse.[10] His first published works, composed between 1360 and 1365, were devoted to logic. From 1365 to 1372 he considered questions pertaining more to metaphysics. But from that point forward he devoted himself to theological issues, though never for a moment putting aside the logical and metaphysical *ancillae* which served the greater task of theology. The roles played by logic and metaphysics were integral to the entirety of Wyclif's thought, insofar as he simply could not conceive of a true logical or metaphysical system which was not ultimately of divine origin. The years 1373–74 saw the completion of his *On Divine Dominion*,[11] which set the stage for his *summa theologiae*, beginning in 1375 with his *On the Divine Commandments*.[12] In addition to this, by 1379 Wyclif had accomplished the rare feat of completing a *postilla*, or commentary, on the entire Bible which students were already regarding as a standard reference.[13] Indeed, it is important to bear in mind as one reads Wyclif's polemically charged works that, despite running afoul of ecclesiastical authority by 1377, Wyclif enjoyed considerable popularity and prestige within the university throughout the decade of the 1370s, and still retained an ardent following after being forced out in 1381.

Wyclif's entrance into the political sphere began when he was the only theologian among a delegation sent by King Edward III to Bruges in 1374 to negotiate a settlement with papal legates regarding the long vexing matters of papal provision to English benefices, taxation of the clergy, and the rights of clergy to appeal to papal courts. The larger question of the authority of secular lords over the Church would become a predominant theme in Wyclif's writings for the rest of his life. He stirred up controversy in this regard with his 1375–76 *On Civil Dominion*,[14] a substantial work written just a couple of years prior to *On the Truth of Holy Scripture*, in which he argued that secular lords are permitted to seize the property of delinquent ecclesiastics. It was at this time that Wyclif entered into the service of John of Gaunt, the Duke of Lancaster, in order to assist him in his struggles against the powerful bishop of Winchester, William Wykeham. Preaching sermons in the furtherance of Gaunt's cause soon provoked a summons to appear before an episcopal court convened at St. Paul's on February 19, 1377 by then–Bishop of London, William Courtenay. He did appear, accompanied by John of Gaunt and Marshall Percy, but the proceedings soon broke down, ending in a chaotic shambles.[15] Wyclif's potent ideas would hardly be forgotten by the powers that be, however. On May 22, 1377 Pope Gregory XI formally condemned nineteen propositions extracted from Wyclif's *On Civil Dominion*.[16] By the end of that year, five bulls issued by the pope had reached England. Providence may have been on Wyclif's side, though, for King Edward III died that year, followed soon after by Gregory, whose own death in 1378 would precipitate the events leading up to the Great Schism. Wyclif endured only house arrest at Oxford. By the time Wyclif was summoned to appear at Lambeth Palace in March of 1378, the bishops received word from the Queen Mother that they were not to pass formal sentence on Wyclif, thus resulting only in the admonishment to desist from expounding his views publicly.[17]

Wyclif remained at Oxford until he faced the condemnation of his eucharistic theology by a university council, in the middle of 1381, effectively ending his university career and forcing him into retirement at his Lutterworth parish, where he continued to write polemical tracts and sermons, often aimed at his former allies in the mendicant orders. Though Wyclif had left the university, Wycliffism had not subsided. Thus William Courtenay, by now Archbishop of Canterbury, convened a council at Blackfriars, London in May of 1382, condemning as heretical or erroneous twenty-four propositions attributed to Wyclif, ranging from sacramental theology to questions of dominion and grace.[18] Wyclif suffered a stroke in November 1382 and a second stroke on December 28, 1384. He died three days later on St. Sylvester's Day, 1384. Despite his steady stream of bitter attacks on popes, prelates, and friars during these final years, Wyclif was permitted to live out his final few years in peace. In 1415, however, following Hus's trial at Constance, the order was given to remove Wyclif's body from sacred ground. This task was finally carried out in 1428, when his remains were exhumed, burned, and the ashes poured out into the river Swift.

Holy Scripture

a) Scholarly Assessments

Taking up the central matter of Wyclif's approach to Scripture, we might briefly consider some assessments offered by modern scholars. While Workman admits, in his 1926 two-volume biography, that Wyclif was not the only medieval churchman to value the authority of Scripture, he is incorrect in arguing that Wyclif had broken with medieval tradition by insisting the Bible be considered in its entirety, words read in their proper context.[19] In fact, such an insistence on Wyclif's part could not have been more traditional. More recent analyses of Wyclif's treatment of Scripture have yielded various conclusions. Smalley found Wyclif a rigid thinker whose attempt to establish the certainty of revelation had, given his metaphysical realism, forced him into arbitrary interpretations of text.[20] Minnis concludes that, driven by his realism, Wyclif placed overwhelming weight on the divine authorship at the expense of the human, thereby putting him at odds with such fourteenth-century biblical exegetes as Lyra and Fitzralph.[21] On the other hand, Evans finds Wyclif's exegesis to be within the conventional bounds of the late medieval biblical interpretation,[22] and Kenny finds Wyclif's arguments for biblical inerrancy within accepted Catholic tradition.[23] Most recently, Ghosh has argued that Wyclif's attempts to defend Scripture's veracity only led him into contradictions of his own making as he sought out the divinely intended sense.[24] I will leave it to the reader to make up his or her own mind, but one may well find that, in spite of his eccentricities, Wyclif actually fits quite comfortably within a continuum of biblical exegesis stretching from Augustine to Aquinas. This tradition of commenting not only affirmed the subtlety of Scripture's discourse, but the necessity of reading the sacred text in light of the faith of the Church, whereby the believer is conformed to the sense which has been imprinted by the Spirit in all of its subtlety and range of meaning.

b) Authority and Authorship

Throughout the Middle Ages the interpretation of the Bible hinged upon the veracity of those writings whose principal author was the Holy Spirit. While there was growing appreciation for the role of human authors in crafting and compiling the biblical texts, they were still regarded as God's inspired agents of revelation. Medieval thinkers had long been concerned with the question of authorship and authority, and the role such questions played when considering the relationship between the various senses of Scripture. Scholars such as A. J. Minnis have examined the increasing precision to be found in the application of theories of authorship in the later Middle Ages, theories which served to safeguard the veracity of the divinely inspired text while at the same time allowing for a certain level of freedom, or autonomy if you will, on the part of the inspired human *auctor*.[25] An *auctor* was not simply a writer, but an authority, one worthy of respect. The writings of an *auctor* thus possessed *auctoritas*, that is to say, truthfulness and wisdom. The greater the *auctor* the more *auctoritas* he possessed. The Bible was the ultimate authoritative text, since its *auctor* is none other than God.[26]

For Wyclif, authority is that which formally determines the author. God alone is Scripture's author in the truest sense of the word, for he is the author in and of himself, while human beings are only authors in a derivative manner, inasmuch as God imparts his power to them for the sake of the Church. All parts of Scripture are thus equally true in light of God's unique authorship. Scripture is the one word of God and human authors are but God's scribes or heralds, charged with the task of inscribing the law which he has dictated to them, and, as such, are deemed authors in only an equivocal sense. The lowest level of authorship thus belongs to the one Wyclif calls the proximate author, that is to say any faithful person to whom God first gave the power to reveal the truth of Scripture to the Church after Christ. Scripture can then be said to maintain a three-fold authorship consisting of God, Christ in his humanity, and lastly, their proximate scribe.[27]

Every truth found in Scripture is of equal authority with any other, since every truth in Scripture is the word of the Lord, and every one of God's words is of equal authority with any other, bearing the highest authority, as they all proceed from the same author.[28] And it is precisely because Scripture is true in all of its parts that it must not be lacerated; phrases should never be isolated from one another in the hope of finding contradictions and impossibilities which, in turn, allow the reader to call its veracity into question. Along the same lines, there can be no question of false parts mingled with the true. Wyclif is convinced that each and every part is true, and fits together, which means that Scripture is to be read in its totality, as an integral whole, and always understood according to the sense of its author.[29]

c) The Literal Meaning of the Text

In Wyclif's insistence upon the inherent veracity and consistency of Scripture he was speaking directly to some of his fellow schoolmen who were, in his estimation, calling the very truthfulness of God into question. The fourteenth-century schools were awash in the logical-grammatical methods they had learned from Aristotle regarding valid and invalid inference, methods of argumentation which allowed for the evaluation of the truth value of a given proposition. Of great concern, therefore, were the rules of proper and improper supposition, that is to say, the difference between the strictly literal meaning of the words on the one hand, and their figurative or metaphorical meaning on the other. When a text is read according to its strict literal construction (*de virtute sermonis* = by the force of the word) it might offer quite different conclusions than when read within the parameters of common usage (*de usu loquendo*), allowing for metaphorical speech when conveying the intended meaning of the author. Yet in their zeal to pursue the natural conclusions of their own methods, some logicians struck a blow at the very foundation of all medieval biblical exegesis, namely the absolute trustworthiness of the divine author. They had put their theories into practice with the result that passages drawn from church fathers and, more astonishingly, from the Bible itself, could be declared false according to the rules of proper supposition (*de virtute sermonis*).

That tensions mounted between the more conservative factions and their free-wheeling colleagues is evinced in a statute issued on December 29, 1340 in which the faculty of arts at the University of Paris condemned the practice of those masters, bachelors, and scholars who were willing to reckon patristic and biblical texts false according to the rules of proper supposition (*virtus sermonis*), even while they knew such sayings were true when read according to their intended sense, one which might well involve metaphorical speech. Yet discourse, says the statute, derives its meaning from imposition and common usage (*usus communis*). The word does not possess force (*virtus*) except by imposition and common usage, which alone constitutes the genuine *virtus sermonis*.[30]

Since the Bible and Fathers often employ figurative language, the literal meaning is to be equated with the author's intention and not simply the arrangement of terms. The statute did not put the matter to rest, however, as such practices extended into the 1370s at both Paris and Oxford.[31] Wyclif's own battles manifested in *On the Truth of Holy Scripture* attest to this.

d) Wyclif's Earlier Defense of the Literal Truth

Well versed in methods of logical-grammatical analysis himself, Wyclif by no means rejected them out of hand. Rather, he applied them in a manner he considered to be in keeping with a centuries-old tradition of biblical interpretation. That the application of these methods to the Bible concerned Wyclif early on at Oxford is evinced in his 1360 *On Logic*, written while still a master of arts. At the request of "certain friends of the law of God," he composed an overview of logic for the sake of defending the "logic of Holy Scripture," equipping the faithful with the tools necessary to explicate the propositions of Scripture.[32] It is taken for granted that logic is an important tool to be put to use in the interpretation of the sacred text, which itself is understood to contain logical propositions. For Wyclif, though, it is never a matter of imposing logical systems upon the text, but rather explicating a text replete with its own logic.

A debate which took place in the early 1370s between Wyclif and the Oxford Carmelite John Kenningham merits brief consideration, as it came just a few years before the 1377–78 *On the Truth of Holy Scripture.* Here Wyclif argues that Scripture is true according to its literal sense (*de virtute sermonis*), which he equates with the intended sense of the divine author.[33] This is precisely because Wyclif believes that the words of Scripture derive their *virtus*, i.e., their import and signifying power, directly from God. Scripture, bearing as it does the imprinted sense of the Holy Spirit, is impressed with this divine force and its subsequent authority.

Wyclif laments that there are sophists, as the students of philosophy were called, who now claim Scripture can be logically construed to prove such ridiculous things as the notion that Christ is a blasphemer. Having recently received his doctorate in theology, Wyclif takes up their challenge, declaring it the solemn duty of the professor of the Sacred Page to conform to Scripture's own manner of speaking, thereby safeguarding the subtle sense of the sacred text. For Scripture still remains the refuge for Christ's faithful, where they can find safety from such sophistical bombast, carnal wisdom, and heretical cunning. It is in Scripture where we acquire a knowledge of real universals, the natural world, and the metaphysics by which we comprehend the eternity of God which will allow us to maintain Scripture's truth according to its intended literal sense (*de virtute sermonis*).[34]

What remains to be decided is what exactly constitutes the literal sense, and how the reader will be able to grasp Scripture's manner of speaking (*modus loquendi Scripturae*). Should one speak just as the Bible speaks? Kenningham says no; we should only seek the sense of the scriptural text, thereby understanding Scripture's manner of speaking and then setting it forth in clear language. Because the truth may be hidden under a multitude of expressions the reader must be alert to cases of improper supposition. Scripture's manner of speaking may in fact be false *de virtute sermonis*, says Kenningham, while still including the suitable, intended senses.[35]

While Wyclif considers it sinister to suggest, as Kenningham does, that we should not imitate the *modus loquendi Scripturae* in its figurative locutions,[36] the Carmelite's admonition is well founded, noting that some of the Church's most infamous heresies were introduced by reading Scripture *de virtute sermonis*. The intention of Scripture may be clear, says

Kenningham, but the strict signification of the words they present can be erroneous. Hence, in these cases one must consider the peculiar characteristics of speech.[37] Herein lies the difference between Wyclif and his formidable opponent. Kenningham limits the parameters of what it means to speak *de virtute sermonis* to strict grammatical conventions which exclude improper or figurative constructions, thereby forcing the reader to press beyond the literal sense where need be in order to grasp Scripture's intended sense. But because Wyclif insists that Scripture possesses a grammar all its own, manifested in its sacred manner of speaking, these same improper or figurative constructions cannot permit falsity *de virtute sermonis*, inasmuch as they are included in the literal sense, which is nothing other than the intended sense of the author. Wyclif considers it axiomatic that to the extent anything is false *de virtute sermonis* it is false, period. If this is the case, then Scripture itself would be false.[38] The proper grammatical construction is whatever the divine author deems fit for conveying the sacred meaning of Scripture, which is most truly Scripture itself.[39]

In his 1375–76 *On Civil Dominion*, Wyclif briefly takes issue with the sophists who claim that many passages of Scripture appear to be false *de virtute sermonis*, as evinced in parables, prophecies, and those truncated sections taken out of context. To this Wyclif responds that it is impossible for any part of Scripture to be found lacking in truth. Thus when it comes to the mystical and parabolical senses the burden is on the sophists to recognize the right sense. It is hardly the fault of Scripture if some ignorant fellow claims to have found an error in one of its manuscripts.[40] The slanderers should first learn Scripture's own supremely correct grammar and logic, and study the sense of the author, before they engage in such defamation.[41] When, for instance, they latch on to a saying found in John 8:48–52 where Christ's adversaries say, "You have a demon," they must realize that every such particle is true when considered in light of the whole passage through which the author of Scripture adequately asserts the truth. After all, this particle cannot be taken to mean that Christ really is demoniac, since it principally signifies that the Jews said to Christ, "Are we not right in saying that you are a Samaritan and you have a demon?"[42] Understanding the sense of Scripture in its integrity means comparing different passages, allowing one passage to teach the reader how another is to be understood within the greater context of this perfect collation, thereby recognizing the way in which the author has chosen to express that sense.[43]

On the Truth of Holy Scripture

a) The Eternal Scripture

Wyclif's metaphysical realism may never be detached from any aspect of his theology, and his doctrine of Scripture is no exception. Largely indebted to the Augustinian realist tradition, Wyclif maintained that God is the first truth, the cause of the eternal exemplars subsisting within the divine intellect. Proposing three grades of universals, Wyclif considers the first to be the eternal exemplar, the universal of causation. The second is similar to the Aristotelian universal, whereby natures are communicated to the many particulars. And the third consists of representations formed in the mind, serving as signs of the prior universals.[44]

In his *On the Truth of Holy Scripture*, Wyclif posits five different levels of Scripture, the highest of which is the book of life subsisting eternally in the divine mind. On the fifth and lowest level there is the bare manuscript, the ink upon parchment which functions as a sign of the eternal truth, that eternal exemplar which is most truly Holy Scripture. In fact, Wyclif contends that the manuscripts may only be deemed Scripture in an equivocal sense.[45] Because the words on the page are merely signs of Scripture's eternal content the reader must transcend the sensible realm and ascend the ontological ladder to the eternal truth.[46] Wyclif finds Scripture itself to be speaking the language of metaphysical realism. For when the great philosopher Moses recounted the creation of the beasts of the earth having been fashioned in their genus and species, he was not speaking merely of the terms which correspond to human conceptions, as the nominalists do, but of universal natures communicated to particulars.[47] Terms only serve as signs, reflecting the real predication which God effects.[48] To say these are no more than humanly devised categories clearly contradicts Scripture, rendering Wyclif's nominalist opponents not simply poor metaphysicians, but heretical at that.[49]

In light of its eternal and perfect nature, it is only right that Holy Scripture would provide the paradigm for all genuine discourse. Human speech must once again be conformed to the logic of Scripture, just as it was in the state of innocence, before sin disrupted that pristine harmony, when humankind had not yet erected its tower of Babel, nor borne the resulting infliction of dissonant tongues.[50] Yet because this celestial logic abides eternally within Scripture it is there to be recovered by the Church. Thus when reading this sacred text, one follows the example of the saints, putting aside foreign logics and grammars, submitting instead to the grammar and logic of Scripture.[51] Only then will the reader begin to understand the eternal truth of Scripture. Reading Scripture is no mere academic exercise; it is a task which lays claim to the entire human person, the whole life of the believer. The reader must purify his heart. It takes a virtuous character to understand Scripture, Wyclif insists, inasmuch as its mysteries are hidden from the proud, those seeking the vainglory of lecture hall celebrity. In a most Augustinian fashion, Wyclif maintains that as Christ is the Light and the Principle of all knowledge one must be conformed to Wisdom himself, the First Teacher. Yet as Scripture itself is Christ the Word, Christ is simultaneously its essence and the very key which unlocks it. If the Christian hopes to understand the logic of Scripture, therefore, he is obliged to conform his own sense to Christ's sense, adapting himself to the reasoning of the most subtle of all logicians. To achieve such an end requires prayer; one must believe in order to understand.[52] Indeed, the whole exegetical task and the entire evangelical life, places conformity to the law of Christ at the center. This law is perfectly revealed in Scripture for the sake of the Church, and most briefly put, says Wyclif, is simply love itself.[53]

b) Defending the Literal Sense of Scripture

For Wyclif, any one of the traditional four senses of Scripture which comprise the *quadriga* might just be the literal sense if this is the sense first intended by the divine author, and thus immediately elicited from Scripture. Although any sense which the letter possesses may be called the literal *de virtute sermonis*, he believes the doctors commonly call the literal sense that sense of Scripture which the Holy Spirit primarily intends, inasmuch as it promotes the faithful soul's ascent to God. Of the three mystical senses, each may offer instruction in either a mediate or immediate fashion, but the literal sense is the catholic sense which is immediately derived from Scripture. And if any of the three mystical senses is so derived then it is the literal sense, inasmuch as it is the primary intended sense. If they are elicited in a mediate fashion, however, then they take their respective places as the allegorical, tropological or anagogical, but not the literal.[54] As long as one bears in mind that the literal sense is the divinely intended sense then this poses no problem. The various senses do not supplant one another, nor do they cease to maintain their essential characteristics. The tropological, for instance, is still the tropological, but it may be the sense which most suitably conveys the divine author's purposes in a given instance, and in that way is reckoned the literal. Wyclif made a similar point in a work of the following year, stating that while the mystical sense of a given passage may not be self-evident to the ignorant reader, if such a sense can be proven by reason, and by other scriptural passages, to be the one intended by the author, then this sense is equivalent to the literal.[55]

While the sophists claim to have located contradictions in the text when read *de virtute sermonis*, this is precisely because they equate the literal or proper sense with the definitions they have learned in grammar school,[56] while Wyclif himself has put away childish reasoning, now recognizing by God's grace that the literal sense is the divinely intended sense, one which utilizes equivocal speech and thereby avoids all contradiction.[57] The holy doctors, says Wyclif, realize that the mystical sense belongs to the fullness of the letter. In this way, Christ is indeed a lamb *de virtute sermonis*, just as Christ can both be "the door" without being "a door."[58] Reasoning according to their childish grammar, the sophists find apparent contradictions, but then if one refuses to follow Scripture's grammar it comes as no surprise that he fails to recognize that the term "hand" is an equivocation meant to designate a bodily organ in one instance and God's power in another. While the uncultured grammarian reads of a lion and sees only a four-legged beast, the theologian recognizes that this term may yet signify further, and thus be referring to Christ, the Lion of Judah.[59] It is all a matter of becoming accustomed to sacred discourse, divine logic. But then, one only comprehends

Scripture by divine dispensation, and those who have not been granted such power must take care that they do not corrupt or condemn the sense of Scripture in their ignorance.[60]

Wyclif's oft-repeated claim that Christ is the Truth, who cannot lie, is actually an answer given to real questions posed in the fourteenth-century lecture halls. One might ask whether or not John the Baptist had lied when claiming not to be a prophet. If not, does this mean Christ's assertion was false when he referred to John as Elijah? Here Wyclif, like Augustine, argues that Christ refers to John as Elijah with respect to his office and not his person. As such, he is called Elijah in likeness, since Jesus speaks truthfully here in terms of prefiguration. Those who reckon this a contradiction prove themselves unwilling to abide by Scripture's deft use of language. But in so doing they turn Christ into the foremost liar, and the greater part of Scripture into a blasphemous falsehood. It is the heretic, says Wyclif, who rejects the subtle equivocations of Scripture, and explicates the sacred texts apart from the requirements of the Holy Spirit and the testimony of the holy doctors.[61] Yet were Scripture false this would have to reflect directly upon its divine author, thus turning God into a liar for having ordained this profane document, this lie designed to deceive his beloved Church.[62] One must never lose sight of the fact that, for Wyclif, nothing less is at stake than the believer's ability to trust in his God. And nothing can be allowed to cast doubt upon the truthfulness of the Holy Spirit and the words of the Savior.

c) Scripture and Tradition

The sophists were not Wyclif's only concern. Their attack on Scripture was symptomatic of what he perceived to be a general trend of exalting human traditions, be they logical or ecclesiastical, over the Bible. For Wyclif, a human tradition was any teaching not grounded in Scripture, itself the sole source of catholic truth. Restoring Scripture to its rightful place and recovering its proper interpretation rests at the heart of Wyclif's call to Church reform. In the latter sections of *On the Truth of Holy Scripture* he turns his attention to the rising tide of papal decrees, human traditions which he believed to be displacing Scripture's unique place of authority in the Church. None of this is to say that Wyclif set Scripture at odds with tradition *per se*, for just as Wyclif constantly appealed to the holy doctors in order to disprove the exegesis of the sophists, so he appeals to these same doctors when verifying what he considers the genuine faith and practice of the Church. Many late medieval theologians, who were after all designated "masters of the Sacred Page," conceived of tradition as a continuum of sacred commentary upon Holy Scripture, and were thus reluctant to recognize the validity of a parallel extra-scriptural tradition that could claim equal status with the Bible.[63] Wyclif was not opposed in principle to canon law, therefore, only the notion that papal statutes could be put on a par with Scripture.[64] Tradition is, for Wyclif, primarily embodied in the commentaries of the holy doctors and the ancient creeds, and only secondarily in canon law. Thus de Vooght is correct in saying that Wyclif never proposed a *sola scriptura* theory which would have precluded the Church fathers as inspired interpreters of the Bible.[65] Indeed, as Wilks notes, Wyclif even approved Gratian's twelfth-century *Decretum* as being legitimate Church law, soundly based upon Scripture, the creeds, and the holy doctors, while taking issue with the papal decrees, the *Decretales*.[66] One might add, however, that Wyclif did demand an interpretation of the *Decretum* which conformed to his own conception of an ideal Church, and thus often accused his opponents of providing distorted glosses on canonical chapters. The sticking point was what constituted the parameters of valid tradition and its proper use. While it is true that no medieval would have dared say canon law superseded Scripture, it is also true that the late Middle Ages witnessed an increasing emphasis placed upon the authority of these extra-scriptural traditions fostered by the Church and ultimately secured by papal authority. Tierney is right to say, therefore, that Wyclif was really reacting against the excessive claims of some canonists who may have asserted in practice what they would never have supported in principle. In demanding that papal decrees always be in conformity with Scripture, Wyclif would have found no opposition.[67]

That said, however, we must also recognize that Wyclif dated the inception of ecclesiastical corruption to the fourth-century Donation of Constantine when, according to legend, the emperor had granted the western lands of the empire to Pope Sylvester. Once temporal sovereignty got its foot in the door of a poor and humble Church all manner of apostasy would surely ensue. And so it did, he believed, in successive stages. Evangelical law was being corrupted and even ignored. And yet if Scripture is the eternal Law of Christ handed down by uncreated Wisdom, it must be infinitely more honorable than any human tradition. Surveying the state of the present Church with the utmost pessimism, Wyclif found historical precedent when predicting the fate of those who forsake Scripture. The dissolution of evangelical law at the time of anti-Christ is leading to the destruction of the Christian people, he claims, just as the infusion of human traditions led to the downfall of the Jews in Christ's own day. If someone seeks a reason for the present chaos afflicting the Church, he need look no further than the papalists who have substituted their own authority and laws for those of Scripture.[68] Even theology, the queen of the sciences, has now been mingled with spurious doctrines and human traditions, as clerics put aside divine wisdom and busy themselves with civil law. But God and his Church cannot abide any rules unless founded upon Holy Scripture, which is the very Catholic faith itself, thereby exceeding all human canons in usefulness, authority, and subtlety.[69]

While Scripture serves as the law for all Christian life today, it also offers a record of Wyclif's idealized apostolic Church: poor, meek, and prepared to suffer martyrdom. He found in the apostolic life so described a model for the present clergy, and measured the contrast accordingly. While the apostles sought no worldly glory, but instead freely submitted themselves to secular authority, modern clerics have forsaken evangelical power for imperial might, as priests are now more interested in maintaining their own temporal dominion than humbly tending their flocks.[70] There is a remedy, of course: since secular lords are charged with the duty of protecting Holy Mother Church it only stands to reason that they have the right to judge the worthiness of the clergy and even revoke the endowments given to the Church by their ancestors.[71] These ideas on Church reform raised in *On the Truth of Holy Scripture* merit further elaboration in the following section of this introduction, as they are indispensable in gaining the perspective necessary for reading Wyclif.

Wyclif the Church Reformer

a) Church and Sacraments

While Scripture provided the blueprint for Church reform, Wyclif's call for such reform was undergirded by an Augustinian conception of the Church's inherent composition. The true Church is the body of Christ, the eternal gathering of God's elect forming the members with Christ at the head. Moreover, as the Church is Christ's bride, so she is mother of all the faithful.[72] Stressing the classic distinction between being *in* the Church and *of* the Church, Wyclif distinguishes between the predestined who comprise the true members of Christ's body, and those whose damnation is foreknown to God, comprising the body of the devil. While many of the foreknown may presently hold the highest ecclesiastical offices, this in no way qualifies them as members of Holy Mother Church. They are but chaff among the wheat waiting to be winnowed out at the final harvest, members of the devil's body currently fornicating with Christ's virgin bride.[73] Yet Wyclif realized that on this side of eternity we cannot be certain who is numbered among the predestined. In fact, there are some members of the true Church currently in a state of mortal sin, while some among the foreknown enjoy present righteousness, though without the gift of final perseverance.[74] And it is precisely because the separation of wheat and chaff, predestined and foreknown, remains a purely eschatological phenomenon, as it was for Augustine, that the present order of the Church need not fear disintegration. Wyclif expressly refuses to draw a direct connection between present mortal sin and final damnation, recognizing the turmoil which would result when applied to prelates, even as we may harbor suspicions regarding their guilt. It is true, though, that he considered an ecclesiastic's accumulation of secular privileges an infallible sign that he is indeed a member of the devil.[75] Nevertheless, these eschatological considerations do not preclude the foreknown priest, even if in a present state of mortal sin, from duly administering the sacraments to God's faithful within the Church militant.[76] As Christ often makes good the priest's defect, so all sensible sacraments when rightly administered have a salutary effect.[77] Wyclif was quite careful to keep the Donatist heresy at arm's length and, with few possible exceptions, was consistent in maintaining the objective quality of the sacraments—*ex opere operato*.[78]

b) Role of the Papacy

It must be admitted that Wyclif employed the theory of an invisible Church, that *civitas dei* presently mingled with the *civitas terrena*, as broad sword by which to sever the bonds of papal authority in principle, while not in fact. Eschatological divisions, as he was well aware, are not the grounds upon which sacramental efficacy or present official tenure can rest. Yet precisely because nobody knows with certainty whether he is a member of Christ's faithful body (itself a perfectly traditional position), it stands to reason that the Vicar of Christ dare not declare himself Head of the Holy Catholic Church, or even claim membership in the true Church for that matter.[79] Papal infallibility is a myth, since popes may err in matters of faith and morals, and the curia itself even apostatize. After all, if the angels could sin, and the first parents fall from the state of innocence, it seems all the more likely that the pope and his college of cardinals will lapse in these perilous times.[80] At any rate, the Roman pontiff is only the head of a particular church at best, and even then is worthy of reverence only insofar as his conduct stands the test of Holy Scripture.[81] To the extent that the pope fails to follow Christ he unjustly occupies the papacy and proves himself a diabolical anti-pope.[82] Such claims were especially pertinent in time of the Schism as Wyclif claims the faithful are under no obligation to believe either Urban VI or Clement VII unless they speak the faith of Scripture.[83] Indeed, nothing could be more insane, he says, than for the faithful to believe every bishop of Rome is the pope, or that every layman is bound to do what he commands, or even that Christians are bound to accept his interpretation of Scripture as authoritative, since there are thousands of Christians who possess the faith of Scripture directly from God and thus independently of the pope.[84] In the midst of so much uncertainty, Wyclif insists that every Christian must be a theologian, which means not only knowing the Law of Christ, but placing it above all else, as it alone leads to love of God and neighbor, and thus final beatitude.[85]

As far as Wyclif is concerned, the current state of the papacy could not have been more at odds with early Christian faith and practice. Prior to Constantine's Donation the holy martyrs had not subjected themselves to a pope, but only to Christ the head.[86] Nor would any of the saints ever have presumed to call themselves head and lord of Mother Church.[87] Hence, when interpreting the critical passage of Matt. 16:15–19 it is hardly surprising that Wyclif determines Christ to be that rock upon which the Church is built, so signified in Peter's confession of faith. As the pope's claim to be head of the universal Church goes by the wayside, so too the claim of plenitude of power. For the power of the keys is all but extinguished, since when Matt. 16:19 is read *de virtute sermonis*, that is, according to Christ's intended sense, Peter's successors are found to have no power to bind and loose anything on earth *except to the extent* that it is bound or loosed in heaven.[88]

c) Dominion

Wyclif's theory of dominion directly serves his program of Church reform. Here Wyclif adopted an already existing principle, namely that all dominion, or lordship, ultimately rests with God, and is subsequently dispensed to human beings who justly partake of that dominion as long as they remain in a state of grace.[89] The human dominion over the earth which was lost in the Fall has been restored to the righteous by virtue of Christ's passion, even surpassing that of the state of innocence.[90] Because rightful dominion demands the proper use of what one has been entrusted with by God, abuse is a sin against divine dominion amounting to theft, thus calling for forfeiture.[91] Dominion belongs to God alone, and is his to grant; human beings only administer it.[92] But where the classic papal conception of this doctrine placed the pope at the top of a descending scale of power, administering God's grace and dominion, Wyclif substituted the king as God's vicar.[93] It is the king who bears the image of Christ in his majestic divinity, while priests exemplify the humanity of Christ, in its humility and weakness.[94] As the kingdom is one body it is for the King of England to regulate his clergy, especially the bishops, and see that they live in accordance with the law of Christ.[95] In fact, Christ himself had instructed his clerics to be subject to princes, and granted to Peter, and those who were his successors by spiritual imitation, only evangelical dominion.[96]

While a person in a state of grace, as an adopted child of God, possesses rights to the whole world, a person in a state of mortal sin has no rights to dominion at all.[97] For true dominion is founded upon the very grace the unjust person lacks, rendering his dominion false and usurped.[98] But civil dominion must be founded upon evangelical justice, which is lacking to those in a state of mortal sin.[99] And because dominion is grounded in moral righteousness, even a member of the predestined currently in a state of mortal sin forfeits present dominion[100]—hence, the rights of temporal lords to disendow clerics who habitually abused their wealth. For God only approves of such temporal holdings insofar as they contribute to the execution of divine law. Where they prevent clerics from following Christ's law they are to be withdrawn.[101] All the while, Wyclif was hoping against hope that prelates would come to see the life of poverty as more closely approximating the state of innocence, thereby recognizing evangelical poverty as a privilege to be embraced.[102] Let popes free themselves from worldly affairs and live divested of wealth, imitating Christ in his patient suffering that they might achieve the greater joy of being inscribed in the Book of Life.[103] How much better things would be if only we could recapture those halcyon days before Constantine endowed Sylvester and his successors with the Lateran Palace and all the insignia of imperial power.[104] While it is true that Wyclif's theory of dominion logically applied to clergy and laymen alike, he really only pressed it in the clerical direction, since his primary concern rested with Church reform. That such ideas met with papal condemnation is hardly surprising and, in point of fact, the Crown had no intention of upsetting its long-established relationship with the Church. Whether or not McFarlane is right that Wyclif's proposals were so unrealistic as to unwittingly undercut any chances of real reform in his own age,[105] the truth remains that the genuine *reformatio ecclesiae* Wyclif hoped for could only have taken place, as Wilks observes, with royal support. That such support would not be forthcoming was a reality to which Wyclif himself was resigned by 1379.[106]

The Eucharist

Finally, something must be said about Wyclif's eucharistic doctrine, not only because this precipitated his fall from grace, but because it is inexorably linked to his approach to scriptural interpretation, having to do specifically with authorial intention and the literal sense. In late 1380, an Oxford council convened by the university chancellor, William de Berton, condemned two of Wyclif's central eucharistic doctrines: the substantial remnance of the bread and wine after consecration; and that Christ's body does not exist in the host substantially or corporeally, but rather in a figurative manner.[107]

By 1380 Wyclif made no secret of the fact that he considered the doctrine of transubstantiation to be an especially noxious product of scholastic recklessness, yet another example of the present Church's willingness to abandon evangelical law. He found it to be a metaphysical impossibility in absolute violation of Scripture. For not only do Scripture and the saints make it clear that accidents cannot exist apart from their proper subjects, but the annihilation of substance would signal the annihilation of the whole created universe and even God himself, who is not about to destroy his own creation through his own sacraments.[108] The sad irony is that his former allies, the mendicants, are now deemed especially culpable as they preach transubstantiation to the laity, leading them into the idolatry of equating Christ's body with the accidents of the bread.[109] Rather than posit a substantial change, Wyclif argues that Christ's body assumes different modes of presence which, in turn, serve to signify greater ones. Thus while truly and really present in the host in a virtual, spiritual, and sacramental manner, his body yet possesses more true and real modes of being in heaven, where he is substantially, corporeally, and dimensionally present. Yet he is the one and same Christ, functioning in this unique sacrament as a sign of himself. Of course, these distinctions of presence are lost on those dullards, he says, ill-suited as they are to understand the mysteries of the Eucharist and the subtlety of Scripture.[110] Because Christ's body is simultaneously truth and figure in the Eucharist, this "infinite sign" makes present his body in a way the signs of the Old Law and images of the New could not.[111] Wyclif firmly believes, however, that his doctrine of the spiritual rather than corporeal consumption of Christ's body is in keeping with not only the logic of Scripture and that of the holy doctors, but with the decrees of the Roman Church as well. And notwithstanding erroneous glosses imposed upon these texts, he is convinced that the true faith still abides within the Church.[112]

At root, eucharistic theology is an exegetical matter for Wyclif, one which calls for the correct discernment of authorial intention. Transubstantiation creates all manner of exegetical difficulties, not the least of which is that it forces Christ to speak falsely, talking of bread while meaning only its accidents. But Christ, the guarantor of the truth of Scripture, would not deceive the faithful by positing the existence of accidents without proper subjects which the doctrine of transubstantiation demanded. Christ is the "author who cannot lie," says Wyclif, and while his presence in the host is "true and real" it does not depend upon a substantial change in the elements.[113] Hence, as the schoolmen debate the precise manner in which the accidents of the bread are upheld, Wyclif concludes that all of their readings render the words of Scripture a lie. Once one is permitted to deviate from the authority of Scripture and gloss the biblical text so as to claim that what it calls bread should be understood as quantity or some other accident, then the ancient faith, indeed the entire history of Christ's life, could also be so glossed to deny the literal sense of the text (*ad literam*).[114]

Following the consecration of the host, argues Wyclif, the bread demonstrated in the proposition "This is my body" still remains bread while at the same time is admitted to be the body of Christ. It is the bread that is demonstrated by the pronoun "this," and when read accordingly this proposition is true. Christ the Truth would never engage in sophistic duplicity; when giving consecrated bread to the apostles he meant that it remained such when they ate it. And yet in calling that bread his body, he did not intend an identical predication, but wished to convey a sacramental signification which revealed the truth of his presence in a way that identical predication could not. Christ's body assumes a sacramental presence, one by which he is uniquely present in the consecrated host. Denying that the substance of the bread is identical with Christ's body, however, does not mean it is falsely called the body of Christ, since in speaking of the bread as his body Christ did so truly and properly.[115] Whatever meaning the author intends is the proper meaning. Here Christ was employing a manner of speaking often found within Scripture, one intended to convey that the bread efficaciously and sacramentally signifies his body.[116] Once again, the literal or proper sense is determined by the author. Grasping this sense entails conforming oneself to that sense which the Holy Spirit has imprinted upon Scripture.[117] For if the pronoun "this" is false then "author of Scripture" speaks deceitfully, mocking his church in this instance—something clearly impossible insofar as all of Christ's sayings are true.[118] Still, says Wyclif, some heretics feel free to impose superfluous senses upon Scripture which the Holy Spirit does not warrant, nor the faith of Scripture support.[119] In claiming that the apostles' recognition of Christ in the breaking of the bread designated only the fracture of an accident apart from its subject, they have fallen under the sway of anti-Christ who not only destroys grammar, logic, and natural knowledge, but even obliterates the "sense of the gospel."[120]

Comments on the Translation

a) Text and Date

The present translation is based upon Buddensieg's critical edition of *De veritate sacrae scripturae*, itself part of an ambitious project undertaken by the Wyclif Society between the years 1882 and 1922, publishing in critical edition a considerable percentage of some three hundred Latin works attributed to Wyclif. This edition is drawn from four manuscripts of Oxford, Cambridge, Dublin, and Vienna, the last of which Buddensieg chose for his standard text. There is no doubt as to the authenticity of this treatise which Wyclif composed over a period stretching from late 1377 into the end of 1378.[121] *On the Truth of Holy Scripture* appears as the sixth treatise within Wyclif's twelve-part *Summa Theologiae* (1375–81), coming just after the completion of his *On Civil Dominion* which led to papal condemnation and the subsequent Lambeth trial that took place as this work was being written.[122] *On the*

Truth of Holy Scripture spans a tumultuous period from the death of Gregory XI to the election of Urban VI in April of 1378, and the ensuing schism with the election of the Avignon pope Clement VII in September of that same year.

Volume One of the critical edition contains Chapters One through Fifteen; Volume Two contains Chapters Sixteen through Twenty-Four; and Volume Three contains Chapters Twenty-Five through Thirty-Two. Buddensieg has already noted some major divisions within the text, and I have followed his lead in breaking this abridged translation into four parts while providing representative portions of every chapter in each part. The first part, consisting of Chapters One through Eight, deals with the absolute veracity of Scripture. The second part consists of Chapters Nine through Fifteen, discussing the authority of Scripture. Part Three is the shortest, comprised of Chapters Sixteen through Nineteen, and speaks to Scripture's divine origin. Finally, Part Four, consisting of Chapters Twenty through Thirty-Two, defends the superior nature of Scripture which must then serve as the paradigm for the ordering of Christendom.

The nature of the present TEAMS series dictated that this translation be an abridgment not to exceed much more than two hundred pages. All counted, the three-volume critical edition of *De veritate sacrae scripturae* consists of almost one thousand printed pages. Hence, while considerable portions had to be omitted, it was imperative that the integrity of the work be preserved. Though no abridgment can hope to pose as a substitute for the original, it can aspire to capture the original work's character and substance. To this end, the translation always adheres to the structure of Wyclif's treatise, maintaining the order of all of the thirty-two chapters, as well as the order of their contents. Passages have been omitted, of course, but nothing has been rearranged. Ellipses will alert the reader to such omissions, but page numbers of the critical edition are placed in the translated text, allowing for swift reference to the original Latin.

b) Translation Theory

Anyone familiar with Wyclif knows that his writing style is often prolix, repetitive, and even convoluted at times. Yet there is much to be foraged in those dense woods. Deciding just what to leave out can be a daunting task. Thus certain criteria were established to facilitate this process: omissions were made if an argument has been made at length earlier in the work, such that its inclusion would be redundant; if an argument amounts to a digression which may be of interest in itself, but is not directly pertinent to biblical exegesis; if it is a matter of providing yet further examples to illustrate an already established point. And lastly, because there are so many direct quotations from patristic sources these too must be omitted at times so as to provide maximum space for Wyclif's own words.

When translating biblical passages quoted by Wyclif, I follow his biblical quotations as given. A few words should be said in this regard. First of all, medieval editions of the Vulgate varied, and Wyclif's text might well reflect such variation in places. Secondly, and perhaps more importantly, as a fourteenth-century doctor of theology, a *magister sacrae paginae*, Wyclif would have had lengthy passages, even whole books, committed to memory. As such, the *magister* could cite a chapter number or opening phrase and assume that his audience would fill in the rest. We must not assume that Wyclif had the biblical text open before him as he wrote. And if when quoting from memory a few words are missing or rearranged he would not regard this as harmful to the text's integrity and veracity. Precisely because the medievals were so confident that the whole text falls within the parameters of the sense of the Holy Spirit, these minor deviations are permissible. In fact, my editorial decision to provide verse numbers may well be considered a violent anachronism perpetrated against the very spirit of a late medieval text.

Like so many of Wyclif's works, *On the Truth of Holy Scripture* is saturated with logical and metaphysical terminology. Because the goal of this translation is to provide an introduction to Wyclif's methods and theories of biblical interpretation for those who may be relatively unacquainted with the more arcane aspects of late medieval theology, I have tried to translate the technical terminology with English words and phrases which will convey their content. On this score, though, something must be said regarding the translation of a few crucial phrases which recur throughout the work, and are indeed essential to Wyclif's entire program of scriptural interpretation. Because Wyclif understood the literal sense of Scripture to encompass the whole meaning intended by the divine author this can include not only figurative language, but the mystical senses of Scripture as well. Thus what is meant by the phrase "literal sense" varies. On the one hand it may simply correspond to the literal-historical sense which comprises the first level of the *quadriga*, thereby distinguishing it from the mystical senses. On the other hand it includes whatever sense the divine author has chosen to convey the sacred meaning, and that might include the allegorical, tropological, or anagogical. When Wyclif argues that Holy Scripture is always and everywhere "literally" true he is referring to its "intended literal sense," which admits no possibility of contradiction.

The fact remains, however, that Wyclif employs a range of terms with sometimes very different connotations. Moreover, he will use the same Latin phrase to denote quite separate ways of reading the text. One of my chief responsibilities as translator is to keep these straight and alert the reader to nuances. I translate the phrase *ad literam* as "literal sense," or "literally," while furnishing the Latin in parentheses. When the more frequent term *literalis* occurs, I translate it also as "literal sense" but do not offer the Latin. These two phrases are relatively straightforward. Where it becomes more complicated is with the phrase *de virtute sermonis*. As we have observed, when Wyclif argues that Scripture is true *de virtute sermonis* he means according to the intended sense of the divine author, which may include figurative language. But when his opponents, the sophists, argue that contradictions can be found in the biblical text when read *de virtute sermonis* they mean the literal sense governed by the standard rules of proper supposition, thereby excluding figurative language. Hence, when Wyclif uses the phrase *de virtute sermonis* he may be referring to his own understanding, in which case I translate it as "intended literal sense." But where he is citing the arguments of his opponents, I have translated the phrase as "strictly literal sense." In either case I provide the Latin in parentheses.

As a final note, I would just add that modern students should recognize a similarity between this fourteenth-century debate regarding the proper application of widely accepted logical methods and those discussions of today concerning the appropriate use of historical-critical methods in biblical studies. Reading the work of a theologian six hundred years past may well yield some substantial connections to scriptural interpretation and authority in our own day.

Notes

1. Parliament passed *De haeretico comburendo* in 1401 while Arundel was Archbishop of Canterbury, allowing for the burning of Lollard heretics. The Carmelite Thomas Netter attacked Wycliffism in his *Doctrinale Antiquitatum Fidei Catholicae Ecclesiae* (1757; repr. Farnborough, 1967).

2. See *The Acts and Monuments of John Foxe*, ed. George Townsend, vol. Z (1843–49; repr. New York, 1965).

3. For detailed Wyclif historiography see James Crompton, "Fasciculi Zizaniorum I & II," *Journal of Ecclesiastical History* 12 (1961): 35–45; 155–66; James Crompton, "John Wyclif: A Study in Mythology," *Transactions - The Leicestershire Archaeological and Historical Society* 42 (1966–67): 6–34; Margaret Aston, "John Wycliffe's Reformation Reputation," *Past and Present* 30 (1965): 23–51; Leslie Fairfield, "John Bale and the Development of Protestant Hagiography in England," *Journal of Ecclesiastical History* 24:2 (April, 1973): 145–60.

4. See Buddensieg's introduction in *De veritate sacrae scripturae*, ed. Rudolf Buddensieg, vol. 1 (1905; repr. New York, 1966), pp. xxi–xli; see also Gotthard Lechler, *John Wycliffe and his English Precursors,* trans. with notes by Peter Lorimer (London, 1878), pp. 8–20, 428–66.

5. Lechler, *John Wycliffe*, pp. 287, 436.

6. On Wyclif's influence on the Lollards see Anne Hudson, *The Premature Reformation: Wycliffite texts and Lollard history* (Oxford, 1988).

7. For the thirty errors of Jan Hus see *Enchiridion Symbolorum*, ed. Heinrich Denzinger (Rome, 1976), pp. 1201–30. And for Wyclif's forty-five errors see ibid., pp. 1151–95.

8. For the most up-to-date biographical sketches of Wyclif see Michael Wilks, "John Wyclif: Reformer," in *Dictionnaire de spiritualité ascétique et mystique: doctrine et histoire*, vol. 16 (Paris, 1994), pp. 1501–12; reprinted in *Wyclif: Political Ideas and Practice: Papers by Michael Wilks*, ed. Anne Hudson (Oxford, 2000), pp. 1–15; and Anne Hudson, "John Wyclif," in *Dictionary of the Middle Ages*, ed. Joseph Strayer (New York, 1982–). For a full length biography see H. B. Workman's *John Wyclif: A Study of the English Medieval Church,* 2 vols. (Oxford, 1926); and Anthony Kenny's compact but erudite *Wyclif* (Oxford, 1985).

9. See J. I. Catto, "Wyclif and Wyclifism at Oxford 1356–1430," in *The History of the University of Oxford,* vol. 2, ed. J. I. Catto and Ralph Evans (Oxford, 1992), pp. 175–261; William J. Courtenay, "Theology and Theologians from Ockham to Wyclif," in *A History of the University of Oxford,* vol. 2 (London, 1924, 1927), pp. 1–34; J. A. Robson, *Wyclif and the Oxford Schools* (Cambridge, 1961), pp. 97–112, 221–31; Hastings Rashdall, *The Universities of Europe in the Middle Ages*, vol. 3, new edition in three volumes, ed. F. M. Powicke and A. B. Emden (Oxford, 1936), pp. 114–29.

10. W. J. Courtenay, *Schools and Scholars of the Fourteenth Century* (Princeton, 1987), pp. 348–55.

11. *De dominio divino: libri tres*, ed. R. L. Poole (1890; repr. New York, 1966).

12. *Tractatus de mandatis divinis*, ed. Johann Loserth and F. D. Matthew (1922; repr. New York, 1966).

13. See G. A. Benrath, *Wyclifs Biblekommentar* (Berlin, 1966); Beryl Smalley, "John Wyclif's *Postilla Super Totam Bibliam*," *Bodleian Library Record* 5 (1953): 186–205; Beryl Smalley, "Wyclif's *Postilla* on the Old Testament and his *Principium*," in *Oxford Studies Presented to Daniel Callus,* n.s. xvi (16) (Oxford, 1964), pp. 253–96.

14. *De civili dominio* I, ed. R. L. Poole (1885; repr. New York, 1966); *De civili dominio*, II–III, ed. Johann Loserth (1900–1904; repr. New York, 1966).

15. See Joseph Dahmus, *The Prosecution of John Wyclyf* (New Haven, 1952), pp. 7–34.

16. For the nineteen condemned propositions see *Enchiridion Symbolorum*, pp. 1121–39.

17. On the Lambeth proceedings see Dahmus, *Prosecution*, pp. 35–73.

18. See Dahmus, *Prosecution*, pp. 89–128.

19. Workman, *John Wyclif*, 1:149–55.

20. Beryl Smalley, "The Bible and Eternity: John Wyclif's Dilemma," *Journal of the Warburg and Courtauld Institutes* 27 (1964): 73–89.

21. A. J. Minnis, "'Authorial Intention' and the 'Literal Sense' in the Exegetical Theories of Richard Fitzralph and John Wyclif," *Proceedings of the Irish Academy* 75 (1975): 1–31.

22. G. R. Evans, "Wyclif's Logic and Wyclif's Exegesis: The Context," in *The Bible in the Medieval World: Essays in Memory of Beryl Smalley*, ed. Katherine Walsh and Diana Wood (Oxford, 1985), pp. 287–300; G. R. Evans, "Wyclif on Literal and Metaphorical," in *From Ockham to Wyclif*, ed. Anne Hudson and Michael Wilks (Oxford, 1987), pp. 259–66; G. R. Evans, "Wycliffe the Academic," *Churchman* 98:4 (1984): 307–18.

23. Kenny, *Wyclif*, pp. 59–61.

24. Kantik Ghosh, "Eliding the Interpreter: John Wyclif and Scriptural Truth," in *New Medieval Literatures*, vol. 2, ed. Rita Copeland, David Lawton, and Wendy Scase (Oxford, 1998), pp. 205–24.

25. A. J. Minnis, *Medieval Theory of Authorship* (London, 1984), pp. 74–117.

26. Minnis, *Medieval Theory of Authorship*, pp. 9–12.

27. *De veritate* I, p. 398.

28. *De veritate* I, pp. 390–92.

29. *De veritate* I, pp. 79–83, 112–14.

30. *Chartularium Universitatis Parisiensis* 2, 1, ed. Heinrich Denifle (Paris, 1889–1897): 505–07.

31. See W. J. Courtenay, "Force of Words and Figures of Speech: The Crisis over *Virtus Sermonis* in the Fourteenth Century," *Franciscan Studies* 44 (1984): 107–28.

32. *Johannis Wyclif Tractatus de logica*, vol. 1, ed. M. H. Dziewicki (1893; repr. New York, 1966). See especially the prologue.

33. *Fasciculi Zizaniorum Magistri Johannis Wyclif cum Tritico*, ed. W. W. Shirley, Rolls Series (London, 1858), pp. 4–103, 453–80. While Wyclif employs the variations *de virtute sermonis* and *de vi sermonis*, both mean the literal sense, which for him is the divine author's intended sense.

34. *Fasciculi Zizaniorum*, pp. 453–54.

35. *Fasciculi Zizaniorum*, pp. 27–28.

36. *Fasciculi Zizaniorum*, pp. 68–69.

37. *Fasciculi Zizaniorum*, pp. 41–42.

38. *Fasciculi Zizaniorum*, p. 459.

39. *Fasciculi Zizaniorum*, pp. 462–63.

40. *De civili dominio* I, p. 422.

41. *De civili dominio* I, p. 423.

42. *De civili dominio* I, p. 423.

43. *De civili dominio* I, p. 424.

44. *Tractatus de universalibus*, ed. Ivan Mueller (Oxford, 1985), pp. 15–16.

45. *De veritate* I, pp. 108–11.

46. *De veritate* I, p. 212.

47. *De dominio divino* I, ed. R. L. Poole (1890; repr. New York, 1966), pp. 102–03.

48. *De universalibus*, p. 49.

49. *De universalibus*, pp. 353–54.

50. *De veritate* I, pp. 49–50.

51. *De veritate* I, pp. 1–6.

52. *De veritate* I, pp. 109–10, 198–202; *De veritate* II, p. 20.

53. *De veritate* I, p. 156.

54. *De veritate* I, pp. 119–24.

55. *Johannis Wyclif Tractatus de potestate papae*, ed. Johann Loserth (1907; repr. New York, 1966), p. 51.

56. *De veritate* I, p. 87.

57. *De veritate* I, p. 114.

58. *De veritate* I, pp. 5–9.

59. *De veritate* I, pp. 10–15, 40–41.

60. *De veritate* II, p. 112.

61. *De veritate* II, pp. 49–50.

62. *De veritate* II, p. 67.

63. On the relationship between Scripture and Tradition in the Late Middle Ages see Heiko Oberman, *The Harvest of Medieval Theology* (1963; repr. Durham [NC], 1983), pp. 364–77.

64. *De veritate* I, p. 403.

65. Paul de Vooght, *Les sources de la doctrine chrétienne* (Bruges, 1954), pp. 169–83.

66. Wilks, "John Wyclif Reformer," in *John Wyclif, Political Ideas and Practice*, p. 12.

67. Brian Tierney, "'Sola Scriptura' and the Canonists," in *Collecteana Stephan Kuttner* I; *Studia Gratiana* XI (Rome, 1967), pp. 347–66.

68. *De veritate* II, pp. 129–30.

69. *De veritate* II, pp. 268–70.

70. *De veritate* II, pp. 181–82, 226–29.

71. *De veritate* III, pp. 1–2, 64–65.

72. *Johannis Wyclif Tractatus de ecclesia*, ed. Johann Loserth (1886; repr. New York, 1966), pp. 1–11.

73. *De ecclesia*, pp. 72, 76, 89, 117.

74. *De ecclesia*, pp. 28, 111, 141, 200–01, 409.

75. *De ecclesia*, p. 185.

76. *De ecclesia*, pp. 442–48.

77. *De ecclesia*, pp. 457–59.

78. Possible exceptions are found in 1381 *De eucharistia minor confessio* in *Fasciculi Zizaniorum*, pp. 115–16; and his 1384 *De antichristo* I, xlviii, ed. Johann Loserth (1896; repr. New York, 1966), pp. 175–76.

79. *De ecclesia*, pp. 5–6, 28–29.

80. *De civili dominio* I, pp. 372–73.

81. *De civili dominio* I, pp. 415–16.

82. *De potestate papae*, p. 262.

83. *De potestate papae*, p. 248.

84. *De potestate papae*, p. 261.

85. *De civili dominio* I, pp. 402–03.

86. *De ecclesia*, p. 35.

87. *De ecclesia*, pp. 23–24.

88. *De civili dominio* I, pp. 281–83.

89. *De civili dominio* I, pp. 5–8, 25.

90. *De civili dominio* I, pp. 62, 66.

91. *De civili dominio* I, pp. 45, 101.

92. *De civili dominio* I, p. 28.

93. *Tractatus de officio regis*, ed. Alfred Pollard and Charles Sayle (1887; repr. New York, 1966), pp. 4–5. See Michael Wilks, "Predestination, Property and Power: Wyclif's Theory of Dominion and Grace," *Studies in Church History* 2 (1965): 220–36.

94. *De officio regis*, pp. 13, 137. This distinction had already been employed by the Anglo-Norman Anonymous ca. 1100.

95. *De potestate papae*, p. 377.

96. *De ecclesia*, pp. 322, 365.

97. *De civili dominio* I, pp. 1–2, 47.

98. *De civili dominio* I, p. 20.

99. *De civili dominio* I, pp. 21–22.

100. *De ecclesia*, p. 141.

101. *De civili dominio* I, pp. 266–71.

102. *De ecclesia*, pp. 176–80.

103. *De potestate papae*, pp. 80, 87, 92–93; *De ecclesia*, pp. 361–64.

104. *De civili dominio* I, p. 285.

105. K. B. McFarlane, *John Wycliffe and the Beginnings of English Nonconformity* (London, 1952), pp. 187–88.

106. Michael Wilks, "*Reformatio Regni*: Wyclif and Hus as Leaders of Religious Protest Movements," *Studies in Church History* 9 (1972): 109–30.

107. For the charges and a list of council members see *Fasciculi Zizaniorum*, pp. 110–13.

108. *Tractatus de apostasia*, ed. M. H. Dziewicki (London, 1889; repr. New York, 1966), pp. 65, 144; *Tractatus de eucharistia tractatus maior*, ed. Johann Loserth (1892; repr. New York, 1966), pp. 53, 71, 189.

109. *De eucharistia*, pp. 15, 19, 57.

110. *Fasciculi Zizaniorum*, p. 117.

111. *Fasciculi Zizaniorum*, p. 119.

112. *Fasciculi Zizaniorum*, p. 119.

113. *Fasciculi Zizaniorum*, pp. 115–16. On this see I. C. Levy, "*Christus qui mentiri non potest*: John Wyclif's Rejection of Transubstantiation," *Recherches de Théologie et Philosophie médiévales* 66:2 (1999): 316–34.

114. *De apostasia*, pp. 48–49. *Iohannis Wyclif Sermones* II, Sermon 48, ed. Johann Loserth (1888; repr. New York, 1966), p. 350; *De eucharistia*, pp. 139–40, 157–58.

115. *De apostasia*, p. 106; *De eucharistia*, p. 35.

116. *De eucharistia*, pp. 50, 116, 296.

117. *De eucharistia*, pp. 216–17, 296.

118. *Joannis Wiclif Trialogus cum Supplemento Trialogi* IV, ed. Gotthard Lechler (Oxford, 1869), pp. 251–53.

119. *Trialogus* IV, p. 254.

120. *Trialogus* IV, p. 261.

121. For information regarding text and date see Buddensieg's introduction to *De veritate sacrae scripturae*, 1:xlviii–lxxi. See also W. R. Thomson, *The Latin Writings of John Wyclyf* (Toronto, 1983), pp. 55–57.

122. Wyclif mentions this in *De veritate* I, p. 374.

On the Truth of Holy Scripture

Part One: The Veracity of Scripture

(*De ver.* I,i): Scripture's Use of Metaphorical Language

(1) It remains to discuss briefly those errors and agreements concerning the sense of Scripture which are being disseminated these days even more so than usual. For Scripture is the foundation of every Catholic opinion, and within it resides the very salvation of the faithful. Moreover, it is the exemplar (2) and mirror designed to examine and extinguish every sort of error or heretical evil. Surely even a small error in this principle could bring about the death of the Church.

First of all, some wish to refute the truth and logical conclusions of Holy Scripture in a number of ways.[1] Now in this matter I have often said that Scripture is true in all of its parts according to the intended literal sense (*de virtute sermonis*). This is why professors of Holy Scripture ought to imitate its manner of speaking, adhering to its eloquence and logic, more so than any foreign pagan writing.

The first objection raised against my position is based upon Book 4, Chapter 8 of St. Augustine's *On Christian Doctrine*, where he appears to say that we should not imitate the authors of Holy Scripture in their manner of speaking.[2]

I respond to this by offering proof drawn from Augustine's testimony concerning logic, metaphysics, and whatever other sort of truth which should be affirmed as more valid (3) than some proof elicited from the declarations of Aristotle, or any other pagan, who remains a stranger to the light of our faith. Now I contend that what Augustine meant in this chapter is that there are two manners of speaking among the authors of Holy Scripture, namely the obscure and the plain. And in regard to these two ways of speaking he offers two conclusions. First, that whether they are explicating Scripture itself or expressing the appropriate meaning which rests beyond the text of Scripture, the interpreters of Holy Scripture should not imitate the aforementioned authors in those instances of obscure discourse. Augustine posits six reasons for their obscure speech which are beyond our own manner of speaking.[3] Whereupon, that text of Augustine reads:

> We should never think that we must imitate them in these things which they had spoken with a useful and salutary obscurity for the sake of exercising and polishing the minds of the readers in a certain manner, and for breaking up the monotony and sharpening the desire of those who wish to learn, while also concealing things, whether in order that the minds of the ungodly would be converted to piety or excluded from the mysteries.[4]

See how we lack the authority of obscure speech because of the six causes, (4) on account of which they spoke so obscurely. Therefore, when explicating such passages, it is better that they speak with special clarity, lest they end up merely reciting the texts, rather than explaining them. And it thus follows in Augustine's text: "They spoke in this manner so that those coming after them, who would properly understand and explain them, would find another grace in the Church of God, certainly of a different sort, and yet closely following it."[5]

The second conclusion of Augustine is found in his *On the Plain Locutions of the Authors of Scripture*:

> Concerning the texts of the authors of Scripture, which can be understood without difficulty, we are permitted to adopt their example of rhetoric and logic, thus speaking in conformity with them. Yet in doing so, we ought to imitate

> them as humble disciples, and not as if we have been made their equals in authority.[6]

The first part is indicated in Chapters 7 and 8 of Luke, and the second part is expressed in these words, when he says, "Their expositors should not speak as though they considered themselves to be of equal authority with the very ones they are elucidating."[7]

In light of this, a third point is clarified. It is not plausible to argue that because we should not put ourselves on a par with the authors of Holy Scripture while explaining their obscure language, nor claim to be their equals in authority of discourse when expressing their plain speech, that we should not, therefore, imitate their logic or eloquence. For Augustine indicates that we should. Surely we have grace not only for a time, but subsequently as well, in the manner of disciples.

(5) In regard to the exposition of the senses of Scripture, the Church and the holy doctors readily grant that according to the intended literal sense (*de virtute sermonis*) Christ is a "lamb, sheep, calf, bull, serpent, lion, worm," though he is such according to the mystical sense, which belongs to the fullness of the literal sense. Nor should one be troubled by that saying of Augustine in Chapter 6, Book 4 of *On Christian Doctrine*, where he states that, "another eloquence is neither suitable for these authors, nor appropriate for others."[8] Now this is literally true (*ad verba*), since every rhetorician has his own eloquence, but the sense is that this eloquence is not suitable for others in an authentic fashion, but rather by way of imitation, on the grounds that they are their disciples, in keeping with that passage in 1 Pet. 4:11, **If anyone speaks, let it be as if these are the words of God**. Otherwise, the Church would never say in her service, in conformity with Scripture, that the Lamb of God inclines his ear to us. And such would be the case for the greater part of the ecclesiastical service which has

been elicited from, and thoroughly informed by, the field of Scripture through the holy doctors. If this were not so then the holy doctors would not follow the logic of Scripture in their own writings, having put aside foreign logics. Indeed, there would exist no other means by which we could learn the Lord's Prayer or the Creed, since both are infused with the eloquence and logic of Scripture. Rather, that logic would have been inserted in vain were it not permissible for us also to learn it, and consequently practice it. This may be clearly confirmed, insofar as the holy doctors, and especially Augustine, can be cited to prove the contrary, as they have in fact taught the very opposite most effectively. We must trust more in the deeds than the words of those who followed Scripture with the utmost strictness, not only in the real philosophy of life, as he thoroughly teaches, but in the philosophy of preaching, as evinced below. Who, therefore, who would say that they mean we should not follow them in logic, when they in fact teach the very opposite? (6) For we are unable to obtain so perfect a logic or eloquence as Scripture possesses, but instead possess only a humble derivative, one which is made more perfect the more it conforms to it. And this is why Augustine says we have a consequent grace.

No one should be troubled by the fact that lords speak in one way and servants in another, since when there is this sort of diversity it is better that one pay attention to what belongs to the subject matter rather than what pertains to manner or form of speech, as Christ says in his own person: **I am the first and the last** (Rev. 22:13). And yet the Christian saying this in his own person would be a blasphemer on account of the subject matter. Therefore, let us retain that form of Scripture's elocution which is suited to our subject matter, so that just as Christ designates his own Father singularly, evinced in John, we might designate our own fathers and brothers singularly, as Christ teaches us in Matt. 6:9–13 in the Lord's Prayer. And let us refrain from imitating the pompous elocution of the secular lords, for I tell you that this is just the sort of fatuous speech which is sapping the strength of the Christian religion.

On this account, the form of Scripture's elocution is the exemplar of every other credible manner of speaking.

(7) The second argument is drawn from the testimony of Augustine's *Sermon 47 on John*, where he says that,

> Christ is called many things by way of similitudes and other devices which would take too long to recount. If, however, you were to discuss the properties of these things which it seems you have become accustomed to see, he is neither a rock, because that is hard and he is not without sense; nor is he a door, since a carpenter did not construct him; nor is he a cornerstone, since he was not created by a sculptor; nor is he a shepherd, since he is not a guardian of four-legged sheep; nor he is a lion, since he is not a wild beast; nor is he a lamb, since he is not a farm animal. He is all of these things, therefore, by way of similitude.[9]

With regard to this citation, I suppose that those arguing from a proof based upon the testimony of Augustine will accept his statements without a mistrustful difference either way. Now I ask you, how could I put faith in a proof based upon the testimony of Augustine if I only cite him in these matters which agree with my own sense, while in those others which disagree with my own opinion I would then cast him aside? For in this way, those holding two contradictory opinions would superfluously accept him based upon the testimony of his statement. (8) In fact, a little later on in the same *Sermon 47* he says,

> Discern, therefore, how the Lord Christ is both the door and the shepherd. He is the door as he throws himself open, and the shepherd entering in through him, but inasmuch as he is the shepherd he extended this even to his members. Now Peter is a shepherd and Paul is a shepherd, and indeed

> the rest of the apostles are shepherds, and the good bishops are shepherds. Yet no one rightly calls himself the door, since he reserved this title for himself alone.[10]

Therefore, he properly called himself the door, just as he is also the foundation, as Augustine demonstrates from Scripture in 1 Cor. 1 and 3. Whereupon, it follows in Augustine's text, "He never became the cornerstone for two flocks, but rather for two walls. And for this reason he is both the door and the cornerstone."[11] Look, if someone arguing in this way were to ponder the logic and words of Augustine, he would expressly grasp how it is that Christ is the door and yet is not a door. And the same applies in similar cases. Hence, according to Augustine's discourse there is evidence that Christ is not a door, and thus he himself is not the door. But there is in fact better evidence that is in keeping with the discourse of the very same Augustine that Christ is the door. For Scripture says this, thereby authenticating Augustine. Thus Christ is the door. Augustine expressly stipulates it either way, and our faith establishes the affirmative, (9) since in John 10:7 the Truth, who cannot lie, says, **I am the door**.

But two things must be stated here. One is a defense of Augustine, lest so subtle a doctor be thought to have erred in these expressions, owing to an ignorance of logic. The second pertains to the understanding of Scripture in such matters, and how it ought to be understood.

Augustine's logic is founded upon the authority of Scripture, and also upon the well-known logical principle that in equivocations there is no contradiction. For it not only pertains to a name, but to a thing as well as a name. Christ says to his brethren in John 7:8–10, **You go up to this festival day. I, however, will not go up to that festival day**; and thereupon it follows in the text, **And then he went up to the festival day, not openly, but as though in secret**. God forbid that anyone would believe the Truth had either lied in this instance or some other, or had asserted a falsehood. Again, in the same vein, the Truth says in Luke 19:26, **From the one who has not, even that will be taken away from him**. And in Prov. 13:4 his father Solomon was instructed by him that **the slothful person desires and does not desire**. Let no Christian ever think that these three examples of Scripture, (10) together with ones similar to them, are asserting anything according to such a form which would result in them savoring of falsehood rather then being engaged in the pointing out of a mystery. It is, therefore, a general and exemplary mystery. And thus the humble Christian should not be ashamed to concede such things according to the equivocal sense, even though they appear to be contradictions to the puffed up sophists and those other people who have even less understanding of these things.

Although there are any number of examples, for the sake of establishing this meaning I will draw upon a three-fold testimony from Augustine. Now when commenting on Ps. 120,[12] he explicates that passage in Prov. 18:21, **Death and life are in the hands of the tongue**. He says,

> We acknowledged tongues in vain; those of the flesh are moved in the mouth, and by striking the palate and teeth they distinguish the sounds by which we speak. The hands of the tongue are shown to me. The tongue, therefore, does not have hands, and yet it does have hands. What are the hands of the tongue? The powers of the tongue. And so it is that in this very way death and life are in the hands of the tongue: **By your mouth you will be justified and by your mouth you will be condemned** (Matt. 12:37).[13]

There are many such sayings in Scripture where the equivocation of terms can be observed. As I have often said, anyone who is unwilling to understand the grammar belonging to some part of Scripture, unless it conforms to that which he learnt as a child, (11) will not only remain quite ignorant of the mysteries of Scripture, but will end up entangling himself in a great number of improprieties. For in these sayings the Lord teaches his own logic and grammar which remains hidden to unbelievers. Let me ask you, how would the grammarian come to recognize that the term 'hand' is an equivocation employed to signify the bodily organ in one instance, while 'power' in another instance, that created or uncreated principle of operation, unless he had earnestly sought out this equivocation in Scripture? There are many ways in which Augustine proves from Scripture that the hand of the Lord is his power. Hence he states, "Listen more attentively, brother, lest up until this point you have been thinking in the fleshly sense that God is distinct in members. Listen clearly to the way in which the hand is called power."[14]

The second testimony of Augustine is culled from his comments in the second sermon *On Psalm 26*, where by raising doubt as to whether the utterances of the Psalmist are our own utterances or the utterances of the spirit of God, he argues with respect to the parts:

> If they were not our utterances, since they are the utterances of sorrow and tears, we would be lying, inasmuch as the Psalm is speaking of nothing but the words of miserable laborers. But it is not fitting that these utterances would belong to him, since he must be venerated, and then we would not be speaking the truth in our own locutions.[15]

And further on he explains it under these words:

> It is fitting that the merciful one speaking to the miserable would employ the voice of the miserable for us; and so this is true on both sides: it is our voice, and it is not ours. (12) Thus the utterance is of the spirit of God, and yet it is not of him. The utterance is of the spirit of God, because we would not learn those things if not for his inspiration. They are not, however, his own. For he is neither miserable, nor does

> he toil. On the contrary, those things pertain to us, because they are utterances which indicate our own misery. And yet again, they are not our own, because it is on account of his gift that we deserve to lament.[16]

Look at this saint! He is such a humble logician, and still so subtle. No fear of the sophists prevented him from conceding conclusions based upon the authority of Scripture which might seem to contradict themselves in the eyes of those foolish ones who know nothing of equivocations. He wishes to say, therefore, that these are not our utterances, but principally Christ's, though they are not Christ's utterances, but personally our own.

In order to understand this one must first observe how Augustine speaks with the utmost wisdom when he says that the Church is one man whose head is Christ, and the members are the predestined faithful. Whereupon he says in his commentary on Ps. 140 that just as in our body the head speaks for the rest of the members, so Christ speaks for the members of his mystical body, as in Acts 9:4, **Saul, Saul, why do you persecute me**; and in Matt. 25:40, **Whatever you have done unto the least of these, you have done unto me**. The voice of the Lord now speaks in the first of the members, and now in the person of the head, as clarified in *On Christian Doctrine* and often in his commentary on the Psalms.

(13) The third example is a saying of Augustine's drawn from his *Sermon 47 on John* where he demonstrates how Christ did not die according to his divinity or soul, but according to his body. In so relating this he says,

> I do not know whether my soul does not die. If it is not killed by you it does not die. How can you ask: am I able to kill my soul? In the meanwhile, so that I would not speak other sins: **The mouth which lies kills the soul** (Wisd. of Sol. 1:11). How then, you say, I am sure it does not die? Hear the Lord himself granting assurance to the servant: **Do**

> **not fear those who kill the body, and afterwards have nothing which they might do. But fear him who has the power to kill the body and the soul in Gehenna** (Luke 12:4–5). See, the soul dies, and see the soul does not die. Just as for your flesh to die is to lose its life, which is the soul, so for your soul to die is to lose its life, which is God. Certainly, the soul is immortal, and still it is dead, just like the voluptuous widow, as the Apostle says (1 Tim. 5:6).[17]

Therefore, just as this widow can be said to be both alive and dead, so it is with the soul, while it has been deprived by God, as he explained when commenting on that passage in Ps. 131, **Blessing, I will bless its widow** (Ps. 132:15).

(14) Look at what sorts of conclusions the saint elicits from Scripture; see how they are keeping with the form of the words! Now there are any number of such sayings belonging to this saint, and to others as well, who concede conclusions of this kind based upon the authority of Scripture. It is made clear in these three sayings, for example, which are not recited in an altogether sterile fashion when they explain the meaning of the Scriptures surpassing the grammar and logic which they teach.

In light of what has been said, one reckons that the authority of Augustine does not militate against conceding the figurative locutions of Scripture simply, when he does this in his very own person. Nor is he to be reproached for being ignorant of logic, despite the opinion of some people who know nothing of Aristotle's logic and the mystical equivocation of the Scriptures.

It remains to be seen, moreover, how someone might discern the sense in which these figurative sayings of Scripture should be comprehended. As I have often said, they should be understood according to the mystical sense, the spiritual sense, the symbolic and proportional, just as the holy commentators on Scripture so often say. Clearly, in the case of something attributed to God which is signified by a proposition of mystical theology whereby one of the extreme terms is the name of a creature,[18] we should observe those conditions and properties established by the analogy, in keeping with the genus found in the creatures whose name is accepted.[19] Therefore, this sort of predication could be attributed to God in the equivocal sense, by honoring only the perfect aspect of the analogy, while putting aside those imperfect properties belonging to the genus. (15) And so it is when the names of creatures belonging to one genus are proportionately attributed to the nature of a creature of another genus, whether for the sake of commendation or vituperation. Eliciting that sense is the proper task of philosophers, as I have demonstrated in Book 3, Chapter 27 in *On Civil Dominion*,[20] under the authority of Augustine in his *Against Simplicianus*.[21] For example, according to the uncultured grammarians the term 'lion' signifies a roaring four-legged beast, while according to the theologians it signifies still beyond this, designating Christ in one instance and the devil in another, as Gregory demonstrates in Chapters 4, 17 and 18 in Book 3 of the *Morals*, having deduced this from Scripture.[22] Now the fifth chapter of the Apocalypse (Rev. 5:5) says, **See, the Lion of the tribe of Judah, the Root of David, opens the book and loosens its seven seals.** And 1 Pet. 5:8, **Like a roaring lion your adversary the devil walks about seeking the one he might devour.** In order to express (16) the equivocation of the sense, one prophet says that Christ is a lion, and the other, that the devil is likewise as a lion. And so it is with other terms in Scripture.

Let us consider the nature of that beast, and then let us see whether we can discover a resemblance in Christ.

In the natural world the lion is the king of the beasts, that one who roars in the mountains, to whom the other animals are naturally subject. By further comparison, he is the strongest, given the magnitude of his breast and head. And yet with his roar he brings to life a sleeping cub within the space of four days, such that he is then roused to movement.

Corresponding to these three, Christ is the first born of the tribe of Judah. **On his thigh is inscribed, "King of kings and Lord of lords,"** as it is said in Apocalypse 19 (Rev. 19:16); the one to whom **every knee should bend in heaven, on earth and in hell**, as the Apostle says in Phil. 2:10; and the one for whom the trumpets will sound at the last judgment **when all the nations will be gathered before him**, as Matt. 25:32 clearly states. This is the lion most powerful in his spiritual aspects, **when all power in heaven and on earth** is chiefly given to him, as is said in the last chapter of Matthew (Matt. 28:18). That is the power pertaining to the heart or spirit which is commonly applicable to the divine person who is in the midst of any of his members, as said in Matt. 18:20. For it is the necessary means of proportional merit for any Christian, just as the heart and chest hold together the mid-section of the human body with respect to strength. Certainly, Christ was very often holding together the mid-section, just as when life of the Church was first (17) worthily formed in his mystical body the life and heat of love flooded into the rest of the members, as the faith of Scripture makes clear. Likewise, he called Lazarus to life with his roar when he stank in the tomb for four days. In John 11:43, after he had wept, his great voice resounded as he cried, **Lazarus, come out**! Nowhere else does one read of a lion roaring so powerfully, so strongly, and from such a distance, as this voice. For his shout was not only heard by the soul, but even terrified the demons who held it captive in the depths of hell. The epics of the poets do not allow that such a thing was even possible for the thunder. Whereupon, the soul of Lazarus, held against its will by demons, then appeared. And he brought to life the dead body, restoring its motion and vital functions. For it is said in John 12:2 that, **Lazarus was one of those sitting at the table**. That roar of our lion heralded the middle roar of which we read in Matt. 27:50–52, **Crying out with a great**

voice, Jesus released his spirit, and behold, the veil of the temple was rent in two parts from the top to the bottom, and the earth shook, and the rocks were split, and the tombs were opened, and many bodies of the saints who had fallen asleep were raised. That roar, which the Apostle calls the mighty cry, is greater than the earlier one and signifies the greatest roar of all at the final judgment, when the dead from the four corners of the earth **will hear the voice of the Son of God** (John 5:28). Thus he will bring them to life with a mighty cry either way following the mortification of the children of Christ in accordance with the sins of the four affections, the four ages and four times.

(18) Accordingly, it is appropriate to search within the lion for properties proportional to the devil, since in rapacity he is the strongest of the beasts, while pertaining to death he is the attacker of men. Fire proceeds from the collision of his hard bones, and he endures continuous fever due to the fury of his cunning. And so I say that the devil is the king who reigns over all the sons of pride, having **power to which nothing on earth can be compared**, as is said in Job 41:24. To the ends of the earth his evil has endured, so fiercely and cruelly doing men harm. Therefore, now that anti-Christ and his divisions are on the verge of victory he attacks the members of Christ even more ferociously than ever. [. . .]

(*De ver.* I,ii): The Logic of Scripture and Pagan Philosophers

(20) I can refute the previous objections in a three-fold manner.[23] First, in light of the fact that the most absurd method employed in disputation is that of refutation, to which Augustine's aforementioned response at the beginning pertains. Therefore, neither Scripture, nor the teaching doctor, can lapse into this method.

In this matter it is evident that there are those such as the sophists, ignorant of logic and wishing for vainglory, who burst forth with assertions of this sort: "Look how you were proven to have contradicted yourself. Today I learnt in the lecture halls that one ought to concede that there are contradictions found within the Sacred Page." They will mock with derision, hints and insults whenever their arguments fail. Still, these are things which the pious Christian humbly endures on account of his love for Christ and the edification of the Church. He would rather suffer reproach for the sake of Christ than be ashamed before Christ on the final day because he had failed to imitate him. For in Luke 9:26 Christ says, **He who is ashamed of my words, this one the Son of Man will be ashamed of before the angels of God.**

Do not be ashamed, therefore, of this evidence: Holy Scripture speaks in this way; therefore, I, as its humble disciple, should speak under its authority in a similar manner. Love, which is intended either way in Scripture, moves even modern doctors to employ a magisterial eloquence derived from Scripture, even if it might appear contrary to the human sciences.

[. . .] (22) In light of these things, it is clear that the humble disciples of Scripture are not refuted by conceding contradictions, given this conclusion: (23) Scripture most effectively teaches that in equivocations there are no contradictions. Therefore, just as the sophist is like a hypocrite more interested in gaining a reputation for knowledge in the eyes of men, than he is in his existence in the sight of God, so on the contrary, the evangelical logician, having put aside worldly fame, would rather be considered a fool in the eyes of the world for Christ's sake, in order that he might be counted wise before God. Now sophists are hateful to God, says the wise man of Ecclesiasticus 37 (Sir. 37:23); just as the Apostle says in Rom 1:22, **declaring themselves wise, they became fools**.

Yet I also confess to such vainglory. For so often, whether in arguing or responding, I fell away from the teaching of

Scripture, wishing to achieve an air of celebrity amid the crowd, while at the same time revealing the arrogance of the sophists. Now, however, I realize that there is no logic ascribed to Holy Scripture, let alone drawn from it, which could appear as a contradiction to the foolish, except that it was inserted there for the sake of indicating some mystery of Scripture, to be followed by the disciples. Hence Christ says in the Apostle (Rom. 15:4), **Whatever was written was written for our instruction.**

Hence, whenever I come across what appears to be a contradiction in Scripture, I immediately recognize that it is intended to educate us in the ways of equivocation, so that we might adapt our speech to that place and time. Therefore, when Christ says, **I am not going up** (John 7:8) he is condescending to human weakness. For by his authority they ought to speak in a similar fashion. Now we commonly say: I have not eaten, I have not celebrated, and similar such phrases, (24) while specifically supplying in thought a certain time which will be properly understood by the ones with whom I am communicating. This way, I can deny that I will be involved in such an action at that time. In my opinion, when Christ was asked by the brothers what hour he would go up to Jerusalem, since he would in fact go up there, he claimed most truthfully that he would not go up, but supply here: "publicly at this hour."

Let us put aside duplicity and adapt our speech to the general understanding of those with whom we are communicating, less afraid of the various sophistical refutations than of some lack of charity on our own part, or that of others. For it is clear, that by preserving this logic we will not lapse into that method which is so unbecoming in the sight of God.

(25) [. . .] It is obvious that Christ distinctly equivocates with his own relatives regarding the festival day given the dictates of their worldly affections.

Third, Augustine points out how Christ goes up on the day of the festival day, not openly, but in secret, as it were:

> He goes up, not as though he wished for worldly glory, but rather in order to teach something salutary, that he might correct people, so they would then turn toward that eternal festival. He wished to avert their love from this age and turn them around towards God. (26) Yet that he went up in secret is not without symbolism.[24]

He does not go up in secret, therefore, only for fear of the Jews, since the hour of his passion had not yet arrived, nor only because he wished to teach his disciples how they too would be required to flee persecution from one city to the next, but rather that he might bring to our attention the flow of present time into the future allegorically, tropologically, and anagogically. It should be observed, moreover, that the Feast of the Tabernacles was celebrated in memory of that time when Israel dwelt in tabernacles in the desert. For having fled from Egypt and the servitude of pharaoh into the promised land, Israel abided in tabernacles, evinced in Exod. 23:14–33. Because, therefore, according to the Apostle in 1 Cor. 10:11, **All these things happened to them by way of a figure, since they were written down for our chastisement, upon whom the end of the ages has come**, it was deemed worthy that, by his own actions, Christ would unlock the mystical sense of this history for us. For the people of faith have been liberated through Christ from Egyptian servitude, in which we served the devil, pharaoh, in the darkness of our sins, when we were fashioning works of clay according to our earthly desires. It was as if we were preparing red bricks for the devil's body or spouse as we gathered up the straw of the earth into the furnace of the soul's temptation and tribulation. And so it is with other figures which belong to history's mystical sense. But Christ, first among the tribe of Judah, walked across the Red Sea, (27) just as Amminadab. He leads us out of the Egyptian servitude through that Baptism of Christ which is reddened by his own blood. Once more, it is as if we are being led by the Lord on a pilgrimage in this age, as we pass through the land of the living, dwelling in tabernacles in the desert. For Augustine says, "He dwells among the tabernacles, who understands himself to be a pilgrim in this world, sighing for the heavenly fatherland."[25] Whereupon, in order that he might signify that complete sense to us, and that our **life his hidden with Christ**, as the Apostle says in Col. 3:3, Christ went up secretly to the Feast of the Tabernacles because, as it says in 1 John 3:2, **Now we are sons of God, and what we will be has not yet appeared.**

I say then, it was for these reasons that it was revealed to us that Christ went to the Feast of the Tabernacles in secret, in case our way of life might be characterized by a craving for secular glory. Second, that we might know that Christians **have no lasting city here** (Heb. 13:14) with respect to allegory. And third, that we would see how the great festival day prefigures the ascension of this man who descended from heaven and the perpetual feast, with respect to anagogy, for as 1 John 3:2 says, **we know this, however, when he has appeared we will be like him**.

Look at how many mysteries the feast and the word of Christ has borne! For what seems uncultured and contradictory to us, actually proves to be wise in this way, so long as we do not ignore the equivocation and the reason why Scripture equivocates. And so I say it is only right that we should be well acquainted with these instances, and be willing to speak of them. For there are no contradictions either in the words of the Lord, nor in what follows from them, but actually a great deal of information. The better and more subtle Scripture is found in the form of words which Christ has instituted, rather than what human arrogance so rashly amends.

(28) I will clarify other apparent contradictions and the employment of such a manner of speaking in the third and fifth chapters below.

Second, some argue that if one accepts the aforementioned response then every doctrinal dispute would be confounded, since someone would be able to express such equivocations regarding a vow, and thus contradict themselves in any given situation, with the result that the philosophy of Aristotle would be destroyed, not to mention the certitude of faith which expresses itself in language.

I respond to this by denying the inference which is thereby drawn.[26] It is, nonetheless, conceded that a man could abuse the knowledge of Scripture's logic, since knowledge must be distinguished from good character whenever it puffs up, according to the Apostle. Thus the Christian should not employ equivocations unless they are firmly grounded in Scripture. For if the verbose sophist insists on chattering to no purpose, then he contradicts the rules of Scripture established by the one who says in 1 Tim. 6:3–5, **whoever teaches otherwise than according to Holy Scripture is to be censured, because he does not agree with the sound words of our Lord Jesus Christ and the teaching that is in accordance with godliness. For he is proud, knowing nothing, but hungering for debates and disputes over words. From these arise envy, dissension, blasphemies, evil suspicions, and struggles among those who are corrupt in mind and bereft of the truth**. Yet our **God is not a God of dissension but of peace**, as the Apostle says in 1 Cor. 14:33. One must surely recognize that a considerable portion of our disputation departs from the rules of Christ's law whenever we dispute for the sake of vainglory, rather than charitably seeking to elucidate Scripture and serve the Church. (29) And so the humility belonging to the logic of Scripture sets the first stage for the destruction of such sophistical contentions. Doctrinal dispute can then be preserved by excluding fallacy through divine logic. In this manner any Christian expressing duplicity can be discerned, and consequently shown to be standing in greater contradiction to himself, both in his deeds and reputation, as opposed to the devout Christian who neither learns, teaches, nor disputes, except for the sake of the honor of his God and the benefit of his Church.

With regard to all of Aristotle's philosophy, it could clearly be saved in its entirety and purified of its errors if these errors were retracted by means of the philosophy of Scripture wherever this is expedient and would otherwise lack its ultimate perfection. For it is impossible that a worldly science would not be deficient, since it lacks the form of the science of the Scriptures. Hence, that philosophy which the Christian piously learns from the books of Aristotle is not studied because it is Aristotle's, but instead, because it belongs to the authors of Holy Scripture. And the same applies to his science, which is also more correctly learned from the books of theology. Now I do not deny that Aristotle was a great philosopher, whose books are legitimately read and meritoriously studied. Nevertheless, we should not learn his errors regarding the eternity of the world, the sea, time, and (30) the other things to which Christians posit a beginning. Rather, we ought to contemplate the principles of Scripture, so that we might better understand how to destroy his errors and demolish his sophisms. Indeed, the Profound Doctor accomplishes this elegantly, along with many other saints.[27] Nor do I think that we have to concede any ground by believing his commentator Averroes when he says in the prologue at the start of the *Physics*,[28] that this error cannot be found among his sayings, or that he had no intention of denying the beginning of the created universe as some would imagine, or even that he later recanted his errors in the book *On the Nature of the Gods*, in *On the Secrets of the Secrets*, and in *On Fruit*, as Master Albert says.[29] (31) Indeed, such questions as these, as well as that question whereby it is doubted whether these books were his own or not, and whether he is saved or damned, along with other similar ones, really seem useless for the Christian. For in this matter I am quite certain that it is not truly philosophical to deny the creation of the world and all of its parts, nor the uncreated Trinity, along with the ideas and other eternal truths.[30] Just as it is not philosophical to assert the opposite of any truth of faith or Scripture, so the same applies in any school or epoch. Here it is so proven: every philosophy is a science; therefore, everything philosophical is scientific. Yet nothing false is scientific, since only that which exists may be known. Therefore, nothing false is philosophical, and consequently no philosophical falsehood exists either to be affirmed or comprehended. And from this it is evident that no philosophy of Aristotle, or of any other philosopher, is incompatible with theology, (32) although the errors of the philosophers are contrary to sacred knowledge. For this reason they must be deprived of the reputation of being true philosophers. Clearly then, nothing true is contrary to logic, provided that it is in keeping with this definition. Now a philosopher is described as a lover of prudence (*sapientia*), though it is evident that nobody is a philosopher inasmuch as he lapses into error. For then he is no different than a fool who hates prudence (*sapientia*) or wisdom (*sophia*), the very opposites of falsehood. Therefore, the greatest philosopher is none other than Christ, Wisdom itself (*sophia*), our God. Consequently, it is by following and studying him that we too become philosophers, while in learning various falsehoods we are straying from philosophy insofar as we drift away from the authentic understanding of the saints, who are the true philosophers. Indeed, if it were philosophical to posit that the world is coeternal with God, whether through proof derived from reason or through proof drawn from authority, it would not be via the first mode, since no reason can prove this. Yet the sophisms which serve to deceive the people who believe this are contrary to reason. Therefore, they should not be believed, nor any other conclusion of this sort which will only lead people astray.

If the conclusion of Aristotle or any other pagan should be believed by authority, all the more so should the opposite be believed, based upon the authority of Christ, the supreme philosopher. Consequently, this is disbelieved.

[. . .] (33) In regard to such matters, it remains clear that nobody who studies the books of Aristotle, whether as a youth or as a full-fledged philosopher, should deny the creation of the world or any other article of faith. Without a doubt, everyone ought to remain staunchly Christian in these matters, (34) yielding to Holy Scripture, which is the Catholic faith.

[. . .] All people should appeal to Scripture's logic and manner of speaking, for then, **together and without contention they would glorify God with one voice**, as the Apostle advises in Rom. 15:6. (35) For then they would receive the faith to speak just as humankind did in the state of innocence. In this matter I trust in St. Peter's command in 1 Pet. 4:11, **If anyone speaks, let it be as if these are the words of God**. And so too do the holy doctors teach that the words of the priest should be as the gospel. Third, some raise the objection that Augustine is known to have been a Platonist, thus erring in philosophical matters which are contrary to Aristotle, chiefly those having to do with logic and metaphysics of abstractions. As such, no evidence can be based upon proofs derived from authority. The argument runs: If Augustine asserts something then it must be true; Augustine speaks according to his own logic; therefore, the Christian should speak in conformity with that logic.

Yet in response to this I often say that a proof drawn from the testimony of Augustine is not infallible, since Augustine himself was capable of committing errors. This is why he frequently forbids us to place any faith in his sayings of this sort. But a dialectical argument based upon the testimony of Augustine is still deserving of greater faith than an argument based upon the testimony of Aristotle or Plato.[31] I wish, therefore, that those people who hold dialectical arguments in such low esteem would only cite the authors of Holy Scripture, because, apart of the authors themselves, Augustine is the foremost among all the doctors of Holy Scripture. And so, by the same rationale, having neglected his testimony, these people would have to disregard the testimony of the others.

With respect to any errors which might be attributed to Augustine, they remain very few in number. In fact, as far as this goes, I have studied the saint (36) and have not yet found an error in his books of logic or metaphysics which he did not later reconsider. The fact that he was a Platonist and thus contrary to Aristotle presents no problem. First, because Plato, according to Augustine, was the more profound in questions of sapiential philosophy. Moreover, as he so often stated, nothing ought to be believed simply on the grounds that it is Platonic, but only insofar as it is supported either by the powerful principles of reason, or the testimony of the Scriptures. We ought to accept the statements of Augustine on these three counts especially: first, due to the testimony of Scripture; second, the strength of his reason; and third, his reputation for sanctity attested to by the church.

(38) [. . .] With one voice the Church sings his praises. For here in St. Augustine God has provided his Church with a catholic doctor to elucidate the mysteries of Holy Scripture. Indeed, as if they were his abbreviators, preeminent doctors such as the venerable Anselm, Hugh of St. Victor, and Master Lincolniensis,[32] have, so to speak, drained from his books the entirety of his thought. "If you would ask," said Lincolniensis, "what moves me to grant that God is form, I say that it is the preeminent authority of the great Augustine."[33]

(39) [. . .] In every case I am in conformity with both the logic and the metaphysics of Augustine, which are all the more excellent for belonging to Holy Scripture, the very first rule of all human perfection. Hence, it surely seems to me the

height of presumption and blind pride for children such as ourselves, ignorant as we are in logic and metaphysics, to condemn or repudiate the knowledge of such a saint without definitive evidence.

The same applies, to a certain extent, when considering Ambrose, Jerome, Gregory, Bernard and other similar saints, especially in matters of logic and the meaning of the Scriptures. For we ought to listen to those who so assiduously beseeched God that they might come to comprehend his sense.

(*De ver.* I,iii): The Superiority and Sufficiency of Scriptural Logic

(40) Furthermore, as this matter appears to be especially important, I will once again offer a three-fold reply.

First of all, if Christ is a lion, since he is not a lion except according to the mystical sense, which alone can be applied to him, it follows that Christ is properly a lion. To the degree that the Lord is properly the chief of his own genus, brave and powerful in bearing, he is properly a lion, because it is only according to that sense that he is a lion. Still, he is such in the most proper manner of all and, therefore, is most properly a lion. But the consequent contradicts those holy doctors who say that Christ is improperly a lion, because he is such figuratively through similitude.[34] And so it is with other predications which pertain to mystical theology.

In this matter I say that Christ is most properly a lion and, nevertheless, is improperly a lion.[35]

For this reason it should be noted that the question of propriety and impropriety is two-fold, as it is comprised of the figure itself and that which it symbolizes. Christ, therefore, is not properly a lion according to the qualities peculiar to that roaring four-legged beast. And so in this way he is a lion when speaking improperly concerning the impropriety of the figure.

Nevertheless, he is a lion in the proper sense when one is speaking of the analogous property of what is symbolized, since **no one in heaven or on earth is worthy to open the book and loosen its seven seals except the Lion of the tribe of Judah and the lamb that was slaughtered**, as it says in Apocalypse 5 (Rev. 5:2–9). That Christ is a lion, rather than presenting a conflict, actually proves to be in harmony with Scripture and the holy doctors. Notwithstanding that, at the same time, (41) Christ is not a lion, a point which Augustine makes clear in *Sermon 47 on John*.[36] Thus it is equally consistent to maintain that Christ is as much a lion properly as improperly. For I do not see how there is any other sense in which Augustine could reasonably say that Christ is properly the door. He reserves the status of being the door to him uniquely, not communicating this property to others, while being a shepherd is common both to him and his vicars. Augustine says, "None of us may properly call himself the door, for he has properly retained this for himself."[37] And so it follows. Hence, it is sufficiently clear that the Lord said this as proper to himself. Whereupon, in Chapter 7, Part 2, of his *Angelic Hierarchy*, Lincolniensis recounts many names which are suitable as much for corporeal things as for the spiritual. He says, "These names apply, suitably and properly either way, although not identically."[38] St. Gregory retains a similar manner of speaking in Book 30, Chapter 4 of the *Morals*, finding that God is improperly and figuratively called such things. He says,

> On this account, all things can be said figuratively, because none of these things can be believed essentially. Therefore, whenever such a mystical predication of the Scriptures occurs, it is good to explain the sense of Scripture lest simple people believe God would assume the nature of a beast in unity of supposition, in the same way that he assumed the essence of a human being.[39]

And things of this sort should not only be spoken according to analogous similitude.

Second, some argue that Scripture should not be comprehended in this way. Better that it be consistent with the grammar one learned as a child. Or at least, if such a sense should be elicited, it is not rejected, but instead (42) will remain the primary sense. Thus it is permissible to deny sayings of this sort, since they are blatantly false.

On this point I have often said that it is a false assumption, precisely because one must learn a new grammar and a new logic when attempting to explicate or understand Holy Scripture. This is clearly the case with Saint Gregory and other saints who explain under the authority of Scripture those new senses of Scripture's terms which are not to be found in their grammar books.

(44) [. . .] Clearly, the theologians of old endeavored to comprehend the sense of Scripture while dismissing unfaithful and childish senses. For just as a child first learns the alphabet, second to spell, third to read, and fourth to understand, he retains in each of these levels his own sense, distinctly oriented toward what he had first learned. But later, given the confusion, he casts off the first sense. Similarly, the theologian, having received grammatical instruction, then learns the grammar of Scripture secondly, adapting to that sense, having left behind the first. And thirdly, having set aside the sensible signs, he devotes his attention to the sense of the author, until at the fourth stage, he might gaze upon the unveiled Book of Life. All sorts of people adhere to such a rule of procedure, whatever the nature of their business or study. If someone wishes to undertake his task more perfectly, he must leave aside the imperfect, since it would only confuse and hinder him as he strives toward his goal. So then, if the prize to be sought above all else is that sense of Scripture which the Holy Spirit introduced, what faithful person would doubt that the leaves

and bark of the words must be disregarded, except insofar as they are previously accommodated to this sense?[40] But if they only lead one astray, they should be condemned as poisonous. This is one reason why Christ and many saints would only inscribe their understanding upon the tablets of the heart, since that way is more perfect.

(47) [. . .] Third, some object to my statements by arguing that if the logic of Scripture were to be maintained always and everywhere then the logic of Aristotle would have to be rejected for the most part. Consequently, the young would no longer learn the logic of Aristotle, but only that of Scripture, since his logic generally tends to violate it.

To this I say that the conclusion does not follow, precisely because the logic of Aristotle, which is correct for the most part, is the very logic of Scripture. For as Augustine says in *Letter 3 to Volusianus*, the logic there, since it is the truth and light of the rational soul, is none other than God himself.[41] And as one reads (48) in *On Christian Doctrine*, Book 3, Chapter 41, "If anything is harmful then here it is condemned, and if useful, here it is found."[42] Therefore, the logic of Aristotle is not to be upheld on the grounds that it is Aristotle's, but only insofar as it belongs to Holy Scripture. Since Scripture alone is the highest author and the first rule, it follows that whatever it affirms must be true, as Augustine instructs in *Letter 9 to Jerome*.[43] By faith, it is surely God, for he is the immediate author of every suitable sense in our manuscripts. One concedes, therefore, that since Holy Scripture contains every sort of logic, then the logic of Scripture subsists in every sort of human being. And whenever they speak this should be understood, since it is the divine logic learnt from the foremost master, the one most resembling that logic learnt in the state of innocence, and consequently the most subtle, useful and certain. If, by the faith of Scripture, the Holy Spirit taught the apostles every truth and logic, which

Augustine says is found in Scripture, it follows that the Holy Spirit taught them that truth. But to what purpose was this except that they would teach others to speak according to its authority in all respects? Surely that Lord is not envious if others would retain his manner of speaking. But by stipulating this he is proven to love communication, while hating the arrogance of exclusivity. Hence, in such great humility, he handed down his logic so that it can be appropriated by anyone.

Again, since in every genre there is one principle which is the meter and measure of all the others, clearly in the genre of logic it is fitting that either the logic of Scripture is the standard of the other logics or vice-versa. And when no foreign logic (49) established the rule that, "if anything is harmful there it is condemned, and if useful it is approved," it follows that this logic would have to be the standard by which all the others are judged.

[. . .] Thus the Catholic church should generally observe the same logic, but she must not observe anything that is not the logic of Holy Scripture. The assumption is obvious, insofar as unity and conformity of speech is commended as much now in this fallen state as it was in the state of innocence. So it was that the confusion of tongues was inflicted as a punishment for pride, as evinced in Gen. 11:1–9. (50) And it is precisely the fall from this logic to which we are principally indebted that so savors of sin and its resulting divisions and quarrels. This is why Peter and Paul commanded everyone to speak the words of God with one voice. It would clearly be to our benefit to put away contradictions and communicate in agreement. The minor premise is evident, for if that alien logic were chosen, then the logic of Scripture would have to be rejected. But this is not good, since the one which endures is unique and must be accepted on the highest authority of Scripture. Otherwise, divine authority would then be impiously cast aside.

It should be noted, however, that while Holy Scripture possesses many kinds of logic this does not mean that everyone should employ Scripture's logic in his own discourse whenever he is engaged in conversation, or conferring with his neighbor. Instead, let him employ one sort of logic here and another sort there, following the instruction of the Spirit of Counsel and the rules of charity. Just as when explicating mystical theology one should employ the plain logic of Scripture, though when speaking to those for whom the mystery of faith is meant to remain hidden, he should utilize Scripture's mystical logic.

In this regard, however, the decretists teach that when a cleric is interrogated in the matter of a fugitive killing, he is allowed either to equivocate or speak mystically in order to avoid offering irregular testimony without telling an outright lie. Though none of this would be permissible, they say, except for the fact that it is authorized by Holy Scripture. For Christ had most subtly equivocated (51) when speaking with the unworthy. Yet I am not convinced that various foreign logics, falsehoods and heresies profit the Church simply because one may quote such aphorisms as "happy is the guilt of the first man," and "it was necessary that Adam sinned."[44] For Rom. 6:1–2 makes it quite clear that one should not behave in this way.

Again I say that the logic of Scripture is lawful and useful for everyone, and for this reason should be imitated. It has been given to the Church of Christ. For as Christ is the head of the Church, so all good things belong to him, and are to be either enjoyed or used.[45] But this is not so of the first mode, since it is neither God, nor man, nor virtue. It was bequeathed, therefore, that it might be given to all the faithful for their use.

With regard to utility and sufficiency it is clear that this is the logic of truth found in Matt. 5:37, **Let your word be yes, yes, and no, no**. Now this is the necessary logic which is sufficient for all of the pilgrim's communication. For by observing it in its totality a person will not sin in his language, and thus undoubtedly results in his] perfection. Therefore, the logic which so succinctly leads to such a useful end, and is the very basis for every science and doctrine, would have to be the most useful of all. Apart from that which teaches us how to extricate poison, I consider every other sophistic subtlety to be both superfluous and harmful, since by its very nature this one leads more succinctly to its ultimate end. Thus **what is more comes from evil** (Matt. 5:37), and it is not necessary for salvation. Rather, the pursuit of dialectical methods is a matter of curiosity, just as we proceed beyond the saints of old, since only the logic of Holy Scripture is necessary for salvation.

Now a fifth principle should be formulated. The Christian should speak the words of Scripture under the authority of Scripture, and according to that form (52) which Scripture itself illustrates. Given this condition, it follows that one ought to imitate Scripture in logic, etc. Such is clearly assumed in the case of Christ's priests, who use the words of Scripture in prayers, the administration of sacraments, and in the preaching and explication of Scripture. For Holy Scripture would be exceedingly harmful if not for the fact that the logic of Scripture is correct with respect to the verbal or literal sense, every bit as much in its historical parts as in the sapiential. And thus from the minor premise of the argument it is clear that the logic of Scripture exists both in the form of its words and in its manner of speaking. But it is certain that just as the Christian should articulate his thoughts under the authority of Holy Scripture in the four previously mentioned cases, so by the same authority, he should adhere to that form of the words, since it remains the principal and humble authority given by the highest master for this purpose. How then could someone who disregards it not incur the indignation of the master! Parisienis touches upon this sin when commenting upon that passage of Scripture in Jer. 2:13, **The people have done two evils things: they have forsaken me, the font of living water, and they have dug up cisterns for themselves which are unable to hold the waters**. He says,

> The science of Holy Scripture, which is divine or heavenly, because it is clear and without worldly troubles, is to be learned above all others on account of its authority and usefulness. But the science of human tradition which is now troubled by worldly concerns and now again not only lacks wisdom but includes blasphemy, must be thrust out just as Ishmael was.[46]

Of this the Lord laments in Isa. 5:24, **They have cast aside the law of the Lord**, on account of which it is mentioned in Isa. 8:6, **Inasmuch as the people cast aside the waters of Shiloah which flow in silence**. And Matt. 15:3 reads, **You have transgressed the commandment of God for the sake of your own tradition**.

(53) The same judgment pertains to the logic of Scripture, since whatever is reprehensible is thus condemned by Scripture. For if the logic of Scripture were not sufficient, but instead greatly diminished, then it could not adequately teach the Christian all the ways of speaking which he needs to know.

And if it is asked where Holy Scripture teaches logic, I answer, in that precept of Christ, **Let your word be yes, yes and no, no** (Matt. 5:37). Now this principle of logic provided by Christ, the highest master, is not of scant significance. For at the same time, he fully instructed the Church, as much in matters of morality, as in the logic of verbal communication. It is only fitting that he would teach this, for in principally abiding by this axiom the speaker will preserve the truth both internally and externally, whether in affirmation or negation. And in so doing, one may exclude false duplicity, provided that an agreement of intention between thought and speech is observed in all cases. Insofar as that which contains all things possesses the science of language, (54) according to which science he taught this logic, what faithful person would dare impose upon it any defect or calumny? For it was not appropriate for Scripture to discuss in particular the other private logics owing to their imperfections and their remoteness from the ultimate goal.

Therefore, this logic which leads straight to the ultimate goal without any troubling ambiguities, is the most certain. Other logics can be recognized for being sporadic and excessively numerous. Sporadic, because, as is evident at Oxford, a foreign logic endures for barely twenty years. And they change so often, since however many masters of logic there are, there are that many logics being rearranged given their craving for conceited distinction. The logic of Scripture, however, stands eternally, because it has been established by the indestructible truth, and thus does not depend upon human favor and esteem.

In light of what has been said a sixth principle can be reckoned. Anyone faced with a decision between two goods should pay heed to the one which is better and easier, and whose selection one would be more pleasing to God. The same applies to the logic of Scripture with respect to the others; therefore, the conclusion. It remains quite certain that the logic of Scripture includes every sort of goodness, and especially that of honesty. Now an Oxford master or doctor delights to have followers of his logic.

Again, some conclusions earlier declared to sound wrong by the logic of a bull sent by Benedict from the curia, are thus called wrong perceptions, even while many people think that they cannot perceive the unintelligible and incongruous conclusions rightly.[47]

(55) Likewise, professors of evangelical truth have complained before the Curia, because it is said that many charters of human invention are found to be impossible. This is all

the more reason why we should be following the logic of Scripture and defending it, thus complaining even more persistently about those people who presume to assail its truth! We should comprehend it in one instance according to its expressed and plain part, and in another instance according to its enigmatic and hidden part, just as the Spirit of Counsel determines what action one should take given the circumstances of time and place. Yet this must always be carried out under the authority of our master Christ, and ultimately for his sake. For I do not see how anyone could be his most beloved child, or his dear disciple, if he refuses to follow his way of speaking, preferring instead to devise some other kind to suit his own strange purposes.

By faith, one maintains that Christ, who is the head of the Church, speaks everywhere in Scripture. And this principle moved Augustine and other saints to speak in harmony. For within that wisdom they found every sort of good. Virtuous indeed is the disciple who imitates his master in his manner of speaking, just as a son imitates his father. If he does not, however, errors will crop up from the start.

(58) [. . .] It seems to me, as I have said elsewhere, that those speaking unfaithfully do not know that it has been granted to us to be heirs with Christ, since **all things are given to us with him** (Rom. 8:32) by the title of grace. This is especially so when we have made our profession, entering into the joy of our most gracious abbot, just as one entering a religious community, which holds all things in common, thereby has all the goods of his order. [. . .]

(*De ver.* I,iv): Mystical Senses, Parables, and the Author's Meaning

(63) Once again there are some who attempt to refute the truth of Scripture in a threefold manner. First of all, they say

that both testaments clearly contain enigmatic and parabolic parts of Scripture which are sufficiently false.

For it is written in Judg. 9:8–15, **The trees once went over to anoint a king to reign over them. And they said to the olive tree, "Reign over us." To which he responded, "Can I abandon my rich oil which gods and mortals use, and be promoted among the trees?" Then the trees said to the fig tree, "Come and accept sovereignty over us." To which he responded, "Can I abandon my sweetness and my delicious fruit, in order to go and be promoted among the other trees?" And the trees also said to the vine, "Come and reign over us." To which he responded, "Can I cease to produce my wine that cheers gods and mortals, in order to be promoted among the other trees?" And then all the trees said to bramble, "Come and reign over us." And he answered them, "If you truly will establish me as king over you, then come and rest under my shade. If, however, you will not, may fire come out of the bramble and devour the cedars of Lebanon."** What could this passage of Scripture be except a fable or a poem? Yet according to Aristotle in Book 2 of the *Metaphysics*, "The poets disguise many things when expressing themselves."[48] (64) The same appears to be true of many of the Savior's parables, as Augustine recalls in his *Against Lying*, Chapter 13, thus writing,

> If, therefore, Jesus signifies nothing else by this than that he intended to go further on (Luke 24:28), it would rightly be judged a lie. But if one correctly understands what he wished to signify in this case, then what he said is discovered to be a mystery. Otherwise, a whole host of lies would exist, because those things which were intended to be signified are not identical to the events as they have been recorded.[49]

(65) [. . .] In this regard I say that all the figurative locutions of Holy Scripture are true, just as St. Thomas states in

On Power, parts 6 and 7. "Metaphorically, the locutions of Scripture are not false."[50] This is also made clear in those authoritative texts adduced from Augustine. The figurative locutions of Scripture are, therefore, most true.

Nevertheless, it should be noted that one thing is a figure of construction while another is a figure of speech. A figure of construction is a concept, synthesis, zeugma, etc.[51] And these are most true, such as "the Father and Second Person are the highest goods." Certainly, Scripture's figurative locutions are metaphorical locutions or similitudes, inasmuch as they pertain to propositions. There are three kinds: allegorical, parabolic and fictional.

It is allegorical whenever, through the history of Scripture, that which occurs according the literal sense (*ad literam*) serves to signify what the future Church ought to believe. For instance, Christ is signified in the killing of the paschal lamb in the Old Testament; killed and consumed at the same time, as documented in Exod. 12. In this way then, Christ is truly called the lamb, sheep, etc. (66) Whereupon, Augustine writes in Chapter 4, Book 8 of *On the Literal Meaning of Genesis*,

> Of course, he is rightly called by the name of that which was meant to signify him before he came. He is the lamb which is sacrificed on the Passover, and yet was symbolized not only in word, but in deed. Was he not the lamb? He was clearly the lamb that was killed and eaten.[52]

Thus I understand in a spiritual manner that eating of which one reads in John 6:53, **Unless you eat the flesh of the Son of Man and drink his blood, you have no life in you.** With respect to that sort of allegorical expression, the Apostle writes in Gal. 4:22, **Seeing that Abraham had two sons**; while he says later that **those things are said by means of an allegory**. Allegory, therefore, always requires a figure in Scripture which occurred in the literal sense (*ad literam*). And it is called such from *alleos*, meaning that which is 'foreign', and *goge*, which means 'leading': thus 'leading to a foreign sense' as it were.

Second, a locution is surely parabolic when a certain likeness is used by Scripture to convey a particular meaning, although the thing itself is not recorded as an historical fact in Holy Scripture. This is evident in many of the Savior's parables found in the gospel. Augustine mentions this kind of speech in Book 8, Chapter 6 of *On the Literal Meaning of Genesis*.[53]

The third kind of locution is a similitude of fictitious device, when something is fashioned in order to signify the truth in a mystical way, even though it is not true according to literal sense (*ad literam*). Augustine notes an example of this in the scriptural passage of Judg. 9:8–15, where the discourse of the four trees should be understood mystically.[54] In this way, the trees are understood to be the people of Shechem (67), while through the olive tree the Hebrews understand Othoniel, who was of the tribe of Judah signified by the olive tree, as in Jer. 11:16, **The Lord called your name plentiful olive tree, fair, fruitful and beautiful.** Through the fig tree they understand Deborah, which is interpreted as 'bee' owing to the propitious fertility which she brought to her nation. For there is a similarity between her work and that of the fig tree as well as the bee, evinced in the history found in Judges 5. Through the vine they understand Gideon who was of the tribe of Joseph, called "the growing one" in Gen. 49:22–26 on account of the expansion he imparted to Israel, as evinced in Judg. 7. For as it said, to these persons of the tribe the community offered a Gentile dominion over them. And even though Othniel should have reigned over his brethren according to Jacob's prophecy, he still did not want to introduce Gentile domination upon his brethren by forsaking the pious duty of worshiping God which must be revealed to his brethren, just so that he might have the pleasure of wielding power. Nor did Deborah wish to abandon the sweetness of divine consolation found in the prophetic spirit, just as Gideon was loathe to relinquish the love of devotion for the sake of introducing some abominable Gentile ritual among the people.

By accepting Scripture in its totality, it becomes clear how Jotham said these things (Judg. 9:8–15), given the growth which he brought to Israel. As such, this passage is free from falsehood, just as Ps. 13 (14:1), **The fool says in his heart, "there is no God."** (68) But it would have been necessary for the sons of Israel to know the first sense, since in 1 Kings 8 (1 Sam. 8:5) they imposed a king upon themselves contrary to divine approval. And it seems to me that the final fictitious part indicates that the priests of Christ, who ought to be vicars of the true vine, should not hold civil dominion, since they consecrate his body and blood to the delight of both God and mortals. Rather, as celebrants, they should bear in mind the one who did not deign to hold civil dominion. For the wine of contemplation that consoles the eye of the priest is evaporated by worldly status and oppressive power. If, in the age before the law, and apart from the example of Christ, a lay person might put aside political affairs for the sake of devotion, all the more ought the priests of Christ follow the example of their master in this way.

The bramble mystically signifies Abimelech, who was of low birth on his mother's side. Now according to Isidore, bramble is a small thicket which emits fire when briskly moved.[55] Mystically, it corresponds to the wicked deed of Abimelech killing his seventy brothers. Beneath the darkness of his sins his accomplices slept when their fervor had expired, after having cut down his noble brothers as though they were cedar trees. So in Isa. 14, and more often elsewhere in Scripture, noblemen are called cedars.

When a doctor digs more deeply into Scripture, which appears so barren, and presses beyond some small aspect of the signified sense, he will find hidden within it the mystical sense concerning the state (69) of the universal Church. In this way the trees are understood to be the baser members of the human race who, on account of their own bestial servitude, subject as they are to their own passions, crave secular power over their fellow man. Such things came about precisely because they fell away from the religion of Christ, and that of the state of innocence, when they abandoned themselves to the assembly of the wicked.

The three fruit-bearing trees refusing the aforementioned rule are those three persons pertaining to the three ages of the state of the Church. By the olive tree is understood that class of person in the age before the law who confessed the divine law in his deeds, having been anointed with the oil of grace apart from the sensible sacraments. For at that time there were no churchmen governing in a civil capacity. The fig tree surely represents that class of person in the age under the law. For at that time, although one could amply cultivate Mother Church as one would a fig tree, he still rejected civil dominion ultimately, as evinced in the case of David and the other saints of the synagogue. And certainly, the vine is understood as the body of the Christian Church, whose head is Christ, the one who did not deign to hold civil dominion. So it is that for the sake of contemplation and a yearning for heavenly things, his priests should also reject this sort of dominion, thereby bringing forth fruit spiritually, in keeping with the passage of Eccl. 24 (Sir. 24:17), **I was as a vine producing a sweet fragrance.** Now Christ, **who is the true vine**, as John 15:1 states, is the most excellent head, as much of the Old Church as he is of the New.

(73) [. . .] At the end of the first conclusion in Part 1 of the *Summa*, St. Thomas says,

> The parabolical sense of Scripture is contained under the literal, for through words one thing is signified properly

> while another thing figuratively. Nor is the literal sense the figure, but instead, that which is symbolized. When, therefore, Scripture refers to the arm of God it is not the literal sense that in God there exists a corporeal member of this sort, but rather that which is signified through this member, namely his operative power. From this it is clear that nothing false can be contained within the literal sense of Scripture.[56]

Look how the holy doctors have endeavored to absolve Holy Scripture from falsehood! They could not have conceived of anything being the literal or verbal sense of Scripture if it were impossible.

(74) Furthermore, concerning the matter of parables, one should consider that according to Januensis, "Parables are called proverbs insofar as even images of the truth are demonstrated within them under the comparative similitude belonging to the figure of the words."[57] Hence, he describes a parable as a comparison of things which belong to different genera. And according to Hugh, the word derives from *para* i.e., 'beside', and *bola*, i.e., 'meaning': 'a meaning which is placed beside', as it were.[58] For it is not the meaning itself which indicates, but the meaning insofar as it set beside another. This agrees with Augustine, as he comments on Ps. 68 (69:12): **I became a parable for them**, "It is called a parable when similitude is granted of something."[59] In light of this one may conclude that all parabolic expressions in the gospel are true according to the sense they are intended to convey, as Augustine says. But the difficulty remains whether parabolic expressions are true according to the literal sense (*ad literam*). Augustine appears to count them as fictions. Yet I have often wondered about this, for it seems fitting that something would not be a parable or a similitude unless it had a solid foundation. As such, there is no similitude between something that is true and something that is not. (75) Likewise, since the example of the prodigal

son is sufficiently possible (Luke 15:11–32), it seems the holy doctor would not say that it is false, especially since the God of truth might retain many truths unknown to us through which he is capable of expressing the truth parabolically, though without positing a falsehood. Furthermore, Augustine in his book *On the Words of the Lord*,[60] along with St. Gregory and other saints, attests to many conclusions that may be drawn from the narratives parabolically, and he recounts them as true, evinced in the case of the rich man buried in hell (Luke 16: 19–31). Since, therefore, the narrative of the two sons is equally possible, it seems fitting that the saints, who so dread to err in the sense of Scripture, would not claim narratives of this sort are untrue without overwhelming evidence.

I have usually said that while there are many fictions, they are still true. Such is the case when Christ indicates that he was going further on, recorded in the final chapter of Luke (Luke 24:28); and still it is true according to the literal sense (*ad literam*), as Gregory explains in Book 2, Sermon 3.[61] Augustine, as mentioned above, touches upon this, and when he says that something would not be rightly understood as an event unless it is something chronicled elsewhere in Holy Scripture. So it is that in Heb. 7:3 the Apostle says Melchisedek did not have a father or mother; but supply here: "whose genealogy is expressly recounted in Holy Scripture." For he must have had them secretly, since according St. Jerome he had been a genuine man.[62]

(79) [. . .] In light of what has been said, the solution to the second objection is clear, even as certain people chose to truncate Scripture in their effort to slander it. They say that while it is surely impossible that Christ could have been a demoniac, nevertheless, one reads in John 8:48, **The Jews answered him, "Are we not right in saying that you are a Samaritan and have a demon?"** Compare also a similar passage in Luke 11:15, **He casts out demons by Beelzebul, the**

ruler of the demons; and the passage from John 9:16, **This man is not from God**, along with similar passages. Yet according to Augustine, in order to acquire the meaning of Scripture one must bind up (80) the small fractures and lacerations into the totality of Scripture.[63] Hence, this objection is similar to the argument of the sophists who contend that by saying this proposition is necessary: no man is a donkey, the following is then said to be impossible, namely that a man is a donkey. And so, by saying this proposition is impossible: no God exists, it is said that God exists, for that is absolutely necessary.

When it comes to such objections it is only right that one comprehend Scripture in its wholeness, as it pertains to the sense of the author. For then it will be found to be true in every respect. Hence, it seems to me that people who argue in this manner are like the ones Jerome speaks of in Chapter 7 of his *Letter to Paulinus*:

> This is only the case with Scripture that all people randomly lay claim to for themselves. They all presume to mutilate and teach it before having learnt it, whether it be the chattering old woman, the delirious old man, or the verbose sophist. Some people caught up in their own arrogance balance pompous words as they philosophize with weak women concerning sacred writings. Oh the shame of it all, for some even learn from women that they should be teaching men. And if this were not enough, possessing a certain facility with words, they audaciously explain to others what they themselves do not understand.[64]

Let us believe, first of all, that Scripture is the truest of all, supremely authentic and most suitable. Second, let us understand it in the proper manner which we have furnished here. And third, let us render judgment upon any false teaching or imposition of slander. For then we will find that Scripture is immune from falsehood.

(81) I have spoken of other things based upon the testimony of the doctors whereby something is said to be false in three ways, just as there are three ways in which something may be said to be true. First, when it lacks the highest truth or being, which is God. And so every creature is said to be false just as it is vain, according to that passage in Eccles. 1:2, **All is vanity**. Yet I would not dare speak in this manner to the imprudent or the simple for fear that they would lapse into error regarding the humanity of Christ and other creatures. Nor does it occur to me only that the authority drawn from Scripture is sufficient for this purpose. Second, a creature is said to be false when it lacks the due form befitting proper conduct, such as rational creatures and their sophistical works. The first falsehood of this sort, however, is sin. The sinner is far more deceitful than the counterfeit coin, or any such product that the deceitful man has created in his sinfulness. The third kind is well known to the grammatical logicians. For them a sign is said to be false when it is assigned to appropriately signify something to which it does not truthfully correspond. Some signs are false contingencies whenever those things which they are intended to signify do not exist. Others are false when those things with which they are meant to correspond never existed. This is the case with impossible propositions based upon a supposition and some absolute impossibilities, which the logicians say signify just as if it cannot exist or be understood as equivocating in an adverb of similitude. Such is the case here: 'there is no God' signifies in this way by demonstrating a manner of signifying, both of the sign and the non-existence of God. (82) Yet it is not possible for God not to exist. And if one asks what I understand by this term, I say that God and every being exists in reality beyond the mode of the signifying sign. For if this were not so, then I could not adequately understand it in some measure. For just as nothing greater than God can be conceived, neither can one conceive

of something having reality in some manner or measure, unless conceived of just as it is in God. Regarding that equivocation of signs, however, there is a great deal of altercation in this aspect.

Based on these premises, I say that the signs recounted are true if they are parts of Holy Scripture, precisely because they are signs imposed by the very author of this Scripture, for the sake of signifying the corresponding truth in its entirety. It is not permissible to mangle Holy Scripture. Instead, one should cite it in its wholeness according to the author's sense. It seems to me that Augustine should be understood in this way when, in Book 8, Chapter 4 of *On the Literal Meaning of Genesis*, he says that the evangelist does not pronounce the Son the lesser on account of his desire to return to the Father.[65] In other words, he does not assert what is chronicled in Scripture as though it were authentic, but says instead that the Lord recited this; and that is authentic. Although such an historical narrative was true, the Lord still recounts it (83) as if it were parabolic or apocryphal. In such a case the parabolic sense is the literal, and moreover, the authentic sense, just as St. Thomas says. Far be it from the Lord to recount this except insofar as it is true according to his own sense, which is the literal sense, and not the historical. It is in this way, therefore, the parts of Scripture should be brought into their proper form, in keeping with the wholeness of the author's sense. And if it should happen that the slanderous charge of falsehood is imposed upon these parts, since it is true that the Jews had said to the Lord, **"Are we not right in saying that you are a Samaritan and have a demon?"** (John 8:48), we will point out that the author does not intend this section to signify that Christ is a demoniac, but rather that the Jews had said such a thing of him. And so it is with similar passages.

Nor is this conditional proposition, 'if no God exists, no God exists', composed from these impossible categories: 'no

God exists, no God exists', if not according to matter and likeness, in which composition they signify the same truth, which signifies its entirety. It is thus denied that if someone says that no man is a donkey he thereupon says that a man is a donkey. And yet if he says that no God exists, he thereupon says that God exists, since all created and uncreated things necessarily declare the existence of God, on account of the vehemence of truth. And so if anyone believes, knows or loves something, it then exists with respect to God in one way or another. For every person believes in and knows God in general, just as every person believes all truth in general, at the very least, even if he disbelieves the Catholic faith in the particular. And God is the analogous good which all things seek.

(84) From what has been said it is clear that not only Scripture, but indeed the entire created universe, signifies God, and consequently the truth. It is more likely that an error in one's perception is going to be the cause of an illusion than the signs of immaculate Scripture. I can think of no reason why those who perversely understand a part of Scripture would falsify it, except that they are like those who hold a mistaken understanding of the sun or some other star, regarding its quantity, motion, or another of its sensible accidents, and thereby falsify it. And by the same rationale, the idea that God moves the infidel philosophers to maintain a spurious sense of him as a punishment for sin would be an impossible and supremely false action. For he signifies to them their own perverse concepts through his eternal ordination, just as he will signify on the Judgment Day, and as he eternally signifies to damned spirits, insofar as he is the principal agent in any action. Someone might say that the reason for diversity stems from the fact that the written or vocal sign is humanly imposed, such that it signifies falsehood of this sort, and thus should be understood in this way and declared false on account of its human imposition. Yet this is clearly not verified

with regard to any part of Holy Scripture, since no one rationally determines that any of its parts would be false. Now Aristotle says in Chapter 1 of the *Posterior Analytics* that it is not demonstration of the universal which leads to error, but rather one's wrong perception.[66] And so it is that no part of Holy Scripture primarily compels someone to consent to falsehood. Instead, ignorance of Scripture derives from sin and induces that intellectual darkness, (85) which the faithful ought to dispel. Nor is any theologian bound to some childish institution which posits the following vocal, mental or written sign: 'no God exists' is impossible on account of its manner of conceiving an impossibility terminating objectively with respect to the attracting sign. And so, by the same rationale, it is understood that one would concede that any other movement to false thoughts or assertions occasioned by sin is all the more false. But one could say together with the philosophers and Scripture that all such signs are proportionately true insofar as they are existent things, conceding that it is false that a man is a donkey, because he is not; and that it is impossible for a man to be a donkey, because he cannot be. For in the case of things which possess real existence falsehood is surely grounded in sin. Hence, just what is evil cannot exist unless grounded in the good, so no falsehood can exist unless it is grounded in truth. For in truth it is false that a man is a donkey, not that man being a donkey would be the form or falsehood by which the subject is false. But the truth that a man is a donkey does not exist makes or causes the statement to be false.

As such, I have customarily offered a response to those people who are seeking a reason for such diversity, whereby the sun and other natural signs which God has instituted for the sake of signifying to humankind may do so falsely, and yet are not false, while humanly instituted signs which falsely signify are actually false. The reason seems to stem from the fact that the agreement in this equivocal signification of truth and falsehood depends upon the signs which are chiefly the product of the childish infirmity of the one who knows them, rather than the things which are signified. But as soon as a person becomes a metaphysician and puts away those signs he will direct the sharpness of his mind towards the things which were signified. For then it is fitting for him to cast aside those childish significations by speaking of the real truth, just as a metaphysician speaks.

On this account, the response to the third objection is clear. Some argue that if any part of Holy Scripture is true then every imperative statement, syllable and letter would have to be true. This is granted, not only on account of existent things, but because they, in turn, are signs of the very same truth which they signify in their entirety. For when many people are dragging a ship any one of them may be said to be dragging the ship. And this applies in the case of concurrent forces at work in actions, whether they be corporeal or incorporeal. In the same vein, every part of Scripture signifies the same faith, hope and love to those who rightly understand it, as Augustine says in *On Christian Doctrine*, Book 3, Chapter 10, and *On The Psalms* 140.[67] This saying of the Apostle in 1 Cor. 11:1 is true, therefore: **Be imitators of me, as I am of Christ**. Here he signifies that the faithful should follow the apostles in the same way they have followed Christ, their guide and captain. One need not fear the offensive launched by the logicians and grammarians, for they are also obliged to submit themselves to learning the new grammar and logic of Scripture.

That meaning would be clearer, however, if we were firmly grounded (87) in the metaphysics which pertains to the essence of Holy Scripture. But, because I have often spoken of this elsewhere, I will put it off until Chapter Six.

It is granted that every part of Holy Scripture's character is true, having been assigned many different senses, insofar as God is the first and last sense of every creature. And according to those senses, the other parts of Scripture are truths advancing, piece by piece, toward that ultimate truth upon which all individual truths converge. Hence, even though it is false that there is no God, the following proposition is true: 'there is no God', since it only signifies what the fool had said: "there is no God" (Ps. 14:1). It is not fitting for the theologian to discuss the distinction of parts of speech and distinctions of propositions in the manner grammarians and logicians speak of them, for he possesses a superior, more suitable metaphysic than those offering rudimentary instruction to children. Moving beyond schoolboy lessons, he should concede that every aspect of Scripture's linguistic expression is intelligible, and capable of signifying in an equivocal manner. (88) Thus Augustine, in Book 7, Chapter 11 of the *Confessions* says, "All things are true in as much they exist, nor is anything false except when what is thought to exist does not."[68] And this agrees with the metaphysics of Aristotle.

(*De ver.* I,v): Natural Sciences and the Intended Literal Sense

(88) Furthermore, a three-fold objection is raised against imitating divine logic: if we ought to imitate Christ in his logic and manner of speaking then, by the same rationale, we should imitate him in fasting for forty days, walking upon the water and performing miracles. If not, it remains to be said how else we should specifically follow Christ.

It is certainly true that Christ did certain things insofar as he is God, certain other things insofar as he is man, and still other things in both capacities. Pertaining to the works of Christ's humanity we should follow him by performing his works in due proportion. Since his logic and eloquence have been given to us for this purpose in the most humble, (89) correct, and simple manner, we ought to learn them by doing as he did. As such, it is clear that we should imitate Christ in these things above and beyond all the other lesser masters.

As evinced by his preaching, Christ's logic savors of humility. Clearly then, we ought to follow him in this way, putting aside bombastic sophistical pretense. For otherwise, we would sin by foolishly choosing the lesser and more troublesome good. He exhorts us to do just this in Matt. 11:29 when he says, **learn from me; for I am gentle and humble in heart**. Augustine comments on this in Sermon 1 of *On the Words of the Lord*, saying, "Do not learn from me to create the world, nor to create all things visible and invisible, nor to perform miracles in this world and raise the dead, but inasmuch as I am gentle and humble in heart."[69]

Giving further attention to a difficult aspect of this matter, since all Christ's actions abide for our instruction it is evident that we should fast for forty days by abstaining from sin and, according to our own ability, from superfluous food for the body. He commenced upon this forty-day fast in order that the Church might follow his example. Furthermore, we should imitate Christ's walking on the water according to its mystical sense. While the flux of worldly affairs is signified by the waters, we should trample upon this sea with the feet of the inner man. And by living in the Spirit, just as Christ walked (90) on air, so we ought to guard against an affection for temporal affairs, in case we become fettered to such things to the point that we are weighed down so heavily that we can no longer aspire to celestial things, and are then dragged back into a wretched state. Whereupon, Augustine says in Sermon 21 of *On the Words of the Lord*,

> While we live here we should be vigilant and choose what we hold on to in the future, lest we would love the world. Because it oppresses its own lovers and does not lead them to the good, it is better that we should toil in it, lest it catch us, rather than fear that it might fail.[70]

When explaining that passage in Matt. 8:23, **When Jesus got up into the boat**, John Abbaevillanus notes how the church is mystically signified by Noah's ark and Peter's boat. For if this vessel hopes to avoid a shipwreck at sea it must be fifteen cubits above the fluctuations of worldly affairs in its foremost parts, just as it was in the beginning of both testaments. For a ship sunken in the land is unnaturally situated by its extended submersion, especially if it becomes mired in the mud of worldly concerns.[71] Surely it is our forsaking of the sense of Scripture when it comes to following Christ, which leads us to disbelieve that sense. Whereupon, the third passage recounting Christ's miracles should lead us to convert both ourselves and our neighbors to the law of God. That deed corresponds to miracles, since it is no less a miracle to make a wicked person righteous than it is to create the world anew, as Augustine says in his brief book (91) *Concerning the Holy Spirit of the Lord.*[72]

(92) [. . .] We ought to defend figurative expressions against falsehood according to the mystical sense, since when they can be predicated according to that sense they are that much more precious. I believe, therefore, that it would be even more unsuitable to deny or falsify mystical theology than historical theology. For while they are both of equal authority, a still greater usefulness rests in that sweeter secondary sense.

Second, some argue by means of a deduction which leads to an impossible conclusion: if Christ is a lion, then a human being is a "sheep, calf, serpent, lion, worm," etc., with the result that something of one species belongs to another species. Surely if the species are commingled in this way then definitions and distinctions of universals will be destroyed, resulting in the destruction of not only linguistic science but the science of real existent things as well.

I respond to this by saying that, since Holy Scripture is supremely true, no impropriety may follow from it, even though a Christian may be led astray on occasion, due to his ignorance of logic and sophisms. It is conceded, therefore, that man is a lion, serpent, worm, etc. And this is the case with any sort of species, just as its principle, since it is clear that Christ is all in all, and the principle of every sort of predication according to his divinity. Nevertheless, he is neither a wild beast, nor some other sort of creature according to his humanity. Hence it is clear that neither universal definitions and distinctions, nor any other aspect of the truth, will be destroyed, having been permitted on that occasion by Christ's law and logic. Yet some people still become entangled in improprieties, while the person who piously acknowledges this will find peace. (93) As the Spirit says in Ps. 118 (Ps. 119:165), **There is much peace for those who love your law, and for them it presents no stumbling block.**

(94) [. . .] That sort of humble and mild concession of the equivocation of signs, which the sophists call a contradiction, actually confounds their useless disputation over words. And it is for this reason that it proves an authentic and dear refuge, as I made clear in the first chapter, based upon the authority of Christ and the testimony of Augustine. Nor will that result in an impropriety, unless perhaps it proves a stumbling block or evokes an ape-like smile among the ignorant.

Furthermore, it must be noted that one is permitted to follow the example of Scripture in speaking figuratively of human beings, as well as other creatures, in accordance with the circumstances of time and place, even though our own figurative propositions are not expressed therein. For in Holy Scripture tyrants are at one moment called lions in Isa. 11:7, and at another moment the people are strong bulls in Ps. 67 (68:30), while prelates are called indolent and mute dogs as in Isa. 56:10. [. . .] (96) Natural philosophy is indeed useful for the comprehension of Scripture. And there is no contradiction in the equivocal senses according to essential and figurative predication, as Aristotle teaches in the *Secrets* Book 3,

Chapter 23, saying that none of the philosophers is a stone, nor does one have the nature of a stone, and still that stone is compared in some ways to a stone of the mountains of minerals.[73] Concerning the equivocation of these senses, the great philosopher Boethius was moved to write in Book 4, Prose 3 of *The Consolation of Philosophy*,

> Since goodness alone can raise someone above humankind, it is necessary that wickedness would cast down the ones it dislodged from the human condition below what is worthy of a human being. As a result, if you were to see someone transformed by his vices, could you not render a judgment regarding him? Of the man burning with greed for the goods of others, and who steals by violence, could you not say he is like a wolf? And the one who is headstrong and restless, keeping his tongue moving in litigation; could he not be compared to a dog?[74]

[. . .] (97) See how mankind, placed as he is between the angels and the beasts, is divinized by his virtues, while by the nature of behavior his vices render him a wild beast, albeit not in bodily appearance. For if this were not so the statement of Christ in John 10:34 could then be denied: **God called them gods, those to whom the word of God was addressed**. Indeed, Scripture itself would be false and inappropriate, since Ps. 21 (22:16) alternatively states, **Many dogs encircle me**. And there is that saying of Christ in Matt. 7:6, **Do not give what is holy to dogs, nor throw pearls before swine**; and the passage from Apoc. 22 (Rev. 22:15), **Outside are the dogs and the sorcerers**. For those quarrelsome oppressors of the poor will never enter the kingdom of the King of Peace.

Concerning all those objections which might be raised in opposition, (98) it is clear that Gregory's and Boethius's distinction of equivocation immediately refutes them. For a man is neither an animal by nature, nor through identical supposition, but by an analogous property in his condition. And the holy doctors speak in agreement in this matter, by the authority of Scripture.

(99) [. . .] And so it is that one will never find such a negation of the mystical sense within the writings of the holy doctors, nor any disparagement of a doctor who grants it. For they do not concede such things are absurd, unlike those proud and envious people do these days whenever their own arguments fail.

In regard to figurative expressions, one should take into consideration the times and circumstances of the listeners, thereby rectifying that form of speaking which occurs in scholastic disputation. Refraining from such things, or if you like, conceding such things in disputation through equivocation, does not result in an impropriety, but instead discloses the equivocation which would undercut the arrogance of disputation prevailing today. For these days it seems that the disputant pays greater attention to acquiring a reputation for subtlety in his conclusion to the respondent, than he does to the glory of God or the edification of the Church, by which the glory of God is proclaimed. (100) But not so the holy doctors, as evinced in their dialogues where they appear to us to have abandoned the form of disputation, as when the essential subject matter of disputation is grasped, and the disputant commends and approves the respondent whenever he lucidly expresses the catholic truth. If at any time, however, one would deviate or wantonly go astray, then he communicates by reason or authority with respect to speculative matters, in order that he might either correct or excel with respect to matters of moral conduct, as Augustine states in *On Christian Doctrine*, Book 3, Chapter 37.[75] This is what is useful in the form of the dialogues of the holy doctors. For I do not see how it could be otherwise, lest their extensive dialogues turned out to be in vain. It seems to me that the disputant recoils from unity, thereby committing apostasy, by a disgraceful combination of motives whereby he is more intent on disproving the response than improving himself by honoring God and bringing glory to the school of Christ; or when he hungers after his own vainglory more than the honor of his God in the elucidation of Holy Scripture, which is itself the law of Christ, the testament of God, and the faith of the Church. If only such apostasy were not so rapidly infecting our theologians!

When I was a young man I rejected mystical expressions partly due to my own pride and partly for the sake of destroying the worthless glory of the sophists. For they would rejoice if they were able to catch one of their fellows in an apparent impropriety.

(101) One might reply that according to this response the certitude of speech would be lost, since, as stated above, anyone could equivocate regarding a vow, and that logic, insofar as it is not a moral virtue, would also be in danger of being abused. In light of this, therefore, the Christian should speak sparingly, and even then he should speak according to the faith of Scripture, or by what it exemplifies. Nor is he to equivocate unless he does so under the authority of Scripture, as he seeks to edify the Church according to that logical principle which Christ passed down: **Let your word be "Yes, Yes" or "No, No"** (Matt. 5:37).

A third objection raised in this matter contends that there are any number of propositions in Holy Scripture which, according to the primary signification of terms, cannot be excused from falsehood according to the strictly literal sense (*de virtute sermonis*), such as that passage in John 7:16, **My teaching is not mine**; John 14:24, **the word which you have heard is not mine**; and Ps. 21 (22:6), **I am a worm and not a human being**, along with other similar passages. Who doubts that such a verbal sense is impossible? And who would doubt that those propositions primarily signify in this way?

Here I have often said that falsehood is assumed whenever there is ignorance of the sense of Scripture, since there is no falsehood on its part which compels the unlettered and the insolent to slander it, as Augustine states in *On Questions of the Old and the New Law*, Chapter 95: "Of the Lord's Scripture, his own senses are apparent to the careful and the devoted, though they are surely inaccessible to the negligent."[76] And below in Chapter 100, he alludes to the saying of Christ in Matt. 11:25–26, **I praise you, Lord, Father of heaven and earth, because you have hidden these things from the wise and the prudent and you have revealed them to infants. Indeed, Father, for such was pleasing in your sight**.[77]

(103) [. . .] The saints understand that contention over words in the teaching of Scripture is useless. For the sense of the author should be humbly searched out, and whatever impedes the understanding of that sense is to be prudently set aside, since the meaning of Scripture is comprehended through devotion. For this reason the doctors often counsel that a sense which is contrary to the intended sense of the author should be dismissed. What is to be gained by verbose disputes, when the truth of the Christian faith does not depend upon the strength of our own manner of speaking (*virtute sermonis nostri*)? Indeed, there is little or no strength (*virtus*) to be found in sophistical speech.[78] This is why I am accustomed to say that each part of Holy Scripture is true according to the divinely intended literal sense (*de virtute sermonis divini*). Certainly, this strength (*virtus*) is the Word of God, the very incarnation of his strength (*virtus*) and wisdom. And John 17:17 speaks of the same wisdom: **your word is truth**; and the Apostle in 1 Cor. 1:24, **we preach Christ, the strength (*virtutem*) of God**.

(104) With regard to that first authority, John 7:16 [**my teaching is not mine**], I have usually said that the word of God is solidified by a two-fold determination. First, that the

teaching of Christ is the truth, which is Christ himself. But it is not such with respect to his own position, but rather on account of his relationship to the Father who begot him. In this manner the distinction of persons is indicated. Augustine illustrates this sense in his *Sermon 29*,

> What is the teaching of the Father except the Word of the Father? But because it is appropriate that the Word pertain to another, he says that his teaching is not his own, since it is the Word of the Father.[79]

Regarding the second authority, I have customarily said that Christ is indicating the distinction between his own personality and the eternal truths which are inscribed upon him, when he says, **Whoever does not love me does not keep my words** (John 14:24). These are the truths which are rationally distinct from the divine essence. And this is not all, for what is especially frightening is that someone would not keep the word (*sermonem*) they had heard spoken to them, since it does not belong to the word of the one speaking, but is the very Word of the Father (*ipsum verbum patris*). And its truth extends beyond the literal sense, in keeping with the intended literal sense (*de virtute sermonis*). In this way we are instructed in the moral sense to offer to our God the primary and entire honor of our efforts, and to recognize him in his name as he is the principal source through whom we accomplish all good works. If only those vicars of Christ, who murmur back (105) against ministerial and vicarious power, would pay attention to that lesson of Christ!

Whereupon, Augustine says in *Sermon 77 on John* that,

> When he adds, **And the word which you hear is not mine, but his who sent me, the Father's** (John 14:24), we should not marvel, nor should we quake with fear. For he is not less than the Father, but he is only of the Father. He is

> not unequal with the Father, but he does not exist unto himself. Nor did he lie in saying, **Whoever does not love me does not keep my words** (John 14:15). Look, he said these were his own words. Can he ever have contradicted himself when he says once again, **The word which you hear is not mine**. Is it possible that for the sake of some distinction when he said his own he said it plurally here as 'words'. Yet where he said 'the word' (*sermonem*), that is, the Word (*verbum*), was not his own but that of his Father, did he want himself to be understood? **In the beginning was the Word and the Word was with God and the Word was God** (John 1:1). Surely this is not his own, but is the Word of the Father, just as he is neither his own image, but rather that of the Father. Nor in the same way is he his own son, but instead that of the Father. He rightly attributed to the author whatever he does as an equal by which he has this very thing itself, such that he is his equal in an undifferentiated manner.[80]

See how this saint, by the strength of the first word (*ex virtute primi sermonis*), notes the case and number, thereby explaining the sense and liberating us from the oppression of the sophists, lest we fear those arguments by which they contend that our Scripture is false or contrary to itself. For the doctor of equivocations, and the grammar and logic of Scripture, demolishes all their objections.

Concerning that passage in Ps. 21 [**I am a worm, and not a human being**] spoken of Christ according to the literal sense (*ad literam*), here this is clearly the figurative sense. (106) As Augustine explains, Christ is of the earth insofar as he was born of the Virgin Mary, having been begotten without copulation, as is the case with worms. Thus in his first tract on this Psalm he says,

> I am not, however, speaking in the person of Adam, for I am properly Christ Jesus, born in the flesh apart from seed,

> in order that I might be in man and yet beyond men, since it is fitting that human pride would imitate my humility in this way. For in humility I became **the scandal of men**, since for the sake of this reproach the curse would be uttered: you are his disciple.[81]

And in the second tract,

> For the worm is a human, but this worm and not a human; whereupon he is not a human, because he is God. Why then would he debase himself in this way so as to refer to himself as a worm? For a worm is born of the flesh apart from intercourse, and in this way Christ is mortal insofar as he was born of the Virgin Mary. Why is he not a human? Because he was God the Word.[82]

See that in both cases there is a mystery to be observed which rests hidden within the logic of Scripture, one that we have rejected in our ignorance. Because Christ is comprised of two natures, he is himself the divinity which is not formally human, because it is not humanity. And so observing the moral sense, we who are purely human should suffer reproach for his sake, since the very one who is so superior to human beings suffered such things on our behalf. There is no contradiction in the following statement: Christ is not a man, and he is a man. For one must understand here that Christ is not formally a man according to his divinity. It should be understood in this way, and not along the lines of an impossible concept (107), as is subsequently clarified. If, from the foundation of the world up until the moment of his Incarnation, Christ is not a man, as Anselm says in his *On the Virginal Conception*,[83] agreeing with the common logic regarding infinite terms, how can that passage of Scripture be refuted according to the intended literal sense (*de virtute sermonis*)?

(*De ver.* I,vi): The Five Levels of Scripture and the Four Senses

(107) Furthermore, some object that it is not unfitting for Holy Scripture to be false. And this should come as no surprise, for if Scripture is nothing but the manuscripts of writers who were themselves unusually false, then it stands to reason that the works which they produced would also be exceptionally false.

Here the assumption is denied. For just as I have demonstrated elsewhere, the law of God subsists beyond all the manuscripts and sensible signs which yield the signified truth. And it is for this reason that it is more suitably called Holy Scripture than the manuscripts themselves. I have been in the habit of describing Holy Scripture (108) as the inscription of sacred truth, whether in its revealing of other truths, or insofar as it is the very revelation of truth itself. I have customarily posited five levels of Holy Scripture. The first is the Book of Life, which Apocalypse speaks of in Chapters 20 and 21. The second consists of the truths inscribed in the Book of Life, according to their intelligible being. Both levels of these Scriptures are absolutely necessary, although they do not differ essentially, but rather according to reason, as I said of this matter in *On Ideas*.[84] On the third level, Scripture is considered in light of the truths which are to be believed in their proper genus. These are inscribed in the Book of Life according to existence and effect. The fourth level considers Scripture in light of the truth which must be believed as it is inscribed in the book of the natural man, that is, in his soul. Some people call this Scripture an aggregate of actions and truths, spoken of in the third manner. For some this is an intellective habit, and for others an intention or species. Yet in the fifth manner, (109) Holy Scripture is understood as referring to the manuscripts, sounds or other artificial signs designed to bring to mind that first truth, in the way Augustine speaks of in his *Letter 39 to Paulinus on Seeing God.*[85] But this can be understood in many ways. It could be understood personally and concretely for the sake of those signs in whatever manner they had signified; or perhaps simply, for those as they would signify the sense of God. And this is the way in which I myself understand the sensible Holy Scripture. Christ understands Holy Scripture in the first manner when he says in John 10:35, **and the Scripture cannot be destroyed, whom the Father sanctified and sent into the world**. From these words he seems to imply that he is the truth itself, when Christ had been established, and became a sanctified human being. For with the oil of grace **he was anointed beyond his fellows**, as is said in Ps. 44 (45:7). God the Father sent this book into the world in order to save the world, as the Apostle states in Gal. 4:4–5, **God sent his Son, born of a woman, born under the law so that he might redeem those who were under the law**. In fact, the whole Trinity, and consequently the very Word himself in his divinity, sent him from heaven. In his humanity he is **the nobleman who went into a distant country to accept royal power for himself and return** (Luke 19:12). This book cannot be destroyed, precisely because the divinity and the humanity are insolubly united in the same person in a seven-fold manner. Every Christian should study this book, since it is all truth. Whereupon, in order that we should learn by this saying to understand that book, rather than the one which is product of human hands, (110) the Holy Spirit ordained in the correct manuscripts the relative pronoun "whom" and not "which" (John 10:35).[86] As such, one comprehends its relationship to the Apostle's manner of speaking in Gal. 3:16: **to your seed, who is Christ**. Whereupon, in his *Sermon 48* Augustine is convinced that this is the literal meaning, thus removing any doubt regarding the sanctification of the Son.[87] He says, "The Father sanctified his own Son and sent him into the world; if the Father sanctified him, then there must have been some time when he was not holy." But he responds by negating the logical inference: For he says, "He sanctified him in the manner by which he begot him; that he might be holy, in begetting him he granted him this, because he begot him holy." Consequently, in disproving the logical inference he thus adds: "If that which is sanctified was not holy beforehand how is that we say to God the Father, 'hallowed be thy name'?" Now the grammarians say that to be sanctified is to 'be or become holy'. Therefore, God made the aforementioned Scripture holy with respect to Christ's humanity, and he begot or caused it to be holy with respect to his divinity. And it is evident from the faith of Scripture that Scripture must be supremely authentic, thereby surpassing sensible signs.

(111) The subtle theologian, however, will not reject the other three Scriptures. That Scripture which is perceptible through voices and manuscripts is not Holy Scripture, except in an equivocal sense, just as we might say the picture or image of a man is called a man on account of its resemblance to the actual man. The first Scripture, however, is the most proper and holy. It is most proper because it is inscribed by the highest wisdom, that inscription which is so proper to God that it cannot be communicated to another nature. For this reason it is a book beyond all measure. It is most holy due to the sanctity of its subject matter, the steadfastness of the meaning inscribed, and usefulness of its purpose. For it was sent into the world for the salvation of human beings. First, one may prove, through a deduction which leads to an impossible conclusion, that Scripture is not merely some sort of sign. For if this were the case, then all Holy Scripture could be damaged by a leather-worker, authorized by a scribe, torn apart by a dog, and corrected by a buffoon, as if it were liable to such defilement. And so any number of people could then render

every Scripture heretical, damnable, and potentially harmful, promoting no virtue or honor, and consequently possessing no authority. Second, it is ostensibly proven this way: Holy Scripture is the descriptive instruction of the truth. Wherever there exists such an inscription which is even more true, then that would have to be more truly Scripture. Yet this is the truth concerning the Book of Life, and thus the truer principle of Scripture abides within it. The truth is present there more permanently, because it is eternal and indelible, a book so majestic because it is **the radiance of the eternal light, the flawless mirror** (Wisd. of Sol. 7:26). (112) In this way an identity is achieved between the written book, the written truth, and the person writing. And while remaining rationally distinct, all three of these are the word of life and the truths in abstraction, as one reads in John 14. And that Scripture is the gospel, of which the doctor of the Gentiles speaks in Gal. 1:11–12, **I make known to you, brothers, the gospel that was evangelized by me, since it is not according to human beings, nor did I receive or learn it from human beings.** I beseech you to tell me, what is that gospel except the revealed truth? And tell me, if you wish to be faithful, whether it is permissible for Christians to speak in conformity with Scripture and the gospel, just as our faith speaks? Would the speech of the layman be more acceptable to you, or that of the grammarians, or perhaps even the pagans?

Third, it is proven from the testimony of Scripture. For in Mark 13:31, Christ says, **Heaven and earth will pass away but my words will not pass away**. Those words, however, are the sayings which he spoke of in the following chapter. And these words are explained in Luke 16:17 when the Savior says, **It is easier for heaven and earth to pass away, then for one point of the law to be revoked**, because in Matt. 5:18 the Truth speaks in the same way: **not one jot, not one point, will pass from the law until all these things come to be**.

And undoubtedly that law, those words, and those sayings are this very Scripture, (113) of which John 10:35 says, **the Scripture cannot be destroyed**. In order that the Scripture be fulfilled Christ came into the world, accomplishing the whole work of the one who sent him, as made clear in Matt. 26, Mark 14 and 16, John 17 and 19. Since the works of Christ are not ultimately dependent upon the works of men, such as parchments, engravings, voices, manuscripts, or other handiworks, one must grant that this is the superior Scripture, of which those sensible scriptures are but images. And concerning them, Ps. 86 (87:6) states, **the Lord will speak in the Scriptures of the people**, which are called the truths of Scripture in Dan. 10:21. And of these the Prophet Ezekiel threatens, **they will not be inscribed in the Scriptures of the Lord of Israel** (Ezek. 13:9); and Ps. 68 (69:28), **Let them be blotted out of the book of the living and not be inscribed among the righteous.**

These are indeed the Scriptures for the sake of whose understanding the Lord **revealed that sense to his apostles** in Luke 24:45; and in which the Pharisees **thought that they have life**, in John 5:39.

(114) In the days when I spoke as a child, I was anxiously perplexed in my efforts to understand and defend these Scriptures according to the strictly literal sense (*de virtute sermonis*), since it was clear to me that they did not derive their truth from the animal hides. Yet at last the Lord revealed that sense to me by his grace, through which I could then understand the aforesaid equivocation of Scripture. Therefore, I understand that Holy Scripture speaks in one instance according to the literal sense (*ad literam*), singularly pertaining to Scripture in the aforementioned first manner, and then again plurally, in regard to the aforementioned second and third manner of Scripture. And so it is with regard to the book. For in Apoc. 20 (Rev. 20:12) it is said, **the books were opened, and another**

book was opened, the Book of Life. These are the books of the soul or conscience, as demonstrated in Dan. 7:10. Hence, the manuscript is called a book in light of its analogous equivocation with the Book of Life, as is clear concerning the book given to Christ in Luke 4:17. Hence, Scripture is more notably accepted on behalf of the three-fold truth inscribed in the book, which now is understood formally, now essentially, and now according to intelligible being, and now according to its existent being. It is by means of these distinctions I have understood Scripture to be indestructibly true according to the literal sense (*ad literam*).

Though Holy Scripture itself makes little or no mention of the aforementioned fourth and fifth levels of Scripture, still this modern generation, intent on seeking after signs (Matt. 16:4), devotes its attention chiefly to this aspect of Scripture, despite the fact that what it possesses is no more fittingly considered Scripture than the lines on a hand discerned in palm-reading, or the configuration of points for prognosticating from the earth. Indeed, it amounts to no more than the trace of a tortoise shell upon a rock, except insofar as it is exemplified by the prior Scripture. (115) Under no circumstances is it deemed sacred, except for the fact that it functions as a guiding process which leads the faithful into the knowledge of the heavenly Scripture. For this reason it is considered holy in an even more remote fashion than vestments and other priestly ornaments are said to be holy. Strip away that sense and you will see that what remains is holy, for the aggregate is Holy Scripture.

[. . .] As such, one may conclude that the Scripture which is perceptible to the senses is called holy insofar as it is the means by which one is directly led to see by faith the will and order of God, which is itself the most sacred Scripture of all. (116) From this it is clear, furthermore, that for a layman, or perhaps someone who is perversely minded, this does not possess the character of Holy Scripture, since it lacks the effect by which it may be called holy. Therefore, the faithful, and theologians especially, should endeavor to preserve its holiness through an upright understanding and affections, not allowing it to become an idol of infidelity in the way that those images which are sacred to us become profane for idolaters. Augustine mentions this viewpoint, as I made clear in Chapter Three of this work. Therefore, if papal bulls or letters, which might in fact be wicked, are still said to be sacred because they are signs of his will or ordinance, how much more should the theologian say that the letters in which he reads of the will of his God are sacred, in keeping with the nine definitions for the word '*ieron*' (sacred) spoken of above?[88] Let us be on our guard lest our own perverse understanding gives rise to dishonor, corruption or some other sort of evil. Thus the Apostle speaks of Christ in 1 Cor. 1:23–24, who is free with regard to either of his natures, as Lincolniensis illustrates in his sixty-ninth *Dictum*.[89] **We preach Christ crucified, a stumbling block to the Jews and folly to the Gentiles, but to those Jews and Greeks who are called it is the power of God and the wisdom of God**. This seems applicable to the perverse theologians who understand Scripture in a sinister manner, for they are in some ways like the faithless Jews. And with regard to those who are puffed up by worldly literature, irreverently and recklessly discussing Holy Scripture, and condemning its logic and eloquence, (117) they are just like those Gentiles who reckoned Christ to be a fool on account of his humility and forbearance. The faithful, however, are the ones he calls as they are of meek and humble heart; people of all sorts, whether clerical or lay, man or woman. By submitting the necks of the interior man to the logic and eloquence of Scripture, they have found in it the power of pious works and that wisdom which is hidden from the proud, as Origen testifies to in *Sermon 20 on Joshua*.[90] This is why Augustine so frequently instructs us to humbly trust in Scripture, as evinced in those books of the *Confessions* where he acknowledges his own pride prior to conversion, and his later humility and infused love which he learned from reading Scripture.

(119) [. . .] Because of its impenetrable heights, Scripture proves to be a secure refuge for those who venerate it, as Augustine says in *On True Innocence* 120. "Just as the night does not extinguish the stars of the sky, so worldly iniquity does not darken the minds of the faithful adhering to the firmament of Holy Scripture."[91]

Holy Scripture retains a four-fold sense within its diverse parts: namely the literal, allegorical, tropological and anagogical, as expressed in this verse: The letter teaches the deeds, the allegory what you should believe, the moral what you should do, the anagogy that for which you ought to strive.

Although any sense which the letter possesses can fittingly be called the literal according to the intended literal sense (*de virtute sermonis*), (120) the doctors commonly call the literal sense that sense of Scripture which the Holy Spirit primarily intends so that the faithful soul would journey upwards into God. In one instance it is the historical, as is clearly the case with the deeds of Christ, and those deeds of the fathers of both testaments. At another time, it is the moral or tropological, evinced in the sapiential parts of Scripture, such as that saying found in Deut. 6:5 and Matt. 22:37, **You should love the Lord your God with your whole heart**, etc. And again it is allegorical, as evinced in that passage of the Apostle in 1 Cor. 10:2, **They were all baptized in Moses**. While in another instance it is surely anagogical, as made clear in that saying of the Savior in Matt. 22:30, and alternatively in Luke 20:35, **For in heaven they neither marry nor are given in marriage, but are like angels of God**. (121) Now these four senses are distinguished in this way according to their own classifications, inasmuch as the classes are not equally the same. For they have some subjective parts of a dissimilar nature and a different reason either way. Nevertheless, they are not distinguished by opposition as, for instance, a man and a donkey. It is the literal sense according to the principle by which the letter primarily teaches the truth. And it is the allegorical sense according to the principle by which Scripture extends beyond the history that it canonizes elsewhere according to the literal sense (*ad literam*), consequently teaching what should be believed by the Church Militant, as the passage in Gal. 4:22–24, **It is written,** in Gen. 17, **that Abraham had two sons; these are the two testaments**. Look at this, for beyond the historical sense, Abraham, who is interpreted as the father of many nations, signifies God the Father. His two sons and their circumstances signify the two testaments, Ishmael the Old and Isaac the New, since in both cases the correspondence is observable. Thus someone reading Scripture according to the primary sense, apart from the secondary, understands only the historical sense, while the one who adds the secondary sense comprehends the allegorical sense by the same letter. It seems to me that this is the meaning of the Subtle Doctor, (122) as he comments on Book 1 of the *Sentences*, Conclusion 3, stating,

> I say that whatever sense in one part of Scripture is not the literal will be the literal in another part. Therefore, even though a given part of Scripture has diverse senses, the entire Scripture still retains all of those senses on behalf of the literal sense.[92]

Nor have I encountered any another doctor whom it is appropriate to trust in this matter, who does not agree, although people who do not understand the distinction of these senses very well might believe they are never commingled. Whereupon, Rabanus, in the prologue of Book 9, truly states that, "In certain passages of Scripture history and allegory must be maintained at the same time, in order that the dull will be nourished by the history and the cleverer ones through the allegory."[93] Yet he does not deny the distinction of the senses or the identity found in many suppositions. Hence, I think that it is quite possible for the faithful reader purely to understand the mystical sense through the text of Gen. 17, while not discounting the history, such that the allegorical sense would be for him the literal. Because the sense of Scripture is the meaning or truth which the Holy Spirit has appointed it to signify, it only seems right that the literal and allegorical senses are the same with respect to diverse characteristics. In fact, of the many scriptural passages lacking an historical sense, their literal and allegorical senses are the same, even though their reason is dissimilar. Indeed, any orthodox sense which is first in the order conceived by a person from Scripture is thereby the literal sense. This is what St. Thomas says of the parabolic sense, (123) whereby the mystical sense, as the symbolized sense, suffices as the literal sense. Certainly that sense, **The word was with God** (John 1:1) is sufficiently mystical. Thus Rabanus is right when he says that in some passages of Scripture only the history ought to be preserved, while in some other part only allegory should be sought, and yet in some others both. Either way, the literal sense must be maintained, sometimes when it is the bare historical, sometimes when the allegorical, and at some other times when they are mixed.

Yet there are times when the moral or tropological sense possess the previously induced historical sense, and other times when it proves to be the literal sense immediately elicited from Scripture, since any sense of Scripture is the moral insofar as it immediately draws us towards the virtues. It is even the anagogical insofar as it teaches that truth which should be expected in the Church Triumphant. Thus when it comes to the three mystical senses, the allegorical teaches in a mediate or immediate fashion what must be believed; the anagogical sense teaches either mediately or immediately what is to be hoped for; and the tropological sense teaches mediately or immediately the work that is to be accomplished meritoriously. And in this way they correspond to the order of faith, hope and love. Those who wish to distinguish the literal sense from the others according to reason or subjective parts ought to say that, in keeping with this principle, the literal sense is the catholic sense, that one which is immediately elicited from Scripture. Thus the other three senses, if immediately derived from Scripture, are then the literal. If, however, they are elicited in a mediate fashion, then these are the allegorical, tropological or anagogical, (124) and not the literal. These four species of senses are mingled together, just as those four concrete species: the faithful, the active, the contemplative, and the heroic. There was a time when I struggled to distinguish these four senses from the opposite direction by employing useless distinctions, and arguing that the true sense was not only the one which the author asserted of Scripture, but was an aggregate formed from both that sense and from our own way of understanding. But I later realized that such a manner of speaking is without foundation and needlessly burdensome. It is sufficient that the sense sometimes would speak of the corporeal virtue of life, since there are five exterior senses and five interior senses. There are surely some other times when it speaks of the created or uncreated intellective power, as in Rom. 11:34, **Who has known the sense of the Lord?** Third, it signifies the act of such a virtue, while it fourthly signifies the object which such a virtue perceives, since the truth which the Catholic perceives from Scripture is called the sense of Scripture. Christ speaks this way in Luke 24:45, **Then he opened up the sense to them so that they might understand the Scriptures**. Although the sense in that instance could be understood to be the cognitive power of the disciples which had been previously concealed, (125) it still seems more appropriate to take this as referring to the meaning written in the law of Moses, the prophets and the Psalms of Christ. For this is the one he spoke of a little earlier as having been necessarily fulfilled (Luke 24:25–27). For that meaning is the Book of Life which Christ authentically **now opens, and now closes** without any impediment, as it says in Apoc. 3 (Rev. 3:7). This is why, according to Parisiensis, the Scriptures are called the **eyelids of the Lord which examine the sons of men**, as it said in Ps. 10 (Ps. 11:4).[94] Above this sense the eyes of the Lord are eternally borne, since at the same time it is essentially that truth which God perceives, his sensitive power, his act of knowing, and he himself as the one who knows. For he is the very sense which we seek in Scripture. Nor would there be a distinction of the aforementioned four senses as they pertain to the aggregate sense, since an aggregate of this sort is not the historical, nor is it the three-fold mystical sense. Nor does Scripture signify it; rather, it is changed according to human ways of understanding.

The fifth mode takes up a certain sense of Scripture on behalf of the act of the person comprehending it, whether it be erroneous or catholic. But I think it is both irrational and groundless to impose such a sense on Holy Scripture.

Let us speak of the sense in the aforementioned fourth manner. It seems appropriate that this alone would be the sense of Scripture which God (126) and the saints read in the Book of Life. It is of one sort or another. For pilgrims, it is concealed for the most part, though it is always true. Otherwise, it would not be the sense of Holy Scripture, but instead would be the most wicked of writings, as I will clarify later. It is invalid to respond by saying that although the sense of the author which abides either way in Holy Scripture is catholic, nevertheless, the literal sense, the verbal, which one really ought to elicit, still remains impossible for the most part.

I have argued against this line of thinking in various ways. First of all, every sense of Scripture is that which Scripture itself signifies. Yet nothing signified by Scripture is impossible, since it could not then exist. Therefore, no sense of Holy Scripture is impossible. For it follows that some sense of Holy Scripture exists; therefore, any one of the senses of Holy Scripture exists. Likewise, every sense is God or is of God; therefore, there is not any sense of Holy Scripture unless it is God or of God, and consequently it is the sense of the author of Holy Scripture. And that would mean that it is impossible according to the sense of the author. Again, either a person should consider such a sense concerning Scripture to be impossible or he should not. If he should, then God ordained that sense of his Scripture, and consequently it would be the sense which God intended. But then that would mean that he ordained that his own Scripture would be impossible. If it should not be conceived of in this way, however, then the sense of Scripture is not impossible, and the error rests instead with the person who wrongly understands it.

(130) [. . .] I have often said that all the evil which was introduced into the human race stems from the erroneous perception of the sense of Scripture, insofar as it is the Catholic faith itself. According to the Apostle in 2 Cor. 4:44, **The god of this world has blinded the minds of the unbelievers**, such that they only comprehend the faith of Scripture indirectly. In this way Christ confounded the devil with three passages from Scripture when the devil had tempted him by quoting Scripture, as is clear in Matt. 4:4–7. It was fitting that the adversary of God should be conquered in this manner, overcoming the one who deceitfully corrupts it, whether through abuse or prescription. Because the temptation of the first human being came about by means of Scripture after which he transgressed and ate, so the conquest of the devil (131) was accomplished first through Scripture. His second conquest

occurred through the spiritual taste of Christ's passion on the tree of the cross, in which matter countless forms should be recorded. It is clear that the whole human race was corrupted by forsaking Scripture's logic regarding the manner in which this negative commandment signifies the sense of the one who issued it. According to Augustine, Adam and Eve believed this prohibition was only spoken in a threatening manner, as he says in Book 11, Chapter 4 of *On the Literal Meaning of Genesis*: "I think Eve had supposed that God intended to signify something else when he said: **If you eat you will die** (Gen. 2:17)."[95]

In light of this, it would seem to me that just as disregard for Holy Scripture is an effeminate weakness, so it is satanic craftiness to refute it by heaping all manner of contradictions and falsehoods upon it. This seems to ring of blasphemy, since according the Apostle in Rom. 15:4, **whatever was written** in Scripture was divinely inspired, and thus **written for our instruction**. Yet God would surely be the greatest deceiver of all if he handed down this Scripture in order to achieve the very opposite purpose, namely that of leading his Church astray, as the opponents of Holy Scripture seem to be implying.

(132) Second, the Truth offers very clear testimony in Matt. 15:1–9 of how the priests, scribes and Pharisees, who were considered knowledgeable in the Scriptures, had transgressed the commandment of God to such an extent through their resoundingly covetous traditions, that the bridegroom of the church says in Ps. 118 (119:29), **It is the time for acting, Lord, for they have squandered your law.** In this vein, Christ **came not to destroy the law but to fulfill it**, as he says in Matt. 5:17. Hence, I am convinced that even in the New Testament, the principal heresy arose among the leaders of the Church due to their perverse understanding of this negative in Luke 22:25–26, **The kings of the Gentiles lord it over them, but not so with you.** For as I explained above in

Chapter Four of this work, since the world ceaselessly aspires to attain secular domination, if the bridle placed upon the very sort of domination which Christ had forbidden to his disciples is now relaxed by his vicars, it is now wonder **if the whole world is in the power of the evil one** (1 John 5:19).

(135) [. . .] The entirety of the evil which is so thoroughly infecting Christendom arises from forsaking the sense of Scripture which is keeping with that form which Christ instituted.

Third, it is evident that the damage done to the Church by the depravity of heresy, the perversity of simony, and all other evils of the Church, proceeded from a failure to imitate Scripture with regard to its form and matter. Such is the case with the heresiarchs Sergius, Pelagius, Julian, Peter Abelard, and all the other fallen heretics.[96]

(136) [. . .] Now just as Holy Scripture is a nest for Christ's faithful chicks, so erroneous readings of it prove a nest for heretics. This is why all Christians, indeed even secular lords, should be well acquainted with Holy Scripture and be prepared to defend it.

Do not be troubled by the false conclusions which are rendered from particular phrases. For heretics quote Scripture for their own purposes and seek the help of secular defenders. And if you come to their aid then you too are a heretic. By mutilating Holy Scripture, heretics deny that it is true. Not conceding it in its wholeness, they interpret it as they like, thereby twisting it to suit their own perverse sense, then seeking the aid (137) of secular lords to foment their crime. Catholics, to the contrary, quote Holy Scripture for its own sake, even passages I would think are impossible for the inexperienced to grasp, for they accept its authoritative truth in its totality, in keeping with the sense which the holy doctors have taught. And so they seek the help of secular lords, among whom the faith of the Church most often prevails, in combating those heretics who oppose Scripture. In fact, they understand the faith of Scripture more correctly and clearly than a number of their great ecclesiastical superiors. For even St. Paul appealed to Caesar in a matter of faith, whose council had an even better sense of the faith than the perfidious priests, scribes, and Pharisees, as evinced in the case of the Gentile philosopher Seneca. This history is made clear in Acts 24 and the two following chapters.

(138) [. . .] Inasmuch as all truth is in Holy Scripture, it is clear that every disputation, every signification of terms, or linguistic science which does not have its origin in Holy Scripture, is profane. According to the grammarians, the profane is common and cursed, that is to say, unholy or sacrilegious. It is at a distance, as it were, from that which is consecrated and corresponds to whatever sorts of logics do not originate in Scripture.

(*De ver.* I,vii): Reading Scripture in Its Totality

(138) The truth of Scripture ought to be comprehended by faith in its totality, since it would not be Holy Scripture otherwise, as Chrysostom teaches in the *Unfinished Work, Sermon 40*.[97] Nevertheless, some instances can arise which lead to improprieties for any Catholic, ones which the falsifiers of the Scriptures will use to frighten them.

First, in this manner: if Holy Scripture were false, since it could not be false except according to the bare grammatical sense, which is commonly impossible, (139) evinced by the mystical names of God, it follows that Holy Scripture would be impossible in large part, and thus supremely false, heretical and blasphemous. There is, however, no foundation in grammar or logic to support the assertion that Holy Scripture could actually be literally false (*ad verba*), or with respect to the literal verbal sense, and yet still remain entirely free from falsehood itself. In this matter it is asked whether some aspect of Holy Scripture may be simply false while some other is true.

If one concedes that Holy Scripture could be supremely false, as in 1 Cor. 10:4, **the rock was Christ**; and **he was the true light** in John 1:9; and the **conquering Lion of the tribe of Judah** in Apocalypse, Chapter 5 (Rev. 5:9), along with other passages similar to these, then it follows, first of all, that the Christian faith, and consequently the very foundation of the sect of Christ, is the most false, damnable, horrible and absurd of all the faiths belonging to other sects. And this hardly seems appropriate to the Catholic. There appears to be no reason why the aforesaid figurative propositions are impossible on account of some impossible concept or sense, except that, by the same rationale, they would be heretical and blasphemous due to some heretical or blasphemous concept. Otherwise, no proposition or opinion would be either heretical or catholic except insofar as it is a sign of such a sense. Hence, the Apostle says in 2 Tim. 4:3, **There will be a time when they will not endure sound doctrine**. Nobody says that such an impossible sense would be catholic or reasonable, for in that case it would be true and then would have to be defended. It is not necessary (140) for the person enunciating a proposition of this sort to assert it according to that sense, nor does it make him a heretic or blasphemer himself. For someone may maintain a heretical conclusion simply as a matter of opinion, or defend it in only a vicarious fashion, even though he would never assert such a thing himself. This is evident, for instance, in the case of an impossible fact which exists only in the intellect. Just as a person can say something impossible although he is not impossible in his own right, so he can utter a heretical proposition although he is not a heretic himself.

(141) [. . .] Just because a sober sense is coupled with a blasphemous one, this does not excuse the proposition formed by such a double sense if its conclusion turns out to be heretical. For if this were the case, then no person's statement could ever be deemed heretical, though according to the Apostle in

1 Cor. 5:6 **a small amount of leaven corrupts the whole lump.** Therefore, just as the pure, sacred sense makes Scripture holy, so a spurious sense renders the manuscript or writing spurious and wrong sounding.

(152) [. . .] The prevailing opinion today among those who provide judgments on matters of law is that whoever happens to be pope is infallible, and consequently whatever he decides or ordains must be just. In fact, his letters are put on a par with, and may even surpass, the authority of Holy Scripture, such that even the gospel is not believed except on his authority. Thus he is able to render Holy Scripture heretical and make catholic what is the opposite of the Christian faith. It is for this reason that the Christian should pay more attention to imitating his life, since a person ought to be trusted more for his deeds than his words, than to the rule of Scripture handed down from Christ through his apostles. Because nobody is allowed to correct him, nor accuse him of any crime, the faithful must resort to him and give heed to his life, just as if it were an example of the entire Christian manner of living. And if one were to object that the pope has adopted a different way of life than Christ and his apostles, they offer a three-fold response. First, they say that the change of times requires this; second, that by the plenitude of his power they may dispense with the obligation to imitate Christ and his apostles; and third, that it is for them to interpret Holy Scripture, to which they apply an extraneous commentary (153) extending beyond the words. For example, I have adduced from Scripture that the priests of Christ should humbly minister to the Church by means of the sacraments, the sacramentals, and the teaching of the gospel of peace. In keeping with the greater part of this humble ministry the majority of them are obliged to attend to what pertains to God. Thus they should live a poor life, devoid of property, thereby imitating Christ in this way. For having been placed in a wicked world, it is that much more necessary.

Neither the change in times, nor a papal dispensation, excuses priests of Christ from this duty, but rather it serves to accuse them if they abandon it. I have selected for this purpose Luke 22:25–26, **The kings of the Gentiles lord it over them, though not so with you**. By the faith of Scripture I have proven that the way of life of Christ and his apostles conforms to this sense, such that life is the best interpreter of Scripture. Second, I have proven this same sense based upon the testimony of the saints such as Chrysostom, Bernard, and others. And third, I have proven this by appealing to the testimony offered by many laws which stipulate that the goods of the Church belong to the poor, and are not given to churchmen for the sake of establishing dominion over others, but are given rather for governance, distribution and service.

(155) [. . .] It is because people have failed to recognize the authority of Holy Scripture that one must first believe in God, and secondly believe in the Catholic church, which is the bride of God according to what the Apostle says in Heb. 11:6, **It is necessary for the one who approaches God to believe that he exists and that he was the rewarder of the good**. Therefore, just as everyone is obligated to believe that he is faithful, so everyone is bound to believe in the society of the faithful. Since neither empire nor kingdom, nor even city or society can endure without law, it is clearly appropriate to trust that God, through the goodness of his providence, bequeathed a law to his Church at some time. For if he does not abandon inanimate bodies, nor vegetative life, nor sentient creatures, but instead ordains a law for them, surely he would not forsake his very own bride.

(156) This law, of whatever sort it was, is none other than Holy Scripture, the Lord's immaculate law which one must comprehend by faith, since it is the highest law, and consequently the most true, complete and salutary. All people are obliged to understand, defend and preserve it, since according

to it all are bound to serve the Lord in hope of eternal reward. The abbreviated form of this law is to turn away from evil and do the good; and more briefly still, I would say, in accordance with the Apostle in Rom. 13:10, **love is the fullness of the law**. All the other private laws, whether of emperors, kings, and cities, or Church constitutions, do not help, but in fact only manage to hinder us, except insofar as they serve and promote this law.

Furthermore, just as we believe in the Lord Jesus Christ, so it is fitting to believe in his gospel, and consequently all the books of the other testament which bear witness to him. Thus it is also fitting that we should trust that our Bible is the law of God which God himself infused with meaning, and which nobody is allowed to infringe upon or refute. How the books of the Bible were canonized by God, and in this way authorized, I clarify elsewhere.

We should believe this law posited in mode, number and measure according to what profits the Church, and thus believe it just as we do God. Whereupon, Augustine teaches in Book 1, Chapter 37 of *On Christian Doctrine*, that many evils arise when people either disbelieve Scripture or maintain some perverted understanding of it. This is what prompts a person to be offended by Scripture, what leads him into contradiction, and worst of all, what persuades him to abandon the very faith which he ought to receive from Scripture. (157) Augustine says, "Faith will falter if the authority of Divine Scripture wavers. Moreover, when faith falters love itself languishes. For if anyone were to fall away from faith, he will necessarily fall away from love."[98] Every intention of Scripture should refer to love of God and neighbor, and consequently to the three theological virtues, as is clear in Book 1 of *On Christian Doctrine*, Chapters 30 and 35, and Book 3, Chapter 14, as well as *On the Psalms* 140, and can also be demonstrated from the intention of divine law.[99] Augustine says,

> Scripture prescribes nothing except charity, neither condemns anything except cupidity, nor asserts anything but the Catholic faith. It condemns vice which uncontrolled cupidity performs in order to corrupt the soul and body, or crime when it does this so as to harm another,

as clarified in Chapter 10, Book 3.[100] And since the love of temporal things interferes with charity, and vice versa, the love of eternal things disrupts the love of earthly things, so then Scripture teaches us to despise temporal things and aspire to the heavenly. Whereupon, in Book 1, Chapter 38 of *On Christian Doctrine* we read that,

> Between temporal and eternal things there is this difference, that the temporal is loved more before it is acquired, and yet becomes valueless when we have attained it. (158) For it will not satisfy the soul for whom eternity is the true and certain resting place. The eternal is surely loved more ardently when it is attained than when it is desired. It is impossible for someone who desires it to estimate that it is greater than it is with the result that it becomes valueless when he finds it to be less.[101]

And so it was Christ's intention that by coming in the flesh his own manner of living would serve as an example in condemning earthly things, as Augustine says in Book 7, Chapter 19 of the *Confessions*.[102] Therefore, whatever Scripture appears to resound of that which is not charity or what pertains to it, this is not the sense of Scripture, but is contrary to it.

With regard to the three arguments, I say there are three pertinent proofs to be set forward: namely, the proof derived from internal illumination, the proof drawn from sensible authority, and the proof received from testimony. The proof drawn from testimony has many levels, according to which the more fitting signs of faithfulness proper to testimonies consist. The proof derived from the authority of Scripture is very fitting indeed. The proof derived from the inspiration of the First Doctor, however, is the most fitting of all, without which none of the others are valid. This is why it is necessary, first of all, for us to rely on faith, whose own proof exceeds that of a dialectical argument.

(*De ver.* I,viii): The Nature of Heresy, and the Five Weapons of Heavenly Logic

(159) Second, I will chiefly prove the same conclusion through a deduction which leads to another impropriety. Namely, that the law of God and the faith of the Church is contradictory, and as such, infinitely flawed and heretical. The syllogism's consequent conflicts with Augustine and all the saints, and is even opposed to the head of the Church, and God its author. The logical inference is clear, insofar as Scripture is not proven false except for the fact that many people who know nothing of the true understanding falsely comprehend it in this way. Yet it is surely the case that many consider parts of Scripture to be contrary and contradictory according to the old grammar, clarified by the authorities expounded upon in the first, second, third and fifth chapters. Heresy is a false dogma, contrary to Holy Scripture, which is persistently defended. Therefore, since people will defend the entirety of Holy Scripture even unto death, it only seems right that the dogma of another contrary writing would be false dogma, etc. For Scripture has any number of parts which many people could wrongly understand, in a contradictory and heretical fashion, as I made clear in the first five chapters.

[. . .] (161) Second, it is objected in this matter that many doctors, and especially decretists, speak in a sufficiently equivocal fashion regarding heresy and, therefore, this description does not generally apply to every heresy.

But that evidence is not very compelling, since according to the philosophers, equivocations are hidden within classifications as well as when the classifications are defined. The term 'man' is very equivocal, since it pertains to an actual man as well as the picture of a man, as made clear in the beginning of Aristotle's book, *Predications*.[103] In one instance (162) it is considered in light of its spiritual principle, and in another instance for the body that was formed by that spirit, and then again for the whole essence. Such is the case with many of the equivocations expressed by Scripture. Notwithstanding that, man is suitably defined according to the univocal sense. And so it is with the signs of other species. That doctors would speak so equivocally about heresy, however, is perhaps due to an ignorance by which they do not know enough to reduce statements to the univocal or analogous sense, since some say every mortal sin is heresy, and others that propounding false dogma is heresy. Some claim that it is an action perceptible to the senses, while others say heresy is an action or disposition within the soul that is imperceptible to the senses. So it goes with many unfounded opinions. I do not believe that falsehood, something which does not exist, is a heresy since, according to the Apostle in 1 Cor. 11:19, **it is necessary that there be heresies**. Consequently, it is necessary that every heresy exist; therefore, there can be no heresy which does not exist. Every heresy is a form by which the infidel is designated a heretic. In this way heresy does not seem to me to be a mortal sin, even though it is likely that every criminal is a heretic, since false dogma proceeds from every mortal sin, etc. Just as I consider every one who commits a mortal sin to be an infidel. For according to Augustine, in his *Sermon 29 on John*, to believe in God is, "by believing in him, to love him, to enter into him, and be incorporated into his members."[104] (163) And from this it is clear that every criminal lacks the first article of faith, for then he does not believe in God, and consequently proposes some dogma contrary to the law of God. For just as the saints hold all good things in common and each one benefits the rest, so the members of the devil hold all evil things in common and each one of them worsens the rest, leading him down the path of wickedness in these matters. And so it is clear that there are any number of levels when it comes to heresy, just as in mortal sin.

Third, it is objected that according to the aforementioned description, not only the dogma of Aristotle and the other pagan philosophers would be heresy, but also the teaching of saints, and even the teaching of the Lord Jesus Christ. Now Aristotle's dogma regarding the impossibility of the Creation, as well as the world being without beginning, is false dogma, contrary to Holy Scripture, as demonstrated in Gen. 1:1, **In the beginning when God created the heaven and the earth**. Yet it was obstinately defended by many disciples of Aristotle and Averroes, and the others. I suppose that, by the same rationale, a dogma belonging to some pious doctor, which he offers as an opinion with legitimate protestation and dread, would also be heresy, thereby rendering him a heretic as well. And the same appears to be true with regard to the words of Christ, which others obstinately defend in a manner which is contrary to the sense of Holy Scripture. In this way, not only would every infidel be rendered a heretic, but also every doctor, however faithful he might be, in the event that some other people perversely seized upon his statements as an opportunity to defend their own heresy.

In this regard I have said that the dogma of the pagan philosophers is heresy in my judgment when, lacking humility (164) in these matters, they have propounded their dogma in both word and deed that is contrary to Holy Scripture, and then have obstinately defended it. It is in this way that I consider all the unfaithful to be heretics. It should come as no surprise that a heretic pretends to be faithful to the Church, just as it is necessary for a schismatic to be within the Church at first, only later obstinately and openly severing himself from it, as the name implies. Likewise, the pagan philosophers all present themselves as faithful men, and consequently as sons of the Church. This is evident in the case of Aristotle who, in Book 3, Chapter 26 of the *Secrets*, proclaims that faith is essential for any system of government. Hence, it is unnecessary for a heretic to be a son of the Church in actual fact, only that he pretends to be a believer. In regard to the schismatic, it does seem necessary that he would first have been a son of the true Church, whether in truth or by pretext. In the case of pagan philosophers, although they were not schismatics, they were still heretics.

(166) [. . .] Second, it is objected that since Holy Scripture in that fifth mode is the written sign, as stipulated in Chapter Six, then it could in one instance signify the catholic sense, while in another instance signify the heretical sense. In light of such a possibility it seems that Holy Scripture will be heretical. Consequently, given Christ's logic in Matt. 11:5 that **the blind see**, etc., Holy Scripture is in fact heretical. Thus the Spirit would be holy and catholic in one instance and heretical in another. And, by the same rationale, so too would Holy Scripture.

Here, it seems to me that the outward signs such as tablets and writings are not heretical, except in a very equivocal manner. Just as urine is said to be healthy because it is a sign of health, so I contend that the writing or utterance of a heretical man can be called heretical or blasphemous. And from such signs a man is able to recognize heresy as well as blasphemy. (167) Whereupon, since the Holy Scripture which is perceptible to the sense states such sensible things collectively and they are conformed to the sense of the Lord, it is obvious that a person who understands these things in a perverted way creates for himself a text which is not Holy Scripture. For when many people understand the same signs in a contrary manner then those signs are the material of one thing in heresy, and are the material of another in Holy Scripture. In this case they would have two things concomitantly: Holy Scripture and a writing which serves to deceive. And then God would surely be a liar, as clarified below. Yet if the decretals, charters or papal bulls, the texts of the philosophers, and other human judgments are defended from falsehood, how much more so the faith of Scripture! For whenever Scripture is spoken according to its own essence then it is automatically understood given its inherent excellence.

Just as Scripture's composition is five-fold, so there is a five-fold armor by which it can be defended from the wiles of those sophists who are intent on imposing falsehood upon it. On this account, it should be noted that just as there are five defensive spiritual weapons (168) which Augustine lists in his brief book *Regarding the Holy Spirit*,[105] concerning the writing of the Apostle in Eph. 6:13–17, namely the **shield of faith, helmet of salvation, breastplate of righteousness, preparation of the feet in the gospel of peace and the belt of truth**, so corresponding to these, heavenly logic possesses five kinds of weapons by which the Catholic can demolish all the javelins and insults of the sophists, who strive in vain to subvert the truth of the Sacred Page according to the strictly literal sense (*de virtute sermonis*).

The first one assigns to God the co-eternal ideas, which are those reasons or exemplars subsisting within him by which the universe was created, according to John 1:3–4, **What was made, in him was life**. In this way one can comprehend how it is that in Gen. 1:3, **God said, "Let there be light"; and light came to be**. This is laden with meaning. First, "to say" refers to the Word of God. Second, "Let there be" refers to the exemplar reason. And third, "it came to be" refers to the creation of the thing, and the existence of the creature. On account of this, one will be able to acknowledge the sheer abundance which surely resides within so many passages of Scripture, its unfathomable profundity and supernal heights, as Augustine often reminds us. This is the helmet of salvation, since according to Augustine in Question 46 of his *Eighty-Three Questions*, "apart from the knowledge of ideas, nobody may be wise or blessed."[106]

(169) The second weapon assigns an actual reality to universals beyond signs. For according to Gen. 1:21, **So God created every living and moving creature, which the waters bring forth in their species, and every flying thing according to its genus**. And knowledge of the these common creatures is a means to understanding the uncreated Trinity, as Augustine teaches in the *Dialogue with Felcianus*.[107] In this regard Anselm states in Chapter 2 of his *On the Incarnation of the Word*, that those who deny such universals are "heretical logicians."[108] Indeed, there is no fallacy regarding the Trinity or the Incarnation which cannot be detected proportionally in the matter of universals. Thus the many passages of Scripture which allude to common things may be defended according to the intended literal sense (*de virtute sermonis*). Undoubtedly then, either this meaning is catholic or it is heretical, though I do not believe that anyone would presume to assert such a thing, since so many saints have defended it. And so this weapon is like the breastplate, according to which genera and species are interwoven through the differences in their subjects.

The third weapon maintains that things which belong as much to one species as to another, although they might be separated by time and space, really form one totality, according to John 1:3, **The world was made through him**. This is, so to speak, the inciting of the soul's feet to strive for evangelical unity and to defend Scripture always according to its intended literal sense (*de virtute sermonis*). (170) This is important when considering the difference of numbers posited by the Apostle in Gal. 3:16, **He does not say, "to seeds," as if many, but rather, "to your seed," who is Christ**. Following such logic the Apostle says in Eph. 5:8, **At one time you were darkness, now, however, you are light in the Lord**. And again in Rom. 15:6 he exhorts, **Let us glorify God together with one voice**. It was by such means that Augustine and the holy doctors granted, along with the Apostle in 1 Cor. 12, that **the church is one body** (1 Cor. 12:12) indeed one person, because she is the **strong woman** spoken of in Prov. 31:10–31, the bride of Christ referred to in Songs (Song of Sol. 1–2). Moreover, she is the mother of the faithful, composed of all the predestined belonging to the past and future, as well as the blessed angels, as Augustine says in Chapter 43 of the *Enchiridion*.[109]

(171) [. . .] Like a most protective shield, the fourth weapon is the lofty metaphysic declaring that all things which once had been, or will be in the future, exist now in the presence of God. They are present in their proper time, not only according to their intelligible being, but with respect to their actual being as well, according to that passage in Eccl. 3:1, **All things have their season, and in their times all things pass under the sun**. And so the Scriptures can be rescued, as the doctors concur, easily destroying the insoluble difficulties raised by those people who attempt to hold present time captive. In this vein, the Truth speaks aptly and truly in John 8:58, **Before Abraham was I am**, and in Luke 13:32, **Go and tell that fox, "Look, I cast out demons and perform cures today and tomorrow, and on the third day I am finished."** And it is in accordance with this sense that Christ cites that passage in Exod. 3:6, **I am the God of Abraham, the God of Isaac, and the God of Jacob**, though spoken long after these saints had died, as made clear in Luke 20. (172) Scripture is filled with such examples, such as John 20:17, **I am ascending to my Father and your Father,**

my God and your God; and 2 Tim. 4:6, **I am already being taken away, and the time of my release approaches**. Whereupon, owing to the certitude of the event, he says in 2 Thess. 2:1–12 that anti-Christ is being revealed at the proper time. And in 1 Tim. 2:6 he says that the **testimony of Christ was confirmed in the proper times**. This is how Solomon speaks in Prov. 25:11, **To speak a word at the proper time is like golden apples on silver dining couches**. It is surely appropriate for all successive actions to follow one another perfectly at the proper time, in the manner spoken of in Ps. 144 (Ps. 145:15), **The eyes of all people place their hope in you Lord, and you give them food at the proper time**. Now there would a great deal of confusion if God permitted the whole created universe to burst forth at the same time. This is the reason why the prophets speak with such variation regarding the differences of times, as Augustine observes in *On Psalm 125*, "It customarily happens that a prophet speaks of the past when foretelling future events."[110] Just as in Ps. 21 (22:16), **They bound my hands and my feet**, were future events even though they were being sung of as if they had already taken place. (173) For God has already brought about all the things which will happen in the future. And Anselm concurs with this in Chapter 5 of *On the Agreement of Foreknowledge and Predestination* where he says, "Just as the present time contains every occasion and those things which are in any occasion, so every time is simultaneously enclosed within the eternal present, as well as those things which are in any time." Therefore, as he says in Chapter 5, "I do not say that my action of tomorrow exists at no time, but today I do deny that it exists, even though it always exists in eternity."[111]

Any number of saints speak with a similar understanding, granting along with Holy Scripture, that God justifies the unrighteous, that **the blind see, the lame walk, the lepers are cleansed, the deaf hear** and **the dead rise**, as Christ says in Matt. 11:4–6.

By means of this weapon one also comes to understand matters of predestination and the necessity of future events, along with the contingencies pertaining to them both. In this way a solution is found for the following argument: Christ, who is God, has asserted this; therefore, it will occur. For inasmuch as the future is necessary so also is the past, since that which does not exist applies to them both. (174) Yet apart from the shield of faith, we could not trust that creatures succeed one another in a changeable fashion, assisted by the immutable God in every past and future instant by reason of his own eternity. Indeed, I do not see how else the scriptural metaphysic regarding God's intuitive knowledge could be salvaged, nor how the philosophy concerning successive actions could be taught.

The fifth weapon is like a wide belt embracing all of these things. It is through a knowledge of the equivocation of terms belonging to Scripture that one realizes that there is no contradiction within equivocal signs, as was explained in Chapter One, both through Scripture and the testimony of Augustine. Those equivocations which remain hidden to the philosophers, are most subtly expressed in our books. And, provided that the theologian comprehends them, he will be able to understand the truth which, by its very nature, does not rest in the veil of words, since it is neither a falsehood nor a contradiction. The one who does not care for the vainglory of the sophists, but instead cherishes the Lord Jesus Christ with a pure love, will employ this exemplary logic of Scripture, as stated in Chapter Three.

I have established a three-fold example for the detection of equivocation. The first is the moral, which is in accordance with the words of the Apostle in 1 Cor. 10:32–33, **Be without offense either to Jews or Gentiles or to the church of God, just as I please all people in all things**; and in Gal. 1:10, **If I were still pleasing human beings, I would not be a servant of Christ**. Upon which Augustine states,

> He, however, who is pleasing to men for the sake of the truth does not himself please them, but rather the truth itself does. Certainly, if a man for his own sake, that is for his own private advantage, seeks to please, (175) it is pride and does not please God. In both ways, therefore, it can rightly be said "I please and I do not please."[112]

(176) [. . .] The second example is the natural: those names of material substances, whenever they concretely signify the material essence to which substantial form is added, or when they simply signify the union of that essence with a form of this sort. Regarding such equivocation, Plato and Aristotle disagreed. According to the first sense, John 2:9 truly states that **the water became wine**. For the same material essence which is presently water will be wine after they have been variously mixed together. This is the case with other sorts of bodies among which Scripture allows conversion. In Gen. 1:1–2, the material essence is called earth in one instance, water in another, and then again the abyss from which primal matter was made, as Augustine observes in Book 12 of the *Confessions*.[113] According to this sense, one should concede that a human being is earth, seed, or some other material from which his body is made. (177) So it was that the priests were partially in the loins of Abraham, as the scriptural passages of Gen. 3:15 and Heb. 7:10 affirm. In fact, all material substances were created simultaneously as Eccles. 18 (Sir. 18:1–5) states. Yet various philosophers argue over that equivocation uncovered in Scripture, as I have said in a certain tract called *On Forms*.[114]

(179) [. . .] The third example is the logical or rational by which one recognizes how a common restricted term pertaining to something singular is distributed or negated while that sense remains. It would not be interchangeable, however, except for the sake of that thing for which it becomes a distinct intellection. For just as Christ is common to humanity

and divinity, in one instance we say that he was made, and then in another instance, that he was not made. Likewise, it is because 'being' (*esse*) commonly connotes any present time, just as 'having been' and 'going to be' are commonly used in order to connote any time in the past or future, that it is limited to a particular time, whether present, past or future. It is for this reason that Scripture often restricts terms to a particular time in order to allow for a special measure of interchange. Consider Gen. 2:20, where it is said, **For Adam a helper was not found like himself**; but supply here: "not yet, before Eve was created." Consider also that passage in Jer. 31:15, **Rachel, weeping for her sons, did not want to be consoled, because they are not**; but supply here: the "sons of predestination," since the sons of Leah were martyred for the sake of Christ, as Augustine explains in *On Questions of the Old and the New Law*, Chapter 62.[115] Now the tribe of Benjamin was cut down on account of the Levite's wife, evinced in Judg. 19. They are not sons of the contemplative part of the Church which the saints understand through Rachel, since the unstable condition of the flesh is absolutely contrary to contemplation. For according to Scripture's manner of speaking, to be a sinner is, to a certain extent, not to exist at all.

One can similarly understand that passage in Apocalypse 10 (Rev. 10:6) where the angel pledges through the Trinity that, **Time will be no more** (180), but supply here: "such that the secret evil would reign," or any other sort of worldliness which the Holy Spirit understood. Instead, it will be destroyed by the faithful people who have been taught by the Spirit of God. And this is designated by the angel having placed his right foot upon the sea and his left foot upon the earth (Rev. 10:2). Indeed, it often happens that the lay people living the active life as reptiles, in the keel of a ship, will take on the wings of the clergy who have been transformed by their greedy devotion to earthly things, just as occurred at the time of Christ and frequently thereafter.

Other negatives within Scripture should be explained similarly, casting aside the vainglory and honor of sophistical pretense, lest the person conceding Holy Scripture in its own form would appear to be refuted. And since all twelve fallacies can be reduced to the first, it is clear that having noted the equivocation which is presented within the Scriptures with the four prior weapons, Scripture itself can be both understood and defended.

I do not think it is right for us to admit any science or conclusion to which Scripture does not bear witness. Thus it seems to me that five important truths are being taught in that passage of Gen. 1:26, **Let us make humankind according to our image and likeness**. First, that God the creator is the Trinity, since otherwise he would not so appropriately say, **Let us make**. Second, that the entire human personality is preserved in the soul, since it said, **Let us make humankind**. Third, that the soul is triune, since it is conformed to the image of its God. Fourth, that the human person was created in grace, since he was made according to likeness of his God. And fifth, that the whole Trinity is one simple essence, since it is said singularly, **according to our image and likeness**. (181) And the same can be said of other parts of Scripture, providing that one's own ignorance does not get in the way.

(182) [. . .] Yet in whatever manner someone might approach these issues I am certain that the aforementioned five kinds of weaponry, habitually established in theology, would safely preserve that person from all the sophistical javelins by means of which certain people vainly strive to impose falsehood upon our Scripture according to the strictly literal sense (*de virtute sermonis*).

I implore all Catholics, however, that they would neither teach, nor defend, any part of this five-fold weaponry as though it were my own, but instead because it belongs to the author of the primary Scripture which is revealed through his saints and given to the faithful for this purpose. Therefore, the sixth invasive weapon, namely the sword of the Spirit, which is the word of Scripture, should not be constrained. Rather, it should be permitted the sort of free operation which it has thus far known. For only then might Scripture recover the authority, reverence, and even the effectiveness, it enjoyed in days gone by.

Notes

1. Wyclif uses here the logical term *consequencia* which is the inference drawn from the relationship between the antecedent (*antecedens*) and consequent (*consequens*) propositions.

2. *De Doctrina Christiana* IV.8.22, ed. Josef Martin, Corpus Christianorum, Series Latina 32 (Turnhout, 1962), pp. 131–32.

3. *De Doc. Chr.* IV.12.27, CCSL 32:135.

4. *De Doc. Chr.* IV.8.22, CCSL 32:131.

5. *De Doc. Chr.* IV.8.22, CCSL 32:131.

6. This may not be Augustine. The citation was not found.

7. Ibid.

8. *De Doc. Chr.* IV.6.9, CCSL 32:122.

9. *In Iohannis Evangelium* XLVII.6, ed. Radbotus Willems, Corpus Christianorum, Series Latina 36 (Turnhout, 1954), p. 407.

10. *In Ioh. Evang.* XLVII.3, CCSL 36:406.

11. *In Ioh. Evang.* XLVII.5, CCSL 36:407.

12. All Psalms are numbered here according to the Vulgate. When the Psalms are quoted I have placed the modern citation in parentheses. Note, however, that in his critical edition Buddensieg emended the text, thus giving the modern numbering of the Psalms within the text itself. I have restored the original numbering.

13. *Enarrationes in Psalmos* CXX.11, ed. Eligius Dekkers and John Fraipont, Corpus Christianorum, Series Latina 40 (Turnhout, 1956), p. 1796.

14. *In Ps.* CXX.11, CCSL 40:1796.

15. *In Ps.* XXVI.2, CCSL 38:154. This quotation varies somewhat from Augustine's own words.

16. *In Ps.* XXVI.2, CCSL 38:154.

17. *In Ioh. Evang.* XLVII.8, CCSL 36:408. Wyclif conflates this passage.

18. Syllogisms are comprised of extreme and middle terms. For example: 'Every man is an animal; Socrates is a man; therefore, Socrates is an animal'. 'Animal' and 'Socrates' are the extreme terms, while 'man' is the middle term.

19. *Genus* is a term of classification beneath which is species. For instance, the human species belongs to the animal genus. Wyclif will also use the term '*genus*' in the broader sense of 'class' or 'kind'.

20. See Wyclif's own *De Dominio Civili* I.xxvii, ed. R. L. Poole (1885; repr. New York, 1966), p. 196.

21. *De Diversis Quaestionibus ad Simplicianum* II, ed. Almut Mutzenbecher, Corpus Christianorum, Series Latina 44 (Turnhout, 1970), pp. 58–91.

22. *Moralium*, PL 75:601, 616.

23. Wyclif concludes the previous chapter saying that he will clarify three apparent contradictions drawn from Scripture.

24. *In Ioh. Evang.* XXVIII.8, CCSL 36:281–82.

25. *In Ioh. Evang.* XXVIII.9, CCSL 36:282.

26. *Consequenciam*. See note 1 above.

27. This is Thomas Bradwardine (d. 1349).

28. Averroes, the great Moslem philosopher from Cordoba (d. 1198), was often referred to simply as "The Commentator."

29. This is Albert the Great (d. 1280). See Albert's *Summa Theologiae* I, T. 3, Q. 18, m. 1, in *Opera Omnia,* ed. August Borgnet, vol. 31 (Paris, 1895), pp. 117–20.

30. Wyclif is referring to the eternal exemplars subsisting in the divine mind.

31. An *argumentum topicum* refers to dialectical argument. Aristotle's *Topics* concerns methods of argumentation. Dialectic proceeds from

opinions which are generally accepted as opposed to those which are self-evidently true.

32. Robert Grosseteste was bishop of Lincoln from 1235 to 1253.

33. See *Roberti Grosseteste Epistolae*, ed. H. R. Luard (London, 1861), pp. 1–2.

34. *Consequens*. See note 1 above.

35. This is a matter of proper and improper speech, i.e., literal and figurative discourse. Wyclif's point is that when the figurative designation aptly applies to the subject then it can itself be considered the literal meaning, such that Christ is a lion according to the text's literal sense.

36. *In Ioh. Evang.* XLVII.6, CCSL 36:407.

37. *In Ioh. Evang.* XLVII.3, CCSL 36:406.

38. This citation was not found.

39. *Moralium*, PL 76:533.

40. The outward sense, grasped at first sight, as opposed to the deeper, spiritual meaning intended beneath the surface.

41. *Epist.* CXXXVII.17, ed. Alois Goldbacher, Corpus Scriptorium Ecclesiasticorum Latinorum 44/45 (Vienna, 1904), pp. 121–22.

42. See actually *De Doc. Chr.* II.41.63, CCSL 32:76.

43. *Epist.* LXXXII.4–8, ed. Alois Goldbacher, Corpus Scriptorium Ecclesiasticorum Latinorum 34.2 (Vienna, 1898), pp. 355–58.

44. It was thus Adam's sin which occasioned the Incarnation.

45. Wyclif appeals here to the Augustinian distinction between *uti* and *frui*, use and enjoyment. All things are to be used in order to draw closer to the only one who is to be enjoyed, namely the Trinity.

46. John of Paris (d. 1306). This citation was not found.

47. This likely refers to Benedict XII's 1340 summoning of Nicholas Autrecourt with five others to appear before the curia in Avignon to answer for various propositions. Autrecourt was later condemned in 1346.

48. See *Metaphysics*, 1091b.

49. *Contra Mendacium* XIII, PL 40:538.

50. *De Potentia* q. VI–VII in *Opera Omnia,* ed. S. E. Fretté and Paul Maré, vol. 13 (Paris, 1895), pp. 178–243. See especially ibid., q. VII, a. 5, pp. 225–29.

51. Concept: conception. Synthesis: word arrangement. Zeugma: one word governing other comparable clauses.

52. *De Genesis ad Literam* VIII.4, ed. Joseph Zycha, Corpus Scriptorum Ecclesiasticorum Latinorum 28.1 (Vienna, 1894), p. 236.

53. *De Gen. Lit.* VIII.6, CSEL 28.1:239–40.

54. Perhaps Augustine's *In Heptateuchum Locutionum* VII.44–46, PL 34:808–09.

55. Isidore of Seville. Perhaps his *Etymologies.* This citation was not found.

56. See *Summa Theologiae* I, Q. 1, a. 10 in *Opera Omnia*, ed. S. E. Fretté and Paul Maré, vol. 1 (Paris, 1876), p. 14.

57. Januensis de Balbis, O.P. (ca. 1280). See his *Catholicon* (Venice, 1495), p. 222.

58. See Hugh's *Eruditionis Didascalicae* VI.4, PL 176:802–05. These words have not been found, however.

59. *In Ps.* LXVIII.15, CCSL 39:914.

60. This may be a general affirmation; a specific citation was not found.

61. *Homilia in Evangelia* II.XXIII, PL 76:1182.

62. *Epist.* LXXIII, PL 22:677–81.

63. These are Augustinian sentiments, but the words have not been found.

64. *Epist.* LIII, PL 22:544.

65. *De Gen. Lit.* VIII.4, CSEL 28:235–36.

66. See *Posterior Analytics*, 85a–86a.

67. *De Doc. Chr.* III.10.14, CCSL 32:86; *In Ps.* CXL.2, CCSL 40: 2026–27.

68. *Confessiones* VII.XI.17, ed. Luc Verheijen, Corpus Christianorum, Series Latina 27 (Turnhout, 1981), p. 104.

69. See *De Verbis Evangelii Matthaei*, PL 38:441.

70. *De Verbis Evangelii Marci*, PL 38:590.

71. John Abbaevillanus (d. 1257). This citation was not found.

72. Perhaps Augustine's *De Spiritu et Littera*, PL 44:199–246.

73. *Secretum Secretorum* is a pseudo-Aristotelian work, a mirror for princes, fully translated into Latin in the thirteenth century. This citation was not found.

74. Boethius, *De Consolatione Philososphiae*, PL 63:799b–800b.

75. *De Doc. Chr.* III.37.56, CCSL 32:115–16.

76. *Quaestiones de Veteri et Nova Lege* XCV, PL 35:2292.

77. *Quaestiones de Veteri et Nova Lege* C, PL 35:2304.

78. Bear in mind that for Wyclif the *virtus sermonis* is that 'force' or 'strength' which imbues discourse with the meaning derived from its author.

79. *In Ioh. Evang.* XXIX.3, CCSL 36:285.

80. *In Ioh. Evang.* LXXVI.5, CCSL 36:519.

81. *In Ps.* XXI.(I).7, CCSL 38:117–18.

82. *In Ps.* XXI.(II).7, CCSL 38:125.

83. *De Conceptu Virginali* XIII in *Opera Omnia*, ed. F. S. Schmitt, vol. 2 (Edinburgh, 1946), p. 155.

84. Wyclif's own *De Ydeis* (ca. 1368, unpublished). This work is found in various manuscripts including Trinity College, Cambridge, B.16.2. See also Williel R. Thomson, *The Latin Writings of John Wyclyf* (Toronto, 1983), pp. 32–34.

85. *Epist.* CXLVII.8, CSL 44/45:281–82.

86. The masculine *quem*, not the feminine *quam*.

87. *In Ioh. Evang.* XLVII.9, CCSL 36:418.

88. I omitted a long quotation from Grosseteste's *Celestial Hierarchy* regarding definitions for the Greek word *ieros* meaning 'holy' or 'sacred'.

89. Wyclif had access to the *Dicta* of Robert Grosseteste.

90. *In Librum Jesu Nave Homilia* XX, PG 12:923–24.

91. See actually *In Ps.* XCIII.29, CCSL 39:1330.

92. Duns Scotus (d. 1308). This citation appears to be erroneous. The correct one has not been found.

93. *De universo libri viginti duo* IX, PL 111:257–58.

94. This citation was not found.

95. Wyclif's citation is incorrect. Perhaps Augustine's *De Genesis ad Literam* VIII.13, CSEL 28:1. Even here, these words are not found.

96. Pelagius (ca. 370–440); Julian of Eclanum (ca. 386–454); Sergius of Constantinople (d. 638); Peter Abelard (1079–1142).

97. *Opus Imperfectum* XL, PG 56:849–59.

98. *De Doc. Chr.* I.37.41, CCSL 32:30.

99. *De Doc. Chr.* I.30.31–33, CCSL 32:23–25; ibid., I.35.39, CCSL 32:28–29; ibid., III.14.22, CCSL 32:91. See also *In Ps.* CXL.2, CCSL 40:2026.

100. Wyclif conflates the words of *De Doc. Chr.* III.10.15–16, CCSL 32:87.

101. *De Doc. Chr.* I.38.42, CCSL 32:31.

102. *Conf.* VII.19.25, CCSL 27:108–09.

103. See *Categories*, 1a.

104. *In Ioh. Evang.* XXIX.6, CCSL 36:287.

105. See *Sermo* CCCXIII, PL 38:1423.

106. See *De Diversis Quaestionibus Octoginta Tribus* XLVI, ed. Almut Mutzenbecher, Corpus Christianorum, Series Latina 44a (Turnhout, 1975), p. 73. These are not Augustine's words but the sentiment is the same.

107. *Contra Felicem* I, ed. Joseph Zycha, Corpus Scriptorum Ecclesiasticorum Latinorum 25.2 (Vienna, 1891), pp. 801–52.

108. See actually *De Incarnatione Verbi* I in *Opera Omnia* 2:9.

109. See *Enchiridion* XXIX, PL 40:246.

110. *In Ps.* CXXV.10, CCSL 40:1852.

111. *De Concordia de praescentiae et praedestinationis* I.5 in *Opera Omnia* 2:254.

112. *Expositio Epistolae ad Galatas*, PL 35:2109.

113. *Confessiones* XII.13.16, CCSL 27:223–24.

114. Wyclif, *De Materia et Forma* (ca. 1370–72) in *Johannis Wyclif Miscellanea Philosophica*, ed. M. H. Dziewicki, vol. 1 (London, 1902), pp. 163–242.

115. PL 35:2260. The "sons of Leah" symbolize the Holy Innocents massacred by Herod (Matt. 2:18).

ON THE TRUTH OF HOLY SCRIPTURE

Part Two: The Authority of Scripture

(*De ver.* I,ix): True and False Scripture

(183) I argue my second point chiefly by proving what is bound to follow from those reasons advanced by the adversaries of Holy Scripture who claim not only that Scripture can falter, but that it is even lacking in authority. Thus it is no wonder why I call this opinion hostile to Holy Scripture, since it opposes Holy Scripture, asserting that it is most worthy of condemnation, contrary to itself, and cursed by God and all the angels. Who indeed would not be opposed to such a law? Now those who express opinions of this sort should thereby confess that they are adversaries of the law and the prophets. That was clarified at the beginning of the preceding chapter. Who would not strive to destroy such a blasphemous writing if it not only contradicted itself, but contradicted God himself, insofar as it was contrary to divine law? Once more, I maintain that Holy Scripture in both its legal and prophetic parts must be understood according to the catholic sense alone, purely according to the sense of the author. Consider the words of Isa. 6:1, **I have seen the Lord sitting upon his lofty and high throne**. It is said that he was martyred by his kinsman Manasseh on this account, who judged the statement blasphemous, since it appeared contrary to the legal codes of Scripture.[1] For Exod. 33:20 states, **No human being will look upon me and live**, with reference to which the Apostle speaks in 1 Tim. 6:16; and John 1:18 says, **No one has ever seen**

God. In light of these texts, the saints agree that the patriarchs had seen God in corporeal nature on those occasions when they looked upon the messenger of God with their fleshly eyes. Thus they perceived God, albeit in a confused manner, just as we see a person while looking at his clothing. (184) For it is incompatible with human fleshliness to gaze upon the divine nature. If, however, Manasseh had been acquainted with that sense of Scripture perhaps he would not have killed the prophet, due to his own blind veneration of the Scripture of Moses. Indeed, all human evil arises from a failure to venerate and understand Scripture correctly.

For this reason, I maintain that the aforementioned passage of Scripture should be understood according to the catholic sense first of all. Furthermore, I posit that if some Catholic fellow, whom we shall call Peter,[2] happens to understand these passages of Scripture according to contradictory concepts based upon the bare grammatical sense, then according to that opinion Peter renders this passage of Scripture false and even heretical. For this would only be such in his own intellect and would not otherwise apply with similar passages. But to render anything false is to falsify it, and Peter thereby falsifies this passage of Scripture. And since it remains Holy Scripture in his opinion nonetheless, then it follows that Peter is falsifying Holy Scripture, which does not seem very pious at all. Now inasmuch as counterfeiting the king's currency or some papal bulls would lead to excommunication and the infliction of corporeal punishment according to human laws, the same judgment seems suitable when it comes to judging something heretical. For to render heretical is to make or denounce something as heretical, whether explicitly or implicitly. And this is just what Peter ends up doing here when he accepts Holy Scripture according to some adverse opinion. In light of this definition it does not appear to fall within the domain of Lord Pope's plenitude of power to render conclusions heretical of even make Holy Scripture heretical, against which he is said to have the power to legislate. (185) For then it would seem to follow that any unskilled grammarian can lawfully render Holy Scripture heretical by an adverse opinion, not only through his own perverse understanding by means of which it is said, but by forcing Holy Scripture to signify a heretical meaning after he has dismissed the prior sense. Now to do this seems neither a great sacrament nor to require preeminence of power. Yet he seems to permit such actions which the Catholic, as it is said, should thus understand.

All manner of blasphemies seem to follow from adverse opinion, which, I believe, the faithful should not tolerate. For it seems to me that all people who hold such opinions are adversaries of Christ's law, and consequently dissent damnably from the law contained within the saying of Christ in Matt. 5:25, **Be reconciled quickly with your adversary while you are on the way with him, lest perhaps your adversary will hand you over to the judge, and the judge hands you over to the attendant, and you are put in prison.** That adversary, according to Augustine in Book 1 of *On the Lord's Sermon on the Mount*,[3] is the law of Christ's commandments, which stands as an adversary to every sinner. Yet this is not turned against anybody, unless he has first turned against it himself. Let your own opinion, therefore, retain the same sense as that law while you make your way along the path towards Judgment Day. And since that law possesses no false, heretical, or blasphemous sense, be careful that you do not hold any such sense with regard to the Lord's law, (186) for then you will fall headlong into the worst perceived conclusion.

[. . .] (189) Now one might argue that an impropriety can follow from contradictions in Holy Scripture in the aforementioned fifth mode, but this is obviously not true. For Holy Scripture is an aggregate formed from the manuscript and the sacred sense or meaning, which the Catholic gathers from the material element, just as from a sign.

For this reason it is clear that, however many manuscripts of Holy Scripture are understood in the catholic manner, even though the content remains the same in number, there are going to be that many Holy Scriptures belonging to the aforementioned fifth level, owing to the various acts of understanding. That mental intellection is more truly Scripture than the line upon the parchment, for the latter is only counted as Scripture on account of its relationship to it. Nor is the Scripture existing in the mind sacred except through that objective Scripture which it perceives. That one by which all Catholics communicate is primarily sacred, since it is the one common faith of the whole Church. In this way any variation of Scripture with regard to the aforementioned fifth manner occurs either by reason of the material sign, the object which is signified, or a mixture of the two formed within the soul's act of perception.

Second, it is obvious that nobody can make heretical, falsify, lawfully regulate, or act against Scripture in the fifth manner, much less against the superior modes of Scripture. It cannot be false for then it would cease to exist, just as it would cease to be sacred insofar as the sacrament is its substantial difference. (190) Hence, the Christian venerates it just as he venerates images for the sake of the protection they offer, and not for sake of the wood or manuscript themselves. To legislate or proceed against it would the same as proceeding against God, which is impermissible. By the same rationale, it is not within our power to force it to signify falsely.

As they pertain to Scripture itself the material manuscripts are of little concern and import to the Catholic. Indeed, if a son is not allowed to violate the testament of his earthly father by interfering with it or imposing some extraneous signification upon it, then by no means is the Catholic permitted to change or destroy the inerrant testament of God the Father.

I have objected elsewhere that every accidental sort of aggregate possesses its designated subject in an accidental fashion. And this would seem to concede that Scripture is only sacred in an accidental fashion, from which follow the aforementioned improprieties. Yet those who thus speak of Holy Scripture from such a good foundation, should eagerly seek their own solution, because I am speaking of the other definition given above.

Third, it is truly objected, therefore, that because the material aspect of Scripture, by which Holy Scripture and the impossibility communicate, is itself part of Holy Scripture, then not only is it untrue, but it is also impossible. On that account, one may assume with Augustine (191) at the end of *On Understanding True Life*,[4] and in Book 15, Chapter 12 of *On the Trinity*,[5] that the sound of the word is the clothing of the word. By the same rationale it is clear that to concede that the aggregate is formed from the voice and concept is the same as conceding that it is formed from the visible sign and concept. On this account one will concede a two-fold Scripture, namely the sacred and the corrupt. The subject matter is true either way, but that aspect of the aggregate which is not part of Holy Scripture remains false. Nor have I found that Scripture signifies this abstraction in such a concrete fashion.

[. . .] (193) Again, those who viciously or wrongly understand Holy Scripture should not grant that it is false on account of their own perverse understanding, since they ought not grant that it retains that concept. Nothing is false except by reason of the falsehood which inheres in it. Falsehood in the proposition, however, is in the one who falsely understands it, and not in Holy Scripture, therefore, etc. If Scripture contained an impossible sense then God would have given it that sense, and consequently it would not be sacred, but would be impossible. This is why the saints forbid such a material document to be understood in that way, for it is not Holy Scripture, but rather some sort of deformed writing. Hence, I do not think that the sense of Holy Scripture could be false, even though some will elicit a false sense from Scripture. Some have been deceived in thinking that doctors like Hugh in Book 6, Chapter 10 of his *Didiscalicon*,[6] as well as other saints, forbid us to understand many passages of Scripture according to the literal sense (*ad literam*), but supply here: when vitiated by an erroneous sense. For if anyone is falsely accused of a crime he is not on this account a criminal, but quite the opposite. Nor then, by this same principle, is Holy Scripture false while it bears the accusations of falsehood leveled against it, as we recounted in Chapter Five.

[. . .] (195) Second, a person must have a thorough knowledge of the logic of Scripture. Otherwise the reader could end up falsifying Scripture, irreverently detesting its form, since he does not know how to defend it against the objections of the sophists. It is certainly fitting, therefore, that the theologian become acquainted with the logic of Scripture, so that he does not find himself overwhelmed by its language. Whereupon, in Book 2, Chapter 14 of *On Christian Doctrine*, Augustine says that, "Scripture's form of speaking becomes familiar through the habit of reading and hearing it."[7] So great is the influence of custom, as general experience bears witness, that in matters of logic and eloquence the form which seemed at first unrefined and unsuitable, will later appear wise and subtle as one becomes better acquainted with it. In this way, the holy doctors (196) had so very much appreciated and utilized the logic of Scripture, as their own words make clear. And here Augustine instructs the Christian to endeavor to speak eloquently, paying heed to the Scripture of our authors, as he clarifies in Book 4, Chapter 5 of *On Christian Doctrine*, "I say that no one should doubt that those who dwell in Christ must observe Scripture's form of speaking."[8] Hence, when commenting upon Psalm 140, Augustine demonstrates from Scripture how we should concede that whatever we do to his members is done to Christ, thus adding, "Things such as these should not be strange to Christians, especially to those from whom the rules have been established by other modes of understanding; and so they will either not be troubled, or will be quickly corrected."[9] See how much confidence and consolation is to be found within Scripture!

Third, frequent reading of the different parts of Scripture seems to be necessary in this regard, as one part of Scripture so often serves to explain another. Just as the varieties of interpretations are always preserved by the truth, reciprocally explaining each other, so it is with the variation of the Evangelists and other Scriptures which add or vary things while still maintaining the same meaning. This was Augustine's principle for annulling falsehood or contradiction among the sacred books, as he states in his tract *On the Consensus of the Evangelists*.[10] Hence, in Book 3, Chapter 10 of *On the Consensus*, he excludes any mendacity from Matt. 27:9, where it says, **Then it was fulfilled, what was spoken through the prophet Jeremiah, saying: and they took thirty pieces of silver, the price of him who was priced, upon whom the sons of Israel had set a price,** etc. That passage, however, is not found in Jeremiah, (197) but is in the form of a judicial sentence located in Zachariah, Chapter 11. Yet Augustine considers three solutions. The first is that the corrected manuscripts have the simple designation "prophets" and not the term "Jeremiah," while the manuscripts which do have the designation "of Jeremiah" are not then Holy Scripture, and should be rejected as deceptive. Yet Augustine does not like that answer, because the majority of manuscripts, even when corrected according to the Greek exemplar, still record it in such a manner. Therefore, a second answer is that Jeremiah, with one voice safeguarded by divine inspiration, had written and spoken all sorts of things which he did not insert into our Scriptures, but left them to be inserted by other prophets. Thus Jerome says that he found within a certain Hebrew book entitled "Jeremiah," the aforementioned authority word for word. After all, we do not possess all the manuscripts of the prophets. Yet the third answer, the one which Augustine decided upon, maintains that the Holy Spirit appointed Matthew to insert the name of Jeremiah in order to denote how all the holy prophets spoke with one spirit as they communicated through their discourse. In this way whatever the Holy Spirit has spoken through a single prophet still pertains to all the rest. On the other hand, what pertains to all of them may be attributed to just one. And so the Holy Spirit moved the mind of Matthew to write in this way in order that the Church would learn that just as there exists so great a power of communion among the saints, so this same concord exists among the prophets such that every saying of Zachariah is most fittingly applied to Jeremiah. And in this way I believe that Augustine was moved to concede that every language belongs to the Church, as recounted in Chapter Three above.

This is why it is so profitable for us to read parts of Scripture frequently for the sake of grasping this concept of agreement and for excluding the appearance of any contradiction. (198) Whereupon, Jerome, in his *Letter 34 to Nepotianus*, instructs him to "read the divine Scriptures often,"[11] just as he elsewhere directs Demetriadus to do the same on account of its multiple benefits.[12] We do well, therefore, to observe the equivocation and logic of Scripture, in keeping with its agreements and procedures.

In regard to the fourth matter, it is clear that unless the disciple of Scripture is of virtuous character his scholarly abilities will remain at the level of a novice and whatever he says will sound wrong. Indeed, since it is appropriate for God to open and close the book, then clearly, whoever is a friend of this master will possess the benefit of discipline which remains hidden from the proud. And it is for this reason that there are so many testimonies of the Scriptures and the holy doctors which surpass rational demonstration. Thus Christ says in Matt. 11:25, **The Father hid the mysteries of Scripture from the wise and revealed them to the lowly**, as the Apostle also says in 1 Cor. 1:27.

Hence, I have become accustomed to saying that the virtuous character of Scripture's disciple rests especially in three things: humble acceptance of the authority of Scripture, conformation to its own reason, and adherence to the witness of the holy doctors.

From the outset, the Christian should believe that the totality of Scripture is unassailably true, and if a faulty understanding does arise, then his own error is the cause. As I stated above, this is in keeping with the rule laid down by Augustine in Book 3, Chapter 16 of *On Christian Doctrine*.[13] (199) For the person who treats Scripture with contempt or wicked designs is the very person who both thinks and asserts that it is false.

[. . .] (200) Concerning the second aspect of honoring Scripture, one ought to employ Augustine's rule found in Book 3, Chapter 16 of his *On Christian Doctrine*, whereby whatever "seems to express criminal or shameful things should be understood figuratively, while whatever commends love . . . "[14] On this basis it is clear that either way in Holy Scripture there exists conformity to reason, and consequently reason is especially necessary for grasping the meaning of the Scriptures. And in this vein, one considers another of Augustine's rules from Book 3, Chapter 27 of *On Christian Doctrine*,[15] where he maintains that within the very same words of Scripture one may discern any number of variant catholic meanings being taught by the Holy Spirit, provided that some other passage of Scripture can show that they are in agreement with the truth. Otherwise, according to this saint, these could not be the senses of Holy Scripture. For the certitude and authority of Scripture should be given preference over human reason on both fronts, since Holy Scripture is the word of the Lord and thus must be of the highest authority.

(201) Regarding the third aspect of the veneration of Scripture, with respect to its witnesses and devoted disciples, I said in Chapter Two that we ought to trust in the testimony of St. Augustine and the other holy doctors. If it is appropriate for a lawyer to trust in false testimony provided in some suspicious case, all the more should the Catholic trust in the testimony of the holy doctors devoted to a cause which has not been corrupted by greed. For they have diligently examined this matter of faith, devoutly calling upon the highest master that they might come to know the truth. Whereupon, I consider it a sign of unfaithfulness that, after something has been proven to be the sense of Scripture based upon the testimony of the saints, one would discredit it, or freely choose not to come to its defense, and yet, with all solicitude and labor, he will adhere precisely to some human judgment which is based upon the testimony of deceitful men, especially in some matter not remotely essential to the Church.

The fifth aspect is the instruction of God.[16] This factor is so crucial that it is impossible for anyone to learn anything at all apart from the wisdom of this first teacher, as Augustine demonstrates in his book, *The Master*.[17] This is evinced by the faith of Scripture in John 1:3, **All things were made through him and apart from him nothing was made**. And this can be demonstrated in the following manner: everything, just as it exists with respect to being itself, is known in that way. But nothing can be true unless it is the First Truth, or participates in it; and thus it is not known. This is why the philosophers say that it is the first thing that is known. Indeed, no individual thing can exist as an entity within a genus, nor can it be true, except through participation in its species; nor any species except through participation in its genus; and no genus except through participation in the first and most common entity, on account of which it abides in that entity and in truth, and consequently in the causality of knowledge. (202) The First Truth is itself the first cause by which every created thing is known, and not only objectively, but through effective design, since apart from its efficiency nothing is created. Truly then, since **Christ is the true light which illuminates every person** (John 1:9), it is evident that it is absolutely impossible for a person's sense to be illuminated such that he could know anything at all, unless he is first enlightened by him. Just as many philosophers believe that it is impossible, based upon this supposition, for the light of a star or candle to make anything known, if it is not first disclosed by the material sun. And Augustine even came across that principle in the books of the Platonists, as he acknowledges in Book 7, Chapter 9, of *The Confessions*.[18]

Clearly then, the other four ways of understanding Scripture are nothing but paths to that one, especially purity of heart attained through the virtues. This is why Lincolniensis says in the prologue to the first part of the *Posterior Analytics* that the master and his signs are only instruments manipulated in an accidental fashion, while Christ is the true doctor, illuminating the mind and making manifest the truth.[19] Thus Augustine states in Book 3, Chapter 37 of *On Christian Doctrine* that it is truly a matter of the greatest importance and necessity that the disciples of Holy Scripture pray in order that they might understand. He says, "In these documents which they study they read that, **Lord gives wisdom, and from his mouth come knowledge and understanding** (Prov. 2:6)."[20] The doctors rightly declare, therefore, that in the highest of all sciences one must commence from the highest human power, namely the will, in which the principle of merit and spiritual purity primarily reside. For as Wisd. of Sol. 7:27 says, **Through a unique outpouring he passes into sanctified souls.** [. . .] (204) Sensible things cannot imprint that knowledge which is of a more perfect quality, except by virtue of Wisdom first moving one toward simple apprehension, second to consensus, and third to contemplation of the truth. This Wisdom is the foremost active intellect,[21] who immediately instructed his apostles and the other faithful on Pentecost, among other days, when he taught them the law. I ask you, what does it matter which sensible signs Uncreated Wisdom chooses to employ when illustrating her meaning, whether it is by adapting the words of so many languages to her logic, or more efficaciously instructing us through her works, or even most effectively through her internal inspiration? The first of the methods we chiefly invoke, however, are the leaves of the fruit of Wisdom which will lead us to her.

It is for this reason that God speaks in such diverse ways; now through prophetic deeds, now through enigmas, and now again through his natural works. Of course, whatever sort of significations he has instituted are rational and proper.

(205) I offer three reasons for this variety. First of all, that we would acknowledge God's universal dominion. For he is the one who constituted every created truth for the purpose of signifying himself and whatever else he deemed acceptable. Second, that Scripture would include within itself every category of suitable speech, since it ought to be the exemplar according to which every type of human being should speak. Third, as we follow our own signs and inventions nonetheless, it would be better if we recognized that the aforementioned variety was introduced as a punishment for human pride.

(*De ver.* I,x): The Authority of the Old Testament

(205) In light of what has been said, one can reckon how authority should be comprehended through the faith of Holy Scripture. It is only fitting that the faithful believe that God exists and that he provides for his Church; as the Apostle says in Heb. 11:6, **In order to approach God it is necessary to believe that he exists, and that he rewards those who seek him.** Now anyone who believes in God believes that he is

supremely powerful, wise and benevolent, since he is triune. And he could not reward those who seek him unless he provided a law for his Church, one that is most essential for its governance. Just as emperors, kings, and leaders of any sort of community establish laws for them, so the ruler of the entire created universe instituted the law of nature by which he governs the created universe. Second, as King of Kings he gave to his Church the law of Scripture or the commandments. (206) And third, the same abbot surely bestowed upon his tiny flock, namely to the apostles and clerics who belong to his special chamber, the law of counsels. And in this way he gave a private law to each part of the ecclesiastical hierarchy by which they might be distinguished from one another. From this double article of faith it follows that God granted such a law to his Church. Otherwise, it would have to be due to impotence, ignorance and envy that he had forsaken his bride by failing to provide her with the necessities found in his law.

From this it seems to follow that the law of God, in whatever form it was given, possesses the highest level of authority, usefulness and reverence. This is clearly the case given the nature of the law-giver himself. For if a defect were found in any aspect of the law that would surely reflect upon its creator, which would be to charge the doctor of our law with blasphemy.

Thirdly, it is essential for one to realize that the law of the Church's manuscripts, commonly called Scripture, is the very law which God gave to his Church. A person must grasp this with a very nimble faith with respect to its demonstration, but one equally steadfast with respect to its defense. I say that the faithful must comprehend this through experience, believing first of all that this man who had conversed with the Twelve Apostles, namely our Lord Jesus Christ, had spent the course of this present life living in the very manner which the gospel relates. The faithful must believe this, since it is fitting for him to extend beyond the general knowledge of the Church, by which he acknowledges that something is the law given by God, to then understand what that law is. Otherwise, the Master teaching the prior common conclusion and not descending to the particular, which would be the proximate principle of operation, would have culpably left his bride wanting in such necessities. And that is not possible. Therefore, it is essential that the faithful would yield to the gospel of Jesus Christ. For in doing so they will comprehend the authority of God's law and Scripture, just as sense and movement enjoyed by the members is derived from the head.

(207) It is appropriate that the body of the Church grasp the teaching it has derived from the head and then communicate this from one member to another. I think this is what the Apostle means when he says in Rom. 10:17, **Faith comes from hearing, heard through the word of Christ**. Now the whole faith, by which it is believed, is sown in Mother Church whereby each of her members is created though the sensible incitement brought about through the sound of various parts of the Church preaching Christ's word. For on the mountain, and often elsewhere, he opened his mouth, and with his voice, made the Holy Spirit resonate so vehemently on the day of Pentecost. And this sound which was disseminated across every land by the members of the Church is, so to speak, the material and original aspect of the Church's faith while the sense is like the formal aspect from which is collected the one substance of things hoped for (Heb. 11:1). Thus whatever sort of sensible sign it may be clothed in, whatever the tone or style, the one faith always abides.

[. . .] (218) Since there are twenty-two books in the Old Testament, which even the Hebrews accept along with the Christians, what would move a sophist to contend that these book are not Holy Scripture?

For one reads in Matt. 19:4–6 and Mark 10:3–8 how the Lord responded to the Pharisees when they questioned him about divorce. He said, **Did you not read that the one who made human beings at the beginning, made them male and female, and said: for this reason a man will leave his father and mother and cling to his wife and the two will be one in flesh?** See how he indicated that the Jews ought to have read that sentence in Gen. 2:24. For here it says that God, who had created man, had thus spoken, thereby denoting that God is the author of our Scripture. It is pointless, therefore, to quarrel over who was the scribe, or the composer of the manuscript, or the reed-pen of the Lord whom God infused with such knowledge. For it is sufficient to believe that God spoke the given knowledge through some of his saints in particular and through individuals generally. And this appears to be what St. Gregory means in Chapter 1 of his *Morals*, concerning the author of the book of blessed Job,[22] a matter which has led to unproductive contention among a number of people.

Likewise, in Gal. 4:21–31 the Apostle relates the history first written in Gen. 20, how **Abraham had Isaac from Sarah and Ishmael from Hagar**. And pertaining to the mystical sense he thus subjoins: **but what does Scripture say? Drive out the handmaid and her son**. (219) In the same manner, from the deeds chronicled in Genesis, the Apostle proves in Heb. 11:1–22 that faith is the foundation of human justification before God. And in similar fashion, in 1 Pet. 3:20, St. Peter cites the history of Gen. 7 regarding Noah's ark and the flood. Just as Christ in John 7:22–24 answers his accusers by citing the passage which states that **Moses gave the law of circumcision to them, and this circumcision was not from Moses, but from the patriarchs**, referring to Abraham, as evinced in Gen. 17. In this regard, because Christ sets the law of Moses before the Jews, which he asserts that Moses had given, he thereby seems to commend the entire law of the

Pentateuch. Otherwise, Christ's allegation would have been erroneous in this matter.

[. . .] (228) Now there are many instances in which some verbal discrepancy abides within a sentence. But I believe this occurred so that we would come to realize that words and manuscripts are only the signs of Holy Scripture, which is the knowledge of the Holy Spirit. We no longer possess the authority to vary the images of the Old Testament Scriptures as the apostles had varied them, because we lack the fullness of the Holy Spirit to instruct us in every truth. For the faith of Scripture tells us how the Spirit taught the apostles on the Day of Pentecost.

All of this can be confirmed by reason. For God's own Church existed in the Old Testament. Hence it was just as essential for them, as it is for us, to have the faith of the Incarnation and the other articles, which remained hidden to the infidels. Because God could not leave his Church bereft of these necessities, he gave the Catholic faith to them in equal measure as he did to us.

The holy doctors draw the conclusion as much from Scripture as from reason that all the patriarchs and prophets possessed the faith of the Incarnation, as well as the other articles, just as the people of modern times. This is clear from Heb. 11:2 and John 5:39, **They are the Scriptures which offer testimony regarding me**. And in Acts 3:18–24, Peter says, (229) **God thus fulfilled what he foretold through the mouth of all the prophets, that his Christ would suffer**. And so he says, **It is necessary that heaven receive Jesus up until that time of the restitution of all things, which the Lord spoke of through the mouth of the all the saints and prophets from ages past.** He says, **Moses said "The Lord your God will raise up for you a prophet like me from among your own brethren. And you will listen to him with regard to all that he has spoken to you. However, it will be**

that every soul which does not listen to that prophet will be driven out from the people." And all the prophets who have spoken from Samuel henceforth have announced these days. From these passages of Scripture it is clear, first of all, that all the prophets spoke unanimously and without contradiction, since he employs the singular here: **through the mouth of all the prophets**. Second, it is evident that all the prophets are unified in their meaning, commonly announcing the day of grace under diverse signs. Undoubtedly then, all the Old Testament Scriptures and all the acts of the patriarchs signify Christ to us, since they are the means God ordained for this purpose. The antecedent signifies the consequent. Hence, according to the Apostle in Gal. 3:16, the words of Gen. 15:18, **I will give that land to your seed**, signifies Christ, and in the same way Gen. 2:24, **The two will be one in flesh**, is explained by the Apostle in Eph. 5:31–32 to mean **Christ and the Church**. And so it is that in Gen. 49:11, **He will wash his stole in wine and his cloak in the blood of grapes**, is explained as referring to Christ, since all the holy sayings and deeds of the patriarchs signify Christ, in keeping his unique preeminence. In this matter I believe that the prophets quite frequently prophesy through works. I have usually understood (230) that testimony regarding Judah in Gen. 49:9 to be speaking principally of Christ according the literal sense (*ad literam*), since a little earlier it is said, **Judah is a lion's cub**, and follows: **and you recline as a lion**, which John expounds upon in Apoc. 5 (Rev. 5:4): **The lion of the tribe of Judah conquers**. Hanging upon the wood of the cross, he let forth a roar like a lion, as I explained in Chapter Three. With respect to Christ one must consider both the flesh which he assumed unto himself personally, and that flesh which is the mystical body of Christ, joined by way of marriage, and subdivided either way. He assumed some aspect of his flesh purely from the Virgin as essential members. They are signified by the stole most closely joined to the cloak and that material he washed with the effusion of his most immaculate blood, as I discussed in Chapter Four. Thus Scripture signifies that through purified wine. But with regard to the outward flesh assimilated by nourishment, which was as a cloak, he pours out less refined blood, which is called the blood of grapes. He did not wash, however, in order to cleanse himself of sin, but rather to cleanse his mystical body, since he merits for himself the stole of obedience and the cloak of love according to Phil. 2:8–9: **Christ became obedient for our sake**, etc., **on account of which God exalted him** with regard to his mystical body. The stole stands for the priests who take upon themselves the yoke of poverty and humility through their obedience to the laws of Christ, while the pallium stands for the laity who at least wear the wedding garment, which is the tunic of love. And in this way the entire mystical body of Christ is rendered dazzling white by the blood of the lamb.

(231) Third, based upon the authority of Peter, it is evident that anyone who does not effectively hear the voice of Christ will be damned, since he speaks every Scripture which must be believed if one hopes to be saved (1 Pet. 1:10–12). The logic of this holy pope is thus quite correct according to the intended literal sense (*de virtute sermonis*) and, as the words are arranged, cannot be disproved by our adversaries.

Returning then to this point, one gathers from Scripture that both Testaments are the word of God, and thus supremely authentic, a fact which the Savior indicates in Luke 24:25–27, saying to Cleopas and his companion, **Oh you are fools and slow of heart when it comes to believing all the things which have been spoken by the prophets, how it was necessary for Christ to suffer that he might enter into his glory. And beginning with Moses and all the prophets he interpreted for them what pertained to him in the all the Scriptures.** And it follows: **These are the words which I have spoken to**

you, since I am yet with you, insofar as it is necessary that all things be fulfilled, which are written of me in the law of Moses and the Prophets and the Psalms (Luke 24:44). With these words he seems to authorize the entirety of Old Testament Scripture in a triple fashion. First because he calls them **fools,** since they speak right past Holy Scripture, and **slow** because their sluggish discernment is due to a lack of faith, since they speak doubtfully of Scripture. Second, insofar as he says, **It was necessary that Christ suffer**, since he did suffer, though absolutely freely and contingently in either respect. And third because he says, **It is necessary that all things be fulfilled which are written in the** legal books, that is to say, the Pentateuch of Moses, in the prophetical books, and in the sapiential books, regarding Christ. Given the fact that the whole of Scripture is divided into these three sections, (232) and each one of them points to Christ, it is clear that Christ must authorize them all. Nor should you be surprised that God, our master, can instruct them so suddenly and concisely in every truth.

(*De ver.* I,xi): Apocryphal Books and Corrected Manuscripts

(232) The first objection raised against this argument contends that the authorities of the New Testament only confirm some particular sayings of the Old Testament books and authors. Where then is the evidence that all our Old Testament manuscripts are authentic? Thus the Hebrews authenticate part of the Book of Daniel and not the whole thing, since they do not include Susanna, and Bel and the Dragon, as Jerome says in his prologue.[23]

It can be confirmed, therefore, that it seems unnecessary for us to believe Ezra had correctly restored the Hebrew Scripture, even having supposed that it was flawlessly conferred in the beginning. And pertaining to the second level, one need not believe that St. Jerome's translation is free from error, since many other interpreters disagree with him. Indeed, in his own time he was reproached by Augustine and his other rivals, as evinced in St. Augustine's *Letter 9 to Jerome*[24] and quite a number of Jerome's prologues. Regarding the third level, given the corruption of the modern texts we have not certified that the books which we do have were duly emended.

(233) As far as this matter is concerned, it is clear, first of all, from what has been said above that faith must commence from the head of the Church. Second, it is essential to establish that he must govern his own Church from the very inception of the world up until its end, as he says in Matt. 28:20, **Behold, I am with you in all days up until the culmination of the age.** And from this the third point follows, namely that to do this he would have to preserve his own law within the Church.

Concerning the manuscripts, one must comprehend them as they have been corrected by the sense and authority of the Church. And with respect to the meaning, one must receive it from the head; for that is faith as well as Holy Scripture.

Yet as we proceed further it becomes clear that our authors of the Old Testament would not be authentic, but suspect in either way, if a falsehood could be located anywhere in their writings. Yet insofar as the New Testament writers cite them, it is clear that the Christian should accept the whole of their testimony, as Christ says in Luke 24. Thus a fallacy is being employed in this argument. Now an opinion is untenable, whose very opposite appears fitting to all, or to many, or to those who are exceptionally wise. Yet the whole Jewish nation dispersed throughout the world, as well as Christians and Saracens, believe that the twenty-two books of the Old Testament, as recounted by Jerome in his explanatory Prologue, are authentic. Hence, backed by the testimony of the New Scripture, it is sufficient for the Christian to trust in them. In order that our faith would be strengthened, the Jews were dispersed among the nations, taking with them their Hebrew manuscripts. (234) Now this happened for three reasons. First, that we might have recourse to their manuscripts as witnesses to the fact that there is no difference in the sense found in our Latin books and those Hebrew ones. Second, so that those among Jewish people who are learned in the faith can offer efficacious testimony by direct word of mouth. And third, so that the truth of Scripture which pertains to them, having been prophesied and fulfilled, might yield faith such that a remnant would believe. Now this was prophesied of them in Lev. 26:33 and Deut. 28:15, that **they would be dispersed among the nations**, if they did not obey the law of the Lord. And so that came to pass, as evinced in 4 Kings (2 Kings 17) and Acts 2:5, where one reads that, **There are religious men living in Jerusalem of every nation which is under heaven**. Yet today it is clear that their dispersion is all the more grave on account of their transgression against the Messiah. This is the reason, according to Augustine in *Letter 42 to Paulinus*, why God ordained that they were to live among his Church in keeping with that passage in Psalm 58 (Ps. 59:11), **You are not to kill them lest my people will forget.**[25] And with respect to its confirmation it is clear that God would have deprived the universal Church of those things which are necessary if he failed to sustain his righteous law among the posterity on account of the sins of the parents. Thereupon, they would indeed be children of desperation, since they cannot live righteously apart from the law.

Regarding Jerome's translation, it seems fitting that it be approved as much by the sanctity of his life, which Augustine recounts in his letter *On the Holiness of Jerome*,[26] as by his expertise in the Hebrew language and the complete agreement of his translation with the Hebrew and Greek manuscripts. (235) For as he recounts in the prologue to Chronicles, the

New Testament cites many Scriptures from the Old which are lacking in the Septuagint translation, inasmuch as they hid many mysteries of their faith from the Egyptian infidels.[27] As such, it is no wonder if St. Jerome suffered the reproach of those filled with envy. Yet his efforts in toiling for the sake of the Church's edification only brought him glory, as Augustine testifies, though he too had once piously grappled with him in scholarly matters.

In light of this, when it comes to those uncorrected modern manuscripts, I say that the defect can arise from sin on the Church's part, since manuscripts are only deemed necessary for a given time, while the sense is always required. And thus it is essential that the Catholic faith abide within the entire Mother Church, since Christ's petition could not have been in vain when he prayed that the faith of Peter would not fail (Luke 22:32). Now if the philosophers say it is necessary for every sort of animal species to have its perfect form, then that is all the more reason why the head of the Church, who is not concerned here with beasts, has established the faith of his spouse, apart from which she cannot live. And that faith is the law of Scripture, which must always exist, whether in the manuscript or in the mind. Although God may punish his Church, even handing some over to their own spurious sense as a punishment for their sin, he can never corrupt his own law, even if those people who could understand and fulfill that law are not present. Since an unjust law is no law at all, and insofar as every law is authorized by God, it is clear that any falsehood or deficiency found within God's law would lead back to God; but that is impossible.

[. . .] (236) Now the solution to the second objection is clarified. It is commonly assumed that there are many truths of Holy Scripture to be found among the writings of the poets, as evinced in the cases of Homer and Virgil Maro, which Jerome recounts in the sixth chapter of his letter placed in the

Prologue to the Bible.[28] The same is evinced with Ovid concerning the old woman, in the Sibylline Oracles, and among so many others who speak evangelical truths. (237) If, therefore, the authors of the Old Testament are authenticated on the whole, because part of their Scriptures is cited on the ground that it is catholic, then the same applies to these poets. Indeed, in Titus 1:12 the Apostle cites a poet named Eumenides under these words: **A certain one of them, one of their own prophets, said Cretans are always liars, evil beasts, and lazy gluttons**. Why then is not his entire book authentic?

Similarly, there were many people besides the Four Evangelists who had written gospels, evinced in the case of Nicodemus, whose authority it seems reasonable for us to accept. After all, he was faithful, holy, and had even been present when these events took place. Now according to Augustine in Book 18, Chapter 38 of *The City of God*, Enoch wrote many prophetic works, but on account of their antiquity we are not sure whether he or someone else was their author, and thus we do not accept them.[29] Why then could this not apply to the authors of the Old Testament books? Although, in the next argument, it would seem that the law of God and the faith of the Church are necessarily to be believed in, it still does not appear that we must believe in the aforementioned fifth level of Scripture and that which is apocryphal.

In this matter three factors ought to be observed. First, that all the faithful must believe every truth in general, while there are some truths (238) which adults are obliged to believe in particular. Concerning this subject there is much to be said.

Second, one should note that when it comes to the substance of the faith, individual manuscripts are of no greater value than the beasts from which they were made. Their true worth rests in the sense and truth which they signify. For if this were the case, then were they burned or otherwise destroyed the faith would perish.

Third, it should be noted that the manner in which the author or witness is cited deserves careful attention, as does his manner of speaking and expression.

With respect to these three observations, it is said of the first that rather than creating a dilemma, it actually proves fitting that the truths of the faith would be declared by the poets, and by all types of human beings, even the Saracens. For according to the Apostle in 1 Tim. 3:7, **It is necessary to provide good testimony to those who are outside**. Truths of this sort are not the faith because these people had uttered them, but rather on account of the fact that they had been spoken by God. Nor is it necessary that all their sayings or writings were authenticated on this account, as is clear in the case of Plato, in whose books Augustine says in Book 7, Chapter 9 of *The Confessions* that he found ten conclusions of John the Evangelist: **In the Beginning was the Word**, etc.[30] Hence when citing the poet Plato or some other author not found in Scripture, we do not cite them as authors who offer proof through an argument based on the faith, but through dialectical argument, based upon human testimony. Testimony of this sort is valid when arguing according to principles admitted by one's opponent, citing a witness to him, whom he accepts as authentic; just as when refuting infidels we quote their own authors to them.

(239) A person's manner of speaking can be divided into three parts. He says some things in an assertive way, some things by way of recitation or interrogation, and some things ironically. The assertive manner is three-fold: offering an opinion, proving through reason, or proclaiming as the meaning of God. And this is proper to the authors of Holy Scripture according to 1 Thess. 2:13, **When you accepted the word of God you heard from us, you accepted it not as the word of human beings, but as it truly is, the word of God which is at work in you, and which you believe.** This is the reason why our prophets say: **Thus says the Lord**. Yet because the

fiction of falsehood could exist in such things, one should thus consider the meaning as well as the life of the speaker. Now since there is one principle in every genre which serves as the measure of all the others, by faith one must suppose that Christ is the First Prophet in and of himself. In light of that fact, we can then discern whether another prophet speaks the meaning of Christ and lives according to his life. If he does, he is truly the prophet. Otherwise, he is not, especially if he fails to meet the second test. Thereupon, he is a false prophet, and whoever is of the opposite condition is a true prophet according to this standard. This meaning is clarified in Deut. 18:15 where the Lord first promises a prophet, **I will raise up for them a prophet from the midst of their brethren**, which is explained as literally referring to Christ (*ad literam*), as I clarified in the previous chapter. Consequently, he adds to this: **The prophet who is so depraved by his arrogance that he would wish to speak in my name things I have not commanded him, such that we would speak in the name of other gods; he is to be killed.** (240) **But if you respond, how am I to understand a word from a tacit thought which the Lord has not spoken,** you will have this sign, **that if what this prophet preaches in the name of the Lord does not come to pass then the Lord did not say these things. Rather, for fear of his life the prophet fabricated them**. Look how the Truth is the test of prophecy, because God speaks all truth. But if the intellect of the prophet has been illuminated and he has ordered his affections for the sake of seeing the truth, and walks according to the morals of which he speaks, then one may believe he is truly a prophet of the Lord. And by faith this is what we ought to suppose of our own prophets. Because, beyond sense experience, we possess a complete knowledge of those things necessary for salvation through the faith of Scripture, it suffices for the Christian to press beyond sense experience and trust in that knowledge, and in Holy Scripture, so that he may then prophesy to his ignorant brethren. On this account, it is said in 1 Pet. 4:11, **If anyone speaks, let it be as if these were the words of God**. By faith we hold that our apostles were prophets entirely of this sort, for according to 2 Pet. 1:18–19, **We heard this voice come down from heaven when we were with him on the holy mountain, and we have the confirmed prophetic word to which you do well to pay heed**. Because the authority of the Church's members rests in these things, they live in conformity to Christ and proclaim his gospel. (241) For in accordance with the humility and poverty of Christ they put aside avarice and pride, and speak of heavenly things.

Returning to the matter, it clearly presents no problem for us if the aforementioned poets had spoken the hidden truths of the faith, just as the demons had spoken them. Nor does it follow from this that they ought to be cited as authors, unless one learns that they had been inspired by the Holy Spirit, as though they were speaking as his scribes. But one would not say this when Christ stilled the prophecies of the demons. And yet there are occasions when it is advantageous to adduce them as witnesses when speaking according to principles admitted by one's opponents, because the spirit of prophecy can sometimes shine even among the infidels.

We believe that the Old Testament authors had spoken by internal inspiration from the mouth of the Lord, and not only by the inspiration of faith, nor only due to the sanctity of their lives, nor only from the authentication received from the entire Church, but because their efficacious Scripture resonates entirely of love and not of worldly ambition, wholly conforming their reason to the desire for heavenly things. No one, therefore, is to be trusted in as a proof from authority, except insofar as he proclaims the word of God. This is the reason why the authors of the Old Testament are cited. And Scripture cites others, as witnesses, speaking according to principles admitted by one's opponent, whether following the persuasive ironic sense, or that of opinion.

The same is said of the Gospel of Nicodemus, although it was apocryphal. (242) It is called apocryphal owing to the '*apo*', meaning 'concerning', and the '*crisis*', meaning 'secret'. It is as if one were to say, "concerning the secrets" and those things which remain unknown to the Church. Now according to others it might be called such on account of '*apos*', meaning 'from afar', and '*crisis*', meaning 'judgment'. For there are such things which are not explicated in the Holy Scripture which is perceptible to the senses, even though they are true. For Jerome recounts in his prologue to 1 Kings, when referring to the Book of Wisdom, Ecclesiasticus, Judith, Tobit and the Book of Maccabees, that we need not disbelieve these books, as if they were false; but neither should the Church Militant explicitly believe in these books as if they were authentic.[31] The same line of reasoning applies to the Gospel of Nicodemus and those others which the Church has decided neither to condemn explicitly, nor explicitly canonize, since it is sufficient for her army to possess the twenty-two books of the Old Testament and the twenty-four of the New, which are correspondingly authenticated according to the two alphabets of Hebrew and Latin. Canonizing any more could reasonably be considered burdensome for the Church.

In light of this, it seems quite likely that many apocryphal books are Holy Scripture, since they are inscribed in the Book of Life. And to this extent we should trust in them explicitly or implicitly, just as our canonical Scripture. Clearly then, it is likely that many such books are sacred truths inscribed in the Book of Life, and since the Church must believe every truth in general or implicitly, the conclusion is obvious.

Second, from these facts I reckon that it is both foolish and pointless for us to grapple excessively over the truth or vicissitudes of the apocryphal Scripture, since we are in full possession of the Scriptures which are sensibly authenticated for us. If it is sufficient for the Church to soldier on faithfully according to the preceding four-fold Scripture, apart from the aforementioned fifth level, (243) it would be absurd to abandon the prior necessary Scripture while giving heed to the fifth. So it is that an adulterous generation seeks after signs (Matt. 16:4)! On this account, all meanings which are found in our sacred manuscripts should be held in greater esteem than those other pages. It is sufficient that one generally believe every truth with love. Whereupon, if other manuscripts contain the truth let us believe it, because it abides in our own manuscripts.

Given these things, a third point follows. Now just as it is possible for a person to possess knowledge of something in general, while doubting the very same thing in the particular, as logicians are well aware, so it is also possible for the same Christian to believe something in a catholic manner, because he does so in general, while doubting the very same thing in the particular. This is clearly the case among Christians who doubt the truths of the faith. Hence, it is not sufficient for someone to believe every truth in general, though he must not disbelieve any article of the Catholic faith in the particular, but should instead believe in the first article. Thereupon, that is a formed faith. For those other adults, just as some Christians, to whom God has given inspiration and the light of understanding for this purpose, it is appropriate for them to believe explicitly in God at the very least, and together with this, to believe in the Holy Catholic Church, and thirdly, that they would hope they were members of the Church. Yet if, along with these gifts, a person dies before acquiring the three theological virtues, these articles of faith, and all the others, then he will not find salvation in the ark. (244) Other people, however, should believe explicitly to a greater or lesser extent, relative to their debt of obligation to God for his gifts and the opportunity of time. But whoever finally acquires a formed faith will be saved.[32]

If someone were to ask which one of these manuscripts or which Scripture it is appropriate for us to believe in according to the aforementioned fifth mode, I say that he should believe in every Scripture, just he should believe in every existent thing in general. But it is no more appropriate for us to believe in any one of these manuscripts in particular than to believe in the beasts from which they were made, or some other sort of sign perceptible to the senses. We believe in these corrected manuscripts, however, only insofar as they are signs of the authentic Scripture which we honor only on account of the resemblance they bear to it. Yet we do not devote ourselves to the manuscripts of the poets, because according to Augustine in *On the Trinity*, Book 4, Chapter 11, "The demons mingle catholic truths with inscriptions of this sort in order to seduce the people into falsehood."[33]

Third, a principal argument raised against what I have said states that many nations admit the faith of Christ with respect to all the viewpoints he asserted or the apostles who accompanied him, as there were Peter, Matthew, Jude, James and John. Yet they will not admit the other Scriptures of Paul, Mark and Luke. The Saracens and other infidels hold this opinion. Why then could not some other sects deny John's vision in the Apocalypse (Rev.), while others deny the Scripture of Peter, Matthew, Jude and James, indeed all their Scriptures at once. Surely, since the judgment is the same concerning the whole and the part, based upon equal evidence they could deny the words of the Lord Jesus Christ and his Incarnation, as the Jews do even to this day. And when it comes to the authorities of the Old Testament (245) they could either deny that they are authentic or refute them according to the strictly literal sense (*de vi vocis*), thereby allowing them to devise whatever impossible glosses they like. And as far as all the Scriptures of the New Testament are concerned they could say that the mother of error had depicted the lion, presumptuously authenticating herself. And one would have to think in this way of the other blasphemous objections. That is the most impudent infidelity of all, trampling upon every prophecy, every sect, and every reason.

With regard to such objections, I think it is superfluous to quarrel so much over their solution, for it is sufficient to say to sophists of this sort that it is faith which moves one to believe the meaning of the New Testament manuscripts. We assent to faith without *a priori* evidence, however, since it is the first principle, although it is supported by reasons *a posteriori*. Let us then **be prepared to provide a reason** (1 Pet. 3:15) and a defense when any particular aspect is opposed. Certainly, if we trust in Christ over those other infidels, we should trust entirely in his deeds, and consequently should trust also in his apostles. And so the Christian religion arose from faith all the way from the aforementioned first level of Scripture to its fifth level. Thus the infidelity of our own so-called Christians begins with their corruption of the aforementioned fifth level of Scripture and leads, step by step, all the way up to a denial of the first. For many of our own people who call themselves Christian actually deny the sense of Scripture in both word and deed. Therefore, since nobody is capable of believing in the Lord Jesus Christ, except that he is drawn and would so will, he should consider the rationality, truth and renown of Christ's law, and then pray in order that he might be drawn to his faith. (246) Nor do I believe that it is possible for any pagan philosopher to discover some objection of falsehood or dishonesty whereby he should not believe the Christian faith above all else.

Admitting the faith of Christ and his apostles, together with their manner of living, as the Saracens themselves do, one may easily bring forth the authority of the rest. For at the end of his Gospel, John testifies that he has written that Gospel (John 21:24), just as he does at the end of his third letter (3 John 9), and at both the beginning and end of his Apocalypse (Rev. 1:1; 22:8). Thus Peter, James, and Jude also imply that each is the author of his own letter at its beginning. And in the last chapter of his second letter, Peter even testifies that the letters of his most dear brother Paul are authentic. He says, **Beloved brother Paul wrote to us according to the wisdom given to him, just as in all his letters speaking of these things which are difficult to understand, and which the unlearned and unstable condemn, just as they do other Scriptures, to their own destruction** (2 Pet. 3:15–16). In light of this, it seems fitting that all fourteen letters of Paul are of equal authority with Peter's two letters, and consequently with the five-fold book of John, together with the Gospel of Matthew, the letter of James, and that of Jude as well. For it was on account of the pseudo-apostles that Paul first states his own name at the beginning of each of his letters. The exception is the letter to the Hebrews, to whom he does not reveal his name until the end of his letter, since it was offensive to them at the beginning. But then, after his good will is understood, he expressly reveals himself to be the editor of that letter. With respect to their own Gospels and the Acts of the Apostles, however, Luke and Mark (247) are thus rendered canonical, in that the Holy Spirit symbolized them among the company of the four Evangelists: Luke by an ox, which is a sacrificial animal, and Mark by a lion, which is made clear in Ezek. 1:10 and Apoc. 4 (Rev. 4:7). Hence he arranged that one would give special consideration to the priesthood of Christ, and the other to his resurrection, just as he sanctified them in their lives which were holy and blameless before God and men.

The second evidence hinges on the rationality and conformity of all of their Scriptures to those of the other two Apostles. Since John, who was the last to write, saw all three Gospels, we should trust that the one who perceived the mysteries of Scripture would have corrected or opposed any lasting error within their Scripture if it would have harmed the Church. Therefore, Peter's approval of his disciple Mark, and

John's approval of Paul's disciple Luke, together with all the rest of the Church, grants the faith that they spoke harmoniously through the same Spirit, although in different places.

Surely the third and most certain piece of evidence in all such matters is the faith which God has infused into sanctified souls, and it is by this faith that they had performed all manner of miracles. That proof destroys all the unfaithful and unhelpful conclusions put forward by those people who are incapable of distinguishing between the natures of truths, how it is that one proof ought to be comprehended by faith, another by consensus, and yet another by demonstration. For this reason it is commanded in 1 Pet. 3:15 that we are **to be prepared to meet the demands of everyone who asks us about our faith**. And Paul did just that in that part of Acts 26 when accused before a pagan judge concerning questions of the law and articles of faith.

[. . .] (258) With regard to the assertion and the rational nature of our faith in these three matters which Mohammed especially repudiates, namely the Trinity, Incarnation, and Passion, it is clear that the books of both Testaments are replete with their testimony. I ask you, how could John, the loftiest of Christ's apostles, have spoken any more explicitly than he does in 1 John 5:7, where he specifically illustrates that point: **There are three who offer testimony in heaven: the Father, the Word, and the Holy Spirit; and these three are one**.[34] (259) And when it comes to testifying to Christ's passion and resurrection, all four Evangelists agree, despite the fact that they lived in different regions: Matthew was in India, Mark in Italy, Luke in Achaia, while John, who confirms the three prior Gospels, was in Asia Minor. And by this faith they performed miracles, strengthened the Church, and were at last gloriously martyred. Reason, however, should compel those who have been nourished in true philosophy, and fitted for battle with the aforementioned five-fold armor, to acknowledge these articles of faith from which the Saracens dissent.

[. . .] (262) Now if we are permitted to examine the most sacred and infinite power of God, how much more so should we scrutinize the power of the Vicar of Christ? (263) It is clearly essential that we discuss the power of Christ's vicars, since the Church is in danger of being lead astray by the disguised power of some pseudo-vicar with the teeth of a wolf and the fleece of a sheep, besieging our churches. Christ appears to command just this in Matt. 7:15, **Watch for false prophets, who come to you in sheep's clothing, although they are inwardly ravenous wolves.** Thus he gives Christians a decisive sign by which to discern them when he adds, **By their fruits you will know them** (Matt. 7:16). Again, since the power belonging to Christ and his vicars is so often displayed in Holy Scripture, Lord Pope is quick to prove from Holy Scripture that as the Vicar of Peter possesses the preeminence of power, it naturally follows that he and his laws grant the license and means by which to examine this power of his with due modesty and honor. Yet insofar as Holy Scripture is true in its entirety, there is no reason why it cannot be examined in its entirety by a catholic doctor. Now I ask you, what would be more suspicious than if I were able to exult my own power beyond the clouds by saying that I can do whatever I please, cloaking this claim in Scripture, and licensing disciples of my tradition to discuss this matter on my terms, while decreeing that no theologian studying Holy Scripture is permitted to venture beyond the terms and limits I have set? This would exceed even the craftiness of Mohammed! Again, this principle having been conceded by God must also be conceded by the successor, since to deny this right would leave the Christian in a quandary. Yet license to discuss such matters has been granted by God, since **all power is from God**, as it is consequently ordained in Rom. 13:1, and so stated in Matt. 28:18 that, **all power in heaven and on earth has been given to Christ**. (264) And again, God uniquely granted Peter the power of the keys for binding and loosing, administering the sacraments, and feeding Christ's sheep, as made clear in Matt. 16:16–19, and in the final chapter of John (John 21:15–19). Thus it is granted to all of his indispensable successors. But if this were the case it would be unnecessary to demonstrate from Scripture that the Vicar of Christ could abuse his power, as when the Apostle says in 1 Cor. 9:1–23 that he has greater power than another, and yet that his power is less than the whole power given to Christ in his humanity. Otherwise, while a theologian is being opposed by an adversary of his law concerning the faith of Scripture, he would stand confused and perplexed, citing with embarrassment that passage in John 1:35, **John was standing by**. Now I am asking you to tell me how the law of Scripture could oblige us to **provide a reason for everyone asking about the faith**, as it says in 1 Pet. 3:15, and yet at the same time muzzle us lest we say something about the power of our ecclesiastical superior especially, since Christ even commanded his rivals in John 7:24 that, **they were not to judge by outward appearances, but were to render a just judgment**? For if he willingly submitted himself to the judgment of Pilate he undoubtedly did so to set an example. Christ, therefore, prohibits rash judging, disputation and accusation, since it is by such judgment that the world argues, and is in no way a prudent course of action. This is confirmed by the fact that all Christ's priests should live on the temporal alms of the laity, while on the other hand, the laity should meet an even greater need by living on the spiritual alms of the clergy. And so they should reciprocally acknowledge one another's power and proper duty, just as it was in the Old Law, as even Christ taught this of himself. (265) However, those who are mutually obligated should acknowledge another's indemnity, lest they fail to absolve what they should. For if they do not then a part of the clergy will be greatly distrusted, unless they rejoice in the knowledge and limitations of their power expressed in the law of Scripture. [. . .]

(*De ver.* I,xii): The Source of False Readings

(268) Returning to our discussion of the authority of Scripture, it appears that those who render it impossible thereby rob it of its authority. I ask you, how could that law be honorable and authentic which is the most impossible and supremely heretical? Yet now, according to adversaries of the law of Christ, among all the laws of the world none would be more impossible than Christian law. But if this were true then its faith and its authority would perish. The minor premise is evident when one considers the whole biblical corpus with regard to both Testaments, and clarifies all of its propositions which are being assailed according to their strictly literal sense (*de virtute sermonis*).

It is confirmed, therefore, that the whole law of Christ is the one, perfect word proceeding from the mouth of God, whose individual parts fit together to create the entire authority and efficacy of Christ's law, according to Matt. 4:4, **A human being does not live by bread alone, but by every word which proceeds from the mouth of God**.

[. . .] (270) In Book 4, Chapter 6 of his *On the Trinity*, Augustine say that, "No one of sound mind would believe what is opposed to reason, nor any Christian what is opposed to Scripture, nor any man of peace what is opposed to the Church."[35] This saint means that if anyone is an adversary of Scripture, then he is not a Christian. And this applies even to Lord Pope, who some people imagine is capable of establishing regulations contrary to it.

Once again, Scripture derives its authority from either total or partial signification. (271) If from the total, then the greater part of Scripture possesses totally impossible signification, which is thus of no authority. And from this it follows that the greater part of Scripture possesses no authority. Yet if it derives from partial signification then, by the same rationale, all writings of the devil, heretics and poets would be supremely authentic, since every creature signifies God first of all. And because this is divinely instituted nobody can obstruct it, but must completely accept it. It is not valid to say, however, that human imposition renders Holy Scripture impossible. On the one hand, because such an institution would be unlawful, since it is repugnant to God, and on the other hand, because having supposed that such an institution is accursed, no Christian would solicit advice from it, just as Scripture, reason and the doctors teach us. Indeed, a letter of this sort kills the soul, as the Apostle says (2 Cor. 3:6). What if our opponents counter by asking why the adversary would understand Scripture in this way? Well, the reason does not appear to be close at hand, for he neither endeavors to edify the Church in this way, nor to commend Scripture, nor even to display truth and subtlety, but rather seeks to do the very opposite. The chronicles record that the acceptance of the fallacies of authors among the infidel philosophers was so great, as Valerius Maximus recounts in Book 8 of *On Remarkable Deeds and Words*, that the veneration given Pictagoras by his audience, (272) was such that they deemed it sacrilegious in disputation to dissent from what they had received from him. Indeed, when obliged to provide a reason for their views they offered only, "he said it is so."[36] How then could a Christian not honor his supreme author to an even greater extent?

And on behalf of the antecedent, it is clear from what has been said even such a trivial thought is harmful to the thinker, and for this very reason, to the Church. Surely, those who fall into the pit which they have dug allege that many Scriptures should not be understood literally (*ad literam*), and on that basis they perversely conclude that they are false according to the literal sense (*ad literam*), because they fail to understand them as they should. And with respect to the second, it is obvious that one does not commend Scripture by calling it is heretical and blasphemous. And since neither is an attribution, it follows that it is an accusation leveled against Scripture. Whereupon, it appears that our own theologians walk into the lecture hall one day dressed as sheep with the purpose of commending the law of Scripture, and all of a sudden acquire the teeth of foxes, adding to this the tail of a viper. They say that Holy Scripture is for the most part impossible and even blasphemous when read according to the literal, verbal, and fleshly sense. These fellows are just like foxes agreeing to peace with the roosters and chickens while standing at the door of their coop, though immediately upon entering they bare their teeth and turn ferocious. Hence, in Luke 13:32 Christ calls Herod a fox on account of such duplicitous hypocrisy. He says, **Go and tell that fox**. (273) Now some will say that they later annul the accusations they have made against Holy Scripture when they go on to bestow the catholic sense upon it. And this is supposed to provide some level of consolation. After all, every argument they know how to make against Scripture, they are then obligated to refute, admitting that Scripture really should not be characterized by that fictitious sense, but instead by the catholic sense which they proceed to explain. Yet if Holy Scripture should not be characterized by that sense, since it only possesses the sense which God confers upon it, it follows that it does not possess that false sense, and consequently this is not its own sense. Nor is it subject to calumny on account of that sense, just as God is not subject to calumny on account of the perverse sense of a heretic.

Although Scripture's accusers might be speaking the truth in this matter, it is still not sufficient for someone after he has leveled accusations against a person, or broken his head open, to admit immediately afterwards that he had lied in that case. Nor does one get off the hook simply by administering medicine to a person whom he has just injured.

[. . .] (278) Let us consider the Lord's Prayer in Matt. 6:9–13, for this seems to imply three heretical falsehoods.

First, that God is **our Father**. Now according to the grammar one learns as a child, a father must be defined as a male being who produces one of like species from his own substance. (279) Otherwise, everything that generates something else would be a father, and so it follows that God is our father in just such a way. And this results in the heresy proposed by those who say that every soul is hewn from the divine essence.

For the sake of that deduction, I suppose that no grammar other than the ancient one they learned outside of Scripture would be acceptable to those adversaries who are extending the generous offer of correcting Scripture. Second, I suppose that in accepting ever so much equivocation or grammatical and logical novelty by the authority of Scripture, this and anything else would have to be accepted through the same.

Having established these facts, it is evident thirdly that it is not due to the childish grammar of these unfaithful Latinists that "father" would thus signify equivocally, as it is elicited from Scripture. For then it could be conceded consequently that our spiritual father begot us in the manner spoken of by the Apostle in 1 Cor. 4:15, **In Jesus Christ through the gospel I have begotten you**; and in John 1:13, **The sons of God are born neither from blood nor the will of fleshly parents**. The adversaries of Scripture's logic wish to deny, as Nicodemus did, since he was an old man, that a human being **is born from water and the spirit**, and thus by means of the seed of faith, according to John 3:5. But if they do this it seems that they should also deny such a new type of sonship, and consequently the fatherhood as well. And on this account, they should also deny that God is the Father, the Church the Mother, and Christ the Brother of those who have been reborn through grace. Yet that would abrogate the faith of Scripture, evinced in Deut. 32:6–7, Prov. 31:2 and Heb. 2:11–12. (280) That, in turn, would lead to the destruction of the hope and love of the Church, since 1 John 3:2 says, **Now we are sons of God**, which is why the Apostle says we are heirs of the kingdom and should love one another as brothers (Rom. 8:17).

I suppose, however, that throughout this entire process the adversary of the law will not admit any proposition or logical inference, unless it agrees with his own grammar and those appendices he chooses to depend upon.

Then follows the second objection to the Lord's prayer: the sanctification of the eternal name of God involves an impossibility, as does the fourth petition for daily bread. It is not possible for something which is already supremely and eternally holy to then become sanctified. Nor can they understand the daily bread in the other petition of Christ, who says in John 6:48, **I am the bread of life**. For inasmuch as they say that Christ cannot possibly be the bread, it follows that the fourth petition would have to be corrected, or even withdrawn, on the grounds that it is heretical and blasphemous. And if they will diligently examine the principal points of Lord's prayer in this way, they will find that any number of its parts implies something blasphemous. Based upon the principle that God becomes our Father when we take on the form of grace, Scripture and the holy doctors say that a man lacking such grace is dead according to Christ's logic in Luke 9:60, **Let the dead bury their own dead**. In keeping with this logic, John speaks of the second death in Chapter 2 of the Apocalypse (Rev. 2:11). And the Apostle says in 1 Tim. 5:6, **The widow who misuses her freedom is dead**; just as St. John says in Chapter 3 of the Apocalypse (Rev. 3:1), **You have the name of one who lives even though you are dead**. (281) Such is the case with many passages of Scripture which have been built upon that foundation. For just as an accidental form arrives and generates an aggregate accidentally, so when it departs an aggregate of this sort is ruined or destroyed. In this manner the saints understand that a person who purifies himself through penance hates his own life which dies to the world and is buried with

Christ. Indeed, when commenting upon the words of Ps. 149 (Ps. 149:7), **In order to render vengeance upon the nations and reproaches upon the people**, Augustine concedes that the preacher of God's word, just as he destroyed sin, thus kills the sinner or man of sin, such that he wounded the old man for the sake of his salvation.[37] And he cites for his purposes the scriptural passage of Acts 10:13 in which the angel says to Peter, **Arise, Peter, kill and eat**. In keeping with that sense, doctors in the time of the law of grace should kill blasphemers and heretics, not permitting them to live upon the land, as commanded according to the literal sense (*ad literam*) in the Old Testament with regard to bodily killing, evinced in Lev. 24:15–23. However, this should be carried out according to the mystical sense during the time of the law of grace. And because these truths are connected, if one were to be denied they would all have to be denied, thereby leading to the destruction of Scripture, according to Matt. 25:40, **Amen I say to you, inasmuch as you have done this to one of the least among my brethren, you have done it to me**. Indeed, that passage of Scripture, (282) which the judge so distinctly asserts, would otherwise be impossible, and consequently would grant what is impossible. Yet this means that the final judgment would be unjust, something not even the damned will dare to say when they ask the question, **Lord, when did we see you as such a poor man**. And that is all the more reason why the Christian will not falsify his own law. This is the charter written by God and granted to us, and the basis upon which we will assert our claim to the kingdom of God. Clearly then, if we were to falsify it we should be disinherited by God's righteous judgment.

[. . .] (287) When communicating by means of the words of Scripture we must limit ourselves to the appropriate sense and stop quarreling over words in a childish and heretical manner. Do not be troubled by the fact that a vocal proposition does not constitute Scripture itself. For Scripture is the aggregate formed by the voice and catholic sense inscribed upon the soul, since the voice is spread out across the air, while the sense is inscribed in the mind. But if the sacred sense is inscribed upon a holy mind then Scripture is holy. Thus it seems that if a corrupt mind contains Scripture then a scripture of this sort, which is the utterance of a sinner, is thereby a false scripture, even though the other prior one remains immaculate. And it is with regard to such an utterance that I understand that statement of the Apostle in 1 Cor. 12:3, **No one is able to say Jesus is Lord, except in the Holy Spirit**. Indeed, unless the Christian has been united with Christ through grace, he does not have Christ as his savior, nor does he speak the sacramental words without falsehood, even if they do benefit those who duly receive them. It is appropriate that a priest confess that he is a member of Christ and, as the saints say, that he is even Christ himself in a certain manner.[38]

[. . .] (299) Second, it seems fair to say that if anything true sounds wrong, the reason for this rests with the person who is listening to it. For God approves every truth, and so it is acceptable to him for this very reason. Accordingly, every person should know this, just as he ought to know that he is obligated to conform his own will entirely to the divine will, approving and rejoicing in the whole of the divine will. And so it follows that the truth should not sound wrong to anyone. If indeed anything true sounds wrong to a person on his part, this is because the truth within him has been damaged. Hence, what should primarily displease him is the principle of falsehood. On this basis it is confirmed that since all truth is righteousness; and as all righteousness sounds good, so then all truth sounds good. Righteousness is the conformity of truth to the divine will. Every such conformity is the righteousness of the Lord and sounds good to his ears. Nothing evil, therefore, is found in truth of this sort, but rather in the person who wrongly hears it, culpably turning it into an opportunity for sin. (300) In fact, since, according to Scripture's manner of speaking, all truth is the will of God, to say that the truth sounds wrong in itself would the be the equivalent of saying that God's will sounds wrong. **Everyone who is of God hears the word of God**, inasmuch as he does his will, as made clear in John 8:47. Now the will of God is the truth which a person performs, as made clear in Matt. 6, and frequently elsewhere. It surely seems that if the truth sounded wrong in itself, when God speaks eternally through singular truths, then there would exist eternal discord within God himself. Yet that is impermissible, since the Father forever hears the good, eternally speaking every good and every truth. Certainly, the Lord God himself is speaking through every person who utters any truth, as is evinced in Ps. 84 (Ps. 85:8–13). Clearly then, to say that the truth sounds wrong in itself is the same as saying that the word of God sounds wrong. That, however, would mean that truth is culpable, and thus God as well.

Third, it seems to me that all wrong-sounding discourse is grounded in falsehood, and consequently in sin. Since, Augustine says in Chapter 1 of the book *From Whence Comes Evil*,[39] that every evil pertains to punishment or guilt, and all punishment originates in guilt, clearly every unsuitable sound originates in guilt. For there would not be the malice of punishment if not for the malice of guilt. This is why a person should take pains to safeguard the truth within his own discourse lest it mingles with duplicity, deception, and falsehood, since they are not compatible. For then he runs the risk of allowing culpable utterances to creep into his discourse. (301) And so it was that in the state of innocence there had been discourse without punishment, and consequently without discord, just as there will be in heaven, where sin is excluded in principle.

It is confirmed, therefore, that when the truth sounds wrong, falsehood by equal measure will sound good. And since every falsehood is a lie contrary to the truth, as Augustine teaches in Chapter 3 of *On Lying*,[40] it follows that lying would sound good. And since every lie is culpable, as clarified below, it follows that what is culpable would sound good. Now it is not possible that anything could be true unless it is meant to be spoken at some time, as clarified below. Consequently, every truth can be spoken without dissonance. On this basis it is clear that dissonance may be communicated accidentally alongside the truth. If this point is established, since no concomitant truth creates from itself dissonance, it follows that what sounds evil does not first originate in the truth, but rather in the very opposite of truth. Otherwise Christ's reproach of the Jews in John 8:46 would not be valid: **If I speak the truth to you, why do you not believe me?** If the unadulterated truth could sound wrong by its very nature, then the Jews would have been able to say, "Although you speak the truth to us, it still sounds wrong on your own part, and so we do not believe you." The cause of dissonance, therefore, must remain with the one who wrongly hears it, as the second corollary states.

[. . .] (302) In light of what has been said, it seems very indiscreet and discordant to say that the truth sounds wrong in itself. Falsehood primarily and inherently sounds wrong, and the subject speaks or hears wrongly only on account of his own participation in falsehood.

(303) Those people, however, who are unwilling to accept figurative locutions or equivocations would not say that truth or falsehood sound wrong, but that it is only the audible corporeal aspect which sounds this way, and it is only perceived through senses. Thus it seems that it would be impossible and heretical, since a truth of this sort either sounds like a falsehood or is perceived as such.

(*De ver.* I,xiii): The Necessity of Speaking the Truth

(303) With regard to the objections and views raised against my position, I will put forward a three-fold argument. The first concerns the fact that the Master of the Sentences explains in Book 3, Distinction 11, that one should not concede absolutely that Christ is a creature, but rather do so with some modification.[41] And in a similar vein he recounts the words of St. Ambrose in Book 1, Distinction 19.[42] On this account, rather than being a hindrance, it is actually appropriate to employ such mitigating clauses when responding, and to beware of linguistic novelties in matters of logic. Why then would we not follow such catholic doctors as mentioned above?

In this matter I offer a three-fold response. First, I say that the proof drawn from the testimony of the Master is ineffective in the proposition since the faith of Scripture, the faith of the Church, and the testimony of the holy doctors teach (304) that predications of humanity made with regard to Christ are to be conceded simply. Surely the following argument is not very impressive: the Master asserts it in this way and, therefore, it is true, as is clearly the case with many of his sayings. Second, one could even say that the Master is apprehensive as he speaks by way of offering an opinion: are those his own words? Now it is customary to ask whether one ought to concede simply that Christ was created. To which one can say that it is stated simply and without further definition, though less fittingly. Or third, one can say with the Master that such things should not be conceded simply unless one supplies in thought what is not expressed, namely the humanity of Christ. Although in that particular instance the Master announces this in a simple fashion for the sake of brevity, this matter should still never be understood simply, nor should the Catholic ever doubt that predications of this sort must not be conceded with regard to Christ, unless his humanity is supplied in thought. In the same way, it should not be conceded of Christ that Christ is a man, the predestined redeemer, or any other predication of creatureliness, except when supplying his humanity in thought. In Chapter 6 of certain treatise, *On the Incarnation*,[43] I have demonstrated from Scripture and the holy doctors that such things regarding Christ are to be conceded simply, as Augustine teaches in Chapter 22 of his *Enchiridion*, and many of the following chapters.[44] And in Book 7, Chapter 19 of the *Confessions*, he concedes that matter simply, saying that "if these things written of Christ were false, then indeed everything is in danger of being a lie."[45]

[. . .] (309) Furthermore, it should be observed that when it came to drawing upon linguistic novelties, the holy doctors of the Early Church quite reasonably forbade, in matters of faith, the introduction of new-fangled terms which are foreign to Scripture, for fear of the poison which could be hidden in them by heretics. Nevertheless, when the sense has been revealed and the signification of terms defined by the Church, then the Catholic can be sufficiently confident when employing such terms, even though they had not been exemplified in the text of Scripture, as the Master records concerning the name of the Person in Book 1, Distinction 23, Chapter 6 of the *Sentences*.[46] And so it is with many of the terms invented by the masters these days. Yet danger still lurks within inventions of this kind, and in the abuse of such inventions. The safest route, therefore, is to employ the terms and logic of Scripture. Or if we press beyond that path, then let us be careful when employing terms which concern the subject matter of faith. It is better that we follow the ancient doctors and the saints, since they are more trustworthy. But above all else, let us abide by Holy Scripture. Hence, Augustine says in Book 1, Chapter 4 of his *Reconsiderations*,

> When I said of the Father and the Son, he who begets and he whom is begotten, is one, I should have said that they

> are one, just as the Truth himself clearly enunciated in John 10:30 saying, **The Father and I, we are one**.[47]

(310) See how this saint, given his zeal for imitating the logic of Holy Scripture, reconsidered and corrected something he had said when found not to be in keeping with Scripture! And so he often reconsiders many things, not because they are false, but because they are either not effectively grounded in Scripture, or because they can be enunciated with still greater conformity to Scripture. The error which this saint detested most of all was the claim that we should not imitate the logic of Holy Scripture, because it is fitting that the Lord would retain some words exclusively for himself. Now according to this line of argument, an apostle would not speak in conformity with Christ, nor a subject in conformity with his ecclesiastical superior. And yet the Church so resonantly cries aloud at Easter: "The Lord is risen indeed," based upon the authority of Scripture in Luke 24:34, and thus of the one speaking those words. Therefore, this is neither impossible, nor does it sound wrong. For then the Church, which should be believed over Peter Lombard, would err shamefully, while the Apostle argues in 1 Cor. 15:14, **If Christ has not risen from the dead, our faith is in vain.**

Second, they base their argument upon Christ's commandment to his disciples in Matt. 7:6, **Do not give what is holy to dogs, nor cast pearls before swine**. In fact, it is a generally held principle among respondents that not all truths should be spoken everywhere. If, therefore, it is permissible for the Christian to keep silent sometimes, then he is also allowed to withhold a complete response.

In this matter I say that the conclusion is true. But we should remember that this teaching of Christ indicates that the Christian should pay close attention to what is being spoken and where, concerning whom, to whom, how, and when.

(311) Hence, whenever Christ responds to the interrogations of his antagonists, he ostensibly convicts them of their slanderous accusation, as evinced in Matt. 12:24–32, when they leveled the charge against him that **he cast out demons by Beelzebul, the chief of the demons.** For here he effectively overcomes their craftiness by the most powerful three-fold reason, sometimes appealing to a proof drawn from authority, as in John 10:34 where he demonstrates his divinity, although in an obscure manner. At other times, however, he responds to a question with a question of his own, as evinced in Matt. 21:23–25, when the Jews ask, **by what power has he performed his signs**, and he inquired of them, **whether the baptism of John was from heaven or from human beings**. Realizing that from either part of the contradiction an impropriety is bound to follow, they confessed that they did not know, at which point he said, **Neither do I tell you by which power I do these things**. And still there are times when he kept silent, as when Pilate asked, **What is truth?** in John 18:38; or when Herod and the priests interrogated him with many words regarding his own teaching, evinced in Luke 23:6–12. And in John 8:48–49, when the Jews charged him with being a Samaritan and a demoniac, he remained silent regarding the first point, even though it was the truth, as evinced in the parable of Luke 10:29–37.[48] Yet wary of blasphemy, he did offer a modest denial of the second charge saying, **I do not have a demon** (John 8:49).

Thus in accordance with the discretion granted by the Spirit of Counsel we ought to imitate Christ by responding in this five-fold manner, taking into account the various circumstances, all the while governed by a guileless eye (Matt. 6:22).

(312) With regard to the first authority, based upon the testimony of Augustine in Book 2, Chapter 20 of his *On the Lord's Sermon on the Mount*, it is clear that by the prohibition against giving what is holy to the dogs (Matt. 7:6) one

understands this to mean the truth of the faith, "which it would be abominable to violate or corrupt, even the attempt to do so rendering the will guilty of this impiety, although what is holy remains inviolable and incorruptible by nature."[49] The pearls, however, are the profound truths which, "concern the covering of allegories as if pertaining to the shells being opened by the searchers as they rummage through Scripture." And thus the truth of the faith is called holy according to a more general principle, inasmuch as it should not be corrupted, while the pearls are called such more specifically in keeping with a principle by which they ought not to be despised. Since dogs and pigs are unclean animals, they signify the sophists, the heretics, and those people consumed with carnal desires. Propelled by the uncleanness of worldly glory and the indulgences of the flesh, these people mangle and trample the truth. To the extent that they are able they will not allow it to remain intact, but will slander and mutilate it with their teeth, or ridicule and defile it amid their corrupt affections. Now the subtle truth of faith is not to be preached among any people of this sort, just as one would not do so among neophytes or the incapacitated. Thus Christ says in John 16:12, **I have many things to say to you, but you are unable to bear them now**. And the Apostle says in 1 Cor. 3:1–2, **I could not speak to you as spiritual people, but as people of the flesh. As if infants in Christ I gave you milk to drink and not solid food**. In this manner, therefore, the truth of Scripture ought to be hidden for the sake of avoiding scandal.

[. . .] (316) It is essential that we discuss specifically where and when a person should speak the truth or keep silent. With respect to this matter, I have at length established three conclusions. First, many more evils arise from not speaking the truth than from its promulgation. It is clear, therefore, that every evil proceeds from not speaking the truth. Now every sin is a sin of omission or is the consequence of that, as I illustrated elsewhere. And since every omission is culpable when one is obliged to declare the truth in word and deed, the same applies to keeping silent. Clearly then, just as all evil originates from such an omission, so too from not speaking the truth. It is in this vein that the prophet Isaiah says, **Woe unto me, because I kept silent** (Isa. 6:5). Hence, the culpable reticence of prelates brings about the total ruin of the people. And here again the prophet Isaiah calls such servile cowards **mute dogs, incapable of barking** (Isa. 56:10). Proclaiming the truth is never culpable, even if there is the possibility that an indiscretion could sometimes accompany it accidentally, thereby leading to the infliction of the evil of punishment.

Second, it seems impossible to speak the truth with **the wisdom of serpents and the innocence of doves** as Christ commands in Matt. 10:16. Yet that is just the manner in which it should be spoken. It is clear, therefore, that it is spoken through the inspiration of the Holy Spirit, mindful of the circumstances, and with a just intention. From which it follows, (317) according to Christ's logical inference in Matt. 6:22, that **the whole body** of one's deeds **will be a light** through the illumination of grace. When, therefore, someone closes a sensible ear and the ear of his mind, lest he hear the enticements of vainglory, he is taking counsel, just as a country or city with respect to its sovereignty. And he closes the other ear, cautiously reflecting on his last days, laboriously earning merit, and bearing in mind that in this brief mortal life, **the one who sows sparingly also reaps sparingly** (2 Cor. 9:6). Then he possesses the wisdom of a serpent from his beginning until his end, by which he prepares his intellect, adding to it the dove-like simplicity which lacks the gall of bitterness and carnality. He strives to feed purely upon the honor of fruitful grain, and finds peace among the stones against the birds of the air, who are the rapacious demons. If he does this, then he possesses the eye of a dove which prepares the affections of his soul. For the dove is surely without gall, lacking claws to wound; nor does he feed on flesh as the raven and the other predatory birds do with their beaks and claws. He subsists instead on pure grains and finds peace in the rock, nesting there so as to escape the attacks of the rapacious birds.

Whoever speaks the truth for its own sake, speaks it laudably, as it should be spoken. Nevertheless, it would not be believed unless he is permitted by turn to pause in his replies, and in keeping with meritorious works, change what he is going to say if so moved by the inspiration he has received from God. But if that Spirit which guides the navigator directly to the port of salvation is absent, then one undoubtedly knows that his own culpable indisposition is to blame. And so I have said on other occasions that it is essential for the faithful (318) to converse in keeping with the five-fold articulation of truth. First, they should speak the truth always in reality, just as one speaks of anything according to its very nature. Second, they should speak the truth in contemplation; third, in prayer; fourth, in preaching; and fifth in vocal instruction. And it is necessary that these four hinge upon the articulation of the truth of Scripture in the aforementioned first mode. For everyone is always obliged to declare his own love in reality.

Third, it appears that refusing to speak the truth is chiefly due to the danger of having one's temporal possessions taken away. Or else it attests to the cowardly and contemptible fear of angering someone who would be severely displeased by hearing the truth, prompting senseless agreement to a lie which is contrary to the truth. Clearly then, since the truth is of far greater value to the pure soul than riches and temporal advantage, to err in some case for the sake of such a fatuous good would be exceptionally loathsome. Whereupon, it was because they revealed the truth that Christ, the Baptist, and all the martyrs were put to death. If Christ had not revealed the greed of the priests, scribes, and Pharisees, instilling in the people the evangelical truth, they would not have so spitefully conspired in his death. And so it was with the Baptist when he rebuked Herod, and the others who preached the truth of Scripture and detested blasphemous falsehoods. Because the evangelical truth should not be suppressed for fear of causing scandal or angering enemies of the truth, it is clear that the Head of the Church, together with his members, was teaching the very opposite as much in his deeds as in his words.

[. . .] (322) Now I hold to the rule that the truth should be proclaimed if it is the faith of Scripture, and the intention of the speaker is both pure and just. Then, confirmed in these principles, whenever someone is moved by the Holy Spirit to speak such truth, he does not fail to do so. Certainly, if the martyrs, who suffered at the hands of the infidels, were willing to suffer imminent death for the sake of declaring the truth, how much more are we bound to correct our brethren among the faithful, where there exists no such imminent danger? This is especially so, since no demonstrated conclusion should be more steadfastly observed (323) than that were a person to die in this way for the truth of Scripture he would surely find his salvation through this glorious martyrdom! [. . .]

(*De ver.* I,xiv): The Proper Occasions for Speaking the Truth

(331) Furthermore, explaining this matter of whether one is obliged to proclaim the truth, a number of objections can be raised. The first is that it is permissible in some cases to keep silent concerning the truth of the faith, however great the necessity pressing upon someone to disclose it. There is even a specific case of canon law pertaining to scandal arising, whether on the part of those who would preach, or those who would listen, or some other person scandalized by the action of such a preaching office. Now in Book 1 of the *Decretals*,

"*De Renuntiatione*," the Church states in the chapter *Nisi cum pridem*, that

> there are six reasons whereby a bishop can seek permission to resign his office, namely being privy to a crime, bodily infirmity, lack of knowledge, the ill-will of the people, grave scandal, and personal impediment to the exercise of sacred orders. In all such cases a note of caution should be observed.[50]

For whatever renders a man unfit to carry out his pastoral duties properly, not only grants him permission to resign his office, but, I believe, demands his resignation. If, therefore, on account of scandal on the part of a bishop, scandal among those under his charge, (332) or even the scandal of his adversary, a bishop should resign his see, then this is all the reason why more should someone should perpetually relinquish the preaching office for reasons of scandal. Consequently, there are numerous cases in which the truth sounds wrong.

In response to that objection, having established the essence of scandal with its distinctions, it should first be observed that a person might be scandalized by the sound of the truth in two ways. It may be due to an occasion in which a person comprehend it wrongly, or an occasion in which it was related to him wrongly; the Apostle distinguishes these two instances in Rom. 7:7–13. Secondly, one should observe that, according to Hostiensis and Bernard, truth is three-fold when considering a proposition, thus having to do with the truth of a good life or righteousness, the truth of doctrine, and the truth of judgment.[51] In light of these suppositions, I propose thirdly that no one should scandalize another in the second manner, that is, by taking the opportunity to present the truth in a wrong manner for the sake of worldly gain, inasmuch as no one should sin for the sake of any such advantage. All scandalizing of this sort is sin, and thus no one should scandalize another for the sake of worldly gain. (333) The Apostle speaks of such practical scandal in 1 Cor. 8:13, and this passage is cited in the aforementioned *Decretal* chapter: **If it would scandalize my brother, I will never eat meat again.**[52] Christ says something similar in Matt. 18:6–7, **If anyone would scandalize one of these little ones who believes in me, it is better for him that a millstone be suspended around his neck and he be plunged into the depths of the sea. Woe to the world on account of scandals!**

Second, I say that a Catholic should allow his brother to be scandalized in the first manner, so that the truth might be illustrated. This is made clear in Book 5 of the *Decretals*, "*De Regulis Juris*." The canon, *Qui scandalizaverit*, states that, "It is more useful that scandal be permitted to arise than that the truth would be forsaken."[53] And this is evinced in the work and words of Christ. For as I made clear in the last chapter, one reads in Matt. 15:12–14 how Christ condemns the ceremonial washing of the Pharisees, when responding to apostles who said, **Do you know that the Pharisees were scandalized when they heard this word?** For he then said, **Leave them alone; they are the blind leading the blind**. This is similarly evinced in Luke 11:39–44. Now the highest master was refuting the scribes and Pharisees in the most acute, clear, and public manner, since he knew them to be perjurers by their accusations which stemmed from a wrong reception of the truth. (334) This is made clear in Matt. 23:13–33 concerning the eight-fold woe he pronounced upon them. As such, I am obviously not impressed by the argument that if my neighbor were to be scandalized by the proclamation of the truth then it should not be declared. Rather we should pay attention to the heart of the one proclaiming it.

Third, I say that just as truth of life, which ought to be common to all, should not be excluded in any possible case, so the truth of judgment when examining judges, or the truth of doctrine when examining doctors, should never be silenced, except for reasons of some insufficiency on the part of the speaker, owing either to lack of resources or context. The first part is evident, insofar as every man ought to be in a state of grace from which he is not permitted to fall away. But the very fact that he remains in a state of grace he thus holds on to the truth of righteousness; therefore, that part is true. And the second part is evident, insofar as all of our sufficiency comes from God, according to the Apostle in 1 Cor. 3:7. If, therefore, God grants us the sufficiency to proclaim the truth of judgment or doctrine, and we leave that undone, then by this act of omission we sin against God, unlawfully accepting his grace in vain. And so it is clearly unlawful for someone to neglect speaking the truth, except if he lacks the sufficiency to do so. And this is the reason why Christ and his apostles so diligently taught the truth of Scripture's faith even to the point of being reckoned insane, as evinced in John 10:20 and Acts 26:24. However, there are times when a given Christian does not possess sufficient resources for this purpose, owing to a lack of bodily power, as is clearly the case with those who are wearied or injured, or other times when he lacks the proper circumstances of time and place, as happens when encountering those who are resting at night or traveling through the wilderness. (335) And yet on another occasion it may be because in this particular case it would be more salubrious for him to follow some other course of action, as is clear with those who are eating or attending to other essential matters, and are thus occupied with the necessity of providing for temporal needs. For **all things have their time**, as stated in Eccles. 3:1. Therefore, as I said above, the Spirit of Counsel is required in such matters in order to determine the specific criteria.

Fourth, as I also say above, when proclaiming the truth a person ought to consider the nature of what is being said, the nature of both persons among whom there should be a relation, and the nature of the adjacent circumstances pertaining to every situation. The first part is clear, insofar as the preaching of the truth is food for the soul. Someone, therefore, who plans to feed a person or a group of people, would make arrangements to feed them with the appropriate food. In this respect the Apostle says in 1 Cor. 3:1–2, **I gave you milk as though infants in Christ, drink, not solid food**. Just as milk properly nourishes infants, who live without guile, so it is fitting that believers would eagerly chew on the plain meaning of Scripture, which so excellently nourishes the neophyte. But, as the Apostle says, **wisdom**, which is solid food, **we speak among the perfected** (1 Cor. 2:6). And it is evident that we should attend to the nature of truth in the ministration of doctrine. Second, we ought to consider the nature of both persons, since the theologian is obliged to propagate the truth of Scripture, not historical events and worldly chronicles, and chiefly those truths of Scripture which he believes will better feed his audience to the honor of God and the edification of the Church, (336) as I said above concerning Christ's teaching in Matt. 7:6. Third, we must truly consider the nature of the adjacent circumstances on the other side. For if the person in need of instruction is more readily compliant, not yet hardened in the depths of vice, then we should persuade him with a moderate sense and gentle words. But if while sunken in the midst of Babylon hope still remains for this person or the people listening, or perhaps those following, then he must be rebuked for the good of Mother Church. Other things being equal, he should be sharply corrected, as evinced in the deeds of Christ and by the Apostle's teaching in Titus 1:9–13, where he advises him that, **One should utterly refute those who are opposed to the teaching of Holy Scripture on account of which**, he says, **they ought to be harshly upbraided.** Yet we must be extremely careful that we do not end up defaming or injuring a person in the process. For when the doctor communicates it should be in keeping with the rules of Scripture, and not always according to the judgment of exhortation. Because there is an infinite number of circumstances for us to consider in such matters, the one who is doing the exhorting should take into account the sanctity of his own life and retain a guileless eye. And from such preparation he should proceed confidently, guided by the inspiration of the Holy Spirit.

[. . .] (338) Do not be disturbed because I so often say that a person possesses the Spirit of Counsel, and indeed that he should believe that he possesses it. For everyone ought to examine his own life, and to the extent that he is not conscious of mortal sin, he should fearlessly believe that he is in a state of charity. Otherwise, a priest would not celebrate, nor would a Christian perform any sort of meritorious work. After all, according to the faith of Scripture in 1 Cor. 13:1–3, no matter what a person does, **as long as he does not have charity**, it will not lead to his salvation.

It is essential, therefore, that each pilgrim treat this examination with the greatest care, since everyone ought to possess the hope of his own salvation, and thus one should fearlessly believe that he is in a state of justifying grace. (339) And since it follows, moreover, that if anyone is in such a state of grace he then has the Holy Spirit to direct him in all works of this sort, it also follows that every person should believe that he thus possesses the Holy Spirit. The infidel, the false Christian, and the damned do not perform these works, but are instead continuously sinning on account of their putrid conscience, as they do the things they should not. Someone who ought to believe the logical inference of this, should then also believe both the antecedent and consequent. Whereupon, in the early Church the faithful generally knew that they possessed the Holy Spirit moving within them, to say nothing of the fact that it is necessary for every creature to be moved by the Holy Spirit, as the faithful philosophers say. But there abides a specific manner of possessing the Spirit through the indwelling of grace, at least according to present righteousness, which they can recognize by the fruit of the Spirit. Now according to the Apostle in Gal. 5:22 there are twelve fruits of the Spirit, and the Christian who has any one of them, or any sort of virtue, undoubtedly possesses the Holy Spirit. Indeed, just as the Christian is obliged to confess that he is a Christian, and is not a Christian unless he possesses the Holy Spirit, so then he is obliged to believe that he possesses the Holy Spirit. I ask you, what could be more recognizable to a person than an act of charity? Thus the apostles had believed in the Scriptures when they heard from Christ in John 20:22, **Receive the Holy Spirit**. And they possessed that very Spirit insofar as the Truth, who could not lie, promised it to them. And so it is when clerics receive the order of priesthood, for they have all duly confessed and yet do not believe that each one of them is aware of it in the same way. But this does not mean that (340) it is permissible for the saints to worry whether the work which they perform is essentially good, because it so happens that a person may merit by performing a work that is essentially evil, such that in sinning mortally he actually performs a work that is essentially good. It is, therefore, one thing to be in doubt concerning a moral good, and another thing to be in doubt with respect to the natural good pertaining to a work. For although it would be lawful for a Christian to believe that he possesses the Holy Spirit, it so happens that pseudo-disciples hypocritically pretend that they too possess the Holy Spirit. And so it is necessary when attempting to discern whether it is deformed that we remember that the truth will be indicated by whether or not their works are in conformity with Holy Scripture. This is why we, who are so far removed from the experience of the Spirit which the saints expressed in the primitive Church, ought to encourage ourselves and others by the authority of Scripture.

And if we are asked whether we possess the Holy Spirit, we can confidently affirm that we believe we possess it. Putting aside presumption, while casting off the fear of having fallen from grace, the companions of the Spirit are truly heroic. And it is with discretion that they can boldly concede they possess the Holy Spirit thus entrusted to them.

I am astonished, therefore, that some of our own people would slander those who say that they possess the Holy Spirit speaking to them in this way. And yet these very same people call their brothers maniacs, and brazenly assert that they know of no one who honors Holy Scripture more than they do. I consistently assert, however, that if a Christian only honors Holy Scripture as any man of the world, then he is God, and consequently greater than any Christian. The Christian honored Holy Scripture in reality, by indestructibly authorizing it, proclaiming its authority to his brethren, and given his love for Scripture, even defending it to the point of enduring the most bitter death. Simply conceding that one loves Scripture is not sufficient for any of our people, even though one might say, "I venerate and esteem the entirety of Scripture with all my strength." For honoring Scripture means being obedient to it in one's manner of living, thus attaining to its perfection through good works born of love, not merely paying homage to it with words alone.

[. . .] (366) With regard to the growth of our faction, by which it is assumed we are throwing the Church into disarray, seeking to separate the members from their head, and striving to destroy the privileges of the Roman Church, I am aware of no such thing. Rather, it is our intention, as much in general as in the particular, that Christ's Church would destroy the sin of scandal, which is the inherent cause of this entire uproar among the people. Clearly then, it is not preaching the evangelical truth for the sake of sin's destruction which is wreaking havoc in the Church, but rather the fostering of sin and obstruction of truth, which results when Scripture's law is not upheld. (367) This is true, despite the fact that it seems all manner of evil is likely to follow from the former, while an abundance of apparent temporal prosperity from the latter. Elijah's response in Third Kings 18 (1 Kings 18:17–18) makes this clear: **Are you that one who troubles Israel? And he said, I have not disturbed Israel, but you and your father's house, who have forsaken the commandments of the Lord**. Thus every Catholic should strive to unite the members to Christ the head, and if this means creating division among the ranks of the enemies of the cross of Christ then so be it. One does this for the sake of securing the true peace of Mother Church, even if it results in disquieting bodily pain. For as Christ says in Matt. 10:34–35, **I have not come to bring peace to the earth, but a sword. Consequently, I have come to separate a man from his father, and a son from his mother, and turn daughter-in-law against mother-in-law.** Christ came, therefore, in order to break apart the deceitful confederation which worldly men forged by their diabolical pride. Indeed, that pride deceives stronger people. And since the devil reigns over all the sons of pride, he ensnares all sinners. Carnal people, however, who have been conjoined through the vice of fleshly pleasure are to be joined together through the penance of Christ. But those who have been married to the world are separated through the poverty of Christ. Someone, therefore, who strives to encourage the people quietly in any of these three categories, is the one who really endeavors to destroy the true peace. For the original peace abiding between God and humanity is torn asunder through sin alone. This is why all the saints of both testaments generally fermented sedition among the people to this end. For they would not be soldiers in the army of Christ if they did not struggle to destroy the peace of the devil which so opposes it. Hence, that very accusation of stirring up turmoil among the people was leveled against the Lord Jesus Christ by the scribes and the priests, accusing him of being a heretic so that they might then put him to death. (368) This is evinced in Luke 23:5 when they said, **He stirs up the people, teaching throughout all of Judea, beginning from Galilee all the way to this place**. And it follows: **The chief priests and scribes stood by constantly accusing him** (Luke 23:10). Clearly then, it does not follow that the Christian who rouses people to fight against the devil, according to the faith of Scripture, is a heretic. Actually, it is a sign of just the opposite.

In light of these things, one is able to examine the benefits of this meaning which I have so carefully disseminated over time. First of all, one can discern that clerics are married to the world and thus to riches, such that this is more fittingly considered their father-in-law than God. For they all grumble more about the privation of temporal goods than they do about the loss of virtues.

One can secondly discern how the world would be wise to withdraw material alms from such men, since no one ought enter into a yoke of matrimony with infidels by confirming such a monstrous marriage. Indeed, it is preferable that it be dissolved.

Third, if God so willed it, these men of every clerical class, whose hearts are touched by the Holy Spirit, could be inspired with a contempt for the world, thereby taking up a life of evangelical poverty for the sake of Christ. Nor do I believe that so great a benefit proceeds from the opinion of one who says that Holy Scripture is heretical and blasphemous.

Furthermore, I must answer the charge that I would abolish the privileges of the Roman Church. For in publicly proclaiming the love and veneration I have for my Mother, the Roman Church, I am seeking to protect her privileges and her insignia, and taking care to see that they are thus secured. (369) I know by the faith of Scripture, inasmuch as it is the indestructible truth, that all of the Church's privileges proceed from God. And so the more obediently she has followed Christ, the more abundantly she has been adorned with privileges. Yet some would entice the Church into paying more attention to worldly rewards and prosperity than suffering persecution for righteousness' sake, such that she will end up prizing Caesar's endowments and palaces more than those of Christ her head. These are the people who remain Christ's cunning enemies, as he says in Matt. 10:34–36, when he taught them that he was not going to bring worldly peace to his bride, but a sword: **A person's enemy is of his own household**. This theme is found elsewhere.

[. . .] (374) Although I was summoned recently to appear before Lord Archbishop at some location within his province, I was afraid to go to him.[54] In fact, I heard that he said in his judgment, **In a short while you will not see me any longer, and once again in a short while you will see me** (John 16:16). I tell you that if a certain doctor goes to Father Pope or the Archbishop he could easily prepare a place of ambushes for me, even one of murder.[55] For many have been instructed, God knows how and by whom, that it would be a work of charity to kill me, whether by burning, or cutting me down, or some other manner of putting me to death. For those arguments which the doctor has already made (375) are commonly rolled around in the mouths of many episcopal clerics who lure the ignorant into unfaithfulness, perverting however many people they can along with themselves, etc.

(*De ver.* I,xv): The Authority of Holy Scripture over All Human Writings

(375) Finally, with regard to the authority of Scripture, in light of what has been said, one clearly reckons that those who falsify Holy Scripture according to some perverse sense not

only detract from its authority, but to the extent that this is possible, diminish and topple its authority, no matter how great a catholic sense they are skilled enough to apply to it. Apart from their dialectical arguments, our adversaries have no evidence for their claim that any writing whatsoever could be counted as Holy Scripture. Therefore a proof derived from the authority of that writing, just as one from Holy Scripture, is nothing but a dialectical proof; for the conclusion is no more certain than its antecedent. Likewise, no conclusion is authenticated by Holy Scripture, except to the extent that it is cited according to the sense of the author. But it is only believed in dialectical fashion by those who hold the opinion that that sense which is signified is in fact the sense of the author. Accordingly, a proof derived from the authority of Scripture is only a dialectical argument for them. Indeed, a conclusion is no better known because it follows from the sense of Scripture than it is known that the given sense is the sense of Scripture, since it is only known in a dialectical manner. Again, since **faith comes through hearing** according to Rom. 10:17, it appears that one is more cognizant of the fact that the master who offers instruction is true, than that the faith which he teaches is true. But the truth of the teacher is comprehended only dialectically, and so then is the truth of faith. If every cause possesses common signification to a greater extent than its effect, then it appears that the faith granted the teacher is greater than the faith granted to his student. (376) But that faith is still only dialectical or probable, since according to the Apostle in 2 Cor. 11:14, **Sometimes the devil transfigures himself into an angel of light**. And so this also applies to the faith elicited from Scripture. But because the moderns think that those sorts of evidence militate equally against everyone, so then they must also militate against those who reject Holy Scripture based upon the strictly literal sense (*de virtute sermonis*). For this reason we must note that although, according to Boethius in Book 3 of the *Topics*, there are any number of proofs upon which an argument can be based,[56] it is sufficient to discuss three at the present time. One is the proof pertaining to form, another pertaining to matter, and yet another pertaining to both. With respect to form there are dialectical proofs, as the modes of syllogism in any of the three figures, just as in Aristotle's *Prior Analytics*.[57] Now *emptimematica* are inductions and examples, and are thus virtually syllogisms. So it is that there are many other ways of arguing in Scripture, which are the very best, even if a special form, although they might seem strange to the uneducated.

In order to rectify those formal proofs, however, it is necessary to exclude thirteen fallacies which Aristotle speaks of in his *Sophistical Refutations*.[58] Having rectified human knowledge in matters pertaining to syllogistic form and fallacies through Holy Scripture, its ultimate responsibility is directly accomplished.

(377) The material element of a proof can vary in three ways, as one proof is derived from the faith of Scripture, another found through rational inquiry, and yet another comes from the testimony of a creature. The proof derived from the faith of Scripture, however, remains the most suitable and convincing possibility, since it is only at that time when the First Master will deign to descend and induce a consensus. This is why it is essential that we comprehend that principal proof in every discipline, as clarified above in Chapter Eight of this treatise. The second proof, found through rational inquiry, is deficient with respect to its possibility in the material element, since a complex universal is experimental whenever it is believed together with an error. This is the case with the essences and passions of things which we discern apart from the authority of Holy Scripture. Proof derived from the testimony of a creature, however, has a number of levels, such as when the inanimate objects of sense experience bear witness, or any

time that human beings do so through the spoken word. And within this category there are any number of levels, according to which the witnesses by faith are the more efficacious. That is evident whenever a syllogism errs neither in matter nor in form, but happens to argue by participating in both in accordance with a manifold variety.

In light of what has been said, any Christian will come to the conclusion that the proof derived from the authority of Holy Scripture, which is proof from faith, is the most fitting possibility of all. It is evident from the faith of Scripture, which one must believe, that a person can acquire nothing superior, nor more certain or efficacious. Indeed, since the entirety of Holy Scripture is the word of the Lord, no testimony could possibly be better, more certain, or more efficacious. For if God, who cannot lie, has spoken something in his own Scripture, which is itself the mirror of his will, then it is true. (378) It is not necessary for the Catholic to grapple over the demonstration of the antecedent, since for him that is Holy Scripture, just as it should be by faith, and by the very fact that the Master is present to teach him the antecedent and awaken him to the assumption. Nor is it necessary to grapple over a further demonstration. As I said above, it is absolutely essential that every person be a theologian, having first set his own affections in proper order. For then the Truth will deign to descend and instruct him in manner free from all deception. Therefore, just as all rivers flow to the sea, so all created authority depends upon the authority of the First Master. Now if asked on what basis such a syllogistic form holds, on what basis is that the greatest particular truth, or from which source follows this sense or that sign, or this testimony and that human reason, it is because he tells me this, and thus it is true. This is said with respect to all of these things, which are true and should thus be believed, precisely because God speaks them. Indeed, since God speaks every truth, clearly his speech is the First Cause of any and all extrinsic truth. And so it seems to me that all other evidence which does not lead back to this principle is deceptive. Therefore, it is called dialectical evidence with respect to the conclusion, when that by which it stands is simultaneously a deception concerning the same thing; and they are such on a multiple level. Evidence or reason is surely infallible with respect to the conclusion when it is simultaneously incompatible with deception, suddenly and at the proper time concerning the same thing, as is the case with that pure vision which the saints in heaven have found in the Word.

These arguments make it clear, therefore, how catholic judgment differs from the judgment of those who falsify Holy Scripture. With regard to the first, it is evident that something untrue is being assumed of devout theologians, since every devout theologian who understands Holy Scripture renders it due reverence and does not understand it in some perverse way according to an erroneous sense. (379) Accordingly, he possesses an evidence which is greater than dialectic, since it is based upon the faith of Holy Scripture. Indeed, he would be willing to die on behalf of that certitude, just as one would in the cause of true martyrdom. Although a witness may provide evidence that the given sense is the sense of Scripture, it is still accidental and secondary, since the sense of Scripture possesses, by its very nature, a prior evidence by faith. I made this clear in Chapter Eight when speaking of the five ways to arrive at the sense of Scripture. Whereupon, the accidental cause commonly concurs with the prior cause to create an effect which is more excellent than that accidental cause. Such is the case with natural heat, informed virtue, movement, and the many other things which make a human being more perfect over time, since it is by definition in keeping with the body and soul to receive such forms. Now in human art the instrument makes something more perfect than itself, while in the case of the virtues, they are more perfect than their effects.

Even sensitive knowledge helps to render lasting intellective knowledge more perfect. But this is accomplished by means of the First Intellect which bestows the ultimate perfection, just as a carpenter's axe fashions a cabinet in an accidental manner together with other causes. Hence, causes of this sort are only accidental and not causes in and of themselves. Rather, they are instruments accomplishing what they do by virtue of the agent to whom they belong. They accidentally produce an effect which is more perfect than themselves. And thus a conclusion is no more certain than its inherent antecedent.

With respect to the second argument it is clear that the minor premise is deficient, insofar as the person who possesses the fifth necessity needed to comprehend the sense of Scripture possesses more than dialectical evidence, since he comprehends that sense through the enlightenment of the First Truth. This evidence hastens with the others as the supporting foundation which will be completed in heaven. Others assist it, however, even though they might be fallacies. This is why I posit that were Peter believed to be a luxuriant man (380) because he was decked out in finery, or perhaps owing to some other natural sign, it is possible that the true faith is begotten, though it is appropriate that one would first introduce the truth based upon the evidence of Scripture before resorting to dialectical evidence. And so it happens that those who neglect the evidence of Holy Scripture are so often deluded. It seems to me that this is the manner in which physicists and physicians proceed in their practices, and all the more so astrologers. Judges, however, rarely draw upon dialectical or probable evidence when deciding cases of human law. Yet the theologian has something which infinitely surpasses these sorts of evidence, since it is by internal inspiration that the Lord speaks his meaning. When opposing those people who deny that this is a statement of the Lord the loftier fellow finds no pleasure in quarreling, since he comprehends this based upon the first evidence, while the other inferior fellow teaches, *a posteriori* according to the aforementioned five-fold rule, that Holy Scripture, which is the Catholic faith, retains that sense. This evidence exceeds all the dialectical evidence which some philosopher or people discern through the intellect or the senses, except perhaps whenever, together with a theologian, they comprehend its own sense through that holy science. Thus in order to prevent some pseudo-disciples from pretending that they have received their understanding directly from God, God established a common Scripture which is perceptible to the senses, by means of which the catholic sense should be comprehended. For God could never abandon his people, but instead will enlighten them through that illumination conferred by sanctity of life and a conformity of one's own sense to that of the holy doctors, in keeping with that age when the Church drank from the font of wisdom. And if that illumination is to endure in Mother Church it is the duty of the theologian to remain within its boundaries. Thus a theologian is not permitted to devise strange ideas which extend beyond the faith of catholic Scripture. Providing that he will abide by this he will never be suspected of heresy. Yet if one asks why the adversary of Scripture cannot speak in conformity with these statements, I say that he is every bit as capable of sanctifying Scripture as he is of corrupting it, if only he so wills. (381) Now it is said in Ps. 18 (Ps. 19:7), **The immaculate law of the Lord refreshes souls**, but Scripture alleged by the adversary is by definition a corrupted falsehood, and for this reason is not sacred.

[. . .] (385) Now if we do not comprehend the words of Christ in their own form, nor the words of the holy doctors, which are an authority for us, how can we hope to understand our own words in their form? Likewise, we must flee from every opinion which induces schism and dissension from the faith of Christ, inasmuch as it is erroneous. But an aforementioned opinion is of this sort, therefore, etc. The minor premise is evident from the effect which we observe after the logic of Scripture has been rejected, while the postillators remain divided in their efforts to explicate Scripture according to contrary senses which vary in their logic. And because observation of Christ's law among the laity follows upon the understanding of the doctors who explicate the sense of Scripture, (386) it is clearly necessary that the exposition of the senses agrees with those which the holy doctors had harmoniously elicited. Otherwise, it would be permissible to twist the sense of Scripture to suit the wishes of the sinner, something which occurs quite frequently these days. I ask you, what could produce a greater deluge of distrust in the words of the Lord than saying that his words are impossible, as are the words of the holy doctors in their exposition of this very Scripture, while my words, though contrary to theirs, are unimpeachably true, having been drawn from a correct logic? As I said above, these are surely not the words of an expositor, but of a destroyer, not the words of a postillator, but those of one who does away with authority. For every expositor explains and defends what he is explicating; he does not deny it. Rather, he submits it as an abridged theorem upon which he might distill the confirmed sense based upon this firm foundation. Exposition is certainly not Holy Scripture though, but rather her herald or handmaid. She does not refute her Lady, but borrows her Lady's very own words, so that she might then reverently explain and disclose her intentions. Again, certain decretal letters, not to mention charters and documents, are composed in such a way that makes it unlawful to add or subtract anything, or even gloss them, except perhaps when confirming the tenor of the words and their sense according to their intended literal sense (*de virtute sermonis*). Yet the logic of Scripture, which is the form of Christ's words, is more perfectly composed, and more duly authorized, since it is granted in its own form, and is, therefore, the rule which should be more fittingly observed. This is clearly assumed from that decretal in *The Sixth Book of Decretals*, "*Exiit, qui seminat*,"[59] where Nicholas III excommunicated those who would distort or corrupt his meaning according to a gloss which deviates from the literal sense (*a litera*). (387) Now it is plainly unlawful to subtract any words from these bulls, charters and instruments. And so the minor argument is clarified by faith, through which we should believe that the Holy Spirit gave us the law of Scripture in the form which he wanted the Church to observe, one whose authority surpasses every created authority, since the efficacy of its meaning is more useful, and the form of its words more venerable, than any foreign meaning or locution.

Once more, as I said above, every Catholic theologian is obligated to study Scripture's manner of speaking in order that he would correctly grasp its sense. But he will not be able to do this unless he becomes acquainted with its logic in order that he might then utilize it, and consequently introduce nothing else which would contradict it. Therefore, it is the duty of every theologian to protect the logic of Holy Scripture from all opposition. Since every logic which asserts that Holy Scripture is heretical or blasphemous is hostile to it, it seems only right that the devout theologian would detest all logic of this sort. Indeed, a logic which opposes the logic of Scripture, teaching that Holy Scripture is so depraved, must be hostile to Scripture. Nor can one pretend that the logic of Scripture is compatible with that logic used by the modern doctors to falsify Scripture, when in fact they are completely at odds with one another.

[. . .] (390) Furthermore, one may debate whether there are levels of authority within the Scriptures. First of all, it seems fitting that every truth would be of equal authority with any other. Now every truth, inasmuch as it is of this sort, is the word of the Lord. And every word of the Lord is of equal authority with any other, because it is essentially the highest authority, as well as the fact that it proceeds from the same author. Therefore, every truth is of equal truth with any other. Again, if truth were to acquire a level of authority from an immediate author, then three falsehoods seem to follow. First, every word of Christ would be of infinitely greater authority than the word of another author of Scripture. Second, it seems that those seven authors of the New Testament, namely Peter, John, James, Matthew, Jude, Mark, and Luke, have written Scriptures of disparate authority and holiness, insofar as they themselves were men of disparate authority and holiness. But that seems inappropriate, since they had spoken with one voice, as is said in Acts 3:11–26. Once again, by this line of thinking it would seem that decretal letters are of equal authority with a letter of St. Peter, thereby surpassing decrees and letters of Paul, and those of the other saints. While, on the other hand, if holiness of life or truth of judgment are the criteria, then it is likely that the writings of the Four Holy Doctors,[60] together with other holy postillators on the Scriptures, would hold greater authority than the decretal letters written by some of the popes or cardinals.

(391) In this matter one must first suppose that authority is that which makes someone formally an author. Second, it is necessary to distinguish in what manner someone is an author in and of himself, as is the case with God alone; and someone else is an author in a participatory and derivative manner, which is the case with human beings to whom God imparts his own power for the benefit of Church. Now those authorities are infinitely distant from one another and exceedingly equivocal. And it is for this reason that one may call the professor of catholic Scripture a secondary power, rather than an authority, since his office is a vicarious one designed for promulgating the sense of the Lord. Third, it is necessary to point out that, insofar as the aforesaid first mode of authority is identical

with the author, so the aforesaid second mode of authority maintains an accidental relationship to the principle, as that from which it proceeds and the end for whose sake it exists. Clearly then, just as truth can be understood in a two-fold manner, so the authority of truth can also be understood in a two-fold manner. In fact, truth can be understood just as one understands the relationship between existent things and their principal being. In this way every truth is God, just as every existent thing is God, or it can be understood with respect to its secondary being, which is existence within a genus. And thus there are many genera of truths.

In this vein, one can understand participatory authority, either in regard to the principle by which it subsists, or with regard to the end for which it has been ordained, or still again with regard to both. By the second manner, prelates standing above their subjects possess greater authority than them, just as one superior in dignity or nature is of greater authority than his subordinate before God.

Based upon these premises, it is possible to establish a four-fold conclusion. First, just as the Holy Trinity possesses in himself his own supreme and pure authority, so every truth spoken outwardly is of equal authority with any other, according to a two-fold rationale. (392) If, in matters of truth, one gives heed to the authority of the one who is speaking, and since God speaks all truths of this sort, who would doubt that every truth is rendered equal in authority with any other? Likewise, as far as equation with the principal intellect is concerned, the same follows, since adequation, like equality, is not susceptible to being either greater or lesser. Truth, therefore, since it is the definitive adequation of a thing with the divine intellect, is not susceptible to being greater or lesser with respect to the principle of truth. On this basis it is correspondingly evident that the entire Scripture is of equal authority according to every single one of its parts. Clearly then, insofar as the entirety of Holy Scripture is the unique word of God, and our authors are only God's scribes or heralds charged with the duty of inscribing his law he has dictated to them, so when compared to God they are only authors in an equivocal sense. And the first reason is in keeping with that judgment.

Now for the second conclusion: although every caused truth is of equal authority with every other with regard to a two-fold rationale, nevertheless, truths which are formally and subjectively distinct are of proportionally disparate authority, since some are more necessary or are prior. The first part is clarified insofar as every truth, just as every existent thing, is God himself, according to the principal reason of truth, as Augustine says in his book *On Truth*.[61] And I made clear in my *On Ideas* that every creature according to its intelligible being is God himself, in keeping with that passage in John 1:1–2, **That which was made, in him was life**.[62] Now the second part is evident from the fact that the accidental and particular authority of a thing is understood to belong to the goodness and priority of God. It is by this manner of speaking that politicians say the superior ecclesiastical dignitary is of greater authority than his vicar, and the father or elder is of greater authority than his son. And so the authority of the priesthood following the order of Melchizedek has its origins in the law of nature.

[. . .] (394) By the third conclusion, the entirety of Holy Scripture, with respect to the authority of the head of the Church, is of infinitely greater authority than any foreign writing with respect to the authentication of its own personal and private author. Therefore, it is clear that on account of his infinite perception, Christ surpasses every one of his brothers. Yet what applies from author to author also applies from authority to authority, and thus the conclusion.

[. . .] (395) The fourth conclusion concerns the proximate creator or author. Any part of Holy Scripture is of infinitely greater authority than any decretal letter. And this is clarified in the following manner: every decretal letter is the creation of some pope, the Vicar of Christ together with his subordinates. Every part of Holy Scripture, however, is immediately and proximately authorized by God; and thus the conclusion. I establish the major premise based upon the definition of the designation, since all of the decretals are human traditions invented following the Donation to the Church for the sake of correcting the errors which might arise in the Church. But this is not the case with any part of Holy Scripture. For it is appropriate that we suppose by the faith of Scripture that the word of God formulated every one of its sciences and handed them down immediately to his scribes, who would never have added any of their own inventions. This is why the prophets so frequently say, **Thus says the Lord**. (396) And when the Apostle is addressing those seeking evidence as to whether the Lord says these things, in 2 Cor. 13:3, he says, **You seek his proof; who is speaking in me but Christ?** By faith we must believe in the entirety of Scripture, since every part of it is linked together as I made clear in Chapters Nine and Ten. In this respect, not only do we have the testimony of Scripture and the operation of the Church, but all the faithful harmoniously attest to this viewpoint. That would certainly be irrational, insofar as Christ ought to have given the law of Scripture to his Church, unless he himself had dictated it within the hearts of the humble scribes, stirring them to follow that form of writing and description which he had chosen. Yet there is no reason for us to believe that this is the case with the other apostles or the Vicars of Peter. But if they collected one meaning of Scripture which had previously been hidden, which would be of equal authority with Holy Scripture with respect to God, according to the first and second conclusion, it is still impossible for it to attain an equal authority with respect to its proximate creator. For if this person or that Vicar of Peter asserts something, thereby making it true, that would mean he would undoubtedly be Christ himself. But to the extent that any secondary author of Holy Scripture is so moved by God to promulgate something in such a way it is supremely authentic with respect to God. Through that distinction one can demolish those laws which seem to imply that all the decretal letters are of equal authority with the gospel. (397) This would be true if they explicated Holy Scripture. Yet this is not so because any Christian says this, but instead because God says this. In fact, the statements of the authors of Holy Scripture are not authentic because they spoke them, but only insofar as God instructed them to speak in this way. This is what the Apostle says in Gal. 1:8 when safeguarding the authority of Christ, **Even if we or an angel from heaven proclaimed another gospel to you other than the one which we have proclaimed, let him be accursed**. And then he adds the reason for this: **I make it known to you, brothers and sisters, that the gospel which was proclaimed by me is not in accordance with human beings. I did not receive it from human beings, nor was I taught it, but I received it through a revelation of Jesus Christ** (Gal. 1:11–12). (398) Nor was it necessary for Paul to seek further evidence that it was so. Just as it is unnecessary for the one who seeks further evidence for what he sees, since the certitude of faith is infused simultaneously with the act of seeing. Therefore, he says in 2 Cor. 12:2, **I know such a man who was taken up into the third heaven**. In order to avoid any equivocation with regard to the creator or author of Scripture, I call the lowest author the proximate author, as he is any faithful person to whom God first gave the power to reveal the truth of Scripture to the Church following the time of Christ. And in this way Scripture has a three-fold author, namely God, the humanity of Christ, and their proximate scribe. God is the immediate author given his requisite priority in the order of ascent, but the Vicar of Christ is the immediate author inasmuch as he is the requisite instrument of authentication in the order of descent. Surely the scribe who receives no revelation is not the author, nor the stationer or any other possessor or creator of signs.

[. . .] (402) Now the apostles were inspired by the Holy Spirit, and thus the meaning which they speak is the word of the Lord. And they proclaimed its great authority for that very reason, and not because it was their own word. How then could a priest of Christ or Vicar of Peter today claim greater authority than even St. Peter dared to assume for himself? And with regard to the authority to govern, clearly what I have said does not diminish the aforementioned papal authority, inasmuch as many holy Vicars of St. Peter living between the time of Peter and the first creator of decretals surely considered the laws of Christ to be quite sufficient for governing the Church. (403) For if these laws were being fully carried out as they should be, the Church would find herself in far better condition than she is today, now that human traditions are increasingly multiplied and so diligently implemented. Nevertheless, I do not deny, but in fact concede, that it is lawful for bishops and Vicars of Christ to formulate statutes designed to help the Church. And whenever they do institute such statutes they ought to be accepted, unless they contradict other statutes or prove contrary to Holy Scripture. But I do think that it is clearly blasphemous to imagine that statutes of this sort, on the grounds that they are issued by the pope, might then claim equal authority with the gospel.

[. . .] (404) Fifth, some argue that not only the letters of Lord Pope, but even the letters of many simple priests should be given as much credence as Holy Scripture. For every word, insofar as it is the word of God, is of equal authority with any other. But many Christians are certain that their own statements are the word of God, and for this reason they should be certain that their own statements are of equal authority with any passage of Scripture. The minor premise is drawn from the remarks made in the previous chapter, namely that every person should be certain, and in reality many are certain that they possess the Holy Spirit who performs all their works, and speaks through them in whatever they might say even if they are not conscious of this as it happens. Therefore, their own statement ought to be of equal authority with any statement found in Scripture. With regard to that objection, I say first, as I said above, (405) that every person should fully believe that he possesses the Holy Spirit, because he should have the habit of charity which excludes every sin, even the venial. Second, I say that it is impossible for a faithful person or an infidel to speak the truth unless it is found in Holy Scripture. This is made clear by Augustine when he says at the end of Book 2 of *On Christian Doctrine* that every truth is contained within Scripture.[63] Thus when any sort of truth is spoken, either by a good person or an evil one, it should be believed to this extent, whether implicitly or explicitly, only inasmuch as it pertains to the authority of the Principal Speaker. Third, on this basis it is clear that although some possess grace, even unknowingly, by means of which they truly believe that their own statement is of equal authority with Holy Scripture, and is even Scripture itself, they should still not authenticate it as if their statement were their very own, nor attempt to authorize something new as if that were of equal authority with Holy Scripture. God bestowed his own law completely through the scribes of the books of both testaments, and he commanded that nothing foreign to be added to it, and nothing be removed from it. How then can a person presume to place his own statements on a par with those bearing the authority of Holy Scripture? Lest he seem to be doing just that, he ought to adduce his statements from Scripture. Hence, those who compose so many decrees and decretal letters should never presume that they are of equal authority with the words of the Lord, inasmuch as they are his own, since this would be to declare blasphemously that they themselves are God. And I believe that Christ prophesied of just this sort of presumption in Matt. 24:5 when he said, **Many will come in my name saying that I am the Christ**. (406) Indeed, everyone who says that his own statements are of equal authority with Holy Scripture seems to be saying implicitly, "I am the Christ." Fourth, I say that the Church should not believe that any Vicars of Peter possess the Holy Spirit for the sake of establishing new canons, which exceed the limits of Holy Scripture, claiming then that they are of equal authority with it. Just as nobody's neighbor should believe that his brother possesses charity and the guidance of the Spirit, unless this can be proven either by his works, or through a special revelation.

[. . .] (407) Fifth, I say that it is impossible to accept the word or statement of a man as he utters his own aggregate formed from a sign and his own meaning, since any statement or deed of a Christian would then be of equal authority with Holy Scripture. It is clear, therefore, that nobody after Christ can achieve equality of authority with him. As such, it is unfitting to place any of the decretal letters on a par with the gospel or the statements of the holy doctors. For, by the same rationale, this could be believed of any papal bulls, which is itself pointless to imagine, since the Church has proven herself deceptive, mistaken, and ignorant, not only in her judicial proceedings, but in other private points concerning the state of the Church, evinced in matters concerning the celebration of Easter, the sacrament of the Eucharist, and many other essential difficulties which remain unresolved. Hence, a succeeding letter of abrogation corrects an earlier mistake. And thus there is a procession of contradictory bulls, as the following one revokes in effect the earlier one, apart from the fact someone previously rendered qualified for clerical office meanwhile is found unfit, not only during a change of popes, but during time of the same pope. Now it is clear that nobody is qualified to hold clerical office unless he is qualified in the eyes of

God. Yet bulls seem to testify that a given cleric is qualified for a given office, even though he is unqualified in the eyes of God. How then could such a bull be of equal authority with Scripture, when in many cases it must be conceded that the pope dishonestly qualifies those whom God disqualifies. On the other hand, in a case now at issue Lord Gregory XI qualified many through bulls which were not effectively carried out, (408) while Lord Urban VI qualifies new people, unknowingly passing over those who are more qualified, since their qualification rested upon the testimony of an earlier pope, who through a growth in merit have by disqualification, continuously and greedily increased the number of bulls that they might then be promoted today, although previously bulls have continuously declared them less qualified.

To say, therefore, that all papal bulls are of equal authority or certainty of truth with Holy Scripture would be blasphemously attributing to the pope the claim of being Christ. Nor have I heard that the popes or their high-ranking experts attempt this. Rather, it is the covetous subjects who, given their hatred of the clergy, soothe their heads with the oil of flattery.

And this viewpoint is proven in many chapters in Distinction 9 of the *Decretum*,[64] and quite often elsewhere. Nor can the new ordinances and opinions of the doctors establish the opposite.

Notes

1. Rabbinic tradition held that Manasseh, king of Judah, had the prophet Isaiah sawed in half. Cf. Heb. 11:37.

2. *Petrus dictus catholicus*. The name "Peter" simply refers to a hypothetical person.

3. *De Sermone Domini in Monte Libros Duos* I.11.32, ed. Almut Mutzenbecher, Corpus Christianorum, Series Latina 35 (Turnhout, 1967), pp. 33–35.

4. *De cognitione verae vitae* XLVII, PL 40:1030–32.

5. *De Trinitate*, XV.12.22, ed. W. J. Mountain, Corpus Christianorum, Series Latina 50a (Turnhout, 1968), p. 493. These are not Augustine's words.

6. Hugh of St. Victor, *Eruditionis Didascalicae Libri Septem* VI.10, PL 176:807c–08c.

7. *De Doctrina Christiana* II.14.21, ed. Josef Martin, Corpus Christianorum, Series Latina 32 (Turnhout, 1962), pp. 46–47. These are not Augustine's exact words.

8. See *De Doc. Chr.* IV.5.7–8, CCSL 32:120–21. These are not Augustine's words.

9. *Enarrationes in Psalmos* CXL.7, ed. Eligius Dekkers and John Fraipont, Corpus Christianorum, Series Latina 40 (Turnhout, 1956), p. 2030.

10. Actually Chapter 7. See PL 34:1173–76. These are not Augustine's words.

11. *Epist.* LII, PL 22:533.

12. *Epist.* CXXX, PL 22:1124.

13. *De Doc. Chr.* III.16.24, CCSL 32:91–92.

14. Ibid.

15. *De Doc. Chr.* III.27.38, CCSL 32:99–100.

16. Note that Wyclif does not explicitly name a fourth aspect.

17. See *De Magistro* XIV.46, ed. W. M. Green, Corpus Christianorum, Series Latina 29 (Turnhout, 1970), pp. 202–03.

18. *Confessiones* VII.9.13, ed. Luc Verheijen, Corpus Christianorum, Series Latina 27 (Turnhout, 1981), p. 101.

19. Robert Grosseteste, *Commentarius in Posterium Analyticorum libros* I.1, ed. Pietro Rossi (Florence, 1981), p. 94.

20. *De Doc. Chr.* III.37.56, CCSL 32:116.

21. The active intellect impresses species upon the possible intellect.

22. *Moralium*, PL 75:517b–d.

23. See Jerome's prologue to the Book of Daniel in *Biblia Sacra Vulgata*, ed. Bonifatius Fischer, Jean Gribomont, H. F. D. Sparks et al. (Stuttgart, 1983), pp. 1341–42.

24. *Epist.* LXXXII, ed. Alois Goldbacher, Corpus Scriptorium Ecclesiasticorum Latinorum 34.2 (Vienna, 1898), pp. 351–87. This is the famous debate between Augustine and Jerome over Paul's confrontation of Peter recounted in Gal. 2:11–21.

25. See instead: *Epist.* CXLIX.9, ed. Alois Goldbacher, Corpus Scriptorum Ecclesiasticorum Latinorum 44 (Vienna, 1904), p. 356.

26. This citation was not found.

27. See Jerome's preface to the Pentateuch in *Biblia Sacra Vulgata*, pp. 546–47.

28. See Jerome's preface to the Pentateuch in ibid., pp. 3–4.

29. *De Civitate Dei* XVIII.38, ed. Bernardus Dombart and Alfonsus Kalb, Corpus Christianorum, Series Latina 48 (Turnhout, 1955), pp. 633–34.

30. *Conf.* VII.9.13, CCSL 27:101.

31. See Jerome's prologue to 1 Kings (1 Samuel) in *Biblia Sacra Vulgata*, pp. 364–66.

32. This is the classic medieval formula: *fides caritate formata*. Faith must be perfected through works of love performed for God and neighbor. While this system of merit in no way impinges upon a doctrine of salvation by grace, it is far removed from the Protestant doctrine of "justification by faith alone."

33. *De Trinitate*, IV.11.14, CCSL 50a:179. Not Augustine's words, though the sense is the same. See also IV.10.3, 178–79.

34.This is a textual variant which is not found in the most reliable New Testament MSS.

35. *De Trinitate*, IV.6.10, CCSL 50a:175.

36. Buddensieg cites: Valerius Maximus, *Factorum et Dictorum Memorabilium libri IX* Book 9 (Berlin, 1854), p. 669.

37. *In Ps.* CXLVIIII, CCSL 40:2187.

38. The priest represents Christ at the altar during the Mass. Note that Wyclif upholds the objective validity of the sacraments here, such that

they are not tainted by the priest's own unrighteousness if properly administered.

39. See actually *De Libero Arbitrio* III.16.45–46, ed. W. M. Green, Corpus Christianorum, Series Latina 29 (Turnhout, 1970), pp. 302–03.

40. See *De Mendacio* III.3–4, ed. Joseph Zycha, Corpus Scriptorum Ecclesiasticorum Latinorum 41 (Vienna, 1900), pp. 414–16. These are not Augustine's words.

41. Book III, D. 11, *Sententiae in IV Libris Distinctae*, vol. 2, 3rd ed., Spicilegium Bonaventurianum V (Rome, 1981), pp. 77–80. *Magister Sententiarum* is Peter Lombard (1095–1160) who produced his *Sententiae* ca. 1155.

42. Book I, D. 19, *Sententiae in IV Libris Distinctae*, vol. 1, 3rd ed., Spicilegium Bonaventurianum IV (Rome, 1971), p. 163. This is actually Ambrosiaster's comment on 2 Cor. 5:19. Cf. *In Epistulas Ad Corinthios*, ed. H. I. Vogels, Corpus Scriptorum Ecclesiasticorum Latinorum 81.2 (Vienna, 1966), p. 237.

43. This is Wyclif's own *Tractatus de Benedicta Incarnacione* VI, ed. Edward Harris (1886; repr. New York, 1966), pp. 85–105.

44. See *Enchiridion* XXXV–XL, PL 40:249–52.

45. *Conf.* VII.19.25, CCSL 27:109.

46. Book I, D. 23, C. 6, *Sententiae in IV Libris Distinctae*, vol. 1, p. 186.

47. *Retractiones* I.4.3, ed. Almut Mutzenbecher, Corpus Christianorum, Series Latina 57 (Turnhout, 1984), p. 14.

48.The "Good Samaritan" parable. Thus Christ is equated with this Samaritan.

49. *De sermone Domini in Monte* II.20.68, ed. Almut Mutzenbecher, Corpus Christianorum, Series Latina 35 (Turnhout, 1967), p. 164.

50. Decr. Greg. IX, L. 1, c. 10, t. 9 in *Corpus Iuris Canonici*, ed. Emil Friedberg, vol. 2 (Leipzig, 1879), pp. 107–08.

51. Perhaps a reference to Bernard of Clairvaux's *De Gradibus Humilitatis*, PL 182:943–46.

52. Decr. Greg. IX, L. 1, c. 10, t. 9, in Friedberg, *Corpus* 2:109.

53. Decr. Greg. IX, L. 5, c. 3, t. 41, in Friedberg, *Corpus* 2:927.

54. Wyclif was summoned to appear before Archbishop Sudbury at Lambeth Palace in March, 1378. Royal intervention forestalled any punitive action being taken against Wyclif. Note that Sudbury was murdered during the Peasants' Revolt of 1381 and replaced by Courtenay.

55. This doctor was likely William Barton, later university chancellor.

56. *Commentaria in Topica Ciceronis* III, PL 64:1083–1108.

57. See *Prior Analytics* 45a–46a.

58. See *Sophistical Refutations*, which runs 164a–184b.

59. Decr. Greg. IX, L. 5, c. 3, t. 12, in Friedberg, *Corpus* 2:1120–21. This is Pope Nicholas III's famous 1279 decretal which affirmed the life of apostolic poverty adopted by the Franciscan Order.

60. Augustine, Ambrose, Jerome, and Gregory.

61. This may in fact be Anselm. See his *De veritate* X in *Opera Omnia*, ed. F. S. Schmitt, vol. 1 (Edinburgh, 1946), p. 190.

62. Wyclif's own *De Ydeis* (ca. 1368, unpublished). See also Williel R. Thomson, *The Latin Writings of John Wyclyf* (Toronto, 1983), pp. 32–34.

63. *De Doc. Chr.* II.42.63, CCSL 32:76.

64. Dec. I, D. 9, c. 1–11, in Friedberg, *Corpus* 1:16–18. In these chapters the absolute superiority of Scripture over episcopal letters is maintained.

On the Truth of Holy Scripture

Part Three: The Divine Origin of Scripture

(*De ver.* II,xvi): The Nature of Lies, Deceptions, and Falsehoods

(1) I raise a third principal argument against the adversaries of Scripture through a deduction which leads to a major impropriety, namely that Christ, our God, the author of Scripture, was the most false, deceitful, and deceptive person of all. Now if a person were to utter or assert a falsehood by means of a proposition, then he himself is false. Yet Christ uttered and asserted the greatest falsehoods by means of a proposition; therefore, he was supremely false. The assumption is evident, inasmuch as it is according to this sense that a person is said to be a deceptive speaker, or false in his words. (2) Otherwise, it could be said that nobody is false, although his own statements are supremely false. The minor premise of this argument is made clear by that passage in John 10:7–11, **I am the good shepherd and the door**, and through that passage in Apocalypse 1 (Rev. 1:8), **I am the alpha and the omega, the beginning and the end**, and also through that passage in John 15:1, **I am the true vine, and my Father is the vine grower**, together with any number of similar passages in which Scripture bears witness to what Christ said and asserted. And yet the adversary says all those things are supremely false. For he asserted those propositions which were supremely false, because he spoke falsehoods assertively, by means of a proposition, to people who would wrongly understand them. And so

by the same rationale, he spoke lies. For in other instances he certainly said things which he discerned to be false, insofar as he understood by his own statements everything which the other person understood. That deduction seems more plausibly directed against the Profound Doctor's concession that God approvingly and causally wills sins.[1] Now, by that same rationale, he would approve of his own statements being lies, and of the fact that he would be deceiving sinners. It appears to follow, therefore, that Christ was the greatest liar of all. For he spoke the greatest falsehoods, opposing his very own discernment, when he knew those things were impossible. And so he intended to deceive by means of those falsehoods. Now according to Augustine in his book, *Against Lying*, a lie is itself, "a false assertion intended to deceive."[2] Whenever a person asserts something which is false according to the sense which he ordains, then it is a false assertion. Yet Christ asserted those false statements. For inasmuch as he ordains every created thing, and since the elicited sense is itself a created thing, it would seem that he ordained that sense. Likewise, a person must be refuted on account of his own false teaching or assertion, (3) but nobody's teaching can have been more false than Christ's teaching, because it contradicted itself, as evinced by these sayings: **My teaching is not mine**, in John 7:16; and **Whoever believes in me does not believe in me**, in John 12:44; and **The Father is greater than me**, in John 14:28; along with ones similar to these.

In light of these comments it follows that there are many reasons why Christ must be refuted. Indeed, if we thus refute Aristotle and the other infidel philosophers or poets in these instances where they contradict the Christian faith, we are not denying that they exist, nor are we denying the fact they have uttered many catholic truths. But inasmuch as they have spoken a falsehood in some matter, we refute them on those grounds. And thus we concede simply that they must be refuted. Otherwise, Peter would not have been denying Christ to the priests, though the doctors say he did, based upon the testimony of Scripture in Luke 22:34. Nor is it necessary for the purposes of denying people, either that the people denied would assert a falsehood, which is denied by its very nature, or that the person who is doing the denying would believe that they were false.

Likewise, to the extent that a law belonging to any lawgiver should be loved, hated, or condemned, so it must have a proportionate effect on that lawgiver. But since the law of Christ is the most wicked and accursed, because it is supremely deceptive, beguiling and blasphemous, it is then the most contemptible and detestable. Therefore, the Christian would chiefly hate and condemn the aforementioned lawgiver.

I have illustrated the major premise at other times from numerous passages of Scripture. Now it is said in John 14: 23–24, **If anyone loves me he will keep my word; whoever does not love me does not keep my words**. Certainly, the rights and privileges of a king are founded upon his laws. Thus to condemn the law of any king would be to condemn his rights and privileges, indeed even to condemn the king himself. (4) This is why St. Gregory says, "anyone who loves the king, loves his law."[3] One does not honor the law, however, by polluting it with some evil sense which proves contrary to the sense of the emperor, for in doing so he would achieve just the opposite effect. It would appear, therefore, that by cursing the law of God, they are not only conceding that the same thing is simultaneously holy and accursed, though such states are thoroughly contrary, but also that the lawgiver who intended to bestow such a law is himself accursed. Now if the logician truly abhors the notion that the same proposition could be true and false simultaneously, the Christian must be all the more horrified at the thought that the law of his God could be simultaneously holy and accursed. But just as it is utterly impossible and not true, so then it would be utterly accursed and unholy. And if someone says that a part could be true at one time and false at another, as is the case with significations drawn from these obligations, then three things must be said in response. First, the entirety of Scripture is true. Second, every passage of Scripture is Holy Scripture because it pertains to God. And third, those who defile the purity of Holy Scripture must be rebuked in no uncertain terms, as I have proven extensively elsewhere. Whereupon, it seems that those who render the law of God heretical would have to say that it is an evil, not only bearing the baseness consisting of punishment, but of guilt as well. After all, the words of the heretic who wrongly understands Scripture are evil and culpable by reason of sin. But the Apostle says in Rom. 7:7, **Is the law evil? By no means!** For then our own God would be as supremely evil as the God of the Manichees, not only because human beings wrongly accept the occasion to sin from him, but because he has severely inflicted every sort of evil punishment. Now just as God should be praised for having bestowed a good law, (5) so he would have to be considered culpable if he were to confer a culpable law. I say that he should be praised for inflicting the evil of punishment, since he does not do so in an evil way, but rather in a manner which both delights him and the righteous. Thus it lacks culpability, inasmuch as he is justly inflicting evil of this sort. Hence, he is not evil by way of guilt or punishment. It is not the subject of punishment with respect to the divinity, nor is it punishment in the formal sense. But with respect to the humanity, which the curse did underlie, it was an evil to him, though he was still not evil, because he was neither culpable, nor was he punished for his own guilt. Therefore, it was evil for him that still did not render him evil. By the same rationale, neither his words, nor any of his actions, were evil, since neither punishment, nor culpability, nor the cause receive every predication of its own effect.

But I have been accused of having once said that Scripture is supremely false and, moreover, that the aforementioned arguments seem to contend indiscriminately against anyone at all. At least, they seem to include the difficulties of Scripture. Therefore, given the number of arguments, there are three difficulties which must be discussed. First, I admit that if I ever said that Holy Scripture is supremely false then this is very distressing to me, and I humbly revoke and retract that statement on the grounds that it is the most wrong sounding, heretical and blasphemous. Second, it is evident that the viewpoint which I am presently explaining is entirely opposed to the conclusions of the aforementioned arguments, since it states that every part of Holy Scripture is inseparably true. For the truth of the mind which is affected by sensible signs is the other part of that aggregate which constitutes Holy Scripture. Philosophers and theologians thus speak of an aggregate accidentally, and in fact Christ teaches this logic or metaphysic in John 8:44, when he says that, **The devil is a liar and the father of lies.** On the one hand, a liar is an aggregate derived from a good and true created nature, since he is a work of God. While, on the other hand, he is comprised of a fictitious falsehood elicited by a sinful nature. Because that aggregate is a detestable monstrosity, (6) on account of one of its parts, the devil is called the father of lies. For, by the freedom of his own perverted choice, that nature turns away from the first truth and procures the lie within himself. This is something Christ could not do, just as he could not sin.

A difficulty still pertaining to the first argument is whether Christ was capable of deceiving anyone. For having established this, it follows together with such truths that Christ would have had a deceitful or deceptive mind. One argues first in this way: it is just, since people are deceived as a penalty for sin, and all such justice is authorized and accomplished by God. Therefore, a fallacy or deception of this sort is accomplished by God. Christ speaks similarly to his disciples in Luke 8:10, **To you it has been given to know the mystery of the kingdom of God, to others, however, in parables, so that seeing they would not perceive, and hearing, they would not understand**. And Isa. 6:10 agrees with that: **Make blind the heart of this people**, etc. Otherwise it would surely be impertinent of God to inquire in Third Kings 22 (1 Kings 22:20), **Who will deceive Ahab?** And it follows later: **The Lord said, "Go forth and do just that."** Whereupon, the Apostle seems to affirm that meaning when he says in Rom. 1:22–32 that, **God handed the philosophers over to their own spurious sense, inasmuch as they knew God and still had not glorified God**. In light of this, it appears that God is the most deceptive of all, insofar as he seems to be infinitely so. Nor is it valid to say that Christ asserted those falsehoods, though not according to the false sense, because Christ was intending for that sense to be comprehended through those signs. Nor is it necessary, moreover, that a person be false in order for his own statement to be false, since he could be consenting to a false sense. This is clear in the case of duplicitous people, (7) and those saying "there is no God," as it is impossible for them, which I discussed in Chapter Eight.

Along these lines, nobody can state anything at all according to a sense which can neither exist, nor be conceived of. But the non-existence of God cannot be conceived of. Therefore, nobody is able to declare any such thing according to that sense, nor could one assert that.

Likewise, those who lie jokingly, or as matter of duty, do not assert the falsehood which they speak, since they contradict it in their mind, where it exists only as an assertion. Yet according to Augustine, they still lie in a culpable manner, since every lie is a sin. And since the greatest lies of all are found in Holy Scripture, all of which God speaks and asserts, it appears that God would be the most deceitful sinner.

Likewise, as often touched upon, such a sense is only an act belonging to the person who knows, or a habit. If, however, it is a heretical or unfaithful sense, then the act of the one who conceives of it is also of this sort. And since that act does not exist unless one so conceives of it, or perceives it, then it follows that such a sense results from a person's own heretical or unfaithful perception. And this means that not only does that passage of Scripture not contain a heretical sense, but that no Christian retains a heretical sense from any passage. Therefore, it is unlawful to elicit such a sense.

Likewise, since such a sense is a created thing, it is the will and the sense of the Lord. For if not, then no faithful person will retain the sense of the author, because he does not formally perceive by means of that act by which God perceives it, just as no Christian perceives what is impossible or blasphemous. And if it is sufficient to elicit such an act, since Christ ordains and elicits that act, it follows that this would have to be the sense of the author. For God would certainly not rebuke or pass judgment according to this sense, unless he knows that sense, in addition to every human evil act which he creates with respect to its substance.

(8) The difficulty which remains in this matter, however, is whether God deceives, misleads, or defrauds anyone as a penalty for sin. And, based upon the authorities cited, it appears that this is the case. If God hardened Pharaoh's heart, as evinced in Exod. 7:3; and kills every person who was killed, as evinced in Deut. 32:39; and makes sport of the one who deserves to be deceived, as he does with the Leviathan in Psalm 103 (Ps. 104:26), why does he not then deceive the sinner by **handing him over to his own spurious sense**, as the Apostle says (Rom. 1:22–32)? Whereupon, in Jer. 20:7, the holy prophet says to the Lord, **You have led me astray, Lord, and I was seduced, because you were stronger than me and you prevailed.** Since seduction and deception, and things

of this sort, can be offered as an excuse for a punishable act, by means of which the created spirit deviates from the truth, why would it be unfitting for God to do this? It seems appropriate, since this is a just creation of God. Yet God does not act in this manner, nor would he punish someone in any way whatsoever, unless it had been accepted as an opportunity for sin. And this is why a sin may be called good, since it provides an opportunity for just punishment. And thus it is said that Jeremiah believed by the authority and sanctification, first granted him in Jer. 1:4–10, that he would not suffer so many punishments, when he was overcome, wounded and afflicted by the priests, scribes, and false prophets, as evinced in Jer. 20, 26, 28, and 37. Nevertheless, he received assistance from the secular power, as evinced in Jer. 37, 38, and 40. And so that sense seems more probable to me than understanding that passage of Scripture in a purely conditional manner: **You have led me astray, if I was seduced.**

This is why the doctors say that for the purposes of imitating God, it is lawful for a Catholic to deceive his neighbor by means of a pious fraud. Yet I still do not think that God wills sins approvingly, nor that he compels people to sin, as the Profound Doctor seems to say.[4] (9) Rather, he approves the resulting good, while condemning the defective aspect.

Hence, in order to understand the Scriptures and the subtlety of this subject matter, one must carefully consider the distinction between the punishments and created things which are works of God, on the one hand, and the defects or sins which are the works specifically belonging to sinners, on the other hand. Second, it is appropriate to distinguish the good which arises from a sin, by the Lord's gracious acceptance, and the sin itself. And third, a theologian can employ a steadfast logic which conforms to Scripture, since nothing is valid which does not originate from this.

On this account, it is commonly said that there are two aspects to be considered in an instance of deception. The first is blindness of intellect, occurring either through the withdrawal of illumination, or through the positive addition of obtuseness, as a punishment for sin. And this is fitting for God, as evinced in many places of Scripture.

Second, there is a two-fold deficiency on the part of the deceiver, by which he says one thing according to one part or potency, and according to another part or potency he says this together with its opposite. And every deception of this sort, since it speaks a lie, cannot be fitting for God. That sort of deception is properly explained as an act of deceit, which is a fraudulent deception. And so every act of deceit is illicit, because it is accomplished through lying and duplicity. Notwithstanding that, God concurs with every positive aspect in the action of the one perpetrating the deceit, by causing and approving of it with respect to the totality of its natural being, just as he does in the case of every created deed.

[. . .] (15) Here I say that nobody understands Holy Scripture falsely, unless he were to sin through lying, because he deceives himself by understanding it in some manner other than he should. Hence, if such a vain thought were to creep in, it would not be the sense of Holy Scripture, nor would it falsify it. As Augustine says in Book 1, Chapter 36 of *On Christian Doctrine*, "If anyone were to perceive something in the Scriptures other than what the writer intended, he is deceived, though these are not lies."[5] The saint, however, has a way of saying that false scripture lies. For otherwise, it would be impertinent to exclude the utterance, writing, or any deed whatsoever, from the charge of lying, were it not for the fact that every lie prevaricates. And, therefore, in *On Lying*, Chapter 5, Augustine excuses the mystical parts of the Old Testament from lying when he says that whatever is said or occurs figuratively, is not a lie. "Every declaration must be referred to that which it declares. Everything done or said figuratively, however, must be understood as declaring what it signifies to those people to whom it was revealed."[6] And in Chapter 10 of *Against Lying*, after demonstrating that Christ is a lion, rock, etc., and having previously demonstrated the manifold cause of veiled signification, he thus states:

> Truths, not falsehoods, are spoken, inasmuch as truths and not falsehoods are signified by either word or deed. They are reckoned to be lies, however, for while the truths spoken are signified, they are not understood. Instead, falsehoods are believed to have been spoken.[7]

See how those of poor understanding convene upon the subject matter of the Lord's word, but neither falsify it, nor turn that word into a lie. For then God would be a liar. (16) And thus, as St. Thomas teaches in the Second Part of Part 2, Question 110, Holy Scripture is "immune from falsehood."[8] The saints have toiled to exclude falsehood entirely from Holy Scripture. But if anyone expounds upon Scripture according to a sense which he believes to be catholic, and yet is deceived in that matter, he is still not excused from an implicit lie, as clarified in Chapter 1 of *On Lying*.[9] Nobody, therefore, should presume to assert such a doubtful point, except conditionally, or by way of opinion.

There is, however, a difference between knowing, believing, and opining, as Augustine says in Chapter 3 of *On Lying*.[10] And Hugh of St. Victor says more explicitly that to know is to understand the truth under the reason presently given by what is making itself known, whether abstractly or intuitively.[11] To believe is to consent without trepidation to the existence of a thing which the believer was ignorant of at first. The person who opines, however, consents with trepidation to something believable. Thus knowing or understanding is the height of one extreme, while opinion is surely the other extreme, between which faith or belief mediate.

And so, those who posit lies concerning Holy Scripture may be placed in three classes. Certain people assert that something false is actually the meaning of the author; and when arrogantly defended it is heresy, according to St. Jerome. The second way is when someone presumes to impose such a sense on Holy Scripture, even if he does so with a certain amount of trepidation. The third way is when someone retains the catholic sense and yet needlessly (17) imposes an impossible sense upon Holy Scripture, on account of which he then declares that passage of Scripture to be impossible. And that genre of lying about Scripture seems to me to be the most pernicious of all, because it blasphemes God, and introduces a great deal of errors. Now we Christians harmoniously confess that we believe the Only-Begotten of the Father ascended into heaven on the Day of the Ascension, insofar as Christ, in Mark 16:14, reproached the unbelief of those who, **had not believed these ones who saw him resurrected from the dead**. Yet that sect of theirs propounds the doctrine that no Christian ought to believe that Christ was raised or ascended into heaven, since he should not concede that. Indeed, as I figure it, he has to concede that the Christian is unable to believe this, since nobody can conceive of the fact that the divinity ascended, or that it was bodily anointed. For then something greater than God could be conceived of, and that will be disproved. Nor can those who hold such an opinion be excused of lying. For according to the saints those people who speak a false proposition have culpably lied, no matter how jokingly, even if neither they nor the people listening to them believe it. This would apply all the more to the one speaking a falsehood or a blasphemy in matters of faith. And the person who understands enough to know that his position is not in keeping with the judgments of the doctors, lies more gravely still, since he has an implicit intention at least of deceiving himself and the Church as well. Everyone sins in this way when he deceives himself. But if a perverted thought concerning Scripture were to creep in against his will he would regret it. For such a superfluous thought leads at least to venial sin, and consequently a lie, even if he were to assert truly that Holy Scripture is not false in this instance, but rather a similar proposition which he is wickedly fabricating. (18) Nor does this mean that it would be better not to understand the grammar of Scripture than it would be to understand it. Nor would it be better for one to refrain from speaking the parts of Scripture and the orations of the Church which are impossible for me than it would be to speak them. For it is good to understand the grammar of Scripture, while it is particularly evil to abuse this science by blaspheming Holy Scripture. And the same applies when it comes to expressions belonging to parts Scripture and those of the Church's orations.

It is conceded that when an occasion for wrong acceptance arises, the grammarian who clumsily understands Scripture sins more by speaking that passage of Scripture according to a wicked sense, than a given layman who speaks it with pious intention. For at least the layman pleases God by believing that it is true, even if he does understand its meaning. And so it happens that the theologian who errs in the sense of Scripture sins more by neglecting to speak that passage of Scripture, thereby bringing about the opposite effect. Accordingly, neither part follows by in and of itself, but it is thoroughly proven that the person lying in this way about Holy Scripture sins gravely, since his lie is neither dutiful nor joking, insofar as it does not pertain to the office of the theologian that he would proceed by such an understanding, or that he would so joke. Rather, the person asserting such a meaning harms himself and others. Therefore, he seems to lie perniciously.

Whenever someone informs the outer material or sensible aspect with a false sense, then the aggregate assembled from the sign and sense is a lie, whether an assertion or consensus is present or not. For a lie which anyone speaks is certainly false. On this basis it is clear that nobody should utter a falsified Scripture, since nobody should lie. Nor is it necessary for devout theologians, who discern Scripture in an orthodox manner, to fear the falsification of their Scripture through wicked circumstantial understandings. For, as stated above in Chapter Eight, those outward signs are not the proposition, nor are they Holy Scripture, but rather an aggregate assembled from those things in addition to the sense.

In light of what has been said, it is evident, first of all, that whenever the slanderers have spoken Holy Scripture, even while understanding Scripture by the first four modes, every Scripture which they then have spoken in the fifth mode will thereupon be false, (19) because the part of any such Scripture is the sense which they elicit. But as long as they persist in their criminal accusations everything they perceive of this sort is corrupted and deceitful. Consequently, the formal part of their aforementioned fifth mode of Scripture is a lie. As a result, such Scripture is not holy for them, but is instead corrupted and deceitful.

And this seems to be the meaning of St. Jerome proposed in the *Decretum*, Case 1, Question 1:

> Marcion and Basilides, and the rest of the destructive heretics, do not possess the gospel of God, because they do not possess the Holy Spirit, apart from which the gospel which is taught is a mere human construct. For we do not reckon that the gospel abides in the words of the Scriptures, but in the sense; not in the outward appearance, but the innermost part; not in the leaves of sayings, but in the root of reason.[12]

Second, it is clear that when a righteous person is speaking any part of Scripture he speaks the truth, because it is Holy Scripture, despite the fact that he is ignorant of the meaning of Scripture, or does not understand it very well, or even if the audience perversely understands what he has said. Any Scripture of this sort certainly signifies God and theological truths to him, and such a sense is part of his Holy Scripture. If, however, he maintains a false sense together with this, then he maintains a false Scripture together with this one, and would thus be sinning, at least in a venial way. Surely every false expression or signification originates from sin. And it is evident that those who employ divine logic are able to declare the meaning of Holy Scripture sacredly and freely, and without difficulty. Whereas the adversaries are compelled to lie, tying themselves up in knots as they grudgingly recite a meaning which they are in fact scarcely able to defend. Blessed be the logic which so clearly liberates its disciples from that miserable servitude. (20) Nor is it valid for these people, together with the philosophers mentioned in Book 4 of *The Metaphysics*, to speak by keeping quiet and express their concepts with nods.[13] For nods and all other signs are undoubtedly every bit as false as spoken words, since an unsuitable sense of Scripture corrupts the whole.

Third, it is evident that the necessity of future events can be proven by the prophecy of Christ and his other instructions. Surely Christ could not lie, since every lie is a sin. Yet it is necessary that he spoke assertively of Peter's denial, the scandal of the world, and the Day of Judgment. It is necessary, therefore, that these things would happen. However, I understand necessity by supposition, whereby either outcome remains contingent, as is the case with any truth during the past. This is something which is clear to logicians. Now it is obvious that the Christian must conform his own sense to the sense of Christ if he is going to understand Scripture. For otherwise, it would not be sacred. Thus it is essential for the Christian to conform his own logic to the logic of Christ and turn away from a contrary logic which would lead him to make inappropriate statements about Scripture. For all manner of evils are bound to follow from that error in the principle of faith.

Let us give heed to the logic of the Foremost Doctor of Equivocations, as St. Jerome teaches, and as established in Distinction 37 of the *Decretum*:

> Those who wrongly understand, and thus pervert the Holy Scriptures, are drunk with wine and strong drink, unscrupulously exploiting worldly wisdom and the snares of the logicians, which should not be called chains so much as phantasms, that is to say, the sorts of shadows and images which are quickly undone and destroyed.[14]

(21) And it follows:

> It is in accordance with tropology that we should comprehend these pseudo-prophets who interpret the words of Scripture in a manner other than the Holy Spirit intends, as well as those demons who, by the conjecture of their own minds, and apart for the authority of divine words, make dubious pronouncements regarding future events as though they were true.[15]

And then it continues: "Whoever does not understand the Scriptures in keeping with its true subject matter, consumes the bitter wine."[16] Let us be on our guard against this most dangerous kind of lying regarding Scripture.

[. . .] (32) Look, someone must not lie even in an effort to save a person from sin. Thus according to the fifth conclusion in the explanation of the last argument, either Lot did not lie when consenting to the fornication of his daughters, but by seeking to avoid sin, or else he sinned by blind piety, consenting to lewdness. Still, his descendants must not imitate him in this course of action. Augustine surely excuses Abraham from lying in that instance when he said to the Egyptians that Sarah was his sister, though not denying that she was his wife, which was literally true (*ad literam*), as evinced in Gen. 20. And so it is with Isaac and Rebecca in Gen. 26. Jacob, however, who covered his bare skin with rough pelts on the advice of his mother, evinced in Gen. 27, speaks the truth according to the mystical and prophetic sense when he spoke in the person of the Gentiles who would later be engrafted on to the tree, owing to the faithlessness of the Jews (Rom. 11:13–24). (33) In keeping with custom, that seed of Abraham is Esau, the firstborn of Isaac, even as Jacob was Esau, that is to say a gemstone by love and firstborn of heaven by right. David, however, lied in 1 Kings 25 (1 Sam. 25: 13–43) when he unexpectedly pledged that he would kill Nabal. But his lie would have been even worse if he had carried it out. Thus he was compelled to sin, just as every sinner is, though he was still capable of refraining from sin all the while.[17] He could have been excused of the lie if he swore the oath with certain stipulations, however, unless God indicated that. Now the Egyptian midwives of whom we read in Exod. 1:15–22, as well as Rahab the prostitute in Josh. 2:1–21, were rewarded by God for having done something essentially good, and not because they had lied, as Augustine teaches us in *Against Lying*, Chapter 15.[18] Indeed, as Augustine argues in Chapter 18, the person who propounds the dogma that one must lie in some cases is asserting this under the pretext of truth.[19] Otherwise, he would have to concede that he either teaches in a false and evil manner, or else that he teaches nothing at all. If, however, one should listen to a doctor only insofar as he speaks the truth, then no one should be listened to because he speaks a lie. Chastity does not teach that one must fornicate, and so also with the other virtues. Neither then does the truth teach that one must lie.

Hence, there is no possible case in which a person is compelled to lie.

(*De ver.* II,xvii): Sacred Subtleties versus Blatant Lies

(33) At this point, I offer a reply to objections concerning the question of lying. Now if it is lawful to deceive, then it is lawful to encourage someone to lie. But it is lawful to deceive, as made clear at the beginning of the last chapter; therefore, it is lawful to encourage someone to lie. (34) Surely God deceived Abraham when he led him to believe that he would kill his son Isaac, as evinced in Gen. 22:1–14. Whereupon, Abraham seems to have committed a lie in this matter, when he said, **Wait here with the donkey, the boy and I are hastening right up there, and after we have worshipped we will return to you**. Although he spoke the truth, this was, nonetheless, not his intention, since he proposed to kill his son. After all, duplicity is still a lie, even if the truth is spoken. In light of this narrative, it seems that Abraham not only intended to mislead his servants, but his son Isaac as well, since he neglected to inform him of the sacrifice. It is impossible to imagine that Abraham did not literally believe (*ad literam*) that he would sacrifice his son. Otherwise, it would have been an exceptional expression of duplicity when he bound Isaac and placed him upon the altar atop the wood pile, extending his hand so that he could lay his sword to the victim, unless he was really of a mind to carry this out. If this were not so he would not have deserved to hear that the Messiah would come forth from his seed, as the Apostle observes in Gal. 3:16–18.

As far as that matter is concerned, I say that a falsehood is assumed, since deception, inasmuch as it is lawful, resounds of the punishment for sin and the useful good which thereupon results. It is certainly lawful for God to punish a sinner, and yet it still is not lawful for him to encourage a person to commit a sin, for that would mean that it is lawful for him to break his own law through some wicked action. Although he could do this if he so chooses, if he were actually to carry it out he would surely destroy himself. Hence, by extending the term, it should be conceded that sinful nature is able to do what God cannot, because it is a lie. Notwithstanding that, a creature cannot create anything positive, unless God has previously created it. But furthermore, a crafty person could lawlessly seize upon some grounds for unjustly deceiving his neighbor. (35) And for this reason it must be noted that the one who is deceiving should retain a pious intention in his mind and truth in his discourse, in order to edify by his deception, even if he has equivocated with deception. Third, it is necessary for him to possess authority or internal motion from God, whereby it would be lawful for him to lead his neighbor astray in this way for the purpose of punishing his sin. Yet the deceiver's conscience and deeds, which follow with the truth of Scripture, will be the judge. If, however, the deceiver is seeking temporal advantage for himself, that will be a sign of an illicit deception. Thus when it comes to swearing a legal oath, the one swearing the oath should be mindful of the purpose for which the oath is being administered. Second, he ought to pay heed to the well recognized sense, applicable to the parties and the witnesses with respect to achieving this laudable goal. Third, he should gage the form of oath as it pertains to such a goal and form of speaking. In private communications, however, it is permissible to equivocate when an unhelpful fraud is not intended, though a useless objection is rejected either way. And from either side, the Christian must pay heed to the logic of Scripture, which is to be preserved above all in the covenant of the Lord's testament.

Third, it must be noted that the saints truly concluded by the faith of Scripture that Abraham was holy. In faith, hope and love, he was foremost among the patriarchs. As a result, it is only fitting that he would have had special knowledge of the Messiah, according to that passage in John 8:56, **Abraham, your father, rejoiced that he would see my day; he saw and was glad.** Thereupon, by the faith of Scripture, it is piously declared that Abraham committed himself to God's guidance in this deed, virtuously expecting the inspiration of the Spirit. Nor did he promise or assert anything by that deed, (36) unless supplying in thought the divine goodwill, just as it is said of the Blessed Virgin, whom some contend was deceived.

Abraham, therefore, was tested by God on a number of levels so that he would take up his very own son, not a stranger, but his very own. This was not the one whom he begot by his foreign wife, but the only-begotten of Sarah. This boy was not the one for whom he cared little, but the only one whom he loved, in light of the gracious promise and the miraculous nature of his birth. This was the son he singularly hoped for with laughter and delight, and so was named Isaac. What is at last described is all the more dreadful, as he would proceed to offer him as a sacrifice upon some distant, gloomy mountain.

This serves to demonstrate the theological virtue of Abraham, whereby he immediately arose in the night without delay, so that his deed could be carried out in greater secrecy and farther removed from distraction. Whereupon, he did not saddle a large horse, nor a mule, nor a multitude of beasts of burden, but simply a donkey. Nor did he take with him a whole host of domestic servants, but only two young men, and the son whom he would sacrifice. Nor was this just a momentary period of testing, since he spent three days continuously standing beside the object of his love, such that he might refrain from carrying out the Lord's command, even as his toil in the desert was so great.

Consider the love of Abraham, how in hope he did such great deeds for the sake of Christ, before having tasted his gratitude of the passion and the particular faith which he had concerning Christ still so far in the future. Then consider our own ungrateful sloth so opposed to Christ, the one whom we clearly perceive, and whose intercession we discern as a past event revealed in so public a charter as the Scriptures. It is no wonder I am ashamed of myself, since not only do I not sacrifice my natural son for the sake of his love, but I do no essentially good works, except rarely because it would delight my body and soul more than some diabolical deed which I quite more frequently commit. (37) Nor do I fully guard against trespasses, for commission of which I incur manifold penalties to this day. But I know it is appropriate for that holy patriarch, who proved to be a future example to Jews and Gentiles, as the Apostle says in Gal. 3:6–18, to excel in faith, since he was neither conscious of any failure to lead a holy life, nor did he disbelieve the promise which God made when instructing him that, **he would go forth from his kindred, and he would cause him to grow into a great nation**, in Gen. 12:1–2. It is no wonder that he excelled in hope and love, dispelling worldly pomp and concerns through his continuous prayer and pure behavior, ceaselessly rejoicing in the Advent of the Messiah. Once again, I realize that we must enter into their toil and completely assimilate ourselves to the Head, if we want to be effectively saved. For just as those believers in the future bridegroom, **were hastening to the fragrance of his anointing oil**, as is said in Song of Sol. 1:2–3, so it is essential for those of us who come after him to hasten to his abundant mercy, imitating his maidens who came before us.

Thus the saints, who have so earnestly studied the Holy Scriptures and the principal aspects which concern the state of the Church, conclude that the life of those patriarchs was more akin to the state of innocence and holier than our own. As such, they do not accuse them of criminal conduct where it would not be appropriate, but to the contrary, specifically absolve them in these matters, which should be for us prime examples of good behavior. Since we are permitted to equivocate with our neighbors when speaking the truth as we ought to do, so there are also occasions when people who wrongly understand are deceived as a punishment for their own sin, as often evinced in the case of Christ. We must concede that the holy Abraham lied by speaking the truth that he and Isaac would return to them, since he knew that they would return on the Judgment Day. Thus he had no intention of misleading them, just as it was not fitting that he intend to deceive them, for he had the intention of bringing about a good result either way. (38) For it was to the honor of God and the benefit of all people that he wanted to kill his own son without any resistance from those who realized what he was about to do. Nor is it problematic if God were to punish him through deception, because his sins outweighed the satisfaction for so great a punishment. Hence, in Chapter 22, Book 2 of the *Reconsiderations*, Augustine thinks it is quite likely that Abraham believed that, "If he killed his son he would soon be resuscitated and restored to him."[20] And so he thinks that his ignorance was a matter of pious deception, as so often happened with the holy patriarchs. Notwithstanding that, it is not as if false faith of this sort is a false cause of salvation, even if it would be meritorious for someone to suffer such deceptions piously. This is what the devout do when they imply by their actions that they wish to act in this way, unless it was clear to them that God had ordained otherwise. Neither can any such faith be catholic, nor can anyone enter into beatitude through that faith. And so Scripture remains true either way. Every lie still remains unlawful, however, even though Scripture truly records that there were many who lied in a culpable manner. Hence, just as one could conclude from such facts that it is lawful to lie, it could then be argued that the sin of the devil, the sin of Adam, and the sin of Judas were lawful, since Scripture records them.

On this basis, the ignorant will conclude that there are many lies in Scripture. Yet it would then be necessary to demonstrate that Scripture records lies of this sort and does not reproach them, but actually commends them. When such a thing is taught by means of an impossibility, then I admit, together with those who teach this, that Scripture would be contrary to itself. Although God did in fact equivocate with Abraham concerning the sacrifice of Isaac, commanding him to carry it out, Abraham still meritoriously condescended to the primary sense of Scripture, offering his son according to the form and arrangement which God commanded. If, therefore, so great a patriarch condescended to the sense of Scripture, how much more have we sons been instructed to do so! Indeed, if it is (39) not lawful to equivocate when swearing oaths by interposing a sense which is foreign to the people, this is all the more reason why we should not interject some foreign sense into the sense of the Lord.

Returning to the sense of the proposed passage of Scripture, it is possible to elicit another double sense from it, extending beyond the literal sense which I explained.

First of all, the series of historical events can also be understood according to the allegorical sense, such that God the Father, by his eternal counsel, spoke his Word, who is the father of many nations. For it said to him in Psalm 2 (2:8), **Ask of me, and I will give the nations to you**, since he would take up his assumed humanity, which he made an object of mockery for us. For it came to be through the hypostatic union, whereby he is the Only-Begotten Son of the Father and Redeemer of the human race. Accordingly, during the night of sinful ignorance, he saddled a donkey, assuming the human nature of both Gentiles and Jews. And it was in keeping with its kind that he guided that nature through three epochs, namely the time before the law, the time under the law, and the time of grace. On both sides he led the two young men along with him, namely the priests and the prophets, who had been unable to redeem the man left half-dead (Luke 10:30–35). But having perceived the third day upon Mount Calvary, these two young men, together with the rest of the human race, expected the one who existed long before the time of John, **until whom there had been the law and the prophets** (Luke 16:16).

Luke 13:32 can be explained according to this sense: **Look, I cast out demons and perform healings today and tomorrow, and on the third day I am finished.** For three years he had sojourned towards Mount Calvary (40) where his humanity was then freed from the old priesthood and prophets. Our Father, however, bound his humanity upon the altar of that mountain, while on the bundle of wood he set the fire of love. For nobody has a greater love than that he would silently lay down his life for his enemies, imploring his Father to forgive them. Yet our Father could not kill him according to his divinity. But he saw past his divinity to his humanity, which adhered to it by spiritual power, and which was prepared to be sacrificed among sinners in the place of the boy. In fact, according to an exposition by St. Augustine, the backside of God which Moses was allowed to see in Exod. 33:20–23 was the humanity comprised of body and soul.[21] It was this that he sacrificed in the place of the boy. He then returned together with him, as well as the two young men extracted from the abode of the dead, and joyfully ascended to the fellowship of the Church Triumphant.

The third sense is the tropological, and it ought to be acknowledged by every Christian, since he himself has been brought to life by the Divine Word and his patriarch Abraham, together with their fellow pugilists. One should first observe how God doubly tests him: calling him inwardly through internal inspiration, and outwardly through the communication of Holy Scripture. This was in order to take up that corporeal nature which is proper to him, and which he loves by nature, according to the Apostle. This is rightly said to be Isaac, for having been chastised according to the rules of Scripture through this mortal life, it makes the person laugh on the final day. The inner man, however, ought to be Abraham, because he spiritually begets many nations by the holy behavior which he exhibited with respect to Christ. After that two-fold test, in the night of ignorance, one should quickly saddle the beast of burden, which is the corporeal nature, with the implements of the virtues, (41) and totally assume the two young men unto himself, namely dove-like innocence and serpent-like wisdom, in keeping with Christ's teaching in Matt. 10:16. The philosophers, who knew aggregates in an accidental manner, determined that the corporeal nature, upon which the inner man rests, as though on a beast of burden, is a nature prior to the one which possesses the innocence of doves and the wisdom of serpents. Therefore, all aggregates of this sort are distinguished in an accidental manner.

Once again, the pilgrim should sojourn for the three days of his life, with the grace of the Holy Spirit continuously leading him. That first day would be the time of youth, by which he meritoriously endures the punishment of an unstable nature incurred by the transgression of the first human being. The second day would surely be middle-age, in which he discerningly assumes for himself a voluntary penance, chastising his beast of burden that it might be meritoriously subjected to the soul. Truly then, the third day would have to be that final stage of life when he is rewarded with the first contemplation that he might see that mountain from afar. And, together with the people who have been forgiven on account of their innocent and wise way of living with respect to the world, he ascends with a purified corporeal nature to a yet higher plane of celestial perception, binding the man of natural life upon the pile of worldly things, and completely submitting with him to the fire of love and **the sword of the Spirit, which is the**

word of Scripture (Eph. 6:17). With these he will sacrifice the prideful man who clings to worldly affairs which overwhelm him as if in the throes of fever. And in this way the inner man will return to that mature fellowship with a glorified corporeal nature. Thus Christ truly says in Luke 14:26–33, **Every one who does not hate worldly and temporal things, even life itself, cannot be his disciple**. Consequently, every member of the Church must follow Christ in proportional sufferings. Otherwise, he will no doubt fail to ascend to heaven with the Head, (42) nor will he dwell with the companions of Bathsheba, that is, at the fountain of bubbling water or the medicinal well. For the Truth says in John 12:25, **He who would wish to save his life will lose it**. Thus the most literal (*literatissime*) parts of Scripture are distinctly arranged according to such a form, whereby they allude to every truth of Scripture according to the literal or mystical sense, since all the individual aspects are connected to one another. Indeed, in a mirror so clear as this there abides neither deceit, nor falsehood, nor direct deception.

[. . .] (49) Based upon those sayings of the saints, which the *Decretum* recites, the point is clearly established that no one should lie for humility's sake, just as no one ought to sin for the sake of virtue.[22]

With regard to the third point, I say that the faith of Scripture makes it perfectly clear that the Baptist did not lie when he denied that he was a prophet. For by the same rationale, the equivocation concerning Elijah and anyone else which Scripture expresses according to the equivocal sense would then be annulled. And this would mean that Christ, the very author of Scripture, would be the greatest liar of all, just as the greater part of his Scripture would be a blasphemous lie. Then it would be more plausible that John's confession was true when he confessed that he was not Elijah, and that Christ's assertion was false and impossible when he said, **If you want**

to understand, he is Elijah (Matt. 11:14). Yet one must not imagine that Christ equivocated with respect to the name of Elijah, except along the same lines that the holy Baptist had when he equivocated regarding the title of prophet, especially when he knew the song of his father written of him: **You, child, will be called a prophet of the Most High** (Luke 1:76).

Since a heretic would explicate Scripture in some other way than that which the Holy Spirit requires, or the holy doctors agree in affirming, namely that Christ and his messenger are equivocating while not contradicting one another, it seems dangerous to annul these equivocal senses of Scripture. (50) Hence, Augustine writes in *Sermon 4 on John* that, "What must be feared is that those of lesser understanding might think when John spoke of these things he contradicted what Christ had said."[23] For in Matt. 11:14 Christ says, **If you want to understand, the Baptist himself is Elijah**. He continues, "God forbid that the messenger would be lying when he speaks that which he heard from the judge."[24] And he later explains that Christ is saying that John is Elijah according to the condition of his office, and not according to his own personal properties. For John was a messenger in keeping with many similitudes preceding the first coming of Christ, just as Elijah precedes the second coming. Thus John speaks according to the unique properties of the thing itself, while Christ speaks truly according to the prefiguration. As such, neither the messenger, nor the judge is false, since he was not Elijah through his characteristic properties, but rather through a similitude. Further on, he illustrates how John was not purely a prophet with respect to Christ, since the one whom the prophets had predicted for such a long time John pointed out with his finger. And so, preserving his humility, John was careful not to lie when, given the intentions of those who were questioning him, he appropriately denied that he was merely a prophet of the distant consecrated Messiah who was still yet to arrive. But truly and humbly recognizing that the Messiah was coming, he confessed that he was the voice of the Word, and the friend of the present bridegroom, and not only of his, but of the whole Church, apart from whom no one else is to be expected.[25]

[. . .] (52) Having explained these four points of evidence,[26] it remains to prove in a three-fold manner that lying is entirely impermissible. And it will be proven through evangelical law. (53) Now having dreamt up some license to lie, one must consequently concede that in a particular case a lie is not a sin, nor does it savor of sin, since God cannot grant someone license to sin. Consequently, it can inhere honestly within an innocent person through some pious intention promoting the benefit of the Church. As a result, it can be very meritorious, and thus inhere in Christ. In fact, it does not savor of the imperfection of sin, as secular dominion does, because it does not involve worldly care, but rather the honesty and advantage of the Church, as it is asserted. On this basis, it appears that Christ could have lied throughout his entire Scripture regarding the everlasting punishment of sin, declaring this to his Church merely to frighten her. Now God, by his absolute power, could surely save all people, even having supposed all the sins they have already committed. So then, by the same rationale, Christ could have spoken threateningly when he said all those things about everlasting punishment. Having conceded this, there would be no infallible evidence left to human beings, except that they must believe every rational creature will be beatified. Now the strongest evidence for this would be the testimony of Scripture. Yet with respect to all the passages of Scripture that could be cited, it can plausibly be said that they are pious lies designed to frighten people into refraining from so much evil.

What should be said in a catholic manner by those holding such an opinion is proven in the following way. This position in no way detracts from divine perfection or the faith of Scripture. To the contrary, it demonstrates a greater benevolence on God's part towards his creation than our adversaries attribute to him. Yet everything of this sort ought to be believed of God in a catholic manner; therefore, this should also be believed in a catholic manner. For if the author of Scripture has piously lied with respect to all the threatening passages of Scripture concerning Gehenna, and will later beatify all human beings and angels following the Judgment Day, then without any greater impropriety, he would indeed be better than he is now. But there is no convincing evidence to support such a possibility inasmuch as it is not self-evident. And thus this point must be conceded both philosophically and theologically. (54) Now with respect to God, his goodness would not thereupon be diminished, and in his universe there would exist an even greater goodness than we presently believe, inasmuch as the beatitude of all the damned would exceed their punishment. For according to those who offer such an opinion, the sense of Scripture is not obviated when one lacks the foundation to prove that not all passages of Scripture, which seem to say the opposite, have actually been spoken in a conditional or threatening sense. Nor does an impropriety follow from elsewhere; therefore, it should be believed. The people who opine in this way could imagine that the saints in heaven know the same meaning, even as Paul knew it in his rapture. Yet they do not promulgate that meaning, because these are **secret words which a person is not permitted to speak**, according to 2 Cor. 12:4. Rather than creating a problem for those who hold such an opinion, this agrees with the notion that pilgrims would be saved by a false faith. For if Christ is able to deceive his most beloved Apostles through a pious fraud, which would be helpful to them and yet harmful to none, by the same reasoning, why could he not deceive all the other people who are going to be beatified?

And so it appears to me that whoever proposes that there exists a license to lie without sin, would consequently have to propose that it is a catholic principle that every rational creature is going to be beatified, even if this should not be proclaimed to the people just yet. But since such a notion is most impossible and supremely heretical, so too seems its foundation, upon which it is conceded that lying is permissible in particular cases. Well then, keep that poison far away from us!

Nor are they troubled by the fact that St. Gregory rejects that opinion of theirs on the grounds that it is heretical, in Book 34, Chapter 19 of his *Morals*.[27] For if one is allowed to gloss piously the saying of Christ in Matt. 25:46, **These will go into eternal punishment, while the righteous into eternal life**, together with other similar statements of God, such that they are only threatening statements, (55) why should not the sayings of Gregory and the other saints be glossed in the same way? Surely any sense of Scripture which is more pious and equally probable must be applied to it, because it has been formulated by God. But that sense of Scripture, so one imagines, is more pious, and as such, is more fittingly applied to Holy Scripture. Second, the aforementioned conclusion is argued on the basis of Church law. Now having proposed a lie exists within the law of Christ, which is itself the principle of the law of the Church, it is necessary that the law will fail on account of a defective foundation. But if one grants the damnable opinion of the previous argument, namely that the faith of Scripture is lacking in truth, then so too is the faith of the Church. Who then would believe that absolution, excommunication, or any of the other spiritual judgments and ecclesiastical punishments, were anything but sophisms? If one believes that the faith of Scripture is lacking in truth, additional arguments would have to be established by which the steadfastness of the Church's pronouncements could be proved. And it is easy to see that a person falsifying Scripture by glossing the threatening aspect could not avoid the conclusion that all the threats of the Church would also have been declared merely to frighten people. I ask you, how then could the Vicar of Christ shackle sinners with the chains of perpetual damnation, if Christ eternally decreed that all these people will finally be saved? And thus the doctors who hold this opinion lapse into the very impropriety which they fear the most, namely that secular lords would be permitted to take all their temporal possessions away from them, inasmuch as they are only subject to punishment in this world, while thereafter in the next world they will not experience any punishment, but only joy.

[. . .] (58) I will again examine the nature of a pernicious lie. Now it is possible that the greatest good of all could proceed from such a lie, since it appears that Christ's incarnation and the salvation of the human race proceeded from the first lie of the devil, proposed in Gen. 3:4, **By no means will you die**. For this reason St. Gregory called Adam's sin necessary, and even a happy transgression. And when every pernicious lie can be one of pious intention, it seems possible for every dutiful and administrative lie to fall under that precept. I do not believe this is something that Lord Pope asserts, although his enemies endeavor to deceive him with the anointing oil of sinners. If he is able to legislate in opposition to Christ, however, then just as Christ can lie in the matter of faith regarding the final judgment, so also could Lord Pope legislate in this way, with the result that the sense of Scripture would become a joke and a pious lie in that instance. On the other hand, by the plenitude of his mercy, Christ could legislate according to his humanity that there be no eternal damnation. And Lord Pope could not do otherwise. Yet they would reckon that a great impropriety, since Christ can communicate that legislative power to his vicar, even as he communicates to him the power of absolution, that is to say, sacramentally promulgating what God himself accomplishes. Would it not then be a great act of piety on the part of the pope to interpret Holy Scripture in this way, and legislate accordingly, since it inclines to the benefit of the Church, as even our adversaries must concede?

[. . .] (59) The third and final argument is based upon civil law. For a disruption of an entire people would follow from the opposite of the conclusion. Now that law examines doubts stemming from the testimony of two, three, twelve witnesses, or even some other number, depending upon the custom of the particular country. If, therefore, it were lawful for them to lie in general, then the conclusion of the judge would be undone given the deficiency of the witnesses since a falsehood proves nothing, as evinced in the case of the testimony given against Naboth (1 Kings 2), against Susanna (Sus. 2), and against Christ himself. For the judge can render no judgment when the proof offered by the witnesses is found to be deficient. Indeed, having granted that false witnesses prove a legal conclusion, all the more must the true witnesses who succeed them prove its opposite.

[. . .] (65) Returning to the subject, I faithfully confess that a person must not lie for reasons of piety, humility, or any other plausible reason, since such things are incompatible with lying by definition.

Now when Christ creates all meritorious works, moving all his members to every righteous act which they might perform, then Christ would also be creating an abundance of lies. Consequently, just as something is true through the authorization and assertion of the truth, so something is mendacious through the speaking of a lie. And so it is proposed that he would piously lie at the time of Peter's passion, by encouraging Peter in the face of his passion, asserting that he is coming to Rome again to be crucified. Thereupon, since he says the opposite to the saints in heaven, because these are singular truths, he would stand in even greater contradiction to himself. And this contradicts the Apostle in 2 Cor. 1:19, for there would be **in him yes and no**, since he would be just like a false prophet, just like a man with a duplicitous mind. Indeed, he would be the most grievous mocker of the Church's members,

(66) were he to say one thing to the Church Militant and its very opposite to the Church Triumphant. As a result, the Christian faith would be chiefly deceptive, because its author is the most false seducer of all. Yet such a notion as this is horrifying to all pious ears.

Let us hold, therefore, to the foundation of Christ's religion, the Lord our God, that he was not able to lie, while his adversary the devil is the first father of lies. The school of the devil, where he instructs his members, abides principally in a lie, just as the school of Christ and his members, since he himself is the Truth, abides purely in a three-fold truth; namely that of life, deed, and word. And the laws of the Church are founded upon that principle of religion. As such, it is impermissible for a Christian, especially a cleric, an administrator of the poor's goods and the alms of the secular men, to administer that office with buffoons and jesters. If he does, he then embraces mendacity within himself. And it is all the more obvious that they should not employ liars, given their lust for temporal rewards. For while the wicked are scattered about in such density, they are not employed for the sake of lying, and consequently sinning.

(*De ver.* II,xviii): Different Ways of Speaking the Truth

(66) Bringing an end to this discussion of lying, a sevenfold argument can be posed in objection to what has been said.

First, it appears that Master Armachus intimates that Holy Scripture could be deceptive and could deceive pious people.[28] Now this is made clear by a series of Gospel passages where Christ predicted the future concerning the Judgment Day and the tribulations of the Church in preparation for anti-Christ, as evinced in Matt. 24 and 25. However, **these things are written, so that you would believe**, according to the final part of John (John 20:31); (67) for Christ says in John 14:29, **Now**

I speak to you before this comes to pass, so that when it has come to pass, you would believe. Therefore, it seems fitting to concede some aspect of the following three options. Either all those things, and by the same rationale, all future events, happen by necessity. Or second, that perhaps Christ was able to assert a falsehood knowingly. Thus he had lied in his Scripture, and consequently had deceived his disciples. Or third, it is not now necessary that Christ thus spoke or asserted those things by way of his humanity, just as it is conceded to be necessary for other creatures.

On this occasion, I say that master Armachus affirmed by faith that just as Christ cannot have lied or sinned, so he cannot have deceived his neighbors. And thus the authority of Holy Scripture is infallible, not only because it deceives nobody in actuality, but because it never could have deceived anyone. Of course, a falsified Holy Scripture could deceive someone. And since this would not be possible, except by divine preordination, then God would have ordained a Scripture that is not sacred, but in fact deceptive, designed to deceive his most beloved children. And such mendacity would undoubtedly lead right back to the author. I ask you, what does matter whether the author asserts a falsehood through a proposition by way of an audible voice, visible script, or any other sensible sign? Neither does it matter whether he asserted those things with respect to his divinity, or with respect to his humanity. For if they were false they would prove that God is a liar as much in deed as in word. It is obvious that Holy Scripture, which is the word of God, cannot have deceived anyone, although sin leads many to wrongly receive it, such that it then becomes an opportunity for further deception and sinning. If Holy Scripture is capable of deceiving and lying, then so is God. Thereupon, it would be supremely contingent either way, since it would lie in this way. (68) Hence, our primary evidence is the one which is intrinsically infallible, the one who would not lie. As a result, mendacity would not only abide within every person, but also in God, though this is contrary to what the Apostle says in 2 Tim. 2:13, **Even if we do not believe, he remains faithful; for he cannot deny himself**. Yet he would deny himself were he to falsify his own word, or deny the truth.

With regard to the third part, it is clear from the faith of Scripture that it would be impossible. For by the testimony of Scripture, **it is necessary that scandals would come** (Matt. 18:7) just as **it was necessary for Christ to suffer** (Luke 24:26). And it is also necessary that these things which Christ said concerning the tribulations of the Church would come to pass, evinced in Mark 13, Luke 24, and Matt. 24. Therefore, since we believe that these things happen by necessity, based upon the intrinsic evidence of the faith of Scripture and the words of Christ, it is clearly necessary that Christ spoke in this way. It is surely impossible to devise a reason why it is necessary that every deed performed by any other person must have been when it slipped into the past, without also asserting that by the same rationale, if not by a greater one, any deed performed by Christ that was completely elapsed and past was necessary beforehand. For neither his voice, nor his writing, nor his act of seeing, knowing, or asserting, nor the Christian faith applied to his words, is any more dependent upon the future than anything else that a member of Christ has accomplished. For as every created necessity declares a constancy and perfection in the good, so God previously would ordain the necessity in his very own words and deeds, rather than the deeds of another. The same consideration applies to external actions in God, and the visions by which the blessed have discerned future events in the Word.

Among the other sorts of subterfuge is the charge that Christ spoke, knew, or asserted nothing simply according to his humanity, along with similar such fictions which do not retain the appearance of faithfulness. (69) This is why we must hold to the first meaning, namely that all future events come to pass by necessity, as the Profound Doctor says based upon Holy Scripture, many reasons, and all manner of testimonies drawn from the holy doctors.[29] The pious doubts of Master Armachanus in that matter were the result of his retreat from the logic of Scripture. For he assumed necessity only applied to that which is not able not to exist; and this is called absolute necessity. Yet Scripture, along with the philosophers, calls every contingent truth necessary by supposition, since it grants an eternal cause with respect to each and every creature with whose position it is formally contrary for the creature itself not to exist. And in this way it is as necessary that Judgment Day and any other future event will exist, as it is necessary that God, the world, and time did exist. Nevertheless, any one of those things is contingent either way with respect to God. Since he is the one who exists before the world it remains possible for him that he is not going to produce any creature, that he is not producing any creature, or that he has not produced any creature from some time. Therefore, we must continue to meditate, pray, and do good works, since those things are the necessary means to attain that end which God has eternally ordained.

Nor do I see how anyone could discern this subtle logic of Scripture unless he posits that all things which have been, or will be, are present to God at the proper time. This is why Scripture so frequently speaks in the present tense of past and future truths. In days gone by, the holy doctors used to maintain the principle that within the entirety of Holy Scripture there was no term, nor accident of a term, placed there which did not bear meaning. Thereupon, from that passage in Gen. 1:26, **Let us make humankind according to our own image and likeness**, (70) they proved that the Trinity is of the most simple essence based upon the disparity of the number of terms. And they made the same argument based upon that three-fold address in Isa. 6:3, **Holy, holy, holy is the Lord**. For they held to the principle that there could be no replication of a term without a mystery. And the same applies to that passage of the Apostle in Rom. 11:36, **From him, and through him, and in him are all things**. Consider also Wisd. of Sol. 11:20, **God arranged all things by measure, weight and number**. And so it is with similar things, all of which are deduced through the heavenly logic of Scripture. Therefore, when Scripture speaks in this way of the extension of time, and also of necessity, its professor should speak in conformity, thereby conceding that it is absolutely necessary. For if Scripture asserts something it must be true.

The second principal argument against what has been said is that if every sophist or logician who argues that his colleague is a donkey is lying. And, by the same rationale, so is the theologian who pursues many arguments all the way to their heretical conclusions, then surely no one would dare assert the following necessary disjunctive conclusions: God exists or there is no God, except if he were lying culpably. And that would be exceedingly serious, since such scholastic exercises are approved of today in order that the faithful person might better know how to guard against the sophistical venom of the infidels. On the basis of this evidence one may deduce that a dutiful or joking lie is a sin, even if the liar is intending to help many and hurt none. Nor will the reason be mentioned why someone would be lying when he says such things that he knows are neither true nor even believed by the one who hears them, indeed not even intending to assert these things, except that, by the same rationale, someone who says a man is a donkey, or some other impossibility, would also be lying.

Here I say that the conclusion does not follow.

(71) On this account, it must be noted that our proposition considers three types of speech, namely a statement which asserts, a statement which recites, and a statement which reproves.

To assert in truth, or speak assertively, is to assent to some statement as being true. To speak by way of recitation is common to questioning and censuring for irony, and to say any other plain thing. But to speak in a reproving manner is to say something as being false for the purpose of refuting it. Christ certainly speaks in this way in Luke 11:19 when he says, **If I cast out demons by means of Beelzebul, in whom do your sons cast out?** And the Apostle does so in 1 Cor. 15:14, **If there is no resurrection of the dead our faith is in vain**. In these instances it is obvious to the faithful that they did not lie. Nor is their statement a falsehood or a lie, since any particular aspect of their statements signifies the truth of the connection.

I do not believe that some part of Holy Scripture could be false. And thus the argumentation of Holy Scripture does not proceed from an impossible part of Holy Scripture, but instead from the impossible statement stemming from lies found outside of Scripture. Consequently, in the Apostle's argumentation the truth is reached from the truth by speaking through signs, since it signifies the truth of the connection either way, in addition to what the infidels have said.

This is why it is entirely far-fetched to conclude from those statements that there is no resurrection from the dead, or that this part of Scripture adequately signifies that there is no resurrection of the dead, even if such a sense is rolled over in the mind of someone wandering aimlessly outside the confines of Scripture. Nor is it fitting for us to think that when God or a saint understands that passage of Scripture that they take it to mean that there is no resurrection of the dead, or that the Catholic faith is void, since they realize that these statements are merely significative. For just as nobody (72) is able to conceive of anything greater then God, so nobody is able to say that the Catholic faith is void. If, however, statements of this sort are understood as a mixture of the material and the significative, then there could arise such a deceitful sense by which someone says that the Christian faith is void, that is to say, he speaks such signs in a way that such things are signified to him, which he then assents to as if they were true.

In light of this, it is evident that Christ did not say, nor did he understand, that he cast out demons by means of Beelzebul, although the false Jews had said so. Thus it is possible for someone accused of causing scandal to say truly that he neither said, nor thought, that another person is a thief. For it is not enough just to speak those signs; an assertion of some supplementary discernment is required.

[. . .] (76) Now those cases where it is proposed that God, under the pretext of beatitude, would command Peter to lie (Mark 14:30), include either part of a contradiction. (77) I do not believe that God can command through deception, if that means a sin would be committed. Just as he cannot have commanded Abraham to kill Isaac, unless by killing him he could obtain merit. For, by the same rationale, he could have permitted Peter to sin, by fulfilling his decree, and consequently deceiving him mendaciously.

Hence, it appears that those who subtly reason that God can command an illicit act, but cannot permit anyone to proceed all the way to the point of fulfilling his command, would leave the Church quite perplexed concerning every prophecy pertaining to the future. For, if the Lord's command is not to be carried out for the sake of some possible good, it is clearly more likely that what is prophesied by the Lord would not come to pass under any circumstances. Now if the divinity is false, or if it is able to assert a falsehood, what becomes of that intrinsic evidence regarding the Judgment Day and the everlasting damnation of the foreknown, along with the rest of these sorts of predictions? Hence, with regard to the prophecy of Isaiah and Jonah, found in Isa. 38:1–9 and Jon. 3:1–10, either God did not assert this, and the prophets had sinfully lied by simply preaching a falsehood; or he asserted their prophecies according to a hidden sense; or what I consider to be more likely, that the prophets asserted such statements literally (*ad literam*), while supplying in thought what is left unsaid, namely that they should happen in this way, unless God decreed that it would take place in another way. Hence, in some cases they were fully illuminated, as in these instances which concern the Catholic faith. While in other cases they were partly in doubt, and still in others they were deceived. Either way, Scripture remains true in its totality, while God also abides in truth either way, without possibility of fallacy or falsehood. [. . .]

(*De ver.* II,xix): The Truth of Prophetic Statements

(99) Returning now to the subject matter of the second argument, taken up at the beginning of Chapter Fifteen, the first thing one should consider is how the adduced authoritative passages are to be understood in a catholic manner. For according to the testimony of the saints, they should not be understood in a blasphemous manner. As Augustine says in his book on Matthew, *Sermon 16*, "With our heart, let us be in agreement, and Holy Scripture will not be found to disagree in any of its parts."[30] Therefore, as I have often said, the following proof is shameful: Scripture is not true according to the literal sense (*ad literam*), nor word for word (*ad verbum*), or when it is wrongly elicited according to the fleshly sense; therefore, Holy Scripture is false with respect to such a sense.

Regarding three authorities, I spoke above in Chapter Thirteen of how it is true according to the intended literal sense (*de virtute sermonis*) that (100) the teaching of Christ is not of Christ, but Christ himself. And since Christ consists of both of the two natures, in this way it is true that the Father is greater than Christ, with respect to his humanity, while Christ is still equal to the Father according to his divinity.

But that passage of John 12:44 presents a new difficulty: **Whoever believes in me does not believe in me**. Whereupon, the doctors explain it in various ways, though they all do so in a sufficiently catholic manner, and without contradicting one another. Doctor Lyra explains it in this way:

> **Whoever believes in me does not believe in me**, namely alone; otherwise, it would be a contradiction. And for this reason it follows, **but in him who sent me**, because one is the faith belonging to the Father and the Son, while the other is the vision which follows from faith. Therefore, it continues, **Whoever sees me sees him who sent me**, because the Father and the Son are one simple essence, although they are distinguished in relative property. However, the nature of the relatives is such that having known one, the remaining one is also known, since they are similar by nature and understanding.[31]

Augustine, however, expresses a more subtle and profound sense in his *Sermon 54 on John*, although remaining in agreement with this position.[32] On behalf of his exposition, it must first be noted that for Augustine it was a well-known matter of faith that Christ is comprised of each one of the three natural principles. And his *Sermon 47* makes this clear.[33] Second, it should be observed that (101) the humanity of Christ, as any creature, as well as the divinity of Christ, are said to exist equivocally. From which it is clear thirdly, that this is not a contradiction, but rather the apex of logical and metaphysical subtlety: **Whoever believes in me**; supplying in thought what is left unsaid, namely according to his divinity, **does not believe in me**; yet supply here: according to his humanity. Surely nobody believes in the nature or the person except with a view to the divinity. It is said in the Creed, therefore, "I believe in God the Father, I believe in Jesus Christ, and I believe in the Holy Spirit." For Augustine says, "Nobody would have dared to say of the apostles: **Whoever believes in me**, etc. Indeed, we believe an apostle, but we do not believe in an apostle, for an apostle does not justify the ungodly."[34]

[. . .] (102) It is a great sin, therefore, to condemn so subtle a logic as Christ's, which is principally disseminated to evoke faith. For to do this, according to Augustine, would be the same as a sick man rejecting medicine.[35] Hence, in opposition to a certain Apollinarian,[36] who was denying that Christ submitted to servitude on our behalf, Ambrose writes in his *Letter 46*, "The Apostle proclaims that he accepted the form of a servant; this is our strength, our hope, and our faith. The one who destroys this, will himself be destroyed." And he continues, "The servant who was made sin, reproach, and a curse for our sake is Christ the lamb, the worm, and many similar things which nobody will hesitate to say, since they were piously recorded."[37] And this sense is illustrated by Scripture in keeping with his two-fold nature. Although those who are fascinated with all things modern continue to murmur against Scripture, there still remains one consolation for us. For just as the eye of someone who squints, or is otherwise deficient, does not corrupt an accurate book, nor then does an error on the part of the other senses falsify the truth of the object. As such, there is no danger that someone's perverse understanding could wind up falsifying Holy Scripture. Still it is possible that someone, though to his own damnation, could fabricate an erroneous Scripture belonging to the Father of Lies, (103) designed to deceive simple people with its sophistry.

[. . .] (107) I do not consider it a valid excuse whereby we pretend that we are not refuting the sense of the author, but rather the erroneous verbal sense; now because we slander Scripture, understanding it according to an unsuitable sense, and now because the sense we dream up we then follow in effect, and now again thirdly, because we deny the Lord's sense of Scripture for the most part. This can be demonstrated by one example taken from the text of Mark 10:33–34, though the principle applies to all similar passages. **Look, we are going up to Jerusalem, and the Son of man will be handed over to the chief priests and the Scribes; and they will condemn him to death and will hand him over to the Gentiles to be mocked and scourged; and on the third day he will rise again.**

In that passage of Holy Scripture the adversary will concede five manifest lies pertaining to the Lord's sense, which are thus demonstrated: The sense of that passage of Scripture which God now comprehends is the same as he ever comprehended. But at any time he comprehended the sense of the first proposition at the present time, and the meaning of the four following propositions he comprehends in the future. (108) Therefore, he still comprehends it in this way now. And it is with respect to that sense that the adversary refutes Holy Scripture on the grounds that it is impossible; therefore, the conclusion. Although the first proposition had probably not been spoken by Christ at the present time for the sake of providing an adequate measure of his going up, since he customarily spoke while sitting or standing, and not, I believe, while walking around like the Peripatetics,[38] it was still true at any time that Christ's assembly went up. Consequently, God knew at any time that they were going to go up. And since it is not possible for him to begin to know or cease to know anything, he must always know that they are going up.

In light of this, it seems that the sense, meaning, and knowledge of God concerning the first proposition is that they are going up, just as at first. And so, according to those people, that passage of Scripture is now impossible with respect to the sense of the author.

Likewise, it is clear with regard to the four following propositions in the future, that any one of them is said to be impossible now, at least in an accidental manner.

Yet it is certain, based upon Christ's manner of speaking, that he utters past and future truths at present, as in John 3:13, **No one ascends into heaven, except for the one who descends from heaven**. Nor would there be any reason why he would now maintain a sense in the future, just as he did formerly, except that, by the same rationale, he would maintain the sense to be true in his own present time. Otherwise, that proposition would never be true at present, nor would the other passages of Scripture through which the Apostles describe the deeds of Christ at present, or others in the future. For after they had been written, they slipped into the past. Thus it would be necessary to express such a sense in the present, the past and the future in a disjunctive way. And that does not savor of the divine sense.

When considering all of those deductions it is appropriate to suppose that God cannot change his sense, knowledge or understanding. Rather, everything which he perceives, understands or comprehends, he comprehends eternally. This is made clear by the faith of Scripture in Mal. 3:6, **I am the Lord and I do not change**. (109) If, however, he were to change his sense according to a change occurring in what is perceived, then the highest level of mutability would abide in that sense, inasmuch as he would be dependent upon the sensible realm to obtain his own sense. Indeed, God's sense of succession would itself be composed successively from sensible instants. While this is appropriate for the human sense, it would be incompatible with the foreknowledge and memory of God if he did not comprehend succession of this sort all at once. Nor would it be in keeping with God's intuitive vision through the eternal principles.[39]

And so it is with regard to many other improprieties which philosophers, as well as theologians, have deduced from Scripture. Nor have I seen the writing of any holy doctor who has not rejected that judgment as damnable insofar as it is repugnant to the faith. Hence, in Book 6, Chapter 10 of *On the*

Trinity, after having illustrated that God is the fullness of all living and changeable principles, Augustine says,

> Therefore, while moments in time disappear and then follow after, nothing disappears and follows after in the knowledge of God. Surely these things which were created are not thus known by God because they were made. Rather, these changeable things were made, because they are unchangeably known by God.[40]

Anselm says something similar to this in the *Monologion*, Chapters 33 and 36.[41] And the Profound Doctor, in Book 1, Chapter 23, adduces many reasons as well as the testimonies of the saints leading to the same conclusion.[42] Having established this, it is evident that the Lord's sense of Holy Scripture is the same as it was prior to the Incarnation. Thus according to the adversaries, all such passages of Scripture would be impossible according to the author's sense.

Our opponent's argument carries little weight against the logic of Scripture. For according to the fourth defensive weapon, since all things are present to God, the prophetic proposition that Christ will rise, is perpetually true. It has been posited in perpetuity, signifying in this way, because it signifies perpetually, even as it does for its proper time. (110) Hence, it is not necessary that in order for the proposition to be true, here on this occasion, that the truth, by means of which it is true, is here on this occasion. For it is sufficient that a truth exists somewhere, which signifies in this manner. Likewise, it is not necessary that in order for the proposition to be true at present, its proper truth, by means of which it is true, abides at present. Rather, it suffices that it exist for a time. Thus it does not follow that if God knows at this moment that Christ will rise, then Christ will rise at this moment. For it is sufficient that this is the case at the time prior to his death. And so it is with other prophecies.

Nor does it follow that if it is not the case at this moment that Christ will rise, therefore, it is false at this moment that Christ will rise, since the consequent is an affirmative proposition, implying that it is false that Christ will rise, with the result that it is not the case that Christ will rise. And it is evident that if it is not the case at this moment that Christ will rise, then this is false at this moment, because Christ will rise after this. Therefore, it is the same thing to say that it is the case, at this moment, that Christ will rise, and that the futurity of Christ's resurrection exists at this moment. Yet this is never in keeping with Scripture, nor with its sense.

And the same is said with respect to all other similar prophecies. Let them be condensed in their totality, insofar as the prophet thus said, etc. And then no part of Scripture will have to bear the slander of falsehood.

That notwithstanding, one should note that some prophecies are threatening, some conditional, some mystical, and certain others simply a matter of divine foreknowledge. One should discern them in their simple or composite sense; a process which requires divine elucidation. So it is with that passage of Isa. 38:1, where it said to Hezekiah, **Put your house in order, because you will die, and you will not live**. (111) But this had been spoken as a threat, so that the one confiding in the Lord would thus repent. Consider that passage in Jon. 3:4, **Forty days as yet, and Nineveh will be overthrown**. This was spoken conditionally in the literal sense (*ad literam*), unless the people would repent; and mystically, in order that the flesh of the people, which inordinately predominated in them, should be held in check through penance. This subject matter is dealt with in the previous chapter.

Those senses which extend beyond the letter are bequeathed to us in Scripture so that we might realize that sin need not remain with the pilgrim, if only he wishes to be broken down in spirit. Now God cannot abrogate his own merciful law through any preordination of his own, but he will turn around and forgive sin, providing that the sinner is duly converted. Nevertheless, God knows who will be converted and who will remain obstinate. For all of these things are equally necessary based upon the supposition that God's ordination and the sense of his Scripture remain blameless either way.

But if someone objects that there is no certitude in the prophecies according to this gloss, since a conditional statement does not posit the sort of certitude in which a predicate belongs to a subject, then surely there can be no prophecy with respect to that sense except history, supposing that the prophet thus spoke, and then there would be a confusion of the parts of Scripture. I say that a falsehood is assumed here, because to those who are illuminated for the sake of understanding the Scriptures prophetically there is certitude in the prophetic sayings in keeping with the level of enlightenment abiding within the prophets. And we even achieve certitude regarding those which were simply affirmed by God.

Future prophecies are also certain for us. For those general ones which come to pass are the faith of the Church. And by applying general prophecies to persons, we know that what was prophesied of them will come to pass, unless they recover their senses sooner. And seeing the continuation of the ingratitude on the part of the sinful people, we will convince them through dialectical evidence based upon prophecy that the given punishment will come about simply, and that it was simply ordained by God. Such is the case concerning the punishment that is going to be meted out to the Church through anti-Christ for having forsaken God's law in this present age. (112) And knowledge of this sort is sufficient for the wayfaring Church.

With regard to the second objection, I have often said that the entire Holy Scripture is the one word of God, and that every one of its parts should be condensed into the totality of that Word in whom the blessed in heaven see the multitude of truths spoken by God. And this point does not oppose, but in fact agrees with, the principle that some parts of Scripture would have a privative sense, others historical, others prophetic, and still others sapiential or mystical. Yet the five-fold method, spoken of in Chapter Eight, is required in order to comprehend such a sense correctly. Therefore, whoever is able to grasp it does so by divine dispensation. But let the person who is not granted such power be careful that he does not subvert, corrupt, or condemn the sense of Scripture.

Hence, for the purpose of teaching the Church that the entire sense of Scripture is the one word of God, it is written in Ezek. 1:1 that, **It came to pass in the thirtieth year, the fourth month, in the fifth day of the month**. Whereupon, the saints who take note of even the conjunctions and accidents of the Scriptures, say that the prophet proceeded to prophesy with a conjunction in order to point out to his descendants that his whole meaning was connected, just as if it was part of the word of the Lord which God spoke to him in the Spirit. Thus all the Lord's scribes surely spoke the one great word with a single voice. Accordingly, the rest of the word, which was distributed to others, the prophet sees confusedly. He then joins to this what he sees distinctly, while he begins to write: and it came to pass in such a year, in such a month, and such a day.

But the third principal objection raised by the sophists is that while none of the complete and whole parts of Scripture is impossible and heretical, the dangling part is, (113) since such parts have been mutilated: "There is no God"; "You will never die"; "That man is a sinner." And such is the case with many of the lies stemming from the body of the devil, which are recited in Holy Scripture. For it does not appear that the Christian mind could ponder an entire passage of Scripture of this sort according to the sense of Scripture, unless it ponders such an aspect according to the impossible sense. Consequently, the Catholic must not be blamed for conceding that

Holy Scripture is impossible according to that part which pertains to the sense he ought to elicit.

To this I say that it is the same thing to concede that Scripture is impossible according to a part of this sort, and to concede that it is impossible together with the other unsuitable appendages which are recited. This is the reasoning of those who say it is neither true, nor authentic, nor catholic according to that part. For as I recounted in Chapter Five, these are the people who separate the true and false parts of Scripture only to claim that more of its parts are false. Now when a human being, and any other bodily entity, receives its beauty from a figure, one still grants that there are any number of quantitative parts which may be deformed in and of themselves. And yet when they are connected with the whole they lack deformity, thereby producing the fully integrated beauty of its totality. So it is with the parts of the Scriptures. Thus when the parts of Scripture have been mutilated in this way, they ought to signify the sense of its totality, even while such an impossible sense is left dangling. Otherwise, it would be possible for the corrupter of Scripture to take a single word drawn from one oration and connect it to a word drawn from another, then claiming that this is Holy Scripture according to any one of its parts, even though it is obviously impossible. That passage of John 7:24 would be perverted just so: **Do not judge according to appearance, but judge by righteous judgment.** From that passage comes the following blasphemous dogma: Do not judge by righteous judgment, but judge according to appearance. (114) After all, the terms themselves are the same in both cases.

Therefore, it appears to be no less of a sin to pervert the sense of Scripture based upon the fixed order of the terms, than it is to maintain an evil sense based upon transposed signs. In these instances one finds neither the senses nor the proper morals, except in a most accidental fashion. If by some perverse custom, the Christian were to lapse into such an impossible thought regarding a part of Scripture, let him bewail his sin and endeavor to restrain his soul, so that he does not ponder such a sense separately, but instead piously proceeds to reflect separately upon the catholic sense.

Undoubtedly, this is quite possible, just as it is possible to think of a person, while not thinking separately of his ugliness, nor of the deformity of part of his shape, having established that he exists in and of himself. But if a faithful person will piously contemplate the anti-Christian sense of some foolish writing or statement which extends beyond the limits of Holy Scripture, he does not include it. Rather, he excludes it, since it would render Holy Scripture impossible. Now just because Song of Songs may provide one with the opportunity for calling to mind carnal copulation with a woman, it does not mean that passage of Scripture is disgraceful or carnal. In fact, it was in order to avoid just such a sense that the Hebrews ordained that only those of mature years should read this song. [. . .]

Notes

1. See Thomas Bradwardine's *De Causa Dei contra Pelagium* I.34, ed. Henry Savile (1618; repr. Frankfurt am Main, 1964), pp. 294–307.

2. *Contra Mendacium* XII.26, ed. Joseph Zycha, Corpus Scriptorum Ecclesiasticorum Latinorum 41 (Vienna, 1900), p. 507. These are not Augustine's words.

3. *Homilia* XXX, PL 76:1220. These are not Gregory's words.

4. *De Causa Dei* III.29, p. 739.

5. *De Doctrina Christiana* I.36.41, ed. Josef Martin, Corpus Christianorum, Series Latina 32 (Turnhout, 1962), p. 30.

6. *De Mendacio* V.7, ed. Joseph Zycha, Corpus Scriptorum Ecclesiasticorum Latinorum 41 (Vienna, 1900), p. 421.

7. *Contra Mendacium* X.24, CSEL 41:501.

8. *Summa Theologiae* II.ii, Q. 110, a. 3, in *Opera Omnia*, ed. S. E. Fretté and Paul Maré, vol. 4 (Paris, 1895), p. 165. These are not Aquinas's words.

9. *De Mendacio* I.1, CSEL 41:413–14.

10. *De Mendacio* III.3–4, CSEL 41:414–16.

11. Hugh of St. Victor, *De Sacramentis* II.18.17, PL 176:614–15. Note that while Hugh writes here on the difference between seeing and believing, Wyclif does not record his words.

12. Dec. II, C. 1, Q. 1, c. 64; in Emil Friedberg, ed., *Corpus iuris canonici*, 2 vols. (Leipzig, 1879–81), 1:381. Cf. Jerome, *Comm. in Epist. ad Galatas* I, PL 26:347. Marcion and Basilides were heretics of the mid-second century. Marcion created his own biblical canon which dispensed with the Old Testament, and adopted Luke as his single Gospel. He retained the Pauline Epistles, but even then redacted them according to his own Gnostic specifications, extracting what he deemed later corrupting interpolations.

13. See Aristotle's *Metaphysics* IV, 1006a–1009a.

14. Dec. I, D. 37, c. 4, in Friedberg, *Corpus* 1:136. Cf. Jerome, PL 24:318.

15. Ibid., in Friedberg, *Corpus* 1:136. See *Comm. in Jer. Proph.* V.29, PL 24:892–93. Note that the Decretum reads '*diuinos*' rather than '*demones*', as does Jerome's text in PL 24.

16. Ibid., in Friedberg, *Corpus* 1:136. See *Comm. in Jer. Proph.* VI.31, PL 24:917.

17. See *Contra Mendacium* IX.20–X.24, CSEL 41:492–502.

18. See *Contra Mendacium* XV.31–33, CSEL 41:511–14.

19. See *Contra Mendacium* XVIII.36–37, CSEL 41:519–22.

20. *Retractiones* II.22.3, CCSL 57:108.

21. Perhaps Augustine's *De Symbolo ad Catachumenos* III, PL 40:663.

22. Dec. II, C. 22, Q. 2, c. 9, in Friedberg, *Corpus* 1:870.

23. *In Iohannis Evangelium* IV.5, ed. D. R. Willems, Corpus Christianorum, Series Latina 36 (Turnhout, 1954), p. 33.

24. *In Ioh. Evang.* IV.5, CCSL 36:33.

25. See *In Ioh. Evang.* IV.6, CCSL 36:34.

26. Wyclif quotes at length Augustine, Gregory, and Chrysostom on the nature of lying, all to the effect that John the Baptist did not lie.

27. *Moralium* XXXIV.19, PL 76:738.

28. This is Richard FitzRalph, Archbishop of Armagh (d. 1360). On this question see Gordon Leff, *Richard Fitzralph: Commentator of the Sentences* (Manchester, 1963), pp. 39–50.

29. See *De Causa Dei* I.27–33, pp. 261–94.

30. *De verbis Evangelii Matthaei*, PL 38:510.

31. *Biblia Sacra cum Glossa Ordinaria et Expositionibus* V.12 (Lyons, 1545), p. 224.

32. *In Ioh. Evang.* LIV.1–8, CCSL 36:458–63.

33. *In Ioh. Evang.* XLVII.1–14, CCSL 36:403–13. By three natures, Wyclif seems to be referring to Augustine's insistence in this sermon that the person of Christ is composed of flesh, soul, and Word.

34. *In Ioh. Evang.* LIV.3, CCSL 36:460.

35. This is certainly an Augustinian precept, but this phrase as such has not been found.

36. Apollinarius of Laodicia (310–390) maintained that the Divine Logos took the place of the human soul in the Incarnate Person of Christ.

37. *Epist.* XLVI, PL 16:1195–96. These are not entirely Ambrose's words.

38. The designation "Peripatetics" refers to the followers of the Aristotle.

39. Wyclif distinguished between *duratio*, which is time understood from God's perspective of the eternal present; and *tempus*, which pertains to humanity's experience of time as a succession of instants.

40. *De Trinitate* VI.10.11, ed. W. J. Mountain, Corpus Christianorum, Series Latina 50a (Turnhout, 1968), p. 241.

41. *Monologion* XXXIII, XXXVI in *Opera Omnia*, ed. F. S. Schmitt, vol. 1 (Edinburgh, 1946), pp. 51–55.

42. *De Causa Dei* I.23, pp. 237–42.

On the Truth of Holy Scripture

Part Four: Scripture as the Law of Christendom

(*De ver.* II,xx): The Superiority of Evangelical Law

(129) With regard to the subject matter of the third argument made at the beginning of Chapter Fifteen, there is no doubt in my mind that the law of Christ should be loved in proportion to its lawgiver. Consequently, it is infinitely more honorable than any human tradition. For as I have often said, since that law was handed down to human beings by uncreated Wisdom, and because it is the most suitable means of bringing peace to the people through its three-fold peace, it is obvious that a disruption or dissolution of this law is attested to by the lack of true peace among the people. Clearly then, this law is by its very nature the cause of true peace. For just as at the time of Christ a commingling of human traditions with the law of Moses heralded the destruction of the people, (130) so the dissolution of Christ's law at the time of anti-Christ attests to the destruction of the Christian people. While Mohammed weakened Christendom through a legal tradition that runs contrary to God's law, as I made clear in Chapter Eleven, so also has there been a multiplication, a dogmatizing, and an appropriation of human tradition following the Donation made to the Church.[1] And this has only served to weaken the law of Christ, thus diminishing the true religion of the Christian people. While on the other hand, it is clear that the observation of Christ's law is by its very nature the cause of true peace, because it is the worship of the true God, a fact to which so

many passages of Scripture bear witness. Now if anyone observes God's law he attains a proportionate peace with God. So it is that by the love of God he finds true peace in all respects, according to that passage in Psalm 118 (Ps. 119:165), **There is much peace for those who love your law, and for them there is no stumbling block.** Though to the contrary, deceitfulness is the disruption of peace, along with the introduction of dissension and disturbance, since this is a privation of God's love. In keeping with this sense it is said in Job 10 (Job 22:21), **Who can resist him and find peace?** And also according to this sense it is said in Bar. 3:10–13, **Why is it Israel that you are in the land of your enemies?** And the response follows: **You have abandoned the fountain of wisdom; for if you had walked in the way of God you would have lived in peace upon the earth.**

There are any number of such sayings to be found in Scripture which echo this refrain. And so it is patently clear that sin accounts for the destruction of humanity's peace with God. Yet when peace abides it is conceded that this **peace surpasses all understanding** (Phil. 4:7), since it is better for the Christian, therefore, etc.

(131) In light of such things it seems, furthermore, that the exercise, indoctrination or institution of human law is leading people to forsake the observation of Christ's law, thus diminishing the effect of this law, which is itself the true peace and Christian religion.

[. . .] (140) Whereupon, in Luke 11:52, Christ speaks directly to the Pharisees and legal experts, saying, **Woe to you, legal experts, who took away the key of wisdom; for you did not enter and you hindered those who were entering!** What he means here is that the Pharisees were taking the key of Holy Scripture away from the laity through the multiplication of their traditions, given the affection they had for their own inventions. They found that there was more money to be made, and more praise to be garnered, in publicly proclaiming things of this sort and seeing that they were carried out, than in following the precepts of the Lord. Oh, if only evil every bit as sinister as this were not springing forth today from a wicked generation within God's holy Church! These are the ones whom the truth calls down upon, or more fittingly, prophesies many woes. And the *Decretum* establishes that we should be on our guard against them in more recent days. For as I recounted above in Chapter Seventeen, by the authority of St. Peter in the ordination of Clement, Case 11, Question 1 of the *Decretum* states that, "Whoever afflicts a doctor of the truth, sins against Christ and provokes God, the Father of all, on account of which he will even lose his life."[2] These days the situation is surely perilous, since the world is far more concerned with temporal matters now that the Bridegroom has journeyed on to heaven.

Those people who corrupt and obstruct the word of Scripture should consider the example of Lincolniensis when he said that the Church is an irrigated garden in which all kinds of virtues are planted, just as plants, trees and shrubs. Surely then, if anyone were so insolent as to enter into this precious garden of the priest and trample this plant under his feet (141) he would cut one off before it had a chance to reach the maturity of the seed, and wholly eradicate another. Do we not believe that the caretaker would excommunicate such a servant, especially if he and his entire family were fed by these fruits? This applies all the more to a caretaker of souls who cherishes the vineyard of his Church to an infinitely greater degree, prizing the trees of the virtues and the seed of faith with a love unceasing.[3] Therefore, let the person who blocks the way of the Lord's discourse, consider the dignity of the word, the value of edifying the people, the excellence of the office, and the severity of the Lord. For then, by the grace of God, he will shudder at the prospect of placing an obstacle in the way of God's word.

A second principal argument which I raise concludes that what is good for any person is more useful and honorable, and is more strictly commanded in all respects. Thus it is reasonably given preference, inasmuch as one sins gravely by neglecting it, as evinced in *De Consecratione*, Distinction 5, "*Non Mediocriter*."[4] This is the case with the law of Scripture when compared to any other laws. As such, that law is foremost among all others and must be chiefly learned by the priests. Its personal usefulness is made clear on the part of the person who learns it, and its general usefulness on the part of Holy Mother Church. On the part of the person who learns it there is a three-fold usefulness. First, it enables him to ward off the attacks of his enemies. Second, he accumulates both merit and reward through his studies. And third, it is the means by which he can generally consider what may be deemed useful in a foreign law. Now he can drive away the devil, exemplified by the office of the exorcist, as well as the teaching of Christ. For when he was tempted by the devil in Matt. 4:1–11, he refuted him three times from Scripture.

Now if I am not mistaken, it is impossible to overcome the devil except through the law of Holy Scripture. With respect to attaining victory over the world, our faith says in 1 John 4:5, **Brothers and sisters, no one overcomes the world unless he believes that Jesus is the Son of God.** (142) This belief is firmly learned from Scripture alone. If you wish, therefore, to trample upon worldly affections, learn how the Son of God lived in this world as one who was hated, exiled, and punished. He lived by punishment, because **He became poor for our sake**, according to 2 Cor. 8:9; **not having so much as a place of his own in the world upon which to lay his head**, according to Matt. 8:20. He was hated, as it says in 1 John 3:13, **Do not be astonished if the world hates you**, etc. For according to John 15:19, **If you were of the world, the world would love its own.** If we consider how the devil's members had called the father of the household "Beelzebul" (Matt. 10:25), while he patiently tolerated these and all other insults, then if we truly belonged to his household we too would suffer such reproach, and repent by conforming to Christ's example. For this was why he assumed that role, as I demonstrated in Chapter 15 of the Fourth Book.[5]

To put it briefly, I say that spiritual profit is infinitely better than temporal, and spiritual profit cannot be acquired apart from the teaching of Holy Scripture. Thus it is clear, given the usefulness of the law, that the law of Christ is of infinitely greater importance for every Christian than all other laws. It is for this reason that Christ says in Matt. 16:26, **What does it profit a person if he were to gain the whole world and yet suffer the loss of his soul?**

In light of this, it is evident that he accumulates this useful good, (143) not only because it is the whole merit of spiritual good for his disciple, but because it is the most useful fruit of Holy Mother Church.

First, peace cannot be established among the people without the promulgation of law, and that is the duty of the priest. Clearly then, apart from the observance of this law, no people can exist, nor can there be peace with God. For apart from this no other peace is valid if lacking the protection of God's word. All of this is clarified by what I have so often said already. Since peace is the single principle which affects the whole human race, according to Augustine in Chapter 12 of *The City of God*,[6] attention must be paid to this law in the conducting of public affairs. Second, by the same rationale, it is clearly impossible to hold dominion over the Church, nor any other community, nor even possess temporal power apart from the instruction and observation of this law. On this account, since Holy Mother Church is intent upon gaining prosperity through temporal power here on this journey homeward, when Song of Sol. 8:3 reckons it greater that **the left hand of the**

bridegroom would be under her head, it seems fitting that she would give the utmost attention to the necessary science in order to achieve this end. Yet it is under that pretext that she so ardently attends to the lucrative sciences. Now it plainly follows that this desire for temporal rights especially disrupts the peace of the commonwealth and corrupts the Church. As such, Holy Mother Church must take great pains to learn these laws and direct the laity to the law of Christ. The deduction fundamentally depends upon that principle of faith which holds that love is the only title by which earthly property is justly acquired, possessed or defended. For that title alone is certified by God. Only love is firmly taught and acquired through the law of Christ, for if another law teaches any love or virtue then it is from God and is thus Christ's law.

(144) Third, the same is made clear by the good of grace and beatitude, which is the goal of every useful good for the pilgrim, according to that passage in Luke 9:25, **What does it profit a person if he were to gain the whole world and yet suffer the loss of his soul?** Aristotle proves the same thing in first and tenth book of his *Ethics*.[7]

Therefore, since the Church cannot acquire the good apart from the teaching of this science, it seems fitting that this science is the most useful thing of all for Holy Mother Church. Whatever science could multiply the theological virtues among the people must itself be sacred theology, leaving aside differences of language or humanly instituted forms. If then, according to Christ's teaching in Matthew 7 (Matt. 6:33), **Every person should first seek the kingdom of God and his righteousness, and all these necessary temporal accessories will be added unto him**, it clearly follows that the science which teaches one how to seek these two things more directly should be chiefly embraced by the Church on account of the fact that it is a useful good. Is there anyone who doubts that every such science is theology, whether grasped through the faithful hearing of human instruction, or by divine inspiration? For if, according to Christ's testimony in Matt. 19:17, **Whoever would wish to enter into eternal life, it is necessary and sufficient for him to keep the commandments**, it seems fitting that the law of God's commandments is sufficient by its very nature. Other mechanical arts, even those called the liberal arts, would be unnecessary and, I believe, in most cases superfluous, if claims to private property had not been culpably introduced. Take away all ownership and culpable affection, and whatever else proves incompatible, and then every case in the Church could only be decided according to the evangelical law of love. Let this law be the principal defender of the rights of Holy Mother Church, and let her then be willing to suffer injury if she must.

(145) In light of this, the correlation seems to follow that all human traditions or voluntary operations which have undermined the free course of evangelical law or withdrawn it from the Church, have thus revoked or diminished the fruit of Holy Mother Church by transgressing against the first commandment of the second table.[8] For they are taking an intrinsically useful good away from her. Yet to the extent that something would be intrinsically good on the one side, so its privation would be that much more evil on the other. Let us be on our guard, therefore, against those who would stand in the way of this blessing which rightfully belongs to our Mother.

It is proven, moreover, that the study and practice of theology will be of greater assistance to any honest person of the Church in acquiring the good more honorably than the study and practice of any other faculty. The good of uncreated Wisdom is more acceptable, whose flowers are the fruit of honor and dignity, as is said in Ecclesiasticus 24 (Sir. 24:17–19), **The foliage of the Lord's words are flowers and his fruit remains the most dignified and beautiful**. For he himself is the principle of beauty and dignity, beyond whose judgment there exists nothing honorable, beneficial, or beautiful. And, by this same rationale, it follows that the most delightful good of all consists in this sacred science, since its end is the contemplation of the highest good. The philosophers consider it axiomatic that if a pure virtue delights in its beautiful object through a clear intuition inasmuch as it is the intrinsic cause, then the purer virtue is even more secluded from distraction. And thus by its intuition of the most delightful object, according to the copious principle of its beauty, which is that much more intense, one rejoices all the more, since the intrinsic cause and its own intrinsic effect mutually correspond. And because, by the faith of Scripture, God is the highest beauty, he is fully comprehensible to the blessed in heaven, apart from fear or any other distraction. Thus it follows that this comprehension is the most joyful of all. And because the goal of theology rests in that clear vision of the Trinity which, based upon Christ's testimony in John 14:6–10, is **eternal life**, it follows that because theology is concerned with this delightful good it surpasses all the other sciences. (146) Surely it is more effective in preparing one for the journey homeward with respect to faith, hope and love. Therefore, since it is appropriate for the predestined to enter into a clear vision, comprehension and abundant love, it would also follow that theology arranges things chiefly for sake of achieving this end. This science is thus more honorable than all the rest on account of the unfailing way in which it proceeds, the nobility of its object, and the principle of its ultimate goal. No other science is good except to the extent that it advances and disposes itself to that end. Consequently, every sensitive or earthly science which opposes, diminishes, or hinders this science is diabolical, since it alone begets and augments the faith of the Church. It is clear that among the sciences this is the only one which begets and rejuvenates the members of Christ. Now the Apostle says in Heb. 10:38, **My righteous one lives by faith**. First of all, I say that spiritual existence comes to members of the Church through faith. Unfortunately, this is not so with those foreign arts which appear to nourish the theological virtues,[9] as in the case of certain demons who were thought to have miraculously cured the afflicted by this sophistical illusion whereby they relieve the wounds of those they were previously afflicting all the more. Of course, we know that it is necessary for every theological virtue to be infused from above, not in a manner befitting the speaking of mendacious words. As such, we are left to conclude that it is only according to the words of the Lord, or of Scripture, that the demons are conjured or natures transmuted, as much by the faithful as by the unfaithful, precisely by the words of the Lord. Whereupon, if God infuses grace into these afflicted traditions this will not be granted by these exterior words by arrangement or occasion, but instead through the mercy of the one who, **where sin abounded, made grace abound all the more** (Rom. 5:20). Therefore, only the words of the Lord are to be disseminated among the people, in keeping with Peter's prescription in 1 Pet. 4:11 that, **If anyone speaks, let it be as if these are the words of God**. (147) Every word of truth which is in keeping with the law of Scripture directly edifies Holy Mother Church, inasmuch as such a word belongs to God's discourse. For this is how Christ most pointedly rebukes the priests, Pharisees and scribes insofar as they do injury to God as they exalted their own traditions and put away the law of God, as evinced in Matt. 15 and 23, and in Luke 5 and 15. For in the word of God abides the power to beget and nourish the children of God. The children of the devil reveal themselves by killing, weakening and hindering the warriors of God's army, thwarting the generation of God's children while multiplying the foreigners. For this not only betrays the Lord's most beloved bride, but tortures the Lord himself, leaving him mangled and infirmed in his mystical body, which is the Church. Yet what could be more heretical and blasphemous than this?

Furthermore, it is clear that this science demands the most attention from the faithful, and especially the priests, by virtue of the Lord's precept. For in the last chapter of John (John 21: 15–19) Christ commands Peter to feed his sheep. There can be no doubt that through Peter he gave all his priestly successors the power of sacerdotal authority. For through Peter he charged them all with this sacerdotal duty. Hence, it was the very intention of the Lord's precept that all priests are successors of Peter, and thus obligated to fulfill this ministry.

I beseech you, let us observe the form of the Lord's precept, how in Peter's final conversation with the Lord it was repeated three times, under no guise or pretext whatsoever. But just as he loved the Lord, so he longed to be loved by him in return. And since there is no salvation when this love is not reciprocated, it is clear that every priest must take great pains to fulfill that duty.

[. . .] (150) The law of love and the principles of faith prove that priests should attend to the art of the work of preaching above all, since it is on this basis that they retain the dignity of their office.

Again, priests of the Old Testament were only obligated to direct their efforts to the law of God, but the priests of the New Testament are under greater obligation to fulfill that duty. For having supposed the major premise, that they would have no other law, this is all the more reason why they should only concern themselves with the law of God. On this basis, the minor premise is clear, namely that our priests have received from God more abundant spiritual gifts and a stricter obligation. And so the sufficiency of the law is the major premise, while the minor is the lack of extraneous material. Surely Christ is superior to the angel who gave the Old Law, and by grace our priests are greater. Now the law of Scripture is fulfilled, explained and facilitated through Christ, for it is made easier, not harder, by the multitude of its conservators. Why then is it necessary for Christ's priests to give such damnable attention to alien laws? For that would be of no use to them unless they were intent on securing their ecclesiastical possessions which have been introduced over and above the gospel. If you are looking for a sign that such laws have been illegitimately introduced, consider that the Donation was made to the Church through theology. (151) And it is precisely because these human laws are multiplied that the multiplication of Christ's law and the peace of the Church is so hindered.

Clearly then, just as the people in Christ's day were destroyed by the traditions of the Pharisees, it is only fitting now that the guidance of Christ's law and the mediation of spiritual leaders will be withdrawn if secular traditions are increasingly multiplied, and the lifestyles of the priests corrupted more and more by worldliness. In his seventh sermon on Joshua, Origen notes how the walls of Jericho were demolished by the noise of the trumpets blown by the priests who had marched around the city seven times, as evinced in Josh. 6:15–20.[10] One reads in Luke 19:1 that the nature of man coming down from Jerusalem entered into Jericho,[11] to whose blind Christ brought sight in Luke 18:35–43. This is an important sign for the present age. Now Jericho is translated as 'the moon' or 'his fragrance',[12] and thus aptly signifies human beings who are violently shaken up in their bodies and affections by the fluctuation of temporal affairs. For they belong to the city of the devil, whose walls are the worship of riches and whose turrets are the celebrated dogmas of heretics, and by whose ramparts worldly dealings are fortified. But the Lord Jesus Christ, whose type Jesus, the son of Nun did bear (Sir. 46:1),[13] brought the walls and turrets of that city crashing to the ground through the trumpet blast of the Apostles, when **throughout every land his sound went forth** (Ps. 19:4). Now the seven forms of evangelical poverty, together with the body of Christ, are effectively illustrated by the arks of both testaments. Those sacerdotal trumpets which are beaten out of metal are surely the organs of the priest's voice through which the sense of Scripture is drawn out for the sake of discouraging worldly desires. (152) Hence, if you are a priest, seeing that you belong to a class especially chosen for this purpose, **lift up your voice as if it were a trumpet**, as it says in Isa. 58:1. Consider it a trumpet, though it is not because you are more than you are that you possess a voice of this sort, since you are but a mere organ of the Bridegroom's voice. Therefore, let not the preachers be proud of their voices, since it is Christ who is speaking through them.

Second, they should connect the parts of their discourse to one another in the likeness of a trumpet, whereby the pages of both testaments are connected, **bringing forth the new and the old** (Matt. 13:52). Thus we, together with the ancient fathers, are the one pipe of the Holy Spirit, not allowing strange words to lead us away from the words of God.

Third, the preacher should proceed by amplifying love according to the form of the trumpet. Just like the Sons of Thunder, he should courageously preach sermons of great authority, sowing those five sayings of 1 Cor. 14 mightily, diversely, and in a circular pattern, to all who are capable of receiving them. For just as a planter sows the seeds across a portion of the circle, treading now upon the higher elevation, and now upon the lower, so too the preacher who endeavors at one time to live the contemplative life and at another time to live the active, should in every case sow the word of God in keeping with a holy purpose. But it must be noted that the people should first be armed like the crowd which follows those seven priests who are making such a joyful noise with their seven trumpets. Every Christian should first be armed with virtues and perform meritorious works, because in Acts 1:1, **Jesus began to work and teach**. Those who pursue the active life and direct their attention to the works of the laity should follow the priestly instruction elicited from Holy Scripture. The entirety of Christendom should harmoniously bellow out a joyful shout to the commander of their army, the Lord Jesus Christ, since they are called upon to fight as happy warriors against the devil's forces, ascribing all power and victory to their commander. This is the chant spoken of in Psalm 88 (Ps. 89:15), **Blessed are the people who know the joyful shout.**

That the seven priests should blow their trumpets continually for six days signifies that the whole priesthood ought to resound in the preaching of the gospel throughout the six ages of the Church Militant, (153) even though the supercilious life-style of this world will not be utterly destroyed prior to the seventh age. Now Jericho signifies the city which loves itself even to the contempt of God, closed off by a three-fold wall composed of fleshly concupiscence, temporal affluence, and worldly prominence. But this wall is brought down by the sound of holy preaching, by the pious shout of prayer, and by the sixth complete encirclement signifying its own shattering. For just as all the warriors of the city of God advance upon the devil's city and take it by assault, so the gold of philosophical wisdom, the silver of secular eloquence, and the vase of natural industry and power which they have found, should be consecrated to the treasury of the Lord. For it has been converted to the sacred use of edifying the Church through a flourishing ritual and way of life by which worldly pride is entirely annihilated. Indeed, only Rahab the prostitute, along with her family, will be saved (Josh. 6:22–25), because only the worldly who live like heathens prove adulterous to Church's Bridegroom. Yet they too will be saved if they do essentially good works, piously repenting, and defending the preachers of the gospel. Now the merciful kindness which prevails above all else makes it possible for those who have proven adulterous to the Lord to obtain forgiveness. This is evinced in the case of Nebuchadnezzar (Dan. 4:34–37), as well as the centurion

Cornelius (Acts 10:44–48). Yet we clerics must fear the invocation of our Joshua most of all: **Cursed is the man in the sight of the Lord who would raise and build up the city of Jericho** (Josh. 6:26). And yet following the Donation to the Church, countless clerics have engaged in the accursed practice of putting on the purple pallium of worldly dominion.[14] Among the laity this is a very good thing, for the golden bar symbolizes the secular wisdom needed to maintain civil rule over the people, while the two-hundred shekels of silver symbolize the much sought after eloquence pertaining to civil laws and ecclesiastical temporalities (Josh. 7:21). And this is the reason why the rights of primogeniture owed to those martyred on behalf of Christ's law were annihilated by the Church's Donation. (154) For these days the charters of this Donation are deemed more catholic than the gospel, while the first and latest works of love now lay dormant. But we must be even more frightened by the fact that within the Christian army the thirty-six men were struck down by the citizens of the city of Ai, on account of the transgression of the priest claiming to be a poor man of Christ (Josh. 7:5). For this is the whole company of the proud led on by the arrogance of the priests. Ai, which is interpreted as the 'life of valleys', signifies the army of arrogant spirits cast down into hell. It is surely inevitable that the Christian army will be conquered by the devil when the leadership of the priests, blowing their metal trumpets, is lost. For according to Lam. 4:13–14, **On account of the sins of her prophets and the iniquities of her priests, who shed the blood of the righteous in her midst, the blind have gone astray in the streets**. Just as in Matt. 15:14 Christ says, **If a blind man leads the blind, both fall into the pit.** It is essential, therefore, to sound the trumpet continually, not by proclaiming the word at one time, while at another time fawning over people in hope of acquiring temporalities; not by yielding to servile fear in one instance and then, putting aside the trumpet of Holy Scripture, growling like beasts plundering the defenseless in a quest for rancid spoils. It would certainly be better that such an eye be plucked out and thrown away from the person of the Church. Or, as I recounted in Chapter Eighteen of this treatise, let him be at least stoned in a spiritual fashion together with Achan (Josh. 7:24–26). For this is in keeping with Origen's rendering of Christ's teaching in Matt. 5:29, **if your right eye causes you to sin, pull it out and cast it away from you.**[15]

The entirety of Holy Scripture, therefore, attests to this meaning both morally and literally (*literaliter*).

(*De ver.* II,xxi): The Necessity of Preaching the Word

(155) Yet in order that this matter of the duty of preaching might be made even clearer, it must be confirmed according to the laws of the Church, filtered through the lens of Scripture and the holy doctors.

First, it seems fitting that in keeping with the dignity of the word of God it must be lovingly communicated to one's brethren. Now according to the Savior's testimony in Luke 11:28, it is ultimately better **to hear the word of God and obey it** than to bear Christ carnally in the womb, since the Blessed Virgin was glorified at first in an accidental fashion, and only secondarily in an essential way. For Christ said, **Blessed are the ones who hear the word of God and obey it**. Case 1, Question 1 instills that meaning under the authority of Augustine:

> I ask you to tell me, brothers and sisters, what seems greater to you, Christ's body or Christ's word? If you wish to respond truly, you ought to say that the word of God is no less than the body of Christ. Since we are so careful when the body of Christ is administered to us that none of it fall from our hands to the ground, let us be just as careful that the word which is bequeathed to you is not lost to the pure

> heart while we are busy thinking or speaking of something else. For the person who would carelessly hear God's word is no less guilty than the person who would carelessly allow Christ's body to fall to the ground.[16]

(156) On this basis it is clear, first of all, that Holy Scripture must be treated with the utmost reverence and never disfigured by an erroneous sense. Second, it is evident that preaching God's word is a more solemn act than consecrating the sacrament, since only one person receives the word of God when accepting the body of Christ. It is a far better thing, therefore, that the people receive God's word than that a solitary person receive Christ's body. And this is the proper duty of the higher ranking clergy, since it pertains to the office of evangelization, while serving tables is reserved for priests and deacons, as evinced in Acts 6, and in the Canon this is testified to by Distinction 25,[17] and the end of Distinction 36.[18] This is the reason why the Archdeacon considers God's word preeminent over the reception of Christ's body, because preaching is more effective in blotting out mortal sins than the Eucharist. He says, "The word of God brings about a restoration in our hearts which results in the forgiveness of sin."[19] It breaks our hearts through fear, for according to Jer. 23:29, **Are not my words as a burning fire and like a hammer breaking a rock into pieces?** Second, according to Psalm 50 (Ps. 51:17), it crushes through sorrow: **A contrite and humble heart, God, you will not despise**. Third, it melts through love, according to Song of Sol. 5:6, **My soul melted because my beloved spoke.** Fourth, it draws upward through desire beyond the hardness of heart, for in Song of Sol. 1:4 the Church says to the word of God, **Draw me after you**. Fifth, it drinks in through delight. Whereupon, Psalm 76 (Ps. 77:3) says, **I was mindful of God and took delight in him, and my spirit fainted.** Sixth, it gives life through inspiration, for in Hebrews 5 (Heb. 4:12), **The word of God is alive**, and in John 5:25, **The Hour comes**

and now is when the dead will hear the voice of the Son of God, and those who hear will live. (157) Seventh, it heals the sick, according to Psalm 106 (Ps. 107:20), **He sent out his word and healed them.** Eighth, it cuts off diseased limbs and inflicts wounds in order to save. Hence, because it inspires fear of punishment and the love of joy it fulfills two functions of justice. It is for this reason that the Apostle says in Heb. 4:12 that it is **sharper than every two-edged sword**. Nine, it illuminates so that the splinters of sin might be seen, for according to Psalm 118 (Ps. 119:105), **Your word is a lamp for my feet and light for my path ways**.

Insofar as the aforementioned preached word is the truth, it is essentially God himself. As such, preaching it must be the most dignified work a creature can perform.

Again, every Christian should diligently attend to this special work above all else, since it was assigned to him by God. Yet that is the work of evangelization which the Lord has imposed upon the priesthood, as clarified in the previous chapter. Therefore, the priest should give heed to that task above all others, and not lapse into idleness. On this basis, the minor premise is clear: that is the work which most directly produces children of God.

This is first confirmed by positing the following example: if someone could, without guilt, beget a natural son who would immediately become the King of England he would take great pains to accomplish such a task. Yet the person who spiritually begets a child of God begets someone greater than any earthly king. For he is a child of God and Holy Mother Church, and is set above all the good things of God, as evinced by the faith of Scripture. And providing that the person begetting such an offspring places no obstacle, then his progeny will doubtless end up profiting him infinitely more than could any of the secular advantages some earthly king might offer. (158) Hence, I am convinced that it is because we have forsaken the faith that we are blinded in this beastly way by the vanity of sensible things, thereby causing us to lose trust in such a principle.

Second, it is confirmed by the words and deeds of Christ, which we should most earnestly endeavor to imitate. Now in Matt. 12:47–50, one reads how the Jews wished to distract Christ from the act of preaching, saying, **Look, your mother and your brothers are standing outside looking for you. And he said, who is my mother, and who are my brothers? And extending his hand upon the disciples he said, whoever would do the will of my Father who is in heaven, he is my father, brother, sister and mother**. Here there can be no doubt that he prefers those who are his spiritual kindred in both word and deed to those numbered among his fleshly kindred. Nor is it permissible for a faithful person wishing to share in the faith of Scripture to deny that a Catholic is required to beget children of God through the preaching of God's word. For this is made clear by John 1:12 and 1 Cor. 4:15. Whereupon, the third letter of John states: **I have no greater grace than these things, that I would hear my children are walking in the truth** (3 John 4).

And if it is objected that a human being is incapable of begetting children of God in this way without special grace: well, in truth, neither is one capable of begetting natural children apart from a special operation of nature. It is, therefore, just as the Apostle says in 1 Cor. 3:9, **We are God's helpers**.

Third, it is confirmed by the law of the Church which states that archbishops and bishops are required to know both testaments, and consequently the entirety of Holy Scripture.[20]

[. . .] (161) If our churchmen will not trust in divine law or reason, let them at least give credence to their own laws and doctors.

Again, inasmuch as the duty of a shepherd is one which requires driving, feeding, and defending his flock, this spiritual duty cannot possibly be fulfilled without a knowledge of Holy

Scripture. This is why it is essential that every spiritual shepherd have a knowledge of Holy Scripture above all else. And since the title of the office is "shepherd," it is clear that God cannot create a shepherd, unless he would then feed his flock. For it surely is impossible for God to fall into a contradiction. The spiritual shepherd ought to fulfill the spiritual office of the shepherd in keeping with that passage in Jer. 3:15, and others generally found elsewhere throughout both testaments: **I will give them shepherds after my own heart**. Now it is clear that the spiritual pastures through which one ought to drive the Lord's flock are truths of Scripture and the way of the Lord, and not the path which leads to hell. By the same rationale, spiritual sustenance is the food of the mind, that is to say, its refreshment, which abides in the preaching of God's word, according to Matt. 4:4, **A human being does not live by bread alone, but by every word which proceeds from the mouth of God**.

[. . .] (172) Hence, with regard to the principle of what it means to be a shepherd, both testaments of Holy Scripture make clear that it consists of feeding the flock with the law of Scripture. (173) Since it is appropriate to understand the shepherd in a spiritual fashion, it is clear that one must understand spiritual sustenance, spiritual driving, and the rest of the shepherd's duties. In this vein, the scriptural passage of Jer. 3:15 says, **I will give them shepherds after my own heart and they will feed you with knowledge and instruction.** And in Ezek. 34:2–10 the prophet describes the duty of the shepherd through the mouth of the Lord, and how **he will lift up his servant David** (Ezek. 34:23), namely Christ, who fulfills the true office of shepherd. Whereupon, in order to teach us that art according to the mystical sense, we read literally of the shepherd's duty (*ad literam*), evinced in Gen. 30:31–43 concerning Jacob, and in Gen. 47:1–6 with regard to the Twelve Patriarchs. So all the shepherds of the

Old Testament symbolize the greatest shepherd of all, who says in John 10:11, **I am the good shepherd**. And whoever does not imitate him by spiritually feeding the people, in keeping with his religion, is undoubtedly not a shepherd.

It is only fitting that the one who is first among the class of shepherds would be the meter and measure of all the others. This very theme resonates within the New Testament, evinced in the last chapter of John. There, under pain of losing Christ's love, the command is issued three times, such that Peter and all shepherds descended from him by way of imitation, must spiritually feed Christ's sheep (John 21:15–19). Whereupon, in 1 Pet. 5:2 Peter issues the order to those who were later placed under his charge: **Feed the flock which is among you**, and the prize bestowed by this ministry will be supplied, so that **when the prince of the shepherds arrives you will receive the imperishable crown of eternal glory** (1 Pet. 5:4). (174) And so again, all the Apostles have taught the same thing in effect. This comes as no surprise, however, given the desire Christ had to save souls, which was the principal reason for his incarnation, passion, and indeed the whole manner in which he lived while on earth. This would be astonishing, though, had he not precisely intended to win souls by his own deeds, and had he not most strictly enjoined that skill which is only taught in Holy Scripture. In this vein, Matt. 25:31–46 tells of how he will beatify those who have performed works of compassion and will condemn those who have failed to do so. The chief works of compassion are undoubtedly spiritual works, from which nobody in this life may be excused. Notwithstanding, it is fitting for curates to perform works of this sort autonomously. Surely material works of compassion are more suitable for laymen than curates, though, as Peter teaches in Acts 3:6, **I have no silver and gold; yet what I do have, I give this to you**.

[. . .] (179) A third fiction states that it is no longer necessary to preach, since the Christian faith has been quite amply disseminated. For every old woman knows the Creed and the Lord's Prayer well enough, and that is surely sufficient for salvation. After all, as they say, it is usually the theologians who wind up being the heretics. Hence, it is prudent to understand what pertains to sensible matters, and thus attend to the worldly affairs which prove a greater benefit to the Church.

I say here that it is necessary to preach all the way to the very ends of the earth. The more strength that sin gathers, the more essential it is to preach, since it is certainly impossible for anyone to sin unless he lacks faith. Now if anyone sins he fails to believe in God, and thus lacks the first article of faith. And since believing in God means firmly adhering to him through love, it is clear that the more someone sins the more he fails to adhere to God as he should. It is confirmed in the following manner: How could anyone consent to sin, as much by act as by habit, if he fully believes both in the goodness and the retribution of God, as well as the falsity of the carnal world and that of the devil? Every sinner sins as a result of a poor choice, choosing what appears good to him because he thinks it is more useful to him than the suitable good he rejects. But he clearly does this because he lacks faith. Therefore, Aristotle says that every evil person is ignorant.[21] (180) If I were effectively to believe that every possible virtue I might acquire would be of greater use to me than all the temporal possessions I could possibly procure, how could I be overcome by worldly temptation? If, moreover, I were to believe perfectly that all fleshly desires are nothing but a fleeting pleasure, and the imaginary stuff of dreams, in comparison with the blessedness of the opposite condition, which is only acquired through the endurance of suffering, how could I ever be overpowered by the flesh? And furthermore, if I were to believe perfectly that every worldly honor is nothing but a pretense withdrawn from genuine excellence, which is itself only acquired through true humility, whereby someone lovingly and obediently reckons every person he meets to be his superior in God's eyes, how could I be conquered by the devil's temptations?

Forsaking the faith of Scripture is the first cause of wickedness. And it is for this reason that the Apostles beseeched their own shepherd in Luke 17:5 that **he would increase their faith**. It seems certain that they had more faith at that time than we do now or, as it happens, those who devise their own fiction. For these people know nothing of the Catholic church, much less her true privileges. The prelates do not even possess suitable knowledge of the individual sacraments. Yet if we retained a proper faith we would love the things of heaven more than those of the earth. It is impossible for anyone to shun or turn away from the law of God, except on account of a lack of faith. Just as faith is the first foundation of the virtues, as evinced in Heb. 11, so infidelity is the first damaging blow enticing one to sin. For the bonds of faithfulness are undone when someone turns away from the Lord or grows lethargic in his duty. That is why the devil first enticed man to abandon his faith, as made clear in Gen. 3:1–6.

(*De ver.* II,xxii): Scripture's Instruction to Pastors

(181) It remains, furthermore, to examine what sort of lifestyle and ministry is appropriate for prelates, according to the faith of Scripture and the testimony of the Church's laws. And that teaching is certainly expressed in our Scripture. Now Holy Scripture would be exceedingly inadequate unless it established a rule for Christians which they could then observe. But we know by the faith of Scripture that it did establish priests of this sort, as evinced in the case of the Apostles and disciples. For this reason it ordained a law for them which would regulate their office.

Let us go beyond the Gospel and the life of the Apostles, therefore, and search for it in the writings of the Apostle. And since no passage of Holy Scripture is contrary to any other, nor any more comprehensive regarding the character of a bishop than the one providing the fifteen conditions which exemplify a bishop, related by the Apostle in 1 Tim. 3:2–7, it is clear that this text completely covers all the necessary requirements for any bishop. This is why Chrysostom, when commenting on this text in *Sermon 10*, says that the Apostle rightly addresses the episcopacy by demonstrating what sort of person is fit to be a bishop.[22]

Whereupon, in order that we might understand this text, it must first be noted that the Apostle includes every sort of priest under the title of "bishop." Otherwise, he would not be handing down a comprehensive rule for the sacerdotal office, nor would he interchangeably call those whom he is instructing in this rule "priests" at one time and "bishops" at another. Nor would canon law explain it in another manner, as evinced by many chapters in Distinction 93.[23]

(182) Second, it must be noted that when the Apostle conveys this rule to Timothy he is actually instructing all succeeding bishops under a single wrapping. This is made clear in Chrysostom's aforementioned sermon when he says that, "While advising Timothy it is as if he is speaking to all bishops by directing them all through him."[24] Consider also Distinction 61, in the chapter "*Miramur*," where Bishop Leo says: "Where is that precept of St. Paul issued through the Holy Spirit by which the sum total of all Christ's priests is educated in the person of Timothy?"[25] Otherwise, the teaching of the Spirit would be incomplete. Therefore, just as we accept the authority of the one God, so too we accept the degree of dignity granted to Peter or another apostle, and to all his successors who rightly imitate him. Thus it is fitting that we should grasp the rules declared to one father of our position or

rank, as if they were truly declared to the entire class holding this rank, as faith makes patently clear.

Third, it must be noted that when the Apostle introduces this rule, he prefaces it with the maxim that aspiring to the episcopate is a legitimate aspiration. On this basis, it is clearly reasonable that we should seek every meritorious position in the Church which God has authenticated and instituted. The episcopate is a position of this sort, evinced by the whole collection of apostles; therefore, the conclusion.

Hence, because the Apostle knew through the Spirit that many seek after such a position for the sake of worldly pomp, and the profits derived from temporal privilege, he modified the formula by which a priest might aspire to the prelacy, as evinced in 2 Tim. 3:2–7. He says, **Anyone who aspires to the episcopate desires a good work**. It is made clear by countless laws that, insofar as priest, bishop, and pope are the titles belonging to an office, anyone who duly desires that office, desires a meritorious work, which would itself be the intrinsic cause of such an aspiration. (183) On this account, as I have said elsewhere, if anyone seeks this position chiefly for reasons of pride or profit, then he mortally sins in pursuing it. Whereupon, Chrysostom says in the aforementioned sermon, "Moses had earnestly wished for this office, though not for the power."[26] The office is called that of "bishop" because one oversees, that is to say, one watches attentively and protects. That sense is commonly explained in the *Decretum*, evinced in Distinction 40.[27] And also below, especially the chapters "*Sacerdotale*" and "*In Sacerdotibus*" in Distinction 61,[28] as well as "*Quoniam Multa*" in Distinction 48.[29]

[. . .] (204) The instilled word of Christ so often stands guard against those whom the Apostles lament, **seek their own interests, and not those which are Christ's** (Phil. 2:21). In fact, another way he could have said, **If you love me, feed my sheep** (John 21:16) would have been: if you love me, realize that you are not to feed yourself, but rather my sheep. (205) And do this because they are my own, and not as if they were yours. And seek my glory in them and not your own, my dominion not yours, my gain not yours, lest you associate with those obsessed with the things of this world. For to their own peril they are in love with themselves, and everything else connected to this vice of evil people. [. . .]

(*De ver.* II,xxiii): Scripture's Censure of Negligent Clerics

(208) In closing, we are still left with the task of adding to this some signs drawn from Scripture through which we can recognize the sort of pseudo-shepherds the Apostle warned us to avoid.

In this process it is essential that we remain on guard against mendacity and the display of favoritism, thereby following the rule of the chief shepherd as much as we are able.

If someone is a professor of Scripture, he is consequently a professor of truth, and should reject mendacity on the grounds that it is contrary to the faith. For inasmuch as anyone is obligated to the First Truth, so he is required to detest falsehood, and thus mendacity as well. Hence, in his *On the Words of the Lord*, *Sermon 138*, Augustine concludes that even evil shepherds who perform essentially good works, such as prophesying or preaching outside the bounds of love, will not presume to lie on the Judgment Day. For as he says, "They will not dare to lie in the court of so great a judge."[30] Consequently, since no lie will escape the sight of the All-Encompassing Truth, (209) anyone would shudder at the prospect of lying, especially the shepherd who cannot truly feed his flock unless abiding in the Chief Shepherd, in whom there will be no possibility of deceit.

This is why Augustine says that when Christ declares in John 10:11, **I am the good shepherd**, he is commending all good shepherds who are only such shepherds insofar as they imitate him and are united in his one body. He says, "I am one, and all those who are in unity with me are one."[31] That is why it is necessary that the dogs of this shepherd would say in Song of Sol. 1:7, **Show me where you shepherd your flock, where you make them lie down at noon**. He states, "Anyone who shepherds outside of you, shepherds against you,"[32] because it is said in Matt. 12:30, **Anyone who is not with me is against me**. And also because Christ's teaching is Christ himself, as evinced in John 7:16, **my teaching is not mine, but his who sent me**, since the Bridegroom feeds his flock through the teaching of Scripture and makes them lie down in the fervor and splendor of love and knowledge. It is thus said to those who do not shepherd their flock in this unity, **Go out and shepherd your own kids** (Song of Sol. 1:8). And at the final judgment it will be said to them: **Amen I say to you, I do not know you** to be of the Church (Matt. 25:12). Just as Samson's companions, you feasted while simultaneously magnifying your treachery and deceit toward the Bridegroom, like mercenaries or thieves (Judg. 14). Yet the Bridegroom is incapable of approving a lie within himself, nor can he allow himself to become the means of defrauding his own members. In fact, he has established very ample means of truth whereby one can turn away from the evil of mendacity and draw near to the fountain of Wisdom, who is the very Lord of Truth.

[. . .] (226) Hence, in an effort to describe the failure besetting the pastoral office Ezekiel speaks also of the five ways in which duty is refused, as diabolic arrogance undeniably besets that proud group. (227) He says, **You did not strengthen the weak, did not heal the sick, did not bind up the broken, did not bring back the abandoned, did not seek after the lost, but you ruled over them with severity and might** (Ezek. 34:4).

With respect to these five censures we must note that what the Apostle says in 1 Cor. 14:19 applies to the curate: **Better**

to speak five words in the superior sense, than ten thousand words in an extraordinary sense.

The first word in which the others are founded is the word of faith, on account of which he says, **you did not strengthen the weak**. First, it is essential that faith be steadfast, because according to the Apostle in Heb. 11:6, **It is necessary for the one who approaches God to believe, and without faith it is impossible to please God**.

Second, after faith has been established, it is essential to teach people that they must turn away from that broad path of sin which leads to hell. Now in a certain way, rejecting what is evil comes before doing what is good. As such, it is significant that he says secondly, **You did not heal the sick**. For sin is the disease of the soul, whose healing only begins when sin is extracted.

Third, the shepherd ought to instruct his sheep to proceed together down the path of good moral conduct, which is expressed under these words: **you did not bind up the broken**. Surely the virtues are connected, (228) inasmuch as they are glue which unites the members to Holy Mother Church according to present righteousness, so that they might recover the communion of saints whose members had been previously wounded among the thorns of the world and the devil's wolves.

Fourth, they should preach the terror of everlasting punishment, which is noted when he says fourthly, **You did not bring back the abandoned**. This is a special medicine employed as an antidote against the errors of the sheep. It is meant to frighten them with the very opposite of consolation, so that they will then return to the flock. Though hardened by their vices, they are led back to Christ by revealing the grievousness and everlasting duration of hell's punishment when compared to a bit of fleeting happiness.

Fifth, they ought to entice the desperate or excommunicated sheep with the hope of beatitude, which is noted in this saying: **You did not seek after the lost**. Since beatitude is the human being's ordained end, and freedom of choice for meriting so great a joy was imprinted upon him by God from a distance, it is incumbent upon the shepherd to find the sheep who is lost in sin.

In fact, the pride which besets the shepherds, thus giving rise to those five derelictions of duty, is really a diabolic lust for domination. That is why the armor of the devil's members is appended: **you ruled over them with severity and might**. This surely applied to the priests of the Old Testament, evinced in 1 Kings 2 (1 Sam. 2:12–34) in the case of Hophni and Phinehas. In fact, it is quite possible today that priests are more interested in their own sovereign lordship than in humble administration; worldly might rather than evangelical power; cruel excommunication rather than the merciful restoration of lost sheep. Whereas it is written against the first in Luke 22:26, **Whoever is the leader among you, let him become as a servant**. (229) And against the second it is written in Matt. 10:1, **Having called together the twelve disciples he gave them power over unclean spirits, in order that they would cast them out and cure every sickness and infirmity**. It is that sort of power which they ought to exercise, therefore, and not imperial power.

Against the third, it is said in Luke 9:54–56, **James and John said, "Lord do you want us to call upon fire to descend from heaven and consume them as Elijah did?" And he turned and rebuked them saying, "You do not know of which spirit you are. The Son of Man did not come to destroy the souls of human beings, but to save them."** And it is in keeping with this meaning that the first Vicar of Christ says in 1 Pet. 5:3, **Not lording it over your charges, but becoming an example for the flock.**

[. . .] (232) Oh, if God would only grant me a docile heart, one marked by perseverance, steadfastness, and love for

Christ and his Church, and even for those members of the devil who so mangle the Church of Christ, that I might rebuke them with a pure love! How glorious a cause it would be for me to put an end to this present misery!

Indeed, this was the cause of Christ's martyrdom, as well as the severe punishment imposed upon the foolish doctor. For as St. Isidore notes in Book 3, Chapter 45 of his *On the Highest Good*,

> The guilty sentence is severely increased for the one who favors a powerful person and so becomes afraid to speak the truth. In their fear, many priests conceal the truth from the powerful, and in their dread are diverted both from good works and the preaching of anything just. But alas, how sorrowful! Henceforth, they are afraid, either because they are caught up in a love for worldly things, or because they are confounded by some criminal deed.[33]

And it seems to me that there is another underlying cause which is two-fold: it is either because they are unacquainted with the skill of rebuking, or because they are afraid that they will lose their worldly belongings. And any one of those four is damnable.

Whereupon, it follows in Chapter 46:

> The priests are condemned on account of the wickedness of the people, if they fail to instruct the ignorant, or do not urge sinners to repent, as the Lord bears witness through his prophet: **I made you a watchman for the House of Israel: if you do not speak in order that the wicked person would take heed to depart from his path, I will require his blood from your hand** (Ezek. 3:17–18). (233) Thus Eli the priest was condemned for the wickedness of his sons (1 Sam. 3:12–14). For although he warned those offenders, he still did not urge them to repent as he should have.[34]

(*De ver.* II,xxiv): Every Christian Must Be a Theologian

(233) An objection is raised against what has been said.

First, it seems that every priest or curate would have to be a theologian, because he preaches the gospel. The consequent is opposed to the approved custom of the Church, by which we know that the king's clerics were not sacred theologians, and yet they still edified the Church on many occasions. And the same seems true of lawyers and decretists, of whom Hostiensis says in his *Summa*, "In some cases their leadership is more useful to the Church than the doctors of theology."[35]

To this I say that the assumption is true, because every Christian must be a theologian, as I have demonstrated elsewhere. For it is essential that every Christian learn the faith of the Church, (234) either through infused knowledge, or along with this, knowledge acquired from human teachers. Otherwise, he would not be a person of faith, and faith is the highest theology of all.

In fact, it is appropriate for every Catholic to be a theologian, but especially the priest, inasmuch as he is of superior rank owing to a certain eminence. Thus in Distinction 23 the chapter "*Qui Episcopus*" says, "The bishop ought to be examined to see whether he is literate and instructed in the Lord's law," that is to say, in both testaments, according to the Archdeacon. He must also be examined to see, "if he is well versed in the senses of the Scriptures," and above all, "if he affirms the proofs of the faith with forthright words."[36] Otherwise, given his ignorance of the sense of Scripture, he could be mistaken and thereby deceive people by preaching some perverted meaning. Now it is taught in Distinction 25, according to the chapter "*Perlectis*," that "It is the duty of a deacon to preach the Gospel and the Apostle. For just as lectors are directed to read the Old Testament, so deacons are directed to preach the New."[37]

As such, royal clerics and men of simple learning sometimes preach more effectually to the people than the aforementioned doctors. And so it is appropriate for doctors of either law to be theologians, preaching in the proper circumstances, especially while they occupy the pastoral office. And so it is that their laws are neither licit nor worthy of study except insofar as they comply with theology.

Hence, both laws begin with the titles, "Concerning the Supreme Trinity and the Catholic Faith" as a sign that theology should be studied first of all, evinced in the Decretals and the Law Code.[38] Indeed, since the Church was obligated to preach the gospel by the Lord's command long before the promulgation of such laws, it still remains the principal duty of the shepherds, as I made clear in the last two chapters. (235) For as nothing accidental annihilates the essence by which it subsists, so it is evident that the Church is obliged to carry out this duty as much today as in times past. Therefore, just as the one judged a pure theologian was duty-bound to preach before such laws were promulgated, or had yet been studied by him, so then the same applies when he would later have an opportunity to study such laws. They should not distract him from so great a perfection, since these laws are accidental to the governance of the Church. For the Church established that the temporal endowments it received would be regulated by pure theologians in many places, but nowhere by human traditions unless they were grounded upon theological premises.

Thus decretists and civil lawyers are variously theologians themselves. Indeed, many of them are better acquainted with the substance of theology, preach more efficaciously, and thus edify the Holy Church in the way of virtues more so than the aforementioned doctors of theology. This happens in small part due to the sin of theologians and the attention lawyers give to theology, which is the lifeblood of their science.

Many saints of simple learning, therefore, proved to be effective preachers, as is evinced in the cases of saints Cuthbert, Wulfstan, Francis, and others like them.

[. . .] (236) The second argument raised against what I have said is that it would then be necessary for a prelate to imitate Christ by devoting all his time to preaching. I recognize that however worthy the prelate, there are many times when it is fitting for him to refrain from preaching, and so he is permitted to refrain from preaching on those occasions. As such, it is lawful for the prelate not to preach in this case. And, by the same rationale, he can be continually excused from the task of preaching.

But that argument only persuades those who concede that if there are some times when Peter does not preach, then Peter does not preach. Yet it is sufficient that he will preach at the proper time, just as there is a proper time for him to sleep. And so, he is obligated to preach at some other suitable time. Therefore, if a bishop does not preach, then he never preaches at any past or future time. At that point, however, I would boldly assert that he is not a bishop.

Lest I appear to be disseminating some novel viewpoint, so displeasing to the satraps, I will supplement it with an abundance of legal testimony in the hope that at least the professors of these laws would not judge my position too severely. For I think it unlikely that the laymen or theologians who are of God would disagree with this. (237) Indeed, the Archdeacon writes of that chapter "*Sit Rector*," in Distinction 48, that, "the prelate who does not instruct the laity is called the **mute dog**," of Isa. 56:10.[39] According to Case 2, Question 7, "*Qui Nec*," he is a "shameless dog, owing to his failure of leadership."[40] And he is even called **a roaring lion and a wolf ravaging its prey**, according to Ezek. 22:25–27.

[. . .] (240) The third argument states that by possessing the knowledge and purpose of preaching the character is imprinted, although he may die in the meanwhile, or damnably omit to preach in the future altogether. Yet because the character of ordination has been impressed upon him he retains his priesthood, and so priesthood abides together with his perpetual refusal to preach. For if this were not the case then there would be very few priests indeed, and Christians would begin to worry whether or not they have legitimate priests who will rightly administer the sacraments to them.

This is why it is fitting to ordain priests from a lesser sufficiency than those who had been ordained in the Early Church. Variation of this sort lies behind the Church's power, as evinced in the case of priests belonging to religious orders who are appropriated by the Church. For they are exempt from the duty of preaching, having exchanged this task for contemplation and prayer.

Here it is generally said that there are many ways of speaking about a priest, as made clear above. (241) But with respect to this purpose, one person is genuinely called a priest, while another in name only, as clarified in a previous response. Indeed, one can conceive of a priest in a two-fold manner: whether pertaining to pure power, or pertaining to the function of performing a task, just as a soldier possesses the power to wage war at the first instant in which God grants the power of soldiering. And concerning such a priest, the Archdeacon says in Distinction 38, in the chapter "*Omnes*," that preaching does not pertain to the essence of the priesthood, but instead to the second manner of speaking about priesthood. And this he calls the executive office to which God instituted him. And so the Archdeacon says, "Knowledge of the Divine Scriptures is said to be the substance of the priesthood,"[41] apart from which it is not duly sustained. And those sorts of priestly functions are spoken of in a certain equivocal manner, although one does not receive the second priestly function to a greater or lesser degree, since it is invisible. But just as any warlike act is suitable for a soldier after he has received his rank with his army's approval, or has acquired his military shoes, so it is appropriate that one would preach the word of God following the reception of any priestly rank.

These days it seems that the requirement for the preaching office is an ability to argue over words. And while one can be sure that many ceremonial aspects were introduced with respect to questions of topic, the form of thematic division, and the form and circumstances of speaking, none of these things are essential for preaching. For the fact remains that anyone preaches the word of God provided that he intends to edify the Church. And so it is that Bede and Francis are said to have preached to the stones and the birds.

[. . .] (268) Now it is true that the sacred canons of Holy Scripture are the most necessary and should be learned first of all. For as I made clear in the last chapter, all other rules are hateful to God and his Church, unless they are founded upon Holy Scripture, which is itself the Catholic faith. After all, Holy Scripture exceeds all human canons in usefulness, authority, and subtlety.

Those who prefer the lesser good to the greater do not err with moderation, as evinced in *De Consecratione*, Distinction 5.[42] Thus it is quite clear, as that canon argues, and is so often recited, that priests commit a great error when they put aside divine law so that they might labor over human laws. A great part of canon law, however, is nothing but an abbreviated form of divine law.

Of course, those who so completely exhaust the water of wisdom in its streams do not lose the title of theologian, nor those who are unable to draw that water so subtly and completely from its proper source. But alas! The queen of the sciences has been mingled with spurious doctrines, because an exceedingly large part of canon law itself has been mixed up with pagan traditions, though not according to that portion which natural law relates so thoroughly, but rather according to the portion which human traditions and ambitions have taught. Though canon law ought to remain purely evangelical, at the time of the Church's Donation it was turned into a law even more vile than the laws of the pagans. And all of this leads one to conclude that clerics should be ruled under civil dominion.

[. . .] (270) There seems to be a three-fold reason why clerics should be prohibited from studying sciences such as civil law. First, because it diverts their attention from the study of divine wisdom. Second, because it generates contention and litigation against the law of a peaceful king, as I made clear in Chapter Twenty-Two with regard to the twelve requirements of episcopal office. And third, insofar as doctrine is more necessary it is rightly given preference. Do we not believe that all these reasons lead to the conclusion that our decretists not only focus their efforts on civil cases, but have neglected the very heart of their meaning? For the third reason remains that Christ wanted his clerics to be governed purely by his own law, which is sufficient by its very nature. How could anyone be so rash in daring to introduce a civil law which only serves to burden the law of Christ and entice his Apostles into the very opposite life?

Surely the law of Christ is sufficient for the collection and distribution of all alms, the rendering of every sort of legitimate obedience, and the fulfillment of whatever ordinances will edify the Church. Or do we not trust that the Apostles had perfectly fulfilled all of these things in accordance with the law of the gospel, even if today they are accomplished according to recently introduced human traditions? We certainly do not believe they retained a prelate or superior unless God had instituted him on account of his distinguished toil and humility, though each one was an obedient master and servant to the other.

And so each gave preference to his neighbor, not contending over the dignity of preeminence in the honor of any position. Nor did any of them covet the preeminence of another after his ascension. Instead, harmoniously relying upon the law of the Head of the Church, (271) they took great pains to ensure that the one among them exhibiting the greatest humility and labor would prevail.

And yet I concede that it is expedient to study many aspects of canon law, but primarily in keeping with that part which more expressly teaches evangelical law. In this way they will all be pure decretists, even if dim-witted theologians. And to the extent that there are more of them proceeding according to the levels of wisdom that God has instilled in them, the more happily will Holy Mother Church march forward.

God thus ordained that secular lords, artisans, and laborers would receive spiritual offerings from their priests and, having obtained these, would then gladly give them material offerings in return. In this way all people would be theologians, since wisdom is the supreme perfection informing the soul.

For as it is said, all the parts of the Church would assist one another with respect that perfection, as if it were the intrinsic cause of making a pilgrimage in softly woven clothes and gold fringes. Thus it is possible for every kind of human being, and every sort of legitimate occupation, to learn where wisdom abides. And it is by journeying along this path that the pilgrim will attain wisdom, though the more he strays from it the more he hastens his own destruction.

(*De ver.* III,xxv): Laymen Are Permitted to Judge Clerics

(1) In light of what has been said, one can figure out the viewpoint I have often introduced into the discussion. For while the world hates to hear it, I tell you that the laity are permitted in some cases both to withdraw and to carry away the Church's property from their ecclesiastical superiors.

(2) On account of the material alms given to them, I call upon all ecclesiastical superiors to come to aid of their subjects with spiritual intercession. This clearly applies to bishops and clerics, along with all sorts of religious alms seekers, who

accepted the Church's belongings from the laity with this intention. Although all the world's goods are the property of the Church necessarily, since all things belong to the righteous, I still suppose, whether on account of reputation or obstinance, that the Church's belongings are understood to be the possessions donated to the Church as either perpetual or temporary alms.

This applies specifically in cases where the ecclesiastical superior, who administers the alms, is in a state of moral sin. I then prove the conclusion, first by the withdrawal of alms, having established that his ecclesiastical superior is a well-known fornicator, or found to be involved in some other notorious crime.

Now a lay subject is not obligated to grant Church property to his ecclesiastical superior, unless he ministers to him and the other subjects of his province according to the aforementioned apostolic form. But if he fails notoriously in this task, the layman has the right to lay claim to such property.

[. . .] (12) Every law firmly establishes that it is appropriate for a cleric to be judged by a layman. For the layman who presents the cleric with his ecclesiastical benefice ought to judge whether he is worthy of it. (13) Indeed, the one choosing the priest to minister and hear confession should be the one to render judgment regarding his discretion and holiness.

Likewise, according to the laws of the Church, the layman ought to accuse a delinquent priest in some cases, and consequently judge whether or not he is evil. Otherwise, the one who knows that this man is a notorious fornicator would not flee from his mass, as the previously cited laws decree.[43] Nor would it be lawful for a layman to correct a priest in a brotherly manner. Yet Christ, the Apostles, and the other saints, had intended that they themselves, as well as their deeds, would be subject to the judgment of laymen, as evinced in John 7:44–52 and Acts 4:5–12. Otherwise, a layman would not be permitted to judge or discern whether a cleric is in fact good. Now someone who judges a person's deeds, judges the person himself. This is why everyone is obliged to judge himself first of all, as the Apostle teaches in 1 Cor. 11:31, **If we judged ourselves, at least we would not be judged.** Hence, in Case 8, Question 1, this excuse is mentioned in opposition to clerics who are unaware of the dignity of their office. Here Jerome says,

> I fear how the Queen of the South, who traveled to the ends of the earth to hear the wisdom of Solomon, is intending to judge the people of this age, and how the Ninevite men who repented at Jonah's preaching will condemn those who have shown contempt for an even greater savior than Jonah (Matt. 12:41–42). For many among the people will judge their bishops, and strip them of their ecclesiastical rank for not fulfilling the duties befitting a bishop.[44]

(14) In this regard, the Archdeacon says that there exists a four-fold judgment: namely, of authority which automatically belongs to God and will apply to the whole Trinity at the final judgment.[45] The second is the judgment of ministry, just as **The Father gave all judgment to his Son**, according to his humanity, evinced in John 5:22. The third is the judgment of approbation. In this way the Apostles will render judgment together with Christ, according to Matt. 19:28. But the fourth is the judgment of operation. And in that manner the evil are judged by the good, while the especially wicked are judged by the evil themselves. Concerning this judgment the *Decretum* says that there is judgment of the righteous, the mediocre, and the wicked.[46]

Therefore, since many priests are the most wicked of all, it is obvious that the good laymen of the Church are fit to judge their evil works.

If this were not so the body of the Church would be deprived of proper governance. For if the healthy and wise member should not render judgment concerning a dangerous illness and the medicine needed to cure the rotting member, then the governance of the Church would perish on both sides. If the laity, and the Queen of the South, and the Ninevite heathens will render a solemn judgment upon the priests who eradicate the law of Christ, as Matt. 12:41–42 makes clear, (15) then there is no reason why pious laymen are not permitted to judge apostate priests in secular court. In this way Solomon judged Abiathar, according to 2 Kings 2 (1 Kings 2: 26–27), just as Daniel judged the fornicators in Daniel 13: 61–62. So too did Nebuchadnezzar judge the king and priests of Jerusalem at the end of 4 Kings (2 Kings 25:6–7), though he is not condemned for this, since Case 23, Question 4 of the *Decretum* maintains that he would be saved.[47] Forty years after Christ's Ascension, Vespasian and Titus cast judgment upon all the priests and Levites whom they found in Jerusalem, quite reasonably executing them in retaliation for the death of Christ. For human justice can be adapted to deal with those situations which frequently occur, as well as those that rarely, if ever, take place.

It is for this reason that the laws of the Church have supposed Christ's priests to be poor and humble men like him, and thus to be judged by one another at their own discretion, and not handed over to secular courts, except in cases where the prelates' own judicial investigations have failed. Hence, all the laws which allege that clerics are not to be hauled in to face secular trial, should be more subtly understood as referring to the priest who justly obeys the order of the clerical office. It is important, therefore, that the people make sure the justice system of the priests does not fail. For it is in their manner of living, ministry, and good governance that the salvation of the people rests, as well as their peace and prosperity in this present age and in the age to come. Why then would not the people's own justice system carefully mull over those things?

[. . .] (33) The hypocrisy of the priests increases even while laws are multiplied to oppose them, but the failure to carry them out can be traced to a double infamy, namely the pretense of holiness and the quest for worldly power. Who doubts that God especially hates the arrogance of the mendicants? Consequently, the laity are all the more obliged to keep an eye out for such deceit and withdraw their alms, taking back what their ancestors mistakenly bequeathed. For by the faith of Scripture it is certain that those powerful members of the clergy, whether taken as individual persons or a collective gathering, who dissipate the religion of Christ under the cloak of sanctity must either be punished here and now by their ecclesiastical superiors, or by the laity. If they are not, they will either be destroyed in a hostile act of devastation, or will amass their crimes only to endure the retribution of divine judgment, as the Apostle says in Rom. 2:3, **Do you reckon, oh every person who judges those who do such things, while you do them yourself, that you will escape God's judgment?** Commenting on what the Apostle says here, Origen states,

> It is not directed to kings, but to those entrusted as leaders of the churches, such as bishops or presbyters who judge and condemn others. It is essential to judge the conscience of such people first, before going on to examine the deeds of their subjects. (34) But if this were put into full effect then all the ambition for seeking ecclesiastical honor would be cut off, and those who want to be rulers of the people would judge themselves worthy of judgment, rather than fit to judge. Because these things are chiefly spoken to those who preside as judges of the people, and since they cannot flee from God's presence, God says elsewhere, **In these who draw near to me I will be sanctified**, as in the case of Nadab and Abihu who offered another's fire, that is to say, not their own, on divine altars (Lev. 10:1–3). Divine

> judgment begins with the sons of the Church, since it is written in Ezek. 9:6, **Begin at my sanctuary**.[48]

And he goes on to say,

> Although these people are blaspheming against God, cheating, plundering, and perpetrating sacrilege or some other evil deed, for all their wickedness in this passage (Ezek. 8:5–18) they seem preferable to those who pass judgment on others while committing more serious offenses than the very ones they punish.[49]

Hence, it seems to me that the houses of the religious orders, the bishops, and the priests, who have forgotten the Lord by failing to observe his law, are fraudulently and mightily storing up riches to suit their own wicked and impenitent hearts, thereby leading themselves and their provinces into ruin. They will be allowed a certain measure of wickedness until that time comes when they must expect the retribution of divine judgment, as made clear by the punishment of the flood and that of Sodom. In keeping with this sense, it is said in Gen. 15:16 that, **The wickedness of the Amorites is not yet complete**. The wickedness of the priests must be revealed, for it is growing cold with the congealing of their temporalities. And this is why neither the clergy nor the people receive the seal of the divine image, since their fleshly hearts have to be prepared like wax liquefying before the intense heat of heaven that they might then receive the celestial imprint.

(*De ver.* III,xxvi): The Right of the Laity to Seize Church Property

(35) At this point, it seems to me that a brief discussion of some objections is in order if that matter is to become any clearer.

Because there is a mutual obligation between clerics and laymen, it would appear that if it is permissible for the laity to withdraw their alms owing to a failure on the part of the clerics to render due service then, by the same rationale, it would be permissible for clerics to withdraw spiritual offerings on account of the laity's disobedience.

But to this I say that although there exists great diversity, there is still a certain amount of agreement. Clerics and laymen are bound by God's law to assist even their enemies continually with spiritual support. Indeed, the law of God obligates a person to make such spiritual offerings. It is no wonder, therefore, that this obligation has greater force than some humanly introduced obligation designed to provide the priest with material offerings over and above the necessities of life. Hence, just as priests are bound in some cases to administer sacraments and sacramentals to enemies of Christ and the Church, and in this manner pray for their enemies, as evinced by the law of Scripture in 1 Pet. 2:15–23, so too are the laity bound to offer spiritual assistance to their ecclesiastical superiors, by withdrawing the temporal dues of the Church. If it is a work of love to remove something combustible from a fire because it might burn the body of my brother, it is all the more charitable, when it comes to spiritual offerings, to withdraw the riches of the world which only serve to drag my neighbor's soul into Gehenna. Whereupon, it seems to me that the laity should never withdraw or carry away clerical temporalities, except in cases when doing so would itself be an act of almsgiving, and in cases when it would be fitting for them to do what they ought by charitable intention, whenever (36) they raise legitimate objections beforehand regarding an unworthy Church ministry and the persistent failure to rebuke prelates who remain unreformed.

There is, however, some similarity. For just as the laity should withdraw Church property from the unworthy, by the same token it is appropriate for Christ's priests to withdraw the word of God from the unfit, for in Acts 13:46 it is said, **Because you judge yourselves unworthy of eternal life, we turn to the Gentiles**. Correspondingly, if the people were found to be obstinate and disobedient to Holy Mother Church, such that they either prohibit, or do not provide, the necessities of life for the evangelist or the one tending to spiritual matters, then they must turn away from them and look toward another people. But this would rarely occur among Christians or pagans who have been specifically instructed by the evangelist in the Apostle's teaching of Phil. 4:12, **I know abundance, and I know how to endure poverty**.

A second objection is raised to the effect that a greater part of the laws adjudicating the Church's benefices, as well as what is owed to the discontented who are vigilantly laboring and competing for them, would be wicked and consequently heretical. And this would also apply to those investigating aspects which pertain to such laws. Surely they do not examine laws of this sort concerning the worthiness of a cleric's administration or the withdrawal of his office.

Here I say that the laws are good and holy, but I fail to see how one can completely excuse those squabbling advocates, procurators or judges. The laws prohibit Church property being given to the unworthy. But if administrators of the law are negligent in their inquiries then the failure rests with them, while the law remains entirely blameless. Hence, if the executors of the laws are sluggish when it comes to examining a cleric's suitability before God, (37) it only seems fitting that this task must revert to the jurisdiction of the laity, who would then administer the goods of the poor. Indeed, it seems that they are bound to withdraw their alms whenever they perceive that the ministry of the clerics is either remarkably unfit or is simply lacking altogether.

[. . .] (39) The third argument states that excommunication is in keeping with rights of the Church and must be used to threaten people who hold back their tithes, oblations, or other alms from those who preside in the Church's presence, no matter whether they are presiding justly or unjustly. (40) Therefore, it is either appropriate to falsify the Church's rights, and thereby Holy Scripture, which is the very foundation of these rights, or else it is absolutely unjust to withhold Church property from the designated rector, however troublesome he may be. Otherwise, any layman could fabricate some deficiency on the part of his ecclesiastical superior, and in due course withdraw what is owed him.

To this I say, as I have explained extensively elsewhere, that excommunication was not invented for the sake of exacting money for the clergy, but for the purpose of frightening the delinquent that they might be saved, and for thrusting poisonous sinners out of the Church. Thus it should never be employed except in love, although it has now been turned into nothing more than a vindictive means for exacting temporal goods.

[. . .] (61) This worldly fiction that wealth should be accepted to the honor and glory of the priesthood is rendered invalid on the grounds that Christ prohibited his disciples from glorying in such things. Nor do human concessions or the rights of the Church prevail, for inasmuch as it is opposed to divine law they cannot bestow Christ's inheritance upon a traitor who has disgraced himself before Christ. (62) It was not necessary for Christ to offer further explanation of the other laws of Scripture in this matter, because the possibility that persons of his own inheritance would be so preoccupied with worthless goods extends beyond the parameters of his ordinance. Notwithstanding that, such proof may be found in many parts of the Old Testament Scripture.

Having established this case, we are able to conclude that these things can be done lawfully. For if the secular Solomon acted in this very way toward the chief priest whom God had constituted, as evinced in 3 Kings 2 (1 Kings 2:26–27), then it is all the more permissible for a person to take away those things of his which were merely granted by human beings.

Now my adversary might locate for me some passage in the New Scripture supporting the dominion of endowment, just as I could find for him cases which support its lawful removal. Yet it is appropriate for possession to precede its privation by nature, but Christ forbids property or worldly possession for his apostles, when he wanted to prepare the oxen in the Old Testament, while in the New he truly wanted to carry off his fatted calves to heaven, according to Matt. 22:4. As a point of fact, horned beasts lack teeth in the upper jaw because the material which would nourish those teeth passes instead to the horns in order to nourish them. In this way the horns of prelates seeking the power of civil dominion render them toothless, just like stammering calves when it comes to fulfilling their preaching duties, since their ingenuity, zeal, and affection pass into worldly concerns. It is for this reason that Christ did not want his apostles to be horned oxen swollen by temporal affairs, but rather fatted calves nourished with a measure of that pure grain which is conveyed from above, while the distribution of temporal goods is administered by secular authorities.

(*De ver.* III,xxvii): The Duty of Secular Lords to Protect the Church

(63) With respect to human laws, it is clear from what I have so often said that any number of them attest to that viewpoint.

For the purposes of grasping their sense I suppose, first of all, that one should be conformed to Scripture's manner of speaking, and that of the theologians, by whose testimony the laws are discerned. Otherwise, the testimony of the saints will be comprehended perversely through the lens of human statutes, as they neglect the saints' meanings and interpose their own.

Second, I suppose that every person should pay greater attention to spiritual matters concerning the salvation of his soul, than to temporal affairs which only pertain to the health of his body in this lifetime. This is made clear by that passage in Matt. 16:26, **What does it profit a person if he gains the whole world and suffers the loss of his soul?**

Third, to accompany these suppositions I will present five human laws through which we can verify the aforementioned viewpoint.

The first occurs in that passage of St. Isidore found in Case 23, Question 5, where it is said that,

> Secular princes possess the highest power within the Church, for the sake of preserving ecclesiastical discipline. Otherwise, they would not be necessary, except in those instances where priests are not powerful enough to accomplish this through the word of doctrine. Then their power will enjoin this through the fear of discipline. Secular princes should recognize, therefore, that they will have to give account to God on behalf of the Church which Christ has given them to defend.[50]

(64) This is where John de Dio notes the eight cases in which a cleric is subject to a secular lord.[51] Therefore, one must either deny the law of the Church and the statement of this holy theologian on the grounds that it is heretical, or else concede that secular authorities have the power and duty defined by God for the purpose of defending the Church chiefly through fear whenever the priests have failed. But I ask you, how can the Church expect to be defended by laymen when one sees wolves and thieves plundering their goods, as the *Decretum* speaks of false pastors,[52] unless one is permitted to take away the spoils by violent means and drag such wolves away from the poor? Likewise, the greater the danger threatening the Church, the more meritorious and necessary it is to come to

her assistance. But the greatest danger facing the Church is found among the pseudo-clerics and internal enemies, as Gregory says in Book 1, Chapter 2 of his *Pastoral Care*.[53] It is, therefore, more meritorious for the laity to help at that time. Consider whether Holy Mother Church would be in greater danger when she is unarmed and forcefully overcome by the laymen, or when, together with this, she is thrown into disorder by the treachery of a bishop who refuses to rebuke his subordinates. Consider, secondly, that if a priest is a good man, and yet is not strong enough to issue a rebuke, given the fierce strength of the Church's enemy, he will then have to rely upon secular power. This is all the more reason that when a bishop is lacking in strength, having been bound by the chains of the devil, it is then preferable to depend upon secular power. Whereupon, in Case 23, Question 5, "*Quali Nos*," Pope Pelagius speaks to a certain patrician named Narse in this way: (65) "There are some bearing the title of 'bishop' in name only who want to appropriate all ecclesiastical holdings for their own use." He later asks him to assist his nuncio in castigating such "pseudo-bishops." For he goes on to say,

> You would not reckon it sinful for men of this sort to be restrained. Indeed, divine and human laws have established that those who are separated from the unity of the Church, and most wickedly disrupt her peace, should be suppressed by secular powers. In this way you can offer a sacrifice to God, and none would be greater than suppressing those who revel in their own destruction and that of others.[54]

Likewise, according to Law 23, Question 5, "The king should repress thievery, punish adultery, and banish the wicked from his land."[55] And the same judgment is made clear above in the same Question, "*Regum Est Proprium*,"[56] and Question 6, "*Quod Erraverat*."[57] Since it is only right that these exceptionally dangerous deeds be repressed, it seems fitting that the secular authorities should be vigilant in pursuing the notorious vices of the priests in order to restrain the very same offenses. This is confirmed by Law 23, Question 5, "*Dicat Aliquis*," where it says:

> Just as we are compelled to display faith and reverence to princes and potentates, so it is incumbent upon these administrators to defend the secular dignities of the churches. But if they have refused to do so they are to be expelled from the communion.[58]

And in the same Question, one reads, (66)

> Without a doubt, administrators of secular dignities should be appointed to defend the churches, protect the orphans and widows, and restrain robbery. For as often as they have been summoned by bishops and churchmen they should listen attentively to their requests and in keeping with what necessity dictates, not neglecting their duty they should correct such matters with a diligent zeal. But if they do have the fear of God before their eyes and are found to be negligent after the second and third admonition, let them understand that they are excommunicated until they have rendered fitting satisfaction.[59]

Although the prelate remains silent on this point, I believe it is the excommunication which God inflicts that is the reason why our Church Militant is beset by wars and misfortune. They should serve God first by honoring Holy Mother Church, in keeping with that form her sacred laws decree. Moreover, they or the faithful theologians ought to be providing thorough instruction, instead of trusting in these scribes and Pharisees who cunningly subvert the benefits of the law with their perverse glosses. For according to these laws, such pseudo-clerics are not clerics, but robbers, indeed worse than the laity, worse than every sort of criminal.

[. . .] (69) Although there are any number of Church laws testifying to the aforementioned viewpoint, (70) these modern scribes blind the minds of secular authorities with all sorts of specious arguments, claiming that a great part of canon law, including the theological portions collected from the saints, has been abrogated today. But then they would have to admit that the whole body of law is now heretical. Moreover, they should say that the pope is able to legislate against God, because that law is utterly contrary to reason. And they ought to say as well that a passage drawn from the law is thoroughly invalid testimony, since none of us know whether the newly circulated law remains idle in this matter or, having been recently created, destroys the law which you are citing. Yet since the new law is valid, and thus rational, it is only fitting that the outdated one which opposes it would now be invalid.

The second pretense contends that while that had been the law at one time, it is now necessary to adjudicate otherwise. For just as severe justice flourished in the Old Testament only to be followed by gentleness, so it is fitting for it to be that way in the New. As such, theologians who are unacquainted with the meanings of the words of the law are laying a scythe to another man's crops, stammering out some sentence which they do not even understand.

Against the first part, I have stated above that it is now more necessary than ever to thwart those who deceitfully manipulate the law, since they are failing to carry out the very law entrusted to them. I have even said that theologians should study their own doctors more thoroughly, reflecting upon the complete works in their original form, as well as the basis for the principles which they elicit from Scripture, as opposed to those doctors who only peruse a theological compendium abridged by theologians. It is necessary, therefore, to establish the foundation for an extraneous signification of terms.

The third pretense more cunningly states that all laws which appear to sound in favor of the laity are really to be understood as referring to a case in which the prelate has erred. But is impossible for the pope to err. Therefore, no one may interpose a rebuke upon a priest unless in accordance with the laws and admonitions of the bishop, extending all the way to the pope. (71) As such, there will never be an instance in which the duty of disciplining a cleric will devolve to the laity.

Inasmuch as one assumes that is true it would never be necessary for laymen to discipline a cleric so long as the prelates would fully discipline themselves and those under their supervision. Yet as I explained above, the rule of Scripture, as well as the notorious deeds of a multitude of clerics, force the world cry to out that prelates do not properly discipline themselves or their subordinates. Thus according to the laws of the Church it is essential for laymen to make use of their own offices based upon the authority of the Head of the Church. For not only is it lawful for them to do so in some cases, but they are in fact damned and excommunicated by heavenly justice if they fail to exercise the power the Lord has bestowed upon them.

With regard to the infallibility of the pope, it is clear from what I have said elsewhere that this notion is exceedingly heretical. Moreover, it is impossible. For God is infallible, as is the Head of the Church, and yet he rejoices in receiving the assistance of the laity. Surely Christ desires this, since in 1 Cor. 3:9 the Apostle writes, **We are God's helpers**. Insofar as earlier holy popes so humbly called upon secular lords to help them with small concerns, evinced in the cases of Gregory, Pelagius, Felix, and others like them, and made clear in the *Decretum* and the registers, what would move modern popes, who find themselves debtors faced with far greater needs, to refuse to call upon them? God forbid that arrogance ends up being the reason why they are so reluctant to subject themselves to secular power, (72) or that profit is the motive for wanting all cases in which riches are at stake to devolve to them, despite the fact that such practices put the Church to shame. For this would surely contend against God and even their own laws.

[. . .] (103) It is appropriate that every son of the Church would assemble at the interlude which takes place in this life-time, since according to the Apostle in 1 Cor. 4:9, **We have become a spectacle to this world, and to angels and human beings**. The game had only just begun during the state of innocence, exemplified directly by uncreated Wisdom, who **plays before God**, since she herself is the art through which God, the earth's creator, eternally plays with the universal order, as it is said in Prov. 8:22–31. After the Judgment Day, however, another game will be consummated which no one will be permitted to enter, unless during the time of this pilgrimage in the aforementioned interlude he played his position well. But, as I have said, it will be for the company of the blessed to render that judgment. Indeed, from their seats on high, the angels and the blessed human beings continuously observe all of our struggles, watching over whatever good or evil we do in the stadium of this life. The priests must insist, therefore, that Holy Scripture be the rule-book for this game. For to the extent that anyone deviates from the original rules of the game he disrupts the interlude. In light of this, it is clearly of the utmost importance that every priest in this interlude be well versed in those pages above all else, and play the game according to a holiness of life befitting the example set by Wisdom in his humanity.

Along these lines, it follows that nothing could be a more terrifying madness than having a prelate who does not understand this game, since he will end up teaching people how to play the devil's game, conveying examples from the book of death.

Therefore, I said in Chapter Twenty-One of this treatise that all the captains of the Church should most suitably provide expert guidance for the priesthood.

(*De ver.* III,xxviii): The Status of Mosaic Law

(104) It remains to consider another incidental facet of the principal subject matter.

Now in my statements regarding the truth of Scripture I have occasionally dealt with the cessation of legal obligations, which is a subject, after the authors of Scripture and especially the Apostle in his letters to the Romans, Galatians, and Hebrews, that master Lincolniensis has excellently treated in a certain little book on that subject.[60]

The Mosaic Law is divided into the ceremonial and the moral injunctions. And inasmuch as the latter pertain to a morality, which is wholly contained within the eternal Decalogue, it is clear that in those aspects no cessation or dispensation occurs. For those principles are not confined to a specific time and location, and thus form the foundation of other moral conclusions.

(105) There are, however, three legal or ceremonial rites whose cessation or variation chiefly offends the Jews or the enemies of Scripture: Sabbath observance, circumcision of the flesh, and the abomination of eating meat with its blood.

For the sake of finding a solution to these and other objections, I suppose that, in light of what has been said concerning the essence of the law, the totality of Christian law is collected from all the truths of Holy Scripture. And each follows at the proper time, one of which is temporary, lasting for its own period, while another perpetually endures, and another abides in eternity with God. And that is the law which Christ said in Matt. 5:17, he **did not come to abolish, but to fulfill**.

Second, I suppose that contradiction or inconsistency should be understood with respect to its own subject matter, form, and time, since there is no inconsistency when diverse subjects are successively designated as contraries, nor when the same subject occurs at the same time with compatible forms, or at different times with opposite forms.

In light of these things, a third point becomes clear. The variety of laws is not inconsistent, but is in fact consonant with the principle that God's law is given to suit different times, places and people. Thus human beings had lived under the natural law prior to the granting of the Mosaic Law. And through that law they were given various ceremonies and precepts having to do with men and women, as well as those pertaining to priests and people. (106) Indeed, they generally suited the disposition of the person or people which God instituted. And since they are all directed toward the Messiah, it finally becomes evident that at the time of the law of grace it is fitting that the figures would cease and other laws take their place. One must grasp by faith that the whole body of God's law proceeds in a most orderly fashion according to its mutable parts without any deficiency in the law of the Lord.

[. . .] (107) With regard to the first difficulty concerning the Sabbath, I have said in Chapter 18 of my treatise *On the Commandments*, that observation of the Sabbath, inasmuch as it pertains to morality, perpetually endures, since we should always take a rest from sin.[61] (108) It is observed in accordance with the figure of the seventh day during that time before the Incarnation, and pre-figuring the repose of the dead Christ in the tomb during the Sabbath, and the repose of those asleep in purgatory in the seventh age. At the time of the law of grace, however, following the fulfillment of the figure, the final Sabbath's rest is then celebrated on the eighth day. For that is when Christ, who created the world on that day, was resurrected, illuminating the world that day through the knowledge of his voice, evinced in the sending of the Holy Spirit. He will come on the same day to render final judgment, awakening the entire race of the saved so that they might find perpetual rest in that eighth age, while the remainder are raised up again to face everlasting damnation.

[. . .] (113) The Apostle utilizes many testimonies drawn from the Old Testament in Heb. 9 and 10 in order to prove that through the giving of the New Law the prophecies are fulfilled in Jesus Christ. This is why the figurative sacrifices must come to an end when the ultimate sacrifice will have been completed. But Christ, **the priest of future good things, entered into the sanctuary once for all, thus obtaining eternal redemption** (Heb. 9:11–12). As such, it is superfluous to add to his figurative sacrifice after the total sacrifice is consummated. (114) The tabernacle of this great priest is the world, and the holy of holies is heaven, as evinced so extensively elsewhere. For Christ did not enter daily with the blood of beasts and the rest of the figures, but once for all, and forever, through his very own blood which was ultimately symbolized by all the previous rituals. Therefore, since that everlasting priest necessarily assists at the right hand of God, living always in order to intercede on our behalf, and prescribing that we who place the entire hope of our concerns on him would not offer up to him the old figures, but rather a devotion of the heart along with the fruit of our labors. For if we do otherwise we would sin by despairing of our mediator and despising the form of his law. How then could we fail to offer him all due reverence at this time, and in the manner that he himself so thoroughly instructed his Apostles that they must be accomplished?

[. . .] (115) This is why I say that, following the promulgation of the law of grace, it is poisonous for Christians knowingly to observe those rites which pre-figured the New Law's sacraments added on top of the Old Law. For someone who does this would be unfaithfully awaiting anti-Christ by implying that these figures have not been fulfilled in Christ. This is the reason for the Apostle's statement in Gal. 5:6, **If you are circumcised, Christ profits you nothing**. (116) Therefore, since Christ's full repose in the tomb on the holy Sabbath was consummated, and that was symbolized immediately by the Sabbath rest on the seventh day, it is clear that keeping the ceremonial aspect on the seventh day should cease. Otherwise, one would unfaithfully await the Messiah's repose in the heart of the earth for the whole Sabbath. Nor am I moved by the argument that both Sabbaths are good and thus they should be observed equally. For in this way no sinful woman would receive the Eucharist in a state of sin, just as a person suffering fever would consume the most ample amounts of the strongest wine and the most nourishing food, and a thief would dishonestly lead a noble and venerable lord into his cottage. It is certain, however, that when it comes to human affairs it is the plight of good natures to be subjected to the worst conditions as is clearly the case when a sword strikes the precious neck of a righteous man. Augustine provides an example in *On True Religion*: "Just as the flame chases away the smoke, the light the darkness, and the master the herald, so the sacraments of the New Law put to flight the figures of the Old Law."[62] But with regard to the existence of these two goods, both should not abide simultaneously. It is on account of the aforementioned three-fold reason that the order which God established ought to be observed.

If it is objected that because Christ observed both of these we too should observe them both, I say similarly that the inference does not follow. For Christ stood on the border line of the two testaments, as it were, there at the end of the Old and the beginning of the New, making both of them one, (117) since **He is the cornerstone** of which Psalm 117 speaks (Ps. 118:22). Nor does it follow that since the mid-point communicating with these two halves connects them to one another that the same applies to any other following point. Just because that middle person who connected the New Law with the Old is its principle and author does not mean that we who are points in the line of the Christian generation which follows him should do likewise. For it is surely sufficient that we would accomplish such things proportionately, by fulfilling in effect what Christ charges us to do in our own time and circumstances. Christ does teach, however, that we are to keep the Sabbath rest on the first day of the week since through its fourth part he rested in the tomb, just as he teaches that the fathers created in the state of innocence were meant perpetually to keep the Sabbath rest on the sixth day of the week. And this is signified by the fourth part of the Day of Preparation, through which Christ lay in the tomb. Thus keeping the Sabbath rest at the time of the state of innocence is signified by the repose of Christ in the tomb on the sixth day of the week.

Just as that time was the fourth part of the day slipping into evening, so too did the Sabbath observance in that period fall into the darkness of sin. And as the fourth part of the third day was progressing toward the brightness of the Lord's Day, so our own Sabbath observance, as though the final hour, which is the whole time of the law of grace, looks forward to the unburdened worship of God in full rest as though it were the eighth day of eternity, which will be the Lord's Day. As the fourth part of the Day of Passover, throughout which Christ lay in the tomb, had its accompanying darkness, so the Sabbath observance of Christians is obscure and symbolic of our everlasting rest, as the Apostle teaches us in Heb. 4:9. We are sure that Christ rested in the tomb over the space of three days, beginning the natural day in the middle of the night (118), just as the Church does in memory of Christ's birth, which is the day that originates all days. Because this was the occasion of the spring equinox and Christ was buried around the time that the sun was going down on the Day of Preparation, it is clear that he had six hours of the Day of Preparation, and thus the fourth part of that day. The Sabbath had completeness to it, however, since the period of the Sabbath rest, as the seventh day, had its own beginning and end. Of the third day Christ had six hours, and thus lay in the tomb over the course of three days, though not for three whole days, nor even two. This is because the middle of the day expired when he lay there for thirty-six hours, as I said in my treatise *On Christ*.[63] Why then should we observe a ritual that is no longer necessary and would only hinder us, thus relinquishing the freedom we have been granted to do what is so easy?

[. . .] (122) Now the Apostle says in Rom. 7:12 that **the Old Law is holy and the commandment is holy and just and good**. Nor is there any doubt that this applies to the totality, for otherwise God's ordination would be deficient with respect to that part. Yet no correction takes place unless there has been an imprudent action, nor does destruction or corruption occur except where something is defective or possesses a contrary. The truth of time, however, since it has no contrary, has no cause for corruption, just as the philosophers say. And so Scripture says in Wisd. of Sol. 1:13 that, **God did not make death**. Nor, by the same rationale, did he make corruption or a change of intention, since according to the Apostle in 2 Cor. 1: 18–19, **There was not in him yes and no, but in him was yes**. For if the legal obligations of the Old Law should thus be changed, then the truth of the following words of Scripture cannot be sustained in their intended literal sense (*de virtute sermonis*). After all, Matt. 5:17–18 determines that, **Christ did not come to abolish the law, but to fulfill it**, and that, **neither one iota or point will perish from the law until heaven and earth pass away**; that is, until the consummation of the world comes to pass on the Judgment Day.

With regard to this matter, I have said elsewhere that the entire Old Law was holy and just, and consequently must be observed in its own time and never destroyed or abolished in any of its parts. The destruction, dissipation and abolishing of the law is what they call an inordinate breaking apart of the law in itself, or in its operation at that time when it should be in existence. But the legal obligations must cease when the law is fulfilled. (123) Therefore, not even the least commandment or ceremony perished from the law. Rather, they elapsed at the fulfillment of the law, which remains up until the Judgment Day with respect to its progress and even more amply by way of an everlasting benefit. Just as it is appropriate for the age of youth would pass into the perfection of human maturity. Yet clearly, any time-bound law which is duly and prudently ordained should still be consummated, just as in the case of a guardian's control over a child heir when it has run its course, according to the Apostle in Gal. 3:15–29. For when the fullness of the time of his reign arrives, he is no longer treated as a servant, but as a master. And so, since the rites and ceremonies of the temporal law are each given their place at the proper time, it is evident that these things must come to an end together with that time; not destroyed, corrected or broken apart, but rather ceasing in their particular aspects when succeeded by the more perfect law.

[. . .] (130) In light of what has been said, a three-fold reason for the cessation of the legal obligations can be reckoned. First, since Christ is the end for whose sake all the Old Testament figures existed then, by the same rationale, it would be superfluous and unfaithful to observe these figures together with the faithless Jews who are still waiting for the incarnation of the Messiah. I say it is superfluous because the burdens of the ancient law hindered the fathers of the Old Testament in their ascent up the aforementioned ladder, inasmuch as they had to busy themselves slavishly with those who were uncultured and farther from salvation. (131) Now, however, **our salvation is nearer than when we had just barely believed in** the Bridegroom's kiss (Rom. 13:11). For we are sons and heirs by participation in the title of our brother, as evinced by the acknowledgment of the angels. Indeed, it would be fatuous and superfluous to climb back down the ladder, in accord with a state that is more difficult, abject, and farther removed from the goal we desire. This is why St. James calls the law of grace the **law of perfect liberty** (James 1:25). Thus, at the synod dealing with the cessation of the law recorded in Acts 15: 10–11, St. Peter says, **Why are you tempting God by placing a yoke upon the necks of the disciples which neither our fathers nor we were able to bear? But through the grace of Jesus Christ we believe that we are saved just as they are,** that is to say, the Gentiles, to whom God gave grace by means of a sensible sign apart from circumcision.

The second reason is that greater faith, love and honor should be bestowed upon Christ, since he is the head of the Church and the end of legal obligations. In fact, we ought to believe that Christ, who at last came in the flesh, is by his very nature capable of drawing forth the faithful without the assistance of such figurative sacraments. Consequently, since his kindness is so powerful that he thus exonerates his children and most beloved brethren, to refuse this liberty would amount to spurning the gift of God, as well as the gratitude which we owe him. Yet this would be altogether contrary to reason, since it is only rational that these things would make him especially beloved. (132) Now the more potent the kindness, more graciously and effectively operating, the more amply should his beneficiaries prize it. As such, the honor which had been previously dispersed among many rituals and figurative sacraments should now be ascribed in unison to such a leader. And this is the reason why the Apostle, in 1 Cor. 1:12–17 and 3:4–9, excludes Peter and Apollo from lordship over their converts. Indeed, it is as if they are nothing, for they are but abject servants of the Lord Jesus Christ, to whom all the Christian's knowledge, love or honor should be attributed. For no creature ought to be known, loved, or honored except Christ, or those who are related to him, insofar as they are his members and those who serve them. Hence, in 1 Cor. 16:22 Paul pronounces a curse upon **those who do not love Jesus Christ**, and in 1 Cor. 2:2 he **decides to know nothing except the**

Lord Jesus. Indeed, it is for this reason that in the early Church **they were baptized in the name of the Lord Jesus Christ**, as evinced in Acts 2:38. And yet the Holy Spirit knew that there would be future schisms in the Church among those saying, **Look here, look there** is the head of the Church, as Christ prophesied in Matt. 24:23 and Matt. 13 (Mark 13:21). Therefore, the Apostles taught that the faith of the Lord Jesus Christ is sufficient for a Christian's salvation apart from any ritual which has been added over and above it.

With respect to the third cause, natural reason will conclude from these things that the Church should not proceed along circuitous and suspect paths which present an occasion for evil when the safe royal road is patently easier. But such is the case with the bare faith of Christ, together with the sacraments of the New Law, (133) since Christ came to unshackle those who were bound and set them free. The Church, therefore, ought to proceed along this path. Since she has been extracted from limbo, and the gates of death have been opened, it is only fitting that she would freely proceed now, setting aside the ladder of rituals, fully committing herself to follow the Bridegroom's course, and thereby his reward. In this way the justification of faith, hope and love are attained through a concise and proper liberty in keeping with the Bridegroom's abridged arrangement, lest the bride allow herself to be treated like a slave by the dictates of servile legal obligations. It only stands to reason that these must be terminated in the wake of the freedom she has found in the Redeemer. For the benefit of redemption abides more graciously in him, and is thus more suited to the bride's progress. In fact, the Old Testament patriarchs knew that they would descend into the abode of the dead until the advent of the Messiah, since it was fitting that **the firstborn from many brothers** (Rom. 8:29) would pass through the gate first among all. Hence, after seeing Joseph's bloody coat, Jacob said in Gen. 37:35, **I will go down to my**

son, mourning in the abode of the dead. Consider the passage below in Gen. 44:18–34, when his sons wished to bring Benjamin into Egypt, as well as 42:38, **If something calamitous were to happen in the land to which you are proceeding, you will bring down my gray hairs with grief into the abode of the dead**. And after Benjamin was arrested, Judah says in the person of his father: **If you take this one and something happens to him along the way, you will bring down my gray hairs with grief into the abode of the dead** (Gen. 44:29). In this vein, Solomon says in Prov. 23:14, (134) **You beat your child with a rod and you will liberate his soul from the abode of the dead**. Look, this is the very abode of the dead from which you have been set free!

[. . .] (136) Christ's Incarnation is the most useful, miraculous and venerable thing of all for the Christian. Therefore, it should be believed in most steadfastly, continuously, and above all else. It is certain, however, that the Incarnation of Christ is the imminent means for the salvation of the human race, for the sake of which occurred the entire bestowal of the law, its observation, and the human pilgrimage. For God would be found lacking in these necessary things, unless he continuously expresses this in a more fitting manner. The faith of the Incarnation is the most useful, however, because without that faith it is impossible for the faithful of the other testament to please God, since he includes within himself the divinity and the salvation of the human race, every bit as much its cause, as its effect, and final purpose. This is why St. John says in 1 John 5:5, **Who is the one who conquers the world, except the one who believes that Jesus Christ is the Son of God?** And Christ says in John 17:3, **This is eternal life, that they might know you, the only true God, and the one whom you sent, Jesus Christ**. In Christ the beatitude of human beings is finally accomplished. [. . .]

(*De ver.* III,xxix): Judaizing and the Correction of Fellow Christians

(144) In light of what has been said, the way to solve the objection raised against Holy Scripture concerning circumcision becomes evident. In this matter Gen. 17:13 states, **My pact in your flesh will be an eternal covenant**. Whereupon, Deut. 27:26 reads, **Cursed is everyone who will not abide by all those things which are in the book of this law, so that he would do them**. But supply here: all the commandments which have been prescribed in that very place. Hence, in Chapter 28:15 it consequently says, **If you do not wish to listen to the voice of the Lord your God, so that you might keep and perform all his commandments and ceremonies which I commanded to you today, then all these curses will come upon you.**

With respect to those objections, and others similar to them, it is clear that circumcision should be perpetually observed according to the mystical sense, namely a spiritual circumcision which is the removal of superfluous thoughts and affections. In this vein, the Apostle says in Rom. 2:29 that, **In secret, a Jew has a circumcision of the heart in the spirit, not the letter**. And in Col. 2:11, **In Christ you were circumcised by a circumcision not made by hands**. Hence, Lincolniensis finds that when the disciple of Scripture hears of circumcision spoken of with respect to Abraham, that it will be **everlasting in his flesh and his seed according to the eternal covenant**, he immediately understands by the aforementioned rules that, "The act of circumcision designates something pertaining to our salvation, and yet a literal circumcision was commanded."[64] And then he examines other passages of Scripture right away in order to find out what the literal circumcision might signify. (145) Since the entirety of Scripture signifies faith and morals, in fact signifying God himself more prominently than anything else, one recognizes right away that an eternal quality should be ascribed to such circumcision. And then all the slandering of Scripture will cease. For in Psalm 118 (Ps. 119:6) it is said, **Then I will not be put to shame, when I will look into all your commandments**. I say that these are the sort which occur to the disciple of Scripture, according to that passage in Jer. 4:4, **Be circumcised to the Lord and remove the foreskin of your hearts**. And in Jer. 9:26, **All the house of Israel is uncircumcised in heart**. And as though he were teaching about the end of the sensible ritual, Moses says in Deut. 10:16, **Circumcise the foreskin of your heart.**

From these statements one reckons that all literal circumcision abides for the sake of signifying the spiritual circumcision which God has given greater weight. It is a destruction or cutting away of the excess of sin from the heart, that is to say, it should be understood as lasting forever with respect to one's disposition. And in every literal circumcision this is principally commanded, in keeping with the prophet Ezekiel's manner of speaking in Ezek. 11:19, **I will remove the heart of stone from their flesh, and I will give them a heart of flesh**. Here the bodily member should signify the soul which is rescued from a hardening in evil and is softened by grace, that is, made tractable and thus capable of receiving the Lord's teaching through obedience and the stamp of his law. Holy Scripture is not falsified, therefore, by some boorish or insipid notion (146) by which some might think that God first removes the bodily member and then transforms it from a material stone into something of flesh. Likewise, one should not think that the literal act of circumcision is a passion, or that the habit of removing the bodily foreskin ought to endure forever, since women are never circumcised in this manner, nor was anyone else before the time of Abraham. Not even the infant underwent fleshly circumcision before he was eight days old, as evinced in Gen. 17:12.

[. . .] (180) It is sufficient to believe that circumcision is no longer generally essential for salvation, nor is it even lawful except in a special case of necessity, in which case it would anagogically symbolize the circumcision of heaven. Gentiles, therefore, should always have renounced circumcision, and the Jews should have done so from the time that they realized through preaching and internal inspiration that judaizing would be superfluous in those matters, since it pertains to one people at one time and to the other people at another time.

Furthermore, I must say that I am not swayed by the argument that the Jews are scandalized when this opportunity is accepted. For if I refuse to be circumcised then I should be circumcised to God. To be sure, no one should sin in order to avoid scandalizing himself or his neighbor. Yet now, in light of the new age and the doctrine of the Church, he has matured in the commandment such that there would no longer be fleshly circumcision. Nobody ought to be circumcised at the present time in order to avoid scandalizing the Jews. In the very early Church, however, the Apostles did permit this for a time, as they took care not to scandalize recent Jewish converts. Still, I do concede that, today and always, if someone has a revelation regarding this matter, or knows that he will be cleansed from sin through this act, and generally, if he knows that he will observe the Lord's commandments together with this action, then he can be lawfully circumcised, since the Apostle says in Rom. 2:25, **Circumcision is of advantage to you if you keep the law**.

All of this is evident from the fact that every such antecedent implies that circumcision would be lawful and even meritorious. Therefore, it is appropriate that we would first establish the antecedent, not **believing every spirit** (1 John 4:1), before the consequent is put into effect. Otherwise, it would be lawful to perform every prohibited work under the guise of such a fallacy. (181)

In light of these things, one can better grasp the controversy which seems to have taken place between St. Jerome and St. Augustine regarding the cessation of legal obligations and Paul's rebuke of Peter.[65] Now it seems fitting that just as Paul was excused for circumcising Timothy in order to avoid scandalizing the Jews (Acts 16:1–3), so then Peter ought to be excused for his withdrawal from his association with the Gentiles for the sake of his circumcised converts (Gal. 2:11–14). As I have often said, it is appropriate for us to believe the person in Holy Scripture who says in Gal. 2:11, **When Peter came to Antioch, however, I opposed him to his face, because he was reprehensible. For earlier, when certain ones came from James, he was eating with the Gentiles. Yet when they arrived he withdrew and set himself apart, fearing those who were of the circumcision**. Certainly, no one is reprehensible except on account of sin. Yet according to the faith of Scripture Peter was reprehensible for having withdrawn from the Gentiles; therefore, he sinned in this instance. There was, however, a difference between his action and the action of Paul. For when Paul circumcised Timothy, (182) he was in this way separately edifying the Jews and teaching the Gentiles. He proved that while the sacrament of circumcision is still permissible for the Jews even after the Ascension, they should understand that it is no longer necessary, though, and must not be imposed upon the Gentiles owing to the intrinsic sufficiency of the Christian faith and sacrament, which Paul undoubtedly showed them through this deed. Peter, on the other hand, had publicly renounced his association with the Gentiles in the city of the Gentiles on account of a few Jews sent from Jerusalem by James, whom he could have readily instructed concerning the communion of faith among Jews and Gentiles. Whereupon, because an error on the part of so great a leader could easily have put many in danger, he absolutely had to be rebuked. This is why Paul subdued the danger: **And the rest of the Jews consented to his hypocrisy, so that Barnabas was led astray by them in hypocrisy** (Gal. 2:13).

Hence, I consider it a slanderous gloss which would altogether excuse Peter from sin on account of the sending of the Holy Spirit, saying that the phrase **he was reprehensible** meant only that he had to be opposed, lest he would engage in further dissimulation, (183) because that would have then been a sin. While at that point it was still nothing but a meritorious work of piety. Yet by that way of thinking, any reprehensible, defective and damnable work might be meritorious. But I do not believe such a notion has any scriptural foundation.

Likewise, the following text seems to demolish such a gloss: **When I saw that they were not walking uprightly with respect to the truth of the gospel, I said to Cephas in the presence of all: if you, since you are a Jew, live as a Gentile and not as a Jew, how do you compel the Gentiles to judaize?** (Gal. 2:14). Now Peter was associating with Gentiles there before the arrival of those Jews, observing the rites of their faith and nothing opposed to them, which is thus to live as a Gentile. How then was it permissible for him and his colleagues to teach the Gentiles to live as a separate association? For that would be judaizing, since it is appropriate for the Apostles, who were Jews by nature, to associate with Gentiles, in keeping with the precept of the Gospel: **Teach all the Gentiles**, in the last chapter of Mark (Mark 16:15); and: **Into whatever home you would enter, remain there**, in Matt. 10:11. Indeed, Peter fulfilled this precept with Cornelius, having been taught by the Holy Spirit, as Acts 10:24–33 makes clear. Inasmuch as God ordained that his faith would be communicated **by hearing**, evinced in Rom. 11 (Rom. 10:17), and that Jews and Gentiles were to be spiritual brothers through a stronger alliance than exists among brothers of the flesh, when would have been a more opportune time to reveal that determination than in the presence of such great prelates? And yet because he was afraid of scandalizing a handful of Jews, with such important doctors standing by, he kept quiet and thus failed to issue that evangelical rebuke.

Therefore, by the faith of Scripture it is fitting to believe that Peter and all the participants in this hypocritical episode did not walk uprightly, that is to say, in an acceptable manner. (184) There can be no question but that Peter and Barnabas had sinned venially when, conscious of their own guilt, they still kept silent, even though they undoubtedly repented by complying with grace.

Just as I have so extensively explained elsewhere, from that small part of the faith of Scripture three elements essential for the governance of the Church become clear. First, it is fitting for an inferior to rebuke his so-called superiors in such cases where their conduct could lead souls into danger. Indeed, Christ did just this with the Pharisees, as did Paul when dealing with the leader of the Church Militant. Hence, commenting upon the first chapter of the letter to Titus, Chrysostom says, "Christ reproached the scribes and Pharisees a thousand times, though not for his own sake, but because the others who were subject to them were perishing by following their example."[66]

Second, it is evident that the superior should humbly accept the rebuke of his inferior whenever evangelical form is observed. Were I to be causing offense to the gospel, how could I refuse even a donkey if he would lead me back in the right direction? Whereupon, one does not read of Peter and Barnabas murmuring against Paul, asserting themselves either as his superior or his equal in office. Nor did they contentiously lodge an appeal from him to the Lord. But if this must be done, Christ, who sowed the seeds of the Church's future faith in his Scriptures, by no means neglected to leave us such an essential example.

(185) Third, it is clear that anyone who properly rebukes his brother ought to rebuke him as if he were a superior. For nobody should rebuke someone else unless the one issuing the rebuke is himself untainted by sin. Indeed, he should take care lest he too stands accused of some great offense, since

"charity begins at home." But inasmuch as he is the one more purified of sin, then he is the superior in God's sight. Taken in this way, in every form of lawful rebuke it is appropriate for the superior to rebuke the inferior.

Hence, to prevent any contention from arising around those things, Christ bequeathed the evangelical law to his Church, so that the person who is rebuked might discern whether or not he caused offense in that matter, and the one issuing the rebuke **would first cast out the beam from his own eye** (Matt. 7:5). And then each of them, having put aside all envy and pretense of superiority, would start with himself when setting things right. Of course, it so often happens that the person issuing the rebuke does what is right, yet does so unjustly and unsuitably.

Therefore, everyone should first make sure that he does his duty in a suitable manner.

(*De ver.* III,xxx): A Mystical Reading of Some Old Testament Laws

(185) With regard to the third Judaic rite, it remains to consider how the Christian should refrain from the eating of blood.

For in Acts 15, where the apostolic synod considered this matter, Peter put forth this definitive judgment on behalf of the holy college: **I determine that those among the Gentiles who are turning to God are not to be troubled,** (186) **but we should write to them that they would abstain from the contaminations of idols, and from fornication, and from what was strangled, and from blood** (Acts 15:19–20). And it follows in the letter which the assembly of Apostles sent to the Gentiles via Paul and Barnabas, Judas and Silas: **It seemed fitting to the Holy Spirit and to us that no more burdens be imposed upon you other than what is necessary, that you would abstain from the sacrifices of idols, and blood, and what was strangled, and from fornication, and keeping**

yourselves away from these things you will do well. Farewell (Acts 15:28–29).

Based upon the synod's most solemn and holy decision, three clarifications seem to have followed. First, that the Gentiles, having rejected circumcision, should have observed the Judaic rite of abstaining from the eating of blood. Second, that the princes of the Church must be careful not to burden their subjects with a whole host of rites extending beyond those observances which have scriptural foundation. And third, all types of sins are included within that definition of fornication.

Since every human soul should be joined to the Bridegroom of the Church in eternal matrimony, it is clear that he must abstain from the sin of the flesh, be it the sin of the world or that of the devil. For anyone who recoils from Christ in spiritual fornication annuls this heavenly marriage. We must never believe that the Apostles allowed the Gentiles to commit any sin, whether that of pride, envy, anger, inordinate laziness, or lust. (187) In fact, the Gentiles were chiefly implicated in the types of sins mentioned above. Therefore, the other sins were all wrapped up into one and prohibited under that form. For at that time carnal fornication was prevalent among the Gentiles. The eating of food sacrificed to idols also offended the consciences of many people at that time, as did the two Judaic ritual prohibitions. The first concerned the illicit eating of beasts, which had been suffocated, and extended beyond the intent to eat them. And there was also the prohibition against the eating of blood, which offended both Jews and Gentiles. Yet that too went beyond the old covenant, or what was essential for the Gentiles. After all, it is not denied that eating food sacrificed to idols is in fact lawful, as clarified in 1 Cor. 10:25, **Eat everything which is sold in the market, examining nothing on account of conscience**. And likewise, it is clear that in the matter of food sacrificed to idols, dealt with in 1 Cor. 8: 4–13, if a Christian were to have reservations about eating those things, or that by eating them he would unfaithfully injure another, then the use of such sacrifices is not permissible. But because that often occurred among the Gentiles, Peter expressly tells them to abstain from the contaminations of idols. For if I comply with faith and love when eating food sacrificed to idols, I abstain from the contaminations of idols, because **all things are pure to those who are pure** (Titus 1:15).

These two rites were commanded and observed in the Old Testament, however. (188) Whereupon it is commanded in Exod. 22:31, **The flesh which has been tasted beforehand by beasts, you will not eat, but you will throw to the dogs**. And the same meaning is made clear in Lev. 5:2, **The soul which would touch anything unclean, or what has been killed by a beast, or is already found dead, or any other reptile, and has thus forgotten its uncleanness, is guilty and has sinned.** This was literally observed (*ad literam*) in order to distinguish Jews from Gentiles, just as one can thereby discern the faithful from the infidels by the idolatry they perform with foods of this sort.

But third, it seems to me that this mystically symbolizes the fact that a person should not do a good work of this type, unless it proceeds from an upright intention and an informing love, such that a virtuous action is the honorable food of the soul. For if it does not so proceed, then even an essentially good work was killed by a beast. The last one, however, is often prohibited in the Old Testament, as in Lev. 7:26–27, **You will also not consume the blood of any animal as food, whether from birds or cattle. Every soul who would eat the blood will be cut off from his people**. And in Lev. 17:10–11, **Any person from the house of Israel, and from the foreigners who sojourn among you,** (189) **if he eats blood, I will set my face against his soul, and I will dispel him from his people, because the life of the flesh is in the blood.**

In light of these things it seems fitting that even after the Apostles had decreed the cessation of the legal obligations,

Christians would still beware the eating of blood and adhere to the same principle which they did in the past, since life is as much in the blood now as it was then. And so it seems appropriate that we too should beware the eating of blood, just as the patriarchs ought to have done. Notwithstanding that, we do see Christians eating blood on occasion when cooked in sausages and in many other ways.

[. . .] (193) Now there are three levels of usefulness which are commonly assigned to the legal obligations. First, that through their exercise they would predict the coming of the Messiah or the works of his own sacraments, though that reason ceases at the instant in which the sacrament succeeds. Second, so that by demonstrating the fulfillment of its task it would remain active in that respect, thereby attesting to the fact that the same God of both testaments is graciously and most truly accomplishing what he promised. And that reason ceases at the very instant there is certitude regarding the occurrence of the faith which was symbolized. But third, so that by remembering the reason why the ceremony was instituted we might enjoy the power it figuratively designated.

And in this manner all the sacraments are everlasting. Thus they should cease doubly in effect, but perpetually remain according to two of the levels having to do with their benefits. Yet if according to faith of Scripture, **the deeds of the blessed follow them** (Rev. 14:13), how could the ceremonies of the patriarchs neither follow them in benefit, nor in effect? One, therefore, is the principle of prognostication, another of attestation, and yet another of the fruition of the ceremony or of another sacrament.

And it is clear that when speaking of their cessation one understands the cessation of the double principle in effect. Though when speaking of their perpetuation one must speak of their perpetuation in terms of the benefit or meaning that was symbolized.

(194) Likewise, when considering the reason for the legal obligations which ought to cease in their literal sense (*ad literam*), Lincolniensis notes that the Old Testament precepts were given for five reasons:[67] in order to prefigure the Messiah, to distinguish a faithful people, to take control of an insolent people, and to provide a humbling recompense for a rebellious people, so that through such obedience God might blunt the swelling pride of those who were saying that the one who would accomplish those things is present, but the one who would command them is absent, as elicited from Exod. 24:3, **All the things which God has spoken to us we will do**. And finally, this was done in order to abolish the blasphemous murmuring against the Lord, by which the person who has fallen into the pit of sin could complain to God that he would not able to climb up by the steps of the commandments of the natural law unless the steps of the law of the commandments, namely the positive law, were thrown down to him, such that they would serve as figures and testimonies of our restoration.

Therefore, since those signs have come to an end with the manifestation of Christ in the flesh, it seems fitting that those legal obligations should also cease at that time. For when the one they symbolized arrives, **You are not under the law, but under grace**, etc., as the Apostle says in Rom. 6:14. (195) From that time forward Jews and Gentiles **are made one people**, as the Apostle says in Eph. 2:14–15, **He is our peace, who made both one, breaking down the middle wall of partition, the hostilities in their flesh, abolishing the law of the commandments in the decrees, so that he might construct the two within himself into one new person.** Then, having put aside carnal affections they should **cast all their care upon Christ**, as Peter teaches in 1 Pet. 5:7. And at that time, The Head of the Church humbled himself and accomplished the act of obedience, fully reversing the act of disobedience on the part of the first parents, since **becoming a man he was**

emptied of equality with God, being obedient to the Father even to the point of death on the cross (Phil. 2:7–8). Whereupon in Gal. 3:13, **Christ redeems us from the curse of the law, becoming for us the curse**. And then the Bridegroom, accomplishing the redemption of the Church and liberating her from captivity, wished to abolish the ladder's steps from the pit so that she would rely more completely upon her Bridegroom, saying with the Apostle in Phil. 4:13, **I am capable of all things in the one who strengthens me**; and Song of Sol. 8:5, **Who is the one that is coming up from the wilderness, abounding with delights, leaning upon her beloved?** Since it now suffices for the bride to make her way without those signs, as the wise grow weary with juvenile imperfection, must not the imperfect be canceled out when perfection arrives? For the natural principle of the philosophers dictates that it is superfluous to retain many things when just a few will suffice. [. . .]

(*De ver.* III,xxxi): Christ as the Fulfillment of the Old Law

(231) Returning to the matter of the cessation of the legal obligations, it still remains to be seen how we must understand the text of the Apostle in Heb. 7:12 where he says, **When there is transference of the priesthood it is necessary for there to be a transference of the law**. We should discuss this question as much for the sake of declaring the truth of Scripture as for establishing the principle behind the cessation of legal obligations.

At first glance that text would appear to be false. For then there would be a transference of English law corresponding to a priestly transference. And since it very often happens that after the death of a bishop there will be two or three transferences of bishops, and consequently priests, it follows that there would be a corresponding transference of our law. And because the transference of reign follows upon the transference of its law, it means that such a priestly transference would threaten to topple the kingdom. Yet the consequence is false.

Along these lines, in the Old Testament there was often a transference of the priesthood without a transference of law. Therefore, that need not be the result. The antecedent is made especially clear by 1 Kings 2:26–27, regarding the deposition of Abiathar, whom the wise Solomon ordered **to go to his estate in Anathoth**, thereby banishing him from the royal city, and consequently taking the high priesthood away from him. And yet this led neither to a transference of law, nor to the destruction of the kingdom. Rather, the punishment of the high priest by the secular prince served to strengthen Solomon's reign. In this instance he surely carried out the will of the Lord, expressed in 1 King 2:1–9, by excluding those deceitful people from the kingdom (232) who would be most likely to bring about the kingdom's destruction. For it is written in Matt. 5:13, **But if the salt becomes tasteless it serves no purpose except to be thrown out and trampled upon by people**. This text is generally true of bishops and priests who ought to salt the life of the people. Whereupon, the common gloss explains how salt of this sort loses its flavor. It says,

> Salt, through water, the heat of sun, and breath of the wind is changed from one nature to another, just as the apostolic men, through the water of baptism, the heat of faith, and the breath, that is, the gift of the Holy Spirit, were transformed from an earthly generation into a spiritual one. God, however, gave the people the sense to discern whether or not a cleric lives this way, and the power to throw the obstinate out of their designated office, and to soundly trample upon the rebellious.[68]

Likewise, at the time of Constantine there was a transference of the priesthood, and yet this resulted in a stabilization of his realm. Of course, this was before the Roman Church had received an endowment of any note. Nor had it yet been decreed that the bishop of this church would necessarily possess primacy among the others, as is supposed today. And it is not valid to say that there was not a transference of the priesthood in this instance, but only an improvement of the same priesthood, owing to the Donation made to the Church. For by the same rationale, the priesthood of Aaron coming after Melchizedek did not occur by transference, but through an improvement of the sacerdotal class, since God always improves things as he proceeds. And along these same lines, the priesthood of the proprietary system is more perfect than one no longer under that system, since God would not otherwise authorize a change from the better to the worse.[69]

In light of any one of these considerations, it seems inappropriate that a transference of the priesthood must result in a transference of the law, since it still remains for all kinds of priests to serve the same law.

(233) Here it is fitting to make a distinction between priesthood, transference, and law.

There are three categories of priesthood in the age of the Church, as I have touched upon in Chapter 21 of my Fifth Book.[70] The first is that priesthood which is in keeping with the natural law, according to which the priests were regularly the first born, abiding by the law of primogeniture. And in this manner Melchizedek was a priest, as evinced by Gen. 14:18.

The second category of priesthood was in keeping with Mosaic law, according to which Aaron and his progeny were priests, as evinced in the process outlined in Lev. 8:1–13. Hence, as a penalty for the sin of the other tribes who had worshipped the calf, the priesthood was transferred from the other tribes to the tribe of Levi (Exod. 32:25–35).

The third category of priesthood is in keeping with the law of grace, according to which Christ, the Apostles, and their successors are priests.

Hence, some people call the first category of priesthood the natural priesthood, the second priesthood the legal, and the third priesthood the one of grace.

The third category, however, comprises the perfection of the two earlier ones, since Christ, the first principle of that priesthood, was king and priest, God and man, the one whom the rites of the earlier two priesthoods were ultimately intended to signify. Therefore, because the Church's Bridegroom improves things as he proceeds, it is evident that the light which is symbolized is preferable to the shadow which symbolizes it.

(234) Second, it must be noted that since the law is two-fold, namely divine and human, the Apostle speaks of the divine law according to which the priesthood should be regulated, and consequently subjected to the Church.

Third, one must note that the transference is two-fold with respect to this purpose, namely personal and general. It is personal whenever one bishop is transferred from the governance of one church or diocese to another. And this is the sort discussed by the laws of the Church. General transference occurs whenever the governance of the whole Church Militant is changed from one kind of priesthood to another.

Thus we conceive of the priesthood, first of all, simply in reference to any one of these three classifications. Second, we understand the law as the divine law which pertains to the governance of the general priest. And third, we think of the general transference. When we understand the Apostle's text from the point of view of causality, it becomes clear that because the priesthood is transferred generally from a legalistic priesthood to a priesthood of grace, it is necessary that the laws by which priests live and govern would also be transferred. For when the legalistic priesthood came to an end, and the prefigured third priesthood of grace was introduced, it was clearly necessary that the legalistic rites would also cease as other new forms corresponding to the new and eternal priesthood were then introduced. And if you ask me where one finds suitable evidence to support the succession of the third priesthood, I say it is found in Psalm 109 (Ps. 110:1) where the lord David addressed the Messiah as Lord, as Christ explains in Matt. 22:41–46 that he would sit forever in his best places. (235) And after that he says again of the same one: **The Lord swore to him, and he will not repent of it: you are a priest forever according to the order of Melchizedek.**

[. . .] (242) Because the First Love puts an end to those legal obligations, guiding the movement of his members as to how and when they should observe or reject these legal obligations, it is essential for all the faithful, in faith, hope and love, to concentrate on this above all else. In so doing, they should believe by faith that Christ, whom we Christians worship, is true God and true man, since he is the Messiah who was promised to the patriarchs.

Although it is appropriate for us to grasp that point first by faith, inasmuch as it is its principal article, it still seems proper for the purpose of understanding Scripture that we would mention a few of its parts which more expressly testify to this. For in keeping with what I said in Chapter Twelve, it is only fitting that every authority belonging to created Scripture originates in him. Therefore, we must first comprehend the gospel of Christ and the Apostles and, moreover, recognize that the other Scriptures conform to his rule. The ultimate conclusion of the entire Scripture, and all of its parts, is that by the most fitting manner, Christ, God and man, is the redeemer of the human race, the author of all salvation, and the one bestowing our final reward. And so he is our redemption, salvation, and reward, indeed everything which is essential for the human race. By a sound analogical understanding of predication he corresponds to the four types of causation: material, formal, efficient, and final. Conceiving of causation analogically beyond the genus, he is the matter from which proceeds the joy of the blessed. (243) He is also the form which all the blessed must clothe themselves with, thereby becoming Christ himself in a certain manner. He is the efficient cause of the first and last aspect of every action, since he says in John 15:5, **Apart from me you can do nothing**. And he is the final end for whose sake the whole universe was ultimately created and constituted in its limits. For in John 1:14 it is said, **The Word became flesh**; and in John 10:35–36, **The Scripture cannot be destroyed whom the Father sanctified and sent into the world**; and below in John 10:30, **I and the Father are one**. When these passages are rightly understood it follows that Christ, whom we worship, is true God and true man, just as any number of passages of the New Law bear witness. And from the same law the testimony of the Old Testament can be deduced. In the last chapter of Luke (Luke 24:27) one reads how Christ, **beginning from Moses and all the prophets interpreted all the things which were written about him** for the two disciples going to Emmaus. And in Acts 3:18 Peter says, **God thus fulfilled what he has foretold through the mouth of all the prophets that his Christ would suffer**. And Acts 10:43 states, **To this person all the prophets bear witness**.

On this basis, it seems fitting that insofar as we should believe the entire New Testament in all matters having to do with Christ, so too should we believe in the Old. Whereupon, as we read in Acts 3:22–24, Peter recounts how Moses said of Christ in Deut. 18:15–18 that, **Moses said, The Lord your God will raise up for you a prophet like me from among your own brethren. And you will listen to him with regard to all that he has spoken to you. However, it will be such that every soul which does not listen to that prophet will be driven out from the people. And all the prophets who have spoken from Samuel henceforth have announced these days.** Based upon the faith of such Scripture (244) we reckon that all the books of the Old Testament either directly and firstly, or mystically and secondarily, signify that our Jesus is the Messiah of the Lord and the man promised to the patriarchs. And, as we read in Acts 9:22, the holy Apostle was instructed in this conclusion after his clear vision of the mysteries, when he preached Jesus to the Jews, **affirming that this man is the Christ.** In short, all the lifestyles of the patriarchs, as well as their deeds, mystically signify the life of Christ, since this life is the end for which the whole created universe strives. It is fitting, however, that the end would be signified through means which lead to this very same end. For God would not otherwise have ordained such means, unless he planned to use them to speak of that intrinsic end which he is so intent upon achieving. Hence, all the patriarchs of the Old Testament were pre-ordained to blessedness, since they had believed in the Messiah whom we now singularly worship. For as it is said in Acts 4:12, **There is no salvation in anyone else** other than our Lord Jesus Christ of Nazareth whom the Jews crucified.

[. . .] (266) Now in Dan. 7:13, after another figure of these four kingdoms (Dan. 7:2–8), it is thus written, **In a vision of the night I was gazing, and behold, with the clouds of heaven he was coming as if the Son of Man, and he will come all the way up to the Ancient of Days, and they presented him within his sight**. If I am not mistaken, no one can more aptly explain this prophetic text than as referring to our Jesus, who, just as he ascended to his ministry among the clouds, will thus come at the final judgment. And so he desired that this would be demonstrated by means of a prophetic revelation.

This is the one who so frequently in the Gospel calls himself the **Son of Man**, and although he would attain equality with the **Ancient of Days** according to his divinity, nevertheless, according to the weakness of the flesh which he assumed from us, **they presented him** in the temple to the Trinity in order to fulfill the ministry of both testaments. And thus the angels were ministering to him in every human deed, so that he might accomplish the task his Father assigned to him.

Hence, for the purpose of confirming that determination of Christ's dual nature, it is immediately added: **And he gave to him power, honor and kingship. And every people, tribe and language will serve him. His power is eternal power which will not be withdrawn, and his kingship will not be destroyed** (Dan. 7:14). I ask you, to whom can that possibly correspond except our Jesus, God and man? (267) Indeed, he himself says in the last chapter of Matthew (Matt. 28:18), **To me was granted all power in heaven and on earth**. For if this were not so he would not be able to crush the aforementioned four kingdoms, nor in his exaltation could he subdue his enemies. And honor follows upon that power, for it is written in Phil. 2:9–10, **He gave him a name which is above every name, so that at the name of Jesus every knee would bend in heaven, on earth, and the lower world**. It is evident that by departing into that distant country he was disposed to accept kingship for himself (Luke 19:12).

I ask you, to whom can this triple servitude apply, this eternal power and kingship, so indestructible, except to the one whom John sees as having inscribed on his thigh: **King of kings and Lord of lords** in Apocalypse 19 (Rev. 19:16)?

If those things are applicable to our Jesus, how can it be appropriate to wait unfaithfully for some other anti-Christ? Whereupon, in Dan. 7:20–23, anti-Christ is presently described by the horn arising at the time of the fourth kingdom. Yet it was amassed from our own potentates in so horrible, cruel and rapacious a manner. For when taking an account of the pagans and our so-called Christians one reads of no less of a struggle for worldly gains than in times past. The ten horns is the entirety of our temporal lords. And then there is the horn which arises from the ten horns, having the eyes and mouth, speaking arrogantly **against the Exalted One and the wearing away the holy ones of the Most High, and reckoning that**

he would be able to change the seasons and the laws (Dan. 7:25). (268) If only this were not the chief of the endowed clergy with all the temporalities of the aforesaid dominion which he amassed!

Thus our clergy are in fact blaspheming when they praise Lord Pope, as I said in Chapter Eight. The sign of this danger is found in that passage of Isa. 59:14–15, **Justice has been turned back and righteousness stands far away, because truth falls down in the street and equity could not enter, and truth lapsed into oblivion, and the one who recoiled from evil was exposed to plunder**. If only such an anti-Christ would not lay waste to northern, western and eastern kingdoms, just as he has polluted Asia, Africa and Europe! I have made up my mind that even though he will reign for a **time** and **times** and **half a time**, divine justice still demands that the aforesaid **power be taken away, broken to pieces and scattered to the ends of the earth** (Dan. 7:25–26).

But by bequeathing those things to the members of the Church, who have been given the task of explaining prophecies, it is determined by the faith of Scripture that any secular or cleric who chiefly obstructs the laws of Christ is the principal anti-Christ. And whatever period or year had been ceded to him to exercise his tyranny is said to be "every time" according to the prophetical sense. Hence, I believe that Daniel understands by **time** the whole period in which the Church had fallen away, from the time of her first endowment up until the time when Mohammed prevailed. And by **times** he understands the variety of times from then up until the time in which secular lords agreed in considering alms only to be what they gave to the poor. And by **half a time** he understands the remaining time when the clergy, through the pretense of their excommunication and the destructive power of censures, madly resist those people who would actually do them a good deed by removing the very thing which incites their criminal behavior.

(269) Yet in whatever way one considers that meaning it remains certain by Daniel's prophetical sense that our Jesus is that great prophet, the savior whom God had promised to the patriarchs. [. . .]

(*De ver.* III,xxxii): A Consideration of Heresy

(274) Finally, as something incidental to this treatise *On the Truth of Holy Scripture*, there remains the consideration of heresy.

Scripture is certainly the standard by which we can best discern heresy through a comparison with its very opposite. In fact, I will say even more resolutely that no one can recognize heresy unless they have knowledge of Scripture.

From this it is clear that only the theologian is suited to judge heresy. And if in the course of his duties a lawyer or decretist renders a determination regarding heresy, he does so inasmuch as he is a theologian, such that he would have been instructed by a theologian regarding what constitutes the sense of Scripture and what is contrary to it.

(275) In Chapter 7 of my Fourth Book, I declared that, "heresy is a false dogma, contrary to Holy Scripture, which is obstinately defended."[71] Although, according to Augustine in the final chapter of his book *On Heresy*, it is difficult, if not impossible, for us to identify all the heresies being circulated, we are still capable of describing it under some sort of analogous definition.[72]

First, it must be noted that a heresy is that thing by which an infidel is formally designated a heretic. In light of this it is evident that heresy is not a falsehood on the part of the thing, but is an evil disposition in the act or habit by means of which the infidel holds an opinion opposed to the Catholic faith. Clearly then, since the entirety of Holy Scripture is true, containing within itself every truth, as Augustine says in his

Letter 4 to Volusianus, and at the end of Book 2 of *On Christian Doctrine*,[73] there is no heresy except that which is false, and contrary to Holy Scripture. A person is not deemed a heretic unless he defends falsehood by word or deed. Nor does offering a merely spur-of-the-moment defense make him a heretic. (276) It is necessary, therefore, that he would obstinately defend his own dogma.

But contrary to that definition, one might first object that many people are heretics while they sleep, keep silent, or explain the truth in detail. And since it is impossible for anyone to be a heretic without the heresy taking substantial form, it seems that false dogma does not fall into the category of heresy.

Here I say that both the Greeks and the Latins are in agreement regarding that category, as I have illustrated by turning to Lincolniensis.[74]

Hence, in order to answer this objection, it must be noted that dogma is common to every teaching, good or bad, whether it was exhibited through any sort of sign, or through the thing propounded as dogma.

Second, we must note that since every natural thing naturally declares itself, as made clear in Book 15 of *On the Trinity*,[75] it is evident that every infidel continuously propounds false dogma in word and deed as long as he is such a person, because he is declaring his own false habit in one way or another. And since every person of this sort is a hypocrite desiring by diabolical inspiration, whether explicitly or implicitly, to pervert part of the Church into following his error, it is clear, according to the principle of one propounding false dogma, that he declares a falsehood. Consequently, his own evil habit, which is heretical, is a false dogma.

On this basis a third answer to this objection is made clear. Now in any one of the three cases touched upon the infidel exhibits false dogma of one sort or another, since he naturally declares himself. Nevertheless, for the sake of his reputation he will not speak of the dogma in public, unless it were a doctrinal discussion brought to his attention. (277) Yet Scripture speaks in another way, as in Job 12:7, where it is said that, **The cattle and the other creatures teach the human being**. Hence, when the infidel teaches that God exists, or some other article of faith, he is teaching the truth by means of false dogma. Indeed, as I said above, his vocal or mental proposition is false, owing to the pollution of the subject, although the truth which is signified remains entirely unharmed. Thus any dogma proceeding from the will, deed, or word of such a person is a false dogma, as is the habit from which it originates.

Whereupon, in order to annul objections, and to speak more easily, in greater conformity with the doctors, I understand by dogma not the bare act or habit but, together with this, a simply relative relationship in act or habit, according to which such an act or habit is so arranged for the purpose of corrupting a person. Hence, in opposition to the sophists, one must be diligent in pointing out which thing is signified by means of false dogma in that description. For that dogma is not formally a sin, but rather a positive form, antecedent or consequent to sin.

Second, an objection is raised against the second section. First, it would be possible for heresy to exist together with this, and that there would be no Holy Scripture. For in fact the one is contrary to the other, and there are many heresies alongside catholic truths whose opposites are nowhere to be found in Scripture.

Blessed be God, who liberated us from those accusations! Now with respect to the first, just as there cannot be darkness unless preceded by at least uncreated light, so there cannot be heresy unless preceded by Holy Scripture, as I said in Chapter Six concerning the five-fold Scripture.

(278) Clearly, an impossibility is assumed in the first instance. And with regard to the second, it is evident since no

Holy Scripture is false. But whatever is sacred is true, such that no part of it is capable of being contrary to another, as I have very clearly stated throughout this treatise. And with respect to the third point, it is evident that every truth is at least implicitly found in Scripture. Consequently, just as every catholic truth is included there, so every heresy is damned there.

Whereupon, since every heresy is an evil which is morally opposed to the faith, and every point of faith is included in Scripture and every vice condemned, it is clear that you will discover all heresies and their opposites in Scripture. In fact, since the principal being of every heresy is truth, and every truth abides in Scripture, it is evident that every heresy abides in Scripture, though not for the sake of approving it, at least not according to the principle by which it is a heresy, but rather for the sake of condemning it. Hence the Apostle writes in 1 Cor. 11:19, **It is necessary that there would be heresies so that those who are approved would be made manifest**. And in Titus 3:10–11 the Apostle argues that, **After the first and second rebuke the heretical person is to be shunned, knowing that someone of this sort is perverted**. Therefore, according to truth or natural being, all manner of heresy is included in Scripture. Yet it does not follow from this that Holy Scripture is heretical any more than it follows that the world itself is heretical in which all heresies exist, though not formally. Indeed, just as every evil action subsists causally in God, although one does not call him evil, so every heresy subsists causally in Scripture. (279) I say "causally" with respect to that positive aspect in a heresy, and according to the final good which God ordained would come from the heresy. Nor would it be appropriate to so describe Holy Scripture, except on account of the greater expression of the exemplar by which the heretic is recognized. Hence, in his book *On Heresies*, Augustine definitively states that, "Heretics are those who attack the rule of truth with individual signs, no more amply than with dogmas."[76] For a heretic disseminates heresy in some way in all of his dogmas, even those in which he propounds the truth. Therefore, lest anyone believe something false of Holy Scripture, inapplicable to the greater explanation, it is said that heresy is a false dogma which is contrary to Holy Scripture. And lest anyone would slander that whole definition, I have cited other texts of Augustine in his book *Against the Manichees*, and proposed in the *Decretum*, Case 24, Question 3, which says, "Heretics are those in the Church of Christ who have a taste for something depraved or diseased, and yet they are unwilling to correct their noxious and deadly dogmas, but would rather insolently resist and defend them."[77] This entire definition makes clear what I established concerning heresy, in addition to those things contrary to Holy Scripture. But in keeping with that definition, it is appropriate that everyone who speaks of heresy accept this understanding.

A third objection is raised concerning the third aspect, that it is "obstinately defended." For by understanding it in conjunction with everything that has been said to this point, it follows that Aristotle and all the rest of the pagan philosophers were heretics, (280) because it is certain that they disseminated false dogma, contrary to Holy Scripture, which they had obstinately defended. That appears to be false when they were never united in the faith of Christ. Thus not only would all infidels and schismatics be heretics, but even a great number of faithful people who utter a false judgment by way of opinion. Still, it is laudable for those maintaining such protestations to then recant in keeping with Church's precept, such that those who obstinately defend their dogma would follow suit. One would then conclude that this dogma was obstinately defended by a follower of this opinion and was, therefore, obstinately defended. And in this way, every protestation of the theologian would perish, or else it would be possible for heresy to inhere formally within him apart from this, such that he would be a heretic. For however much the person piously protests or teaches something false by way of opinion, he is still not obstinately defending it. But however much a single heretic succeeds in disseminating false dogma, contrary to Holy Scripture, it is obstinately defended. Yet it is not taught, since it obstinately resounds of evil at all times. As such, it suffices to define a heretic as an obstinate person, and heresy as obstinacy.

In light of this, it appears to me that Aristotle and every infidel was a heretic at some time, but in what condition he died, or how long he defended his heresy, that I leave to the Searcher of Hearts.

How could we excuse the erroneous opinions of the infidel philosophers regarding the eternity of the world and all its obvious implications, since Christians who defend that judgment less obstinately are heretics? Even the ignorance or failure of their catholic instructor does not excuse them, for they do in fact fall into heresy or mortal sin. Of course, I believe that our own philosophers who gratuitously disseminate false dogma for the sake of vainglory, or some other extraneous cause, (281) are heretics in their own right. This is why it is particularly dangerous to disseminate such opinions simply for the sake of pursuing superfluous ideas.

[. . .] (295) A further difficulty which remains is whether everyone whose damnation is foreknown is perpetually a heretic, while everyone who is predestined for salvation is perpetually catholic. Or is there some alternation between the two, such that one is a now heretic and now again a Catholic? It seems fitting, however, that everyone whose damnation is foreknown, even every devil, would be perpetually a heretic, just as he is a blasphemer, because he has separated himself from the congregation of the faithful through his own evil choice. Such a person was never part of the Church, according to Augustine in Book 3, Chapter 32 of *On Christian Doctrine*.[78] Nor, on the other hand, does the predestined person ever cease to be part of the Church. Consequently, from God's perspective, it is impossible for such a person to alternate between the two.

On this point I say that if an authority were presented to me in keeping with this manner of speaking, then I would concede the conclusion. Nevertheless, (296) with respect to the equivocal sense it just so happens that a person can abide within the grace of final perseverance, or simply abide in a state of grace pertaining to present righteousness. And so, it is possible for a person to be a heretic in a two-fold manner, because in however many ways he can be called one of the opposites, there are that many ways he can be called the remainder. Otherwise, it would not be possible for a heretic to become a Catholic, nor vice-versa. Thus he is a heretic according to his state of present unrighteousness, while he is not a heretic according to God's foreknowledge that he will become a Catholic. Whereupon, those sophists contending over verbal distinctions object that everyone who is a heretic according to foreknowledge is in fact a heretic according to present unrighteousness, since all unrighteousness is present to God. But in this way the sophist can then object that every predestined person would be foreknown, when God knows and eternally disposes him to glory, while everyone who must be damned, and is in a state of grace at any time, he preordains and predestines to grace. Therefore, in such cases we should accept the sense that is in keeping with the way the speakers are employing these terms. In so doing, present righteousness or unrighteousness would only be called righteousness or unrighteousness, which is merely temporal, that is to say, it has an end in time, beyond which time itself continues. And taken in this way, there are many predestined people who propound false dogma and obstinately defend it. Likewise, there are many among the foreknown who virtuously teach true doctrine and persistently defend it at the time. It is similar to the person who is caught up in the fervor of charity and takes a vow to devote himself to doing a good work, only to break his vow by sinning. For in point of fact his vow retained a kind of implicit mortal baseness. So it is with every person whose damnation is foreknown, for no matter how long he abides in a state of grace according to present righteousness, he finally breaks the vow he had made. Therefore, it is only in an equivocal sense that he exists in a state of grace with the predestined person. Nor does the predestined person mortally sin along with the foreknown person, except in an equivocal sense.

[. . .] (309) That is all I have to say for now about heresy in general, (310) so that by the fruit of Scripture's truth one might know how to recognize heretics and guard against them. This will also allow for a clearer understanding of my treatise *On Simony*. For that is a topic which, God willing, I propose to study at some length.

Notes

1. Wyclif is referring to the alleged "Donation of Constantine," whereby the Emperor Constantine had granted the western lands of the Roman Empire to Pope Sylvester in the fourth century. The document of record was later proven to be a forgery by Lorenzo Valla in the fifteenth century.

2. Dec. II, C. 11, Q. 3, c. 12, in Emil Friedberg, ed., *Corpus iuris canonici*, 2 vols. (Leipzig, 1879–81), 1:646.

3. Wyclif engages in a play on the word '*episcopus*', using it to refer to the garden's caretaker in the first instance and the bishop in the latter.

4. Dec. III, D. 5, c. 24, in Friedberg, *Corpus* 1:1418.

5. This refers to the fourth book of Wyclif's *Summa Theologiae*. See *De civili dominio* II.xv, ed. Johann Loserth (1900; repr. New York, 1966), pp. 197–208.

6. See *De Civitate Dei* XII.23–28, ed. Bernardus Dombart and Alphonsus Kalb, Corpus Christianorum, Series Latina 48 (Turnhout, 1950), pp. 380–85.

7. See Aristotle's *Nicomachean Ethics* I (1094a–1103a); X (1172a–1181b).

8. Wyclif refers to the commandment to "honor thy father and mother."

9. The three theological virtues are faith, hope and love.

10. *In Librum Jesu Nave Homilia* VII, PG 12:856–58.

11. This is Christ.

12. Wyclif seems to be referring to a work attributed to Origen: *De Origeniano Lexico Nominum Hebraicorum*. See PL 23:1214.

13. This is Joshua.

14. The pallium is a cloth band traditionally bestowed upon archbishops by the papacy, symbolizing allegiance to Rome. Purple is the imperial color, and legend has it that the Emperor Constantine had placed his own cloak upon Pope Sylvester.

15. See Origen's *Traité des principes*, IV.3, ed. Henri Crouzel and Manlio Simonetti (Paris, 1980), p. 354.

16. Dec. II, C. 1, Q. 1, c. 94, in Friedberg, *Corpus* 1:391.

17. Dec. I, D. 25, c. 1–2, in Friedberg, *Corpus* 1:89–92, 135.

18. Dec. I, D. 26, c. 3, in Friedberg, *Corpus* 1:135.

19. Wyclif refers to the gloss of Guido de Baysio, archdeacon of Bologna (d. 1313). This citation may be from the *Rosarium Decretorum* but was not found. See Dec. I, D. 43, c. 5, in Friedberg, *Corpus* 1:156. This chapter insists upon the duty of the preacher to proclaim the word. The above quote is not found.

20. I have omitted the lengthy quotation from canon law which follows in support of this third point. See Dec. I, D. 38, c. 6, in Friedberg, *Corpus* 1:142.

21. See Aristotle's *Nicomachean Ethics* III.2 (1111b–1112a).

22. *In Epist. I ad Timoth.* X, PG 62:547.

23. Dec. I, D. 93, c. 1–26, in Friedberg, *Corpus* 1:320–30.

24. *In Epist. I ad Timoth.* X, PG 62:547.

25. Dec. I, D. 51, c. 5, in Friedberg, *Corpus* 1:228.

26. *In Epist. I ad Timoth.* X, PG 62:547.

27. Dec. I, D. 40, c. 1–12, in Friedberg, *Corpus* 1:14.

28. Dec. I, D. 61, c. 1–2, in Friedberg, *Corpus* 1:227.

29. Dec. I, D. 48, in Friedberg, *Corpus* 1:174.

30. *De verbis Evangeliii Johannis* CXXXVIII, PL 38:764.

31. Ibid., PL 38:765.

32. Ibid., PL 38:765.

33. See Isidore's *Sententiarum Libri Tres* III.45, PL 83:714.

34. Ibid., III.46, PL 83:714–15.

35. Henry of Segusio, or "Cardinal Hostiensis," was a leading canonist (d. 1271). See his *Summa* (Lyon, 1537). This quote has not been found.

36. Dec. I, D. 23, c. 2, in Friedberg, *Corpus* 1:79–80.

37. Dec. I, D. 25, c. 1, in Friedberg, *Corpus* 1:89–91. The offices of lector and deacon were minor orders in the medieval Church.

38. Wyclif refers to the opening titles of canon law and civil law. Cf. Decr. Greg. IX, L. 1, c. 1, t. 1, in Friedberg, *Corpus* 2:5–7, and Codex Iustianianus, L. I, t. 1, in *Corpus Iuris Civilis* 2:5–12, ed. Paul Krueger (Berlin, 1963).

39. Dec. I, D. 48, c. 1, in Friedberg, *Corpus* 1:153–55.

40. Dec. II, C. 2, Q. 7, c. 32, in Friedberg, *Corpus* 1:493.

41. Dec. I, D. 38, c. 6, in Friedberg, *Corpus* 1:142.

42. Dec. III, D. 5, c. 24, in Friedberg, *Corpus* 1:1418.

43. Wyclif had earlier cited canonical chapters to this effect. Consider for instance: Dec. I, D. 32, c. 6, in Friedberg, *Corpus* 1:117, where it said that one should not attend the mass of a priest who has a concubine. Canon law made it quite clear that while the sacraments administered by a sinful priest were still valid, the laity should avoid contact with such priests when possible.

44. Dec. II, C. 8, Q. 1, c. 22, in Friedberg, *Corpus* 1:597. See Jerome, *Comm. in Epist. ad Titum* I, PL 26:602c–d.

45. See Dec. II, C. 11, Q. 3, c. 78, in Friedberg, *Corpus* 1:665.

46. See Dec. II, C. 11, Q. 3, c. 71, in Friedberg, *Corpus* 1:663.

47. See Dec. II, C. 23, Q. 4, c. 39, in Friedberg, *Corpus* 1:919–20.

48. *Comment. in Epist. ad Rom.* II, PG 14:873–74.

49. Ibid., PG 14:874.

50. Dec. II, C. 23, Q. 5, c. 20, in Friedberg, *Corpus* 1:936. See Isidore's *Sententiarum Libri Tres* III.53, PL 83:726.

51. John de Dio was a thirteenth-century canonist. This citation was not found.

52. See Dec. II, C. 23, Q. 5, c. 40, in Friedberg, *Corpus* 1:941.

53. *Regulae Pastoralis Liber* I.ii, PL 77:15–16.

54. Dec. II, C. 23, Q. 5, c. 44, in Friedberg, *Corpus* 1:943–44.

55. See "*Rex Debet*," Dec. II, C. 23, Q. 5, c. 40, in Friedberg, *Corpus* 1:941.

56. Dec. II, C. 23, Q. 5, c. 23, in Friedberg, *Corpus* 1:937.

57. Dec. II, C. 23, Q. 6, c. 2, in Friedberg, *Corpus* 1:948.

58. Dec. II, C. 23, Q. 5, c. 25, in Friedberg, *Corpus* 1:938.

59. See "*Amministratores*," Dec. II, C. 23, Q. 5, c. 26, in Friedberg, *Corpus* 1:938.

60. See Grosseteste's *Expositio in Epistolam Sancti Pauli ad Galatas* ed. James McEvoy; *Glossarum in Sancti Pauli Epistolas Fragmenta*, ed. R. C. Dales; *Tabula*, ed. R. W. Rosemann, Corpus Christianorum Continuatio Mediaevalis 130 (Turnhout, 1995).

61. See Wyclif's *De Mandatis* XVIII, ed. Johann Loserth and F. D. Matthew (1922; repr. New York, 1966), pp. 206–29.

62. Perhaps a vague reference to *De vera religione* L.98. ed. Josef Martin, Corpus Christianorum, Series Latina 32 (Turnhout, 1962), p. 250.

63. This may refer to Wyclif's *Tractatus de Benedicta Incarnacione* III, ed. Edward Harris (London, 1886; repr. New York, 1966), pp. 33–34.

64. See Grosseteste's *De Cessatione Legalium* I.10.8, ed. R. C. Dales and E. B. King (London, 1986), p. 54.

65. Augustine argued that Peter was indeed reprehensible in this case, while Jerome considered this confrontation an elaborate show performed

for the sake of the gospel. See Augustine, *De Mendacio* V.8–9, ed. Joseph Zycha, Corpus Scriptorum Ecclesiasticorum Latinorum 41 (Vienna, 1900), pp. 422–25. And Jerome, *Comm. in Epist. ad Galatas* I.2, PL 26:363–67.

66. *In Epist. ad Titum* I, PG 62:661.

67. See Grosseteste's *De Cessatione Legalium* IV.8, pp. 35–38, 196–99.

68. Wyclif refers here to the *glosa communis*. There are some similarities to comments found in the *Glossa Ordinaria* on this passage. Cf. *Biblia Latina cum Glossa Ordinaria*, ed. Karlfried Froehlich and Margaret Gibson, vol. 4 (Turnhout, 1992), p. 19.

69. The proprietary church system (*Eigenkirchenrecht*) placed churches under the control of the secular lords who endowed them. It had grown up in the West during the early Middle Ages. Eleventh- and twelfth-century reform efforts led by the papacy sought to free the Church from lay control.

70. This refers to the fifth book of Wyclif's *Summa theologiae*, which is the third book of his *De civili dominio*. See *De civili dominio* IV.xxi, ed. Johann Loserth (1904; repr. New York, 1966), pp. 437–38.

71. See Wyclif's *De civili dominio* II.vii, p. 58.

72. *De Haeresibus*, Epilog. 3, ed. R. Vander Plaeste and C. Beukers, Corpus Christianorum, Series Latina 46 (Turnhout, 1969), p. 344.

73. See *Epist.* CXXXVII,I,3. ed. Alois Goldbacher, Corpus Scriptorum Ecclesiasticorum Latinorum 44 (Vienna, 1904), pp. 99–100. See also *De Doctrina Christiana* II.42.63, ed. Josef Martin, Corpus Christianorum, Series Latina 32 (Turnhout, 1962), pp. 76–77.

74. See Wyclif's *De civili dominio* II.vii, p. 58.

75. *De Trinitate* XV.12.21–22, ed. W. J. Mountain, Corpus Christianorum, Series Latina 50a (Turnhout, 1968), pp. 490–94. Wyclif reflects Augustine's theme in these passages.

76. *De Haeresibus*, Epilog. 3, CCSL 46:344.

77. Dec. II, C. 24, Q. 3, c. 31, in Friedberg, *Corpus* 1:998. This passage is actually drawn from Augustine's *De Civitate Dei* XVIII.51, CCSL 48:649.

78. *De Doc. Chr.* III.32.45, CCSL 32:104–05. Buddensieg inserted the "*vicesimo secundo*" but Wyclif is surely referring to Book 3, Chapter 32, where Augustine explains the second rule of the Donatist, Tyconius: "Of the Bipartite Body of the Lord."

SELECTED BIBLIOGRAPHY

Benrath, Gustav Adolf. *Wyclifs Bibelkommentar*. Berlin: Walter De Gruyter, 1966.

Catto, J. I. "John Wyclif and the Cult of the Eucharist." In *The Bible in the Medieval World: Essays in Honor of Beryl Smalley*, ed. Katherine Walsh and Diana Wood, 269–86. Oxford: Basil Blackwell, 1985.

———. "Wyclif and Wycliffism at Oxford 1356–1430." In *History of the University of Oxford*, gen. ed. T. H. Aston, 8 vols., 2:175–261. Oxford: Clarendon Press, 1984–.

Copeland, Rita. "Rhetoric and Politics of the Literal Sense, in Medieval Literary Theory: Aquinas, Wyclif and the Lollards." In *Interpretation: Medieval and Modern*, ed. Piero Boitani and Anna Torti, 1–23. Perugia: D. S. Brewer, 1993.

Courtenay, William J. "Force of Words and Figures of Speech: The Crisis over *Virtus Sermonis* in the Fourteenth Century." *Franciscan Studies* 44 (1984): 107–28.

Dahmus, Joseph H. *The Prosecution of John Wyclyf*. New Haven: Yale University Press, 1952.

Evans, Gillian R. "Wyclif on Literal and Metaphorical." In *From Ockham to Wyclif*, ed. Anne Hudson and Michael Wilks, 259–66. Oxford: Basil Blackwell, 1987.

———. "Wyclif's Logic and Wyclif's Exegesis: The Context." In *The Bible in the Medieval World: Essays in Honor of Beryl*

Smalley, ed. Katherine Walsh and Diana Wood, 287–300. Oxford: Basil Blackwell, 1985.

Ghosh, Kantik. "Eliding the Interpreter: John Wyclif and Scriptural Truth." In *New Medieval Literatures,* ed. Rita Copeland, David Lawton, and Wendy Scase, 2:205–24. Oxford: Clarendon Press, 1998.

Hudson, Anne. "John Wyclif." In *Dictionary of the Middle Ages*, ed. Joseph Strayer. New York: Charles Scribner's Son, 1982–.

———. *The Premature Reformation*. Oxford: Clarendon Press, 1988.

Hurley, Michael. "'Scriptura Sola': Wyclif and His Critics." *Traditio* 16 (1960): 275–352.

Jeffrey, David Lyle. "John Wyclif and the Hermeneutics of Reader Response." *Interpretation* 39/3 (July, 1985): 272–87.

Keen, Maurice. "Wyclif, the Bible, and Transubstantiation." In *Wyclif in His Times*, ed. Anthony Kenny, 1–16. Oxford: Clarendon Press, 1986.

Kenny, Anthony. *Wyclif.* Oxford: Oxford University Press, 1985.

Lechler, Gotthard. *John Wycliffe and His English Precursors*. English edition and translation by Peter Lorimer. London: Religious Tract Society, 1884.

Leff, Gordon. "John Wyclif: The Path to Dissent." *Proceedings of the British Academy* 52 (1966): 143–80.

———. "The Place of Metaphysics in Wyclif's Theology." In *From Ockham to Wyclif*, ed. Anne Hudson and Michael Wilks, 217–32. Oxford: Basil Blackwell, 1987.

Levy, Ian C. "*Christus qui mentiri non potest*: John Wyclif's Rejection of Transubstantiation." *Recherches de Théologie et Philosophie médiévales* 66/2 (1999): 316–34.

McFarlane, Kenneth B. *John Wycliffe and the Beginnings of English Nonconformity*. London: English Universities Press Ltd., 1952.

Minnis, A. J. "'Authorial Intention' and the 'Literal Sense' in the Exegetical Theories of Richard Fitzralph and John Wyclif." *Proceedings of the Irish Academy* 75 (1975): 1–31.

———. *Medieval Theory of Authorship*. London: Scolar Press, 1984.

Molnar, Amedeo. "Der alternde Wyclif und die Logik der Heiligen Schrift." *Communio Viatorum* 28:3–4 (Winter, 1985): 161–76.

Robson, J. A. *Wyclif and the Oxford Schools*. Cambridge: Cambridge University Press, 1961.

Smalley, Beryl. "The Bible and Eternity: John Wyclif's Dilemma." *Journal of Warburg and Courtauld Institutes* 27 (1964): 73–89.

———. "John Wyclif's *Postilla Super Totam Bibliam*." *Bodleian Library Record* 5 (1953): 186–205.

———. "Wyclif's *Postilla* on the Old Testament and His *Principium*." In *Oxford Studies Presented to Daniel Callus*, 253–96. Oxford: Clarendon Press, 1964.

Thomson, Samuel Thomson. "The Philosophical Basis of Wyclif's Theology." *Journal of Religion* 11 (January 1931): 86–116.

Thomson, Williel R. *The Latin Writings of John Wyclyf.* Toronto: Pontifical Institute of Mediaeval Studies, 1983.

Tresko, Michael. "John Wyclif's Metaphysics of Scriptural Integrity in the *De Veritate Sacrae Scritpurae*." *Dionysius* 13 (1989): 153–96.

Wilks, Michael. *Wyclif, Political Ideas and Practice: Papers by Michael Wilks*, ed. Anne Hudson. Oxford: Oxbow Books, 2000.

Workman, Herbert B. *John Wyclif: A Study of the English Medieval Church.* 2 vols. Oxford: Clarendon Press, 1926.